American Language Hub

LEVEL 1
Teacher's Book

GARY PATHARE

macmillan education

Macmillan Education Limited
4 Crinan Street
London N1 9XW

Companies and representatives throughout the world

American Language Hub Level 1 Teacher's Book
ISBN 978-0-230-49686-6

American Language Hub Level 1 Teacher's Book with Teacher's App
ISBN 978-0-230-49687-3

Written by Gary Pathare

The author has asserted their right to be identified as the author of this work in accordance with the Copyright, Designs and Patents Act 1988.

First published 2020

Teacher's Book credits:
Original design by emc design ltd
Page make-up by SPi Global
Illustrated by Rose Frith (Lemonade Illustration Agency) page W5
Joseph Wilkins (Beehive Illustration) pages W1, W2, W8, W12, W16, W26, W27, W29, W36, W39, W48, W54, W56, W60, W65
Cover design based on an original design by Restless
Cover image by Plainpicture/Cultura/dotdotred

Author's acknowledgement
For Emma Pathare

The author and publishers would like to thank the following for permission to reproduce their photographs:

Corbis W33; **E+** W16, W61; **Getty Images** W27, Getty Images/Asimetrica Juniper W43, Getty Images/Caiaimage W36, Getty Images/Cultura RF W54, Getty Images/E+/GCShutter W4, Getty Images/iStockphoto/HalfPoint W3, Getty Images/iStockphot/Rawpixel W23, Getty Images/iStockphoto/Romrodinka W63, Getty Images/Cultura RF/Tim Macpherson W45, **Hero Images** W23; **Image Source** W13, W16, W57; **Moment RF** W28; **Shutterstock** nikiteev_konstantin/Shutterstock W5, Michael Warwick/Shutterstock W18.

The author and publishers are grateful for permission to reprint the following copyright material:

Extracts from: '700 Classroom Activities New Edition' © David Seymour and Maria Popova 2005, Published by Macmillan Education Limited. Used with permission. All rights reserved.

Extracts from: 'Teaching English Grammar' © Jim Scrivener 2010, Published by Macmillan Education Limited. Used with permission. All rights reserved.

Extracts from: 'Learning Teaching 3rd Edition Student's Book' © Jim Scrivener 2011, Published by Macmillan Education Limited. Used with Permission. All rights reserved.

Student's Book credits:
Text, design and illustration © Macmillan Education Limited 2020
Written by Peter Maggs and Catherine Smith

With thanks to Edward Price and Carol Goodwright for additional authoring and to Signature Manuscripts for the Grammar Hub pages.

The authors have asserted their right to be identified as the authors of this work in accordance with the Copyright, Designs and Patents Act 1988.

The right of Sue Kay and Vaughan Jones to be identified as authors of the Speaking Pages in this work has been asserted by them in accordance with the Copyright, Designs and Patents Act 1988.

Designed by emc design ltd
Illustrated by Rasmus Juul, Rose Frith (Lemonade Illustration Agency), Peter Lubach (Beehive illustration)
Picture research by Emily Taylor
Café Hub videos produced by Creative Listening
Café Hub video scripts written by James and Luke Vyner

Full acknowledgements for photographs in the facsimile pages can be found in the Student's Book ISBN 978-0-230-49680-4.

The authors and publishers are grateful for permission to reprint the following copyright material:

p14 Extract from 'One is dark-skinned and one is white, one has brown eyes and the other blue - but Bobby and Riley are million-to-one TWINS' by Jennifer Newton. Originally published in MailOnline, 5th July 2015. © Associated Newspapers Ltd. Reprinted with permission of Solo Syndication.

p36 Extract from The Open University. © The Open University 2018. All Rights Reserved. Reprinted with permission of The Open University.

p162 Extract from 'A day in the life: Ireland's 800m Olympic hopeful Ciara Everard' by The42 Team. Originally published in The 42, 12th January 2016. Content copyright © Journal Media Ltd. 2018. Reprinted with permission of The 42.

Printed and bound in Brazil

2025
28

Contents

Student's Book Introduction

American Language Hub is a new six-level general English course for adult learners, which takes the complexity out of teaching English. It is designed to promote effective communication and helps to build learners' confidence with regular opportunities for meaningful practice. With its firm pedagogic foundation and syllabus aligned to the revised CEFR, American Language Hub has clear learning outcomes which make it easy to use in a variety of teaching situations.

The engaging photograph and famous quotation help teachers to focus students and familiarize themselves with the ideas in the unit. Teachers can also encourage students to label the picture.

Student's Book unit opener

The first page of every American Language Hub unit is the unit opener. It is an exciting visual opportunity for students to engage with the theme of the unit and see at a glance the CEFR learning objectives for each lesson.

There is a quick warm up speaking activity. Teachers can use this time to prepare the class for their lesson and delay the main start for five minutes until all the students arrive.

Student's Book lessons 1 and 2

Reading and Listening

Reading and listening sections allow students to practice their receptive skills. All sections have tasks that move from global to detailed understanding so students can achieve a good overall comprehension. The key skills focus is clearly marked in the activity titles. The texts and scripts also present target vocabulary, grammar or pronunciation.

Grammar

The American Language Hub approach to grammar is inductive. Students are exposed to new language in context. Each grammar section prompts the student to notice the feature in context and to discover its form and use. Students then have further opportunities for controlled practice before using their new language in more authentic spoken or written output.

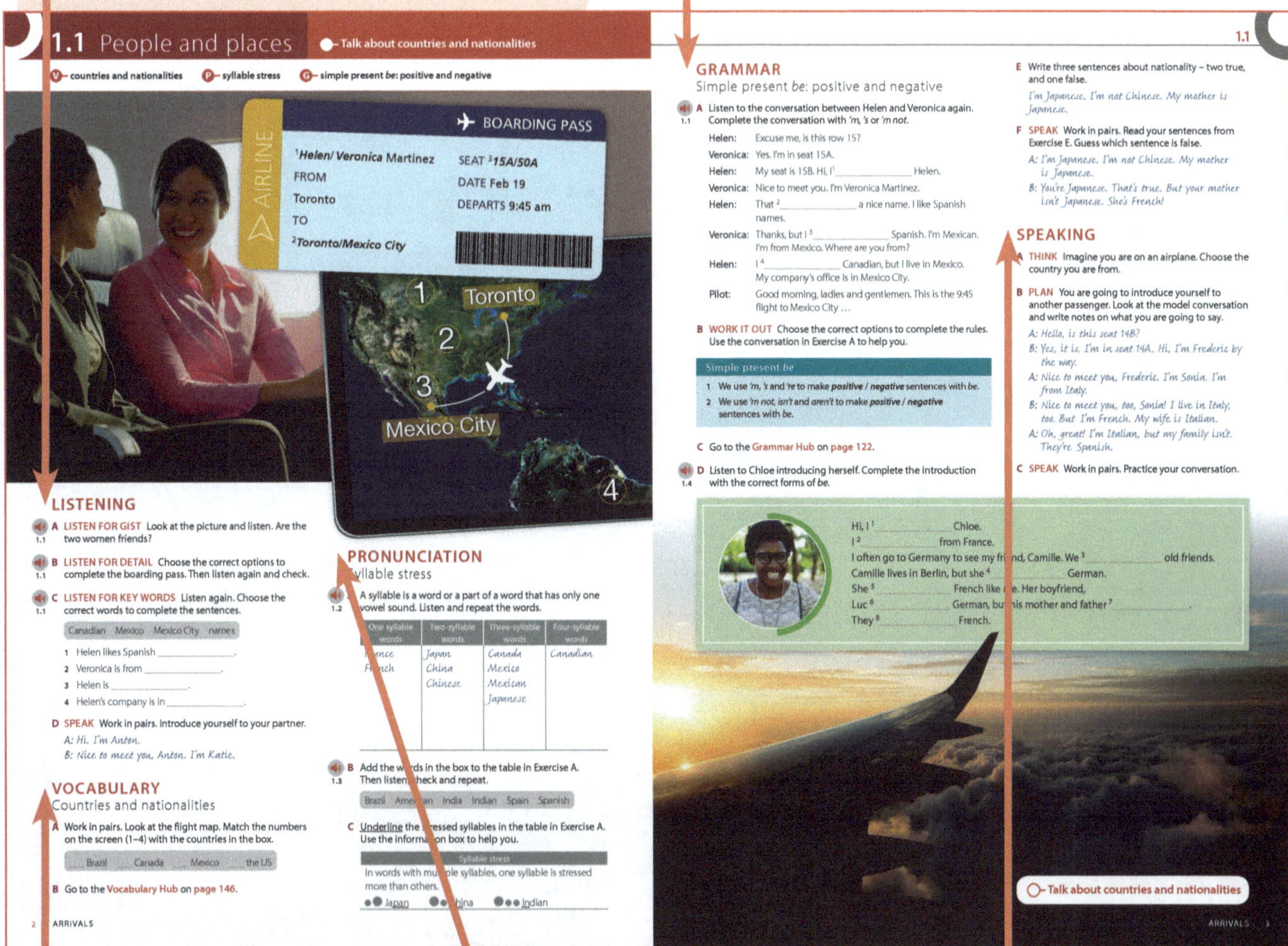

1.1 People and places — Talk about countries and nationalities

V – countries and nationalities P – syllable stress G – simple present *be*: positive and negative

LISTENING

1.1 A LISTEN FOR GIST Look at the picture and listen. Are the two women friends?

1.1 B LISTEN FOR DETAIL Choose the correct options to complete the boarding pass. Then listen again and check.

1.1 C LISTEN FOR KEY WORDS Listen again. Choose the correct words to complete the sentences.

Canadian Mexico Mexico City names

1. Helen likes Spanish ______.
2. Veronica is from ______.
3. Helen is ______.
4. Helen's company is in ______.

D SPEAK Work in pairs. Introduce yourself to your partner.

A: Hi. I'm Anton.
B: Nice to meet you, Anton. I'm Katie.

VOCABULARY
Countries and nationalities

A Work in pairs. Look at the flight map. Match the numbers on the screen (1–4) with the countries in the box.

___ Brazil ___ Canada ___ Mexico ___ the US

B Go to the Vocabulary Hub on page 146.

PRONUNCIATION
Syllable stress

1.2 A A syllable is a word or a part of a word that has only one vowel sound. Listen and repeat the words.

One syllable words	Two-syllable words	Three-syllable words	Four-syllable words
France	*Japan*	*Canada*	*Canadian*
French	*China*	*Mexico*	
	Chinese	*Mexican*	
		Japanese	

1.3 B Add the words in the box to the table in Exercise A. Then listen, check and repeat.

Brazil American India Indian Spain Spanish

C Underline the stressed syllables in the table in Exercise A. Use the information box to help you.

Syllable stress
In words with multiple syllables, one syllable is stressed more than others.
●● Japan ●● China ●●● Indian

2 ARRIVALS

GRAMMAR
Simple present *be*: positive and negative

1.1 A Listen to the conversation between Helen and Veronica again. Complete the conversation with *'m*, *'s* or *'m not*.

Helen: Excuse me, is this row 15?
Veronica: Yes. I'm in seat 15A.
Helen: My seat is 15B. Hi, I [1] ______ Helen.
Veronica: Nice to meet you. I'm Veronica Martinez.
Helen: That [2] ______ a nice name. I like Spanish names.
Veronica: Thanks, but I [3] ______ Spanish. I'm Mexican. I'm from Mexico. Where are you from?
Helen: I [4] ______ Canadian, but I live in Mexico. My company's office is in Mexico City.
Pilot: Good morning, ladies and gentlemen. This is the 9:45 flight to Mexico City …

B WORK IT OUT Choose the correct options to complete the rules. Use the conversation in Exercise A to help you.

Simple present *be*
1. We use *'m*, *'s* and *'re* to make ***positive / negative*** sentences with *be*.
2. We use *'m not*, *isn't* and *aren't* to make ***positive / negative*** sentences with *be*.

C Go to the Grammar Hub on page 122.

1.4 D Listen to Chloe introducing herself. Complete the introduction with the correct forms of *be*.

Hi, I [1] ______ Chloe.
I [2] ______ from France.
I often go to Germany to see my friend, Camille. We [3] ______ old friends.
Camille lives in Berlin, but she [4] ______ German.
She [5] ______ French like me. Her boyfriend,
Luc [6] ______ German, but his mother and father [7] ______.
They [8] ______ French.

1.1

E Write three sentences about nationality – two true, and one false.

I'm Japanese. I'm not Chinese. My mother is Japanese.

F SPEAK Work in pairs. Read your sentences from Exercise E. Guess which sentence is false.

A: I'm Japanese. I'm not Chinese. My mother is Japanese.
B: You're Japanese. That's true. But your mother isn't Japanese. She's French!

SPEAKING

A THINK Imagine you are on an airplane. Choose the country you are from.

B PLAN You are going to introduce yourself to another passenger. Look at the model conversation and write notes on what you are going to say.

A: Hello, is this seat 14B?
B: Yes, it is. I'm in seat 14A. Hi, I'm Frederic by the way.
A: Nice to meet you, Frederic. I'm Sonia. I'm from Italy.
B: Nice to meet you, too, Sonia! I live in Italy, too. But I'm French. My wife is Italian.
A: Oh, great! I'm Italian, but my family isn't. They're Spanish.

C SPEAK Work in pairs. Practice your conversation.

Talk about countries and nationalities

ARRIVALS 3

Vocabulary

American Language Hub teaches vocabulary in topic-related sets to help students categorize the new words they learn. Key vocabulary sets are built on and reviewed in the back of the book.

Pronunciation

In American Language Hub, lessons focus on both word level and sentence level pronunciation. This not only allows students to improve their accuracy, but also fluency through sentence level intonation, which helps students understand how to add meaning through their pronunciation.

Speaking

Each lesson starts with a CEFR unit objective which the lesson is designed to address. Students will often use the grammar, vocabulary and pronunciation from the lesson to complete a speaking activity linked to the unit objective. American Language Hub allows students to safely practice speaking in pairs after most sections. This ensures that they feel confident to take an active role in the final speaking task.

American Language Hub for Teachers

Student's Book lesson 3

Reading and Listening Skill

Every unit includes a task designed to practice a key reading or listening skill. This ensures students are given the tools they need to effectively process a wide variety of texts and scripts. By the end of each book, students will have been exposed to 12 different key skills for reading or listening.

Topics

American Language Hub topics contextualize the language input for the lesson. They have been selected to allow opportunities for personalization.

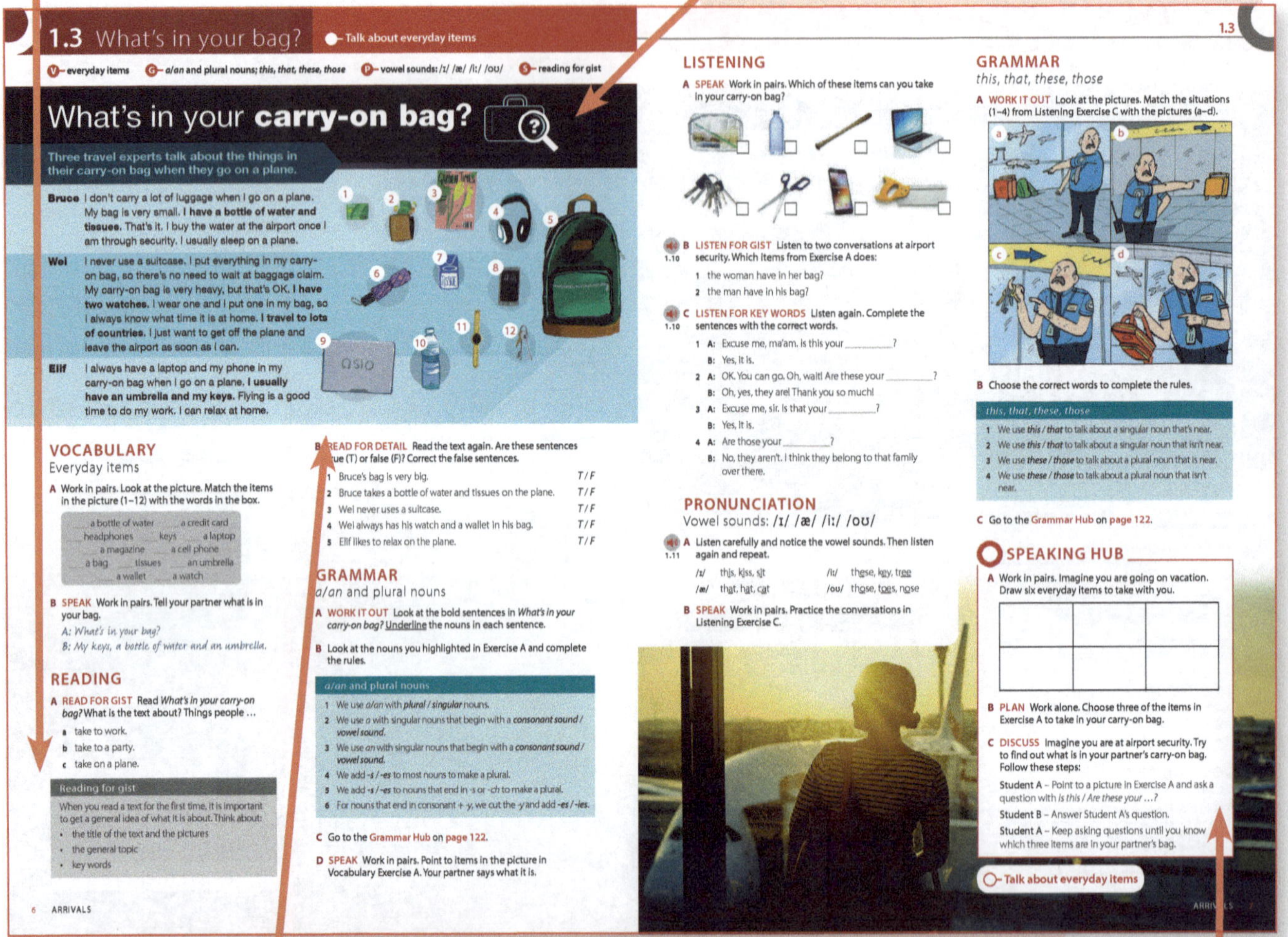

1.3 What's in your bag? Talk about everyday items

V– everyday items G– *a/an* and plural nouns; *this, that, these, those* P– vowel sounds: /ɪ/ /æ/ /iː/ /oʊ/ S– reading for gist

What's in your carry-on bag?

Three travel experts talk about the things in their carry-on bag when they go on a plane.

Bruce I don't carry a lot of luggage when I go on a plane. My bag is very small. **I have a bottle of water and tissues.** That's it. I buy the water at the airport once I am through security. I usually sleep on a plane.

Wei I never use a suitcase. I put everything in my carry-on bag, so there's no need to wait at baggage claim. My carry-on bag is very heavy, but that's OK. **I have two watches.** I wear one and I put one in my bag, so I always know what time it is at home. **I travel to lots of countries.** I just want to get off the plane and leave the airport as soon as I can.

Elif I always have a laptop and my phone in my carry-on bag when I go on a plane. **I usually have an umbrella and my keys.** Flying is a good time to do my work. I can relax at home.

VOCABULARY
Everyday items

A Work in pairs. Look at the picture. Match the items in the picture (1–12) with the words in the box.

___ a bottle of water ___ a credit card ___ headphones ___ keys ___ a laptop ___ a magazine ___ a cell phone ___ a bag ___ tissues ___ an umbrella ___ a wallet ___ a watch

B SPEAK Work in pairs. Tell your partner what is in your bag.

A: What's in your bag?
B: My keys, a bottle of water and an umbrella.

READING

A READ FOR GIST Read *What's in your carry-on bag?* What is the text about? Things people …

a take to work.
b take to a party.
c take on a plane.

Reading for gist
When you read a text for the first time, it is important to get a general idea of what it is about. Think about:
- the title of the text and the pictures
- the general topic
- key words

B READ FOR DETAIL Read the text again. Are these sentences true (T) or false (F)? Correct the false sentences.

1 Bruce's bag is very big. T / F
2 Bruce takes a bottle of water and tissues on the plane. T / F
3 Wei never uses a suitcase. T / F
4 Wei always has his watch and a wallet in his bag. T / F
5 Elif likes to relax on the plane. T / F

GRAMMAR
a/an and plural nouns

A WORK IT OUT Look at the bold sentences in *What's in your carry-on bag?* Underline the nouns in each sentence.

B Look at the nouns you highlighted in Exercise A and complete the rules.

a/an and plural nouns
1 We use *a/an* with ***plural / singular*** nouns.
2 We use *a* with singular nouns that begin with a ***consonant sound / vowel sound.***
3 We use *an* with singular nouns that begin with a ***consonant sound / vowel sound.***
4 We add ***-s / -es*** to most nouns to make a plural.
5 We add ***-s / -es*** to nouns that end in *-s* or *-ch* to make a plural.
6 For nouns that end in consonant + *-y*, we cut the *-y* and add ***-es / -ies.***

C Go to the Grammar Hub on page 122.

D SPEAK Work in pairs. Point to items in the picture in Vocabulary Exercise A. Your partner says what it is.

6 ARRIVALS

1.3

LISTENING

A SPEAK Work in pairs. Which of these items can you take in your carry-on bag?

1.10 B LISTEN FOR GIST Listen to two conversations at airport security. Which items from Exercise A does:
1 the woman have in her bag?
2 the man have in his bag?

1.10 C LISTEN FOR KEY WORDS Listen again. Complete the sentences with the correct words.
1 A: Excuse me, ma'am. Is this your ________?
B: Yes, it is.
2 A: OK. You can go. Oh, wait! Are these your ________?
B: Oh, yes, they are! Thank you so much!
3 A: Excuse me, sir. Is that your ________?
B: Yes, it is.
4 A: Are those your ________?
B: No, they aren't. I think they belong to that family over there.

PRONUNCIATION
Vowel sounds: /ɪ/ /æ/ /iː/ /oʊ/

1.11 A Listen carefully and notice the vowel sounds. Then listen again and repeat.
/ɪ/ this, kiss, sit /iː/ these, key, tree
/æ/ that, hat, cat /oʊ/ those, toes, nose

B SPEAK Work in pairs. Practice the conversations in Listening Exercise C.

GRAMMAR
this, that, these, those

A WORK IT OUT Look at the pictures. Match the situations (1–4) from Listening Exercise C with the pictures (a–d).

B Choose the correct words to complete the rules.

this, that, these, those
1 We use ***this / that*** to talk about a singular noun that's near.
2 We use ***this / that*** to talk about a singular noun that isn't near.
3 We use ***these / those*** to talk about a plural noun that is near.
4 We use ***these / those*** to talk about a plural noun that isn't near.

C Go to the Grammar Hub on page 122.

SPEAKING HUB

A Work in pairs. Imagine you are going on vacation. Draw six everyday items to take with you.

B PLAN Work alone. Choose three of the items in Exercise A to take in your carry-on bag.

C DISCUSS Imagine you are at airport security. Try to find out what is in your partner's carry-on bag. Follow these steps:

Student A – Point to a picture in Exercise A and ask a question with *Is this / Are these your …?*
Student B – Answer Student A's question.
Student A – Keep asking questions until you know which three items are in your partner's bag.

Talk about everyday items

ARRIVALS 7

Skill labels

By focusing students' attention on the skills labels next to each exercise number, teachers can highlight which skills are being practiced and recycled.

Speaking Hub

At the end of Lesson 3, students perform a longer speaking turn which is staged to allow for planning and idea creation. Students should apply their learning from the whole unit in the performance of their long speaking turn.

Student's Book lesson 4

Functional Language

Each video provides a model for functional language so that students are able to access an ever-expanding bank of phrases. This language helps students to communicate effectively in a range of real-world situations.

Café Hub

The final lesson in each unit has a focus on video. Café Hub is an amusing situation comedy series. Meet Milly, Sam, Neena, Zac and Gaby as they take you through their adventures in London. Find out how they start their journey as complete strangers but become the best of friends.

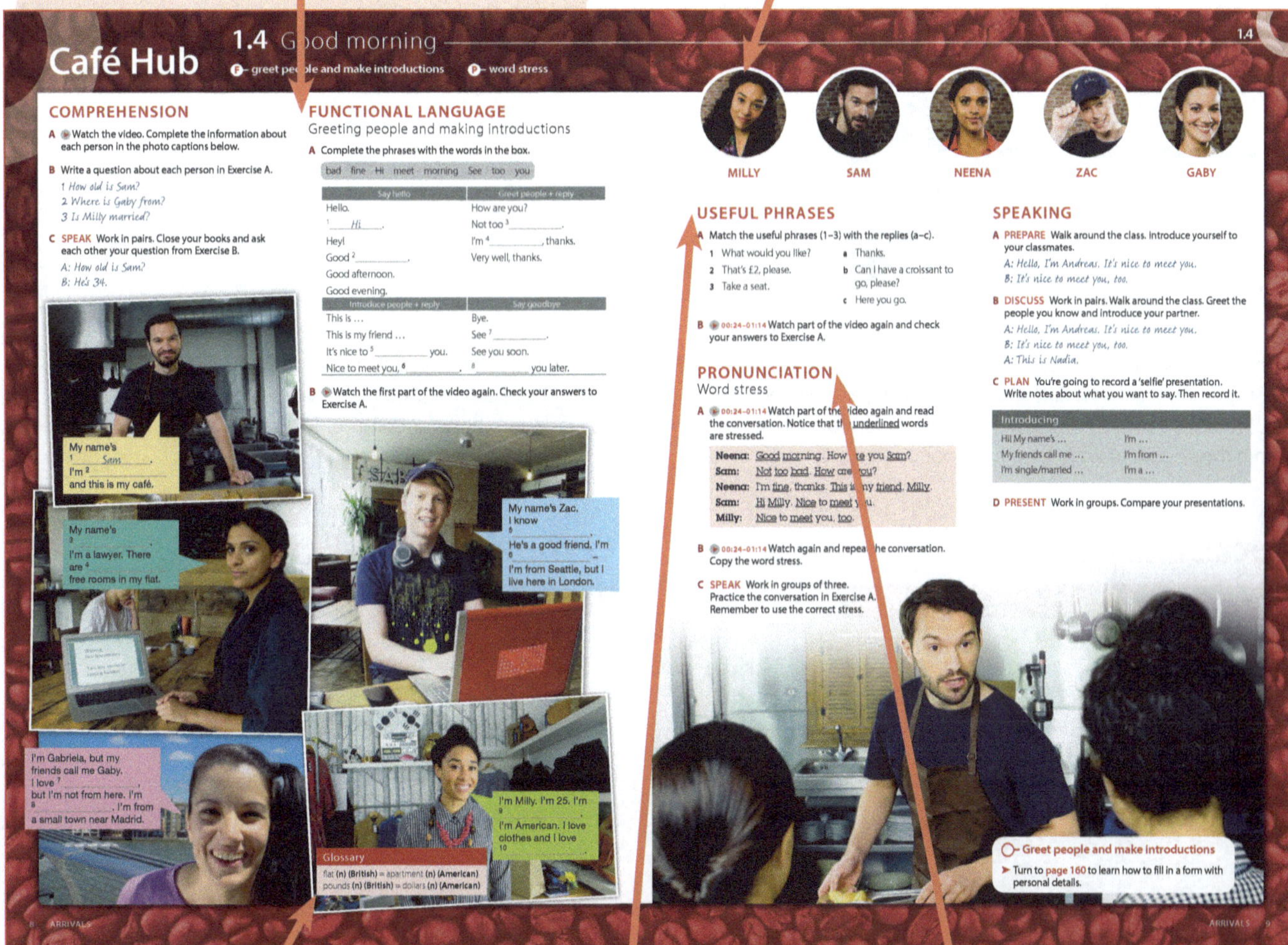

Café Hub

1.4 Good morning

F– greet people and make introductions P– word stress

1.4

COMPREHENSION

A Watch the video. Complete the information about each person in the photo captions below.

B Write a question about each person in Exercise A.

1 *How old is Sam?*
2 *Where is Gaby from?*
3 *Is Milly married?*

C SPEAK Work in pairs. Close your books and ask each other your question from Exercise B.

A: How old is Sam?
B: He's 34.

My name's [1] *Sam*. I'm [2] ______ and this is my café.

My name's [3] ______. I'm a lawyer. There are [4] ______ free rooms in my flat.

I'm Gabriela, but my friends call me Gaby. I love [7] ______, but I'm not from here. I'm [8] ______. I'm from a small town near Madrid.

FUNCTIONAL LANGUAGE

Greeting people and making introductions

A Complete the phrases with the words in the box.

bad fine Hi meet morning See too you

Say hello	Greet people + reply
Hello.	How are you?
[1] *Hi*.	Not too [3] ______.
Hey!	I'm [4] ______, thanks.
Good [2] ______.	Very well, thanks.
Good afternoon.	
Good evening.	
Introduce people + reply	**Say goodbye**
This is …	Bye.
This is my friend …	See [7] ______.
It's nice to [5] ______ you.	See you soon.
Nice to meet you, [6] ______.	[8] ______ you later.

B Watch the first part of the video again. Check your answers to Exercise A.

My name's Zac. I know [5] ______. He's a good friend. I'm [6] ______. I'm from Seattle, but I live here in London.

I'm Milly. I'm 25. I'm [9] ______. I'm American. I love clothes and I love [10] ______.

Glossary

flat (n) (British) = apartment (n) (American)
pounds (n) (British) = dollars (n) (American)

MILLY SAM NEENA ZAC GABY

USEFUL PHRASES

A Match the useful phrases (1–3) with the replies (a–c).

1 What would you like?
2 That's £2, please.
3 Take a seat.

a Thanks.
b Can I have a croissant to go, please?
c Here you go.

B 00:24–01:14 Watch part of the video again and check your answers to Exercise A.

PRONUNCIATION

Word stress

A 00:24–01:14 Watch part of the video again and read the conversation. Notice that the underlined words are stressed.

Neena: Good morning. How are you Sam?
Sam: Not too bad. How are you?
Neena: I'm fine, thanks. This is my friend, Milly.
Sam: Hi Milly. Nice to meet you.
Milly: Nice to meet you, too.

B 00:24–01:14 Watch again and repeat the conversation. Copy the word stress.

C SPEAK Work in groups of three. Practice the conversation in Exercise A. Remember to use the correct stress.

SPEAKING

A PREPARE Walk around the class. Introduce yourself to your classmates.

A: Hello, I'm Andreas. It's nice to meet you.
B: It's nice to meet you, too.

B DISCUSS Work in pairs. Walk around the class. Greet the people you know and introduce your partner.

A: Hello, I'm Andreas. It's nice to meet you.
B: It's nice to meet you, too.
A: This is Nadia.

C PLAN You're going to record a 'selfie' presentation. Write notes about what you want to say. Then record it.

Introducing	
Hi! My name's …	I'm …
My friends call me …	I'm from …
I'm single/married …	I'm a …

D PRESENT Work in groups. Compare your presentations.

F– Greet people and make introductions

▶ Turn to page 160 to learn how to fill in a form with personal details.

8 ARRIVALS

ARRIVALS 9

Variety of English

The Glossary boxes on these pages point out differences between American English and British English.

Useful Phrases

The video also provides an opportunity to learn a variety of useful phrases. Students can use these to bring authenticity to their language output.

Pronunciation

Lesson 4 has a focus on stress and intonation. Students notice the stress and rhythm of British and American English pronunciation in the video before preparing to speak themselves.

American Language Hub for Teachers

Student's Book Hubs

Writing Hub

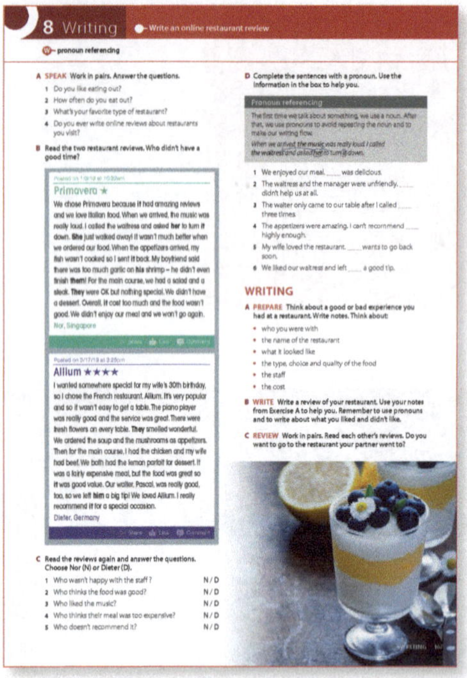

The Student's Book has an individual writing page at the back of the book for each unit. Each writing lesson is aligned to the unit topic and teaches a different writing genre and writing skill. Students can see completed writing models to analyze before they begin to write their own work.

Grammar Hub

Clear explanations and further practice activities for each grammar point in the syllabus are provided at the back of the book. These can be used in class or set for homework to free up classroom time for communication.

Vocabulary Hub

The Vocabulary Hub provides extra practice of key vocabulary presented in each unit. As with the Grammar Hub sections, these can either consolidate work done in class or be used for further self-study.

Communication Hub

The Communication Hub is used to set up longer communicative activities, such as information exchanges, quizzes and role plays.

Workbook

A Workbook is sold separately for American Language Hub. This includes 360 print activities practicing the language from the Student's Book. For each lesson there are corresponding practice exercises of grammar, vocabulary and pronunciation. There is further practice of the reading and listening skills from Lesson 3 and extension practice of the functional language from Lesson 4. There is also a page dedicated to the unit's writing genre and skill. All of these pages develop learning from the main lessons of the Student's Book.

Vocabulary and Grammar

The Workbook practices Vocabulary and Grammar that students have encountered in the Student's Book. By reminding themselves of the words and skills they have recently seen, students are better able to imbed learning and have it ready for recall during speaking practice.

Listening and Reading

The Workbook provides additional listening and reading texts that explore the topics in the Student's Book. These give students the opportunity to develop the key receptive skills from the unit.

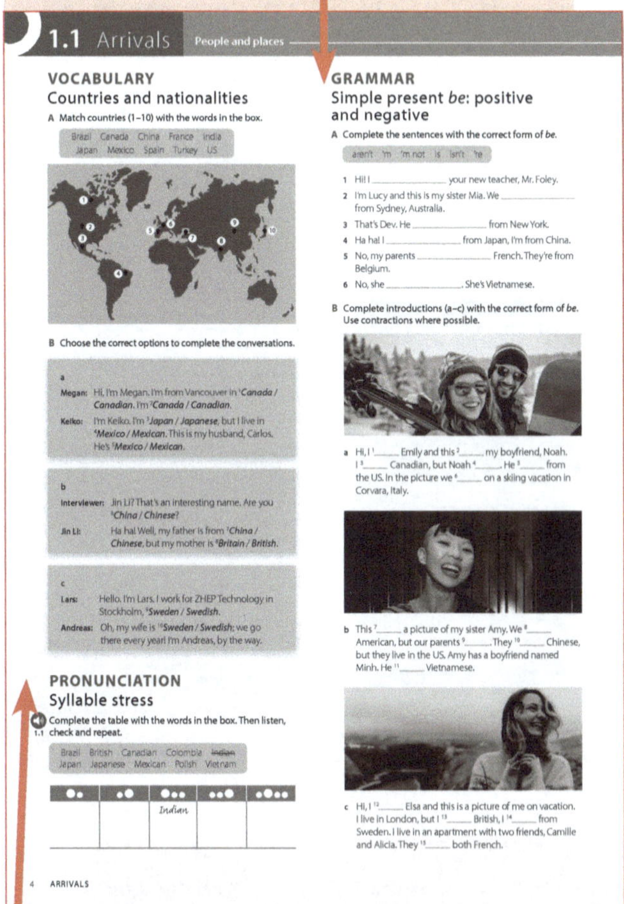

1.1 Arrivals People and places

VOCABULARY
Countries and nationalities

A Match countries (1–10) with the words in the box.

Brazil Canada China France India Japan Mexico Spain Turkey US

B Choose the correct options to complete the conversations.

a
Megan: Hi, I'm Megan. I'm from Vancouver in [1]*Canada / Canadian*. I'm [2]*Canada / Canadian*.
Keiko: I'm Keiko. I'm [3]*Japan / Japanese*, but I live in [4]*Mexico / Mexican*. This is my husband, Carlos. He's [5]*Mexico / Mexican*.

b
Interviewer: Jin Li? That's an interesting name. Are you [6]*China / Chinese*?
Jin Li: Ha ha! Well, my father is from [7]*China / Chinese*, but my mother is [8]*Britain / British*.

c
Lars: Hello. I'm Lars. I work for ZHEP Technology in Stockholm, [9]*Sweden / Swedish*.
Andreas: Oh, my wife is [10]*Sweden / Swedish*; we go there every year! I'm Andreas, by the way.

PRONUNCIATION
Syllable stress

1.1 Complete the table with the words in the box. Then listen, check and repeat.

Brazil British Canadian Colombia ~~Indian~~ Japan Japanese Mexican Polish Vietnam

●•	•●	●••	••●	•●••
		Indian		

GRAMMAR
Simple present *be*: positive and negative

A Complete the sentences with the correct form of *be*.

aren't 'm 'm not is isn't 're

1 Hi! I ________ your new teacher, Mr. Foley.
2 I'm Lucy and this is my sister Mia. We ________ from Sydney, Australia.
3 That's Dev. He ________ from New York.
4 Ha ha! I ________ from Japan, I'm from China.
5 No, my parents ________ French. They're from Belgium.
6 No, she ________. She's Vietnamese.

B Complete introductions (a–c) with the correct form of *be*. Use contractions where possible.

a Hi, I [1]____ Emily and this [2]____ my boyfriend, Noah. I [3]____ Canadian, but Noah [4]____. He [5]____ from the US. In the picture we [6]____ on a skiing vacation in Corvara, Italy.

b This [7]____ a picture of my sister Amy. We [8]____ American, but our parents [9]____. They [10]____ Chinese, but they live in the US. Amy has a boyfriend named Minh. He [11]____ Vietnamese.

c Hi, I [12]____ Elsa and this is a picture of me on vacation. I live in London, but I [13]____ British, I [14]____ from Sweden. I live in an apartment with two friends, Camille and Alicia. They [15]____ both French.

4 ARRIVALS

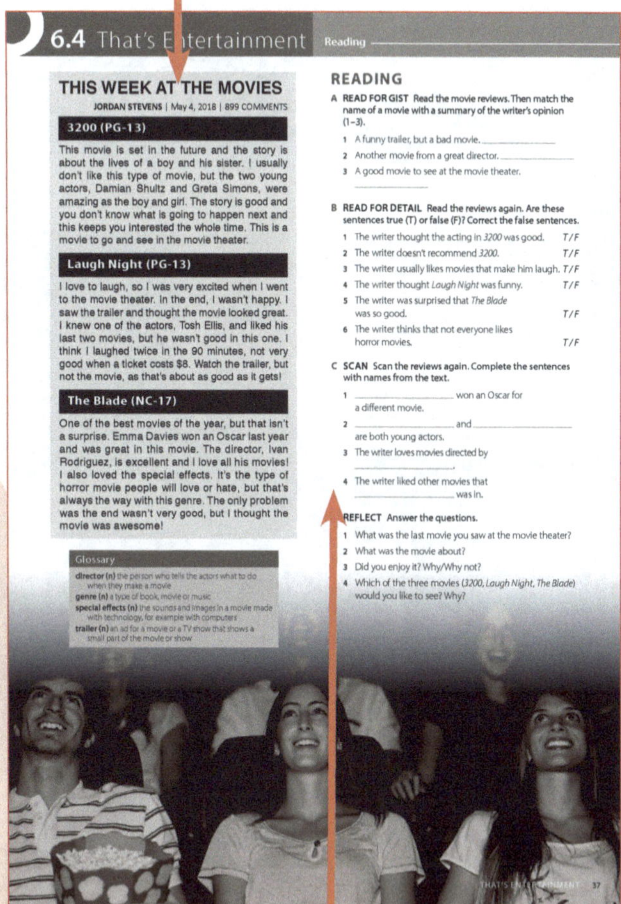

6.4 That's Entertainment Reading

THIS WEEK AT THE MOVIES
JORDAN STEVENS | May 4, 2018 | 899 COMMENTS

3200 (PG-13)
This movie is set in the future and the story is about the lives of a boy and his sister. I usually don't like this type of movie, but the two young actors, Damian Shultz and Greta Simons, were amazing as the boy and girl. The story is good and you don't know what is going to happen next and this keeps you interested the whole time. This is a movie to go and see in the movie theater.

Laugh Night (PG-13)
I love to laugh, so I was very excited when I went to the movie theater. In the end, I wasn't happy. I saw the trailer and thought the movie looked great. I knew one of the actors, Tosh Ellis, and liked his last two movies, but he wasn't good in this one. I think I laughed twice in the 90 minutes, not very good when a ticket costs $8. Watch the trailer, but not the movie, as that's about as good as it gets!

The Blade (NC-17)
One of the best movies of the year, but that isn't a surprise. Emma Davies won an Oscar last year and was great in this movie. The director, Ivan Rodriguez, is excellent and I love all his movies! I also loved the special effects. It's the type of horror movie people will love or hate, but that's always the way with this genre. The only problem was the end wasn't very good, but I thought the movie was awesome!

Glossary
director (n) the person who tells the actors what to do when they make a movie
genre (n) a type of book, movie or music
special effects (n) the sounds and images in a movie made with technology, for example with computers
trailer (n) an ad for a movie or a TV show that shows a small part of the movie or show

READING

A READ FOR GIST Read the movie reviews. Then match the name of a movie with a summary of the writer's opinion (1–3).
1 A funny trailer, but a bad movie. ________
2 Another movie from a great director. ________
3 A good movie to see at the movie theater. ________

B READ FOR DETAIL Read the reviews again. Are these sentences true (T) or false (F)? Correct the false sentences.
1 The writer thought the acting in *3200* was good. T/F
2 The writer doesn't recommend *3200*. T/F
3 The writer usually likes movies that make him laugh. T/F
4 The writer thought *Laugh Night* was funny. T/F
5 The writer was surprised that *The Blade* was so good. T/F
6 The writer thinks that not everyone likes horror movies. T/F

C SCAN Scan the reviews again. Complete the sentences with names from the text.
1 ________ won an Oscar for a different movie.
2 ________ and ________ are both young actors.
3 The writer loves movies directed by ________.
4 The writer liked other movies that ________ was in.

REFLECT Answer the questions.
1 What was the last movie you saw at the movie theater?
2 What was the movie about?
3 Did you enjoy it? Why/Why not?
4 Which of the three movies (*3200*, *Laugh Night*, *The Blade*) would you like to see? Why?

Pronunciation

The Workbook also consolidates the pronunciation topics from the Student's Book through further controlled practice.

Reflect

Each reading and listening page has a Reflect section so that students can use their Workbooks in class if they wish to reflect on their learning with their peers.

American Language Hub for Teachers

Teacher's Book

Interleaved pages

Every level of American Language Hub has a Teacher's Book interleaved with pages of the Student's Book. The answers to all of the Student's Book activities are annotated on the page so there is no need for teachers to flip backward and forward to find information.

Procedural notes

The lessons include procedural notes for teachers. These offer support to teachers on how to deliver the lesson rather than telling them how to teach. The notes are designed to be brief and easy to read.

Extra activities

The Extra activity boxes help teachers extend the content of the lesson, both in and out of the classroom.

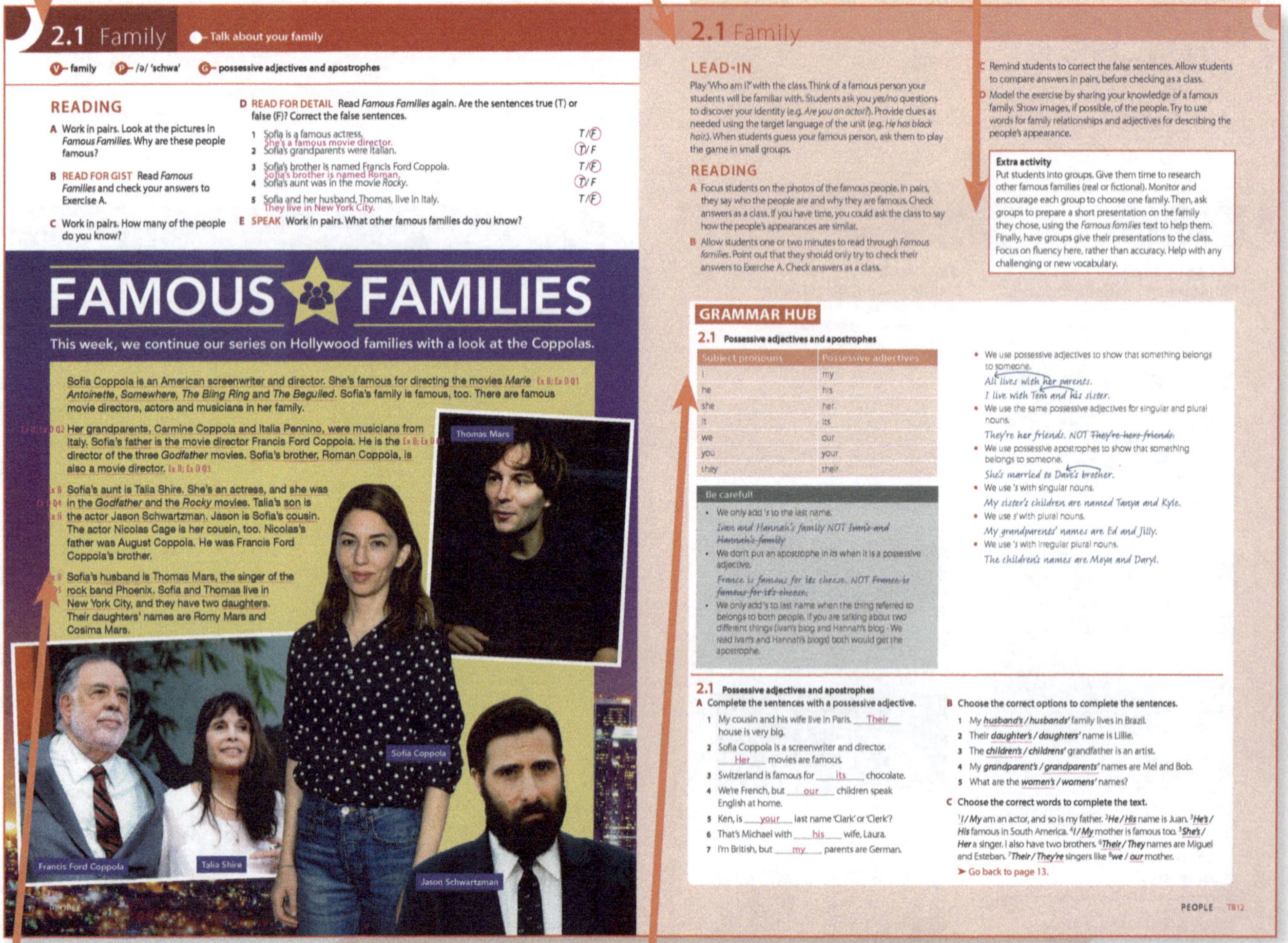

Annotated answers

The answers to reading and listening exercises are annotated on the interleaved pages of the Student's Book. These provide a quick reference tool for teachers.

Grammar explanations

Where the Student's Book asks the students to look at the Grammar Hub, the teacher can find this already annotated on the Teacher's Book page. For ease of use, the Grammar Hub reference activities at the end of the Student's Book have been added to the Teacher's Book pages at the location they will be used in the course. This makes it easier for teachers to grade homework in class or refer to succinct grammar explanations.

Teacher's Book: Macmillan Books for Teachers

Worksheets

The bank of communicative worksheets at the back of the Teacher's Book provide additional controlled and freer practice of every vocabulary and grammar section.

Lead-in

Suggested lead-ins can be used to activate prior knowledge, generate interest in the lesson topic or focus on useful lexis.

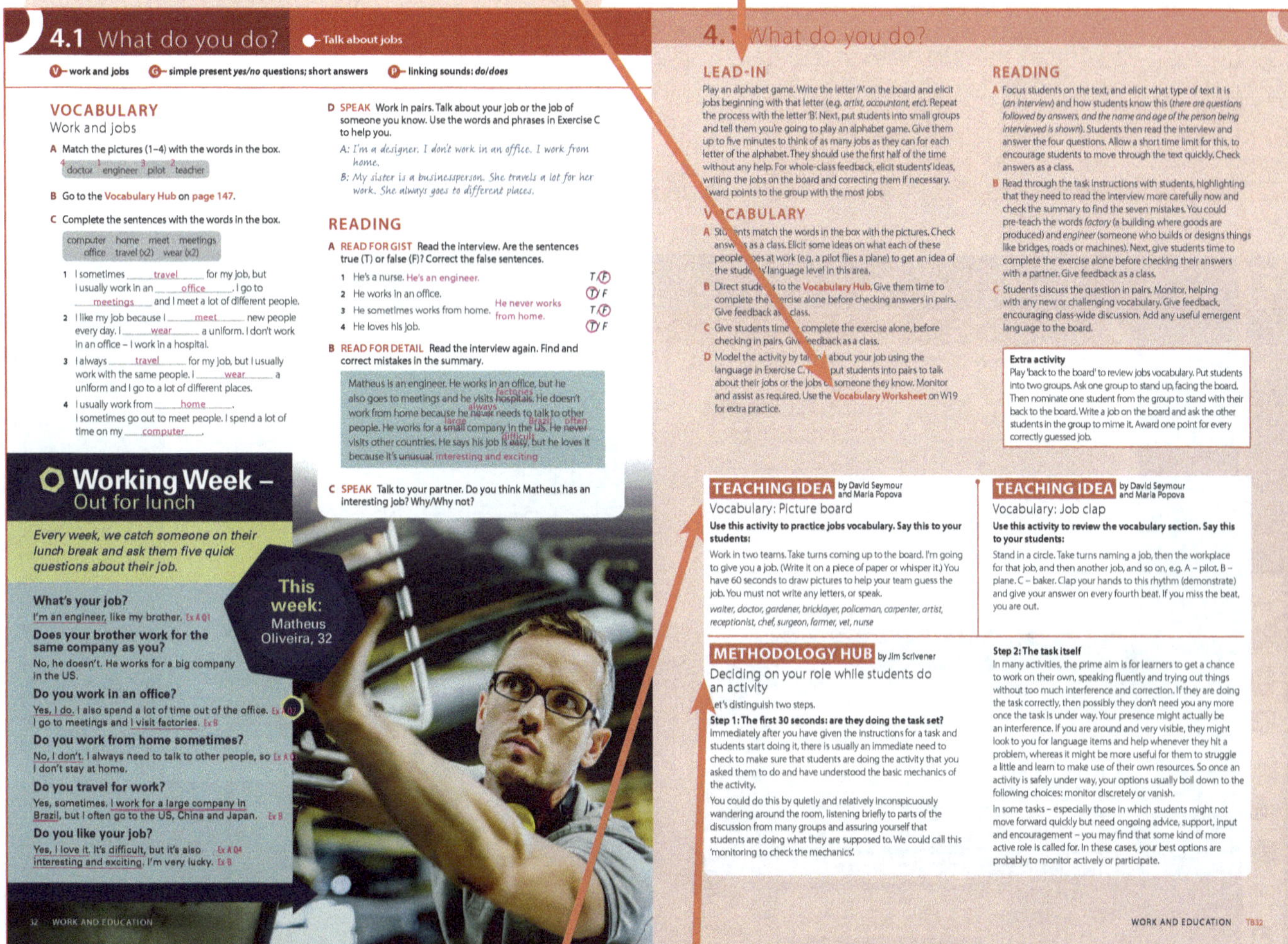

4.1 What do you do? — Talk about jobs

V – work and jobs   G – simple present *yes/no* questions; short answers   P – linking sounds: *do/does*

VOCABULARY
Work and jobs

A Match the pictures (1–4) with the words in the box.

doctor (4) engineer (1) pilot (3) teacher (2)

B Go to the Vocabulary Hub on page 147.

C Complete the sentences with the words in the box.

computer home meet meetings office travel (x2) wear (x2)

1 I sometimes ___travel___ for my job, but I usually work in an ___office___. I go to ___meetings___ and I meet a lot of different people.
2 I like my job because I ___meet___ new people every day. I ___wear___ a uniform. I don't work in an office – I work in a hospital.
3 I always ___travel___ for my job, but I usually work with the same people. I ___wear___ a uniform and I go to a lot of different places.
4 I usually work from ___home___. I sometimes go out to meet people. I spend a lot of time on my ___computer___.

D SPEAK Work in pairs. Talk about your job or the job of someone you know. Use the words and phrases in Exercise C to help you.

A: I'm a designer. I don't work in an office. I work from home.
B: My sister is a businessperson. She travels a lot for her work. She always goes to different places.

READING

A READ FOR GIST Read the interview. Are the sentences true (T) or false (F)? Correct the false sentences.

1 He's a nurse. He's an engineer. T/F
2 He works in an office. T/F
3 He sometimes works from home. He never works from home. T/F
4 He loves his job. T/F

B READ FOR DETAIL Read the interview again. Find and correct mistakes in the summary.

Matheus is an engineer. He works in an office, but he also goes to meetings and he visits ~~hospitals~~ factories. He doesn't work from home because he ~~never~~ always needs to talk to other people. He works for a ~~small~~ large company in the ~~US~~ Brazil. He ~~never~~ often visits other countries. He says his job is ~~easy~~ difficult, but he loves it because it's ~~unusual~~ interesting and exciting.

C SPEAK Talk to your partner. Do you think Matheus has an interesting job? Why/Why not?

Working Week – Out for lunch

Every week, we catch someone on their lunch break and ask them five quick questions about their job.

This week: Matheus Oliveira, 32

What's your job?
I'm an engineer, like my brother. Ex A Q1

Does your brother work for the same company as you?
No, he doesn't. He works for a big company in the US.

Do you work in an office?
Yes, I do. I also spend a lot of time out of the office. Ex A Q2
I go to meetings and I visit factories. Ex B

Do you work from home sometimes?
No, I don't. I always need to talk to other people, so Ex A Q3
I don't stay at home.

Do you travel for work?
Yes, sometimes. I work for a large company in Brazil, but I often go to the US, China and Japan. Ex B

Do you like your job?
Yes, I love it. It's difficult, but it's also Ex A Q4
interesting and exciting. I'm very lucky. Ex B

32 WORK AND EDUCATION

4.1 What do you do?

LEAD-IN

Play an alphabet game. Write the letter 'A' on the board and elicit jobs beginning with that letter (e.g. *artist, accountant, etc*). Repeat the process with the letter 'B'. Next, put students into small groups and tell them you're going to play an alphabet game. Give them up to five minutes to think of as many jobs as they can for each letter of the alphabet. They should use the first half of the time without any help. For whole-class feedback, elicit students' ideas, writing the jobs on the board and correcting them if necessary. Award points to the group with the most jobs.

VOCABULARY

A Students match the words in the box with the pictures. Check answers as a class. Elicit some ideas on what each of these people does at work (e.g. a pilot flies a plane) to get an idea of the students' language level in this area.

B Direct students to the Vocabulary Hub. Give them time to complete the exercise alone before checking answers in pairs. Give feedback as a class.

C Give students time to complete the exercise alone, before checking in pairs. Give feedback as a class.

D Model the activity by talking about your job using the language in Exercise C. Then put students into pairs to talk about their jobs or the jobs of someone they know. Monitor and assist as required. Use the Vocabulary Worksheet on W19 for extra practice.

READING

A Focus students on the text, and elicit what type of text it is (*an interview*) and how students know this (*there are questions followed by answers, and the name and age of the person being interviewed is shown*). Students then read the interview and answer the four questions. Allow a short time limit for this, to encourage students to move through the text quickly. Check answers as a class.

B Read through the task instructions with students, highlighting that they need to read the interview more carefully now and check the summary to find the seven mistakes. You could pre-teach the words *factory* (a building where goods are produced) and *engineer* (someone who builds or designs things like bridges, roads or machines). Next, give students time to complete the exercise alone before checking their answers with a partner. Give feedback as a class.

C Students discuss the question in pairs. Monitor, helping with any new or challenging vocabulary. Give feedback, encouraging class-wide discussion. Add any useful emergent language to the board.

Extra activity
Play 'back to the board' to review jobs vocabulary. Put students into two groups. Ask one group to stand up, facing the board. Then nominate one student from the group to stand with their back to the board. Write a job on the board and ask the other students in the group to mime it. Award one point for every correctly guessed job.

TEACHING IDEA by David Seymour and Maria Popova
Vocabulary: Picture board

Use this activity to practice jobs vocabulary. Say this to your students:

Work in two teams. Take turns coming up to the board. I'm going to give you a job. (Write it on a piece of paper or whisper it.) You have 60 seconds to draw pictures to help your team guess the job. You must not write any letters, or speak.

waiter, doctor, gardener, bricklayer, policeman, carpenter, artist, receptionist, chef, surgeon, farmer, vet, nurse

TEACHING IDEA by David Seymour and Maria Popova
Vocabulary: Job clap

Use this activity to review the vocabulary section. Say this to your students:

Stand in a circle. Take turns naming a job, then the workplace for that job, and then another job, and so on, e.g. A – pilot. B – plane. C – baker. Clap your hands to this rhythm (demonstrate) and give your answer on every fourth beat. If you miss the beat, you are out.

METHODOLOGY HUB by Jim Scrivener
Deciding on your role while students do an activity

Let's distinguish two steps.

Step 1: The first 30 seconds: are they doing the task set?
Immediately after you have given the instructions for a task and students start doing it, there is usually an immediate need to check to make sure that students are doing the activity that you asked them to do and have understood the basic mechanics of the activity.

You could do this by quietly and relatively inconspicuously wandering around the room, listening briefly to parts of the discussion from many groups and assuring yourself that students are doing what they are supposed to. We could call this 'monitoring to check the mechanics'.

Step 2: The task itself
In many activities, the prime aim is for learners to get a chance to work on their own, speaking fluently and trying out things without too much interference and correction. If they are doing the task correctly, then possibly they don't need you any more once the task is under way. Your presence might actually be an interference. If you are around and very visible, they might look to you for language items and help whenever they hit a problem, whereas it might be more useful for them to struggle a little and learn to make use of their own resources. So once an activity is safely under way, your options usually boil down to the following choices: monitor discretely or vanish.

In some tasks – especially those in which students might not move forward quickly but need ongoing advice, support, input and encouragement – you may find that some kind of more active role is called for. In these cases, your best options are probably to monitor actively or participate.

WORK AND EDUCATION TB32

Teaching Idea

Tips and ideas from *The Macmillan Books for Teachers* series are included in the procedural notes to give teachers some new ideas for instant communicative activities in the lesson. These can usually be used without paper preparation as warm-ups to get the class moving or as a flexible stage where there is time to fill.

Methodology Hub

Ideas for professional development from Jim Scrivener's *Learning Teaching Third Edition* are presented in every unit. These are here to help teachers pick up useful tips to add to their repertoire or just reflect on a new way to use American Language Hub with their class.

American Language Hub for Teachers

Teacher's App

The American Language Hub Teacher's Book comes with a Teacher's App, which gives access to the Resource Center, Test Generator and Classroom Presentation Kit.

The Classroom Presentation Kit is designed to be displayed on an interactive whiteboard (IWB) or using a projector, it enables teachers to play video and audio or show interactive activities in class. It is not only user-friendly for the teacher but also for the student, with activities being clearly visible for the whole class. Answer-by-answer reveal enables teachers to elicit student responses and check answers one by one.

Tools

Embedded tools make it possible to highlight and annotate texts to prompt noticing or self-correction. Teachers have the option to turn on an audio script, which is timed to sync with the dialogue, when listening to audio.

Teachers can zoom into each activity with one click. Then they can either move smoothly through the activities or zoom out to see the whole page. They can also create a whiteboard area for additional notes.

Video

Teachers can also access the video and audio for the course, including the authentic video from The Guardian.

Homework

The app allows teachers to assign homework directly to their students' devices and alert them when they have activities to complete.

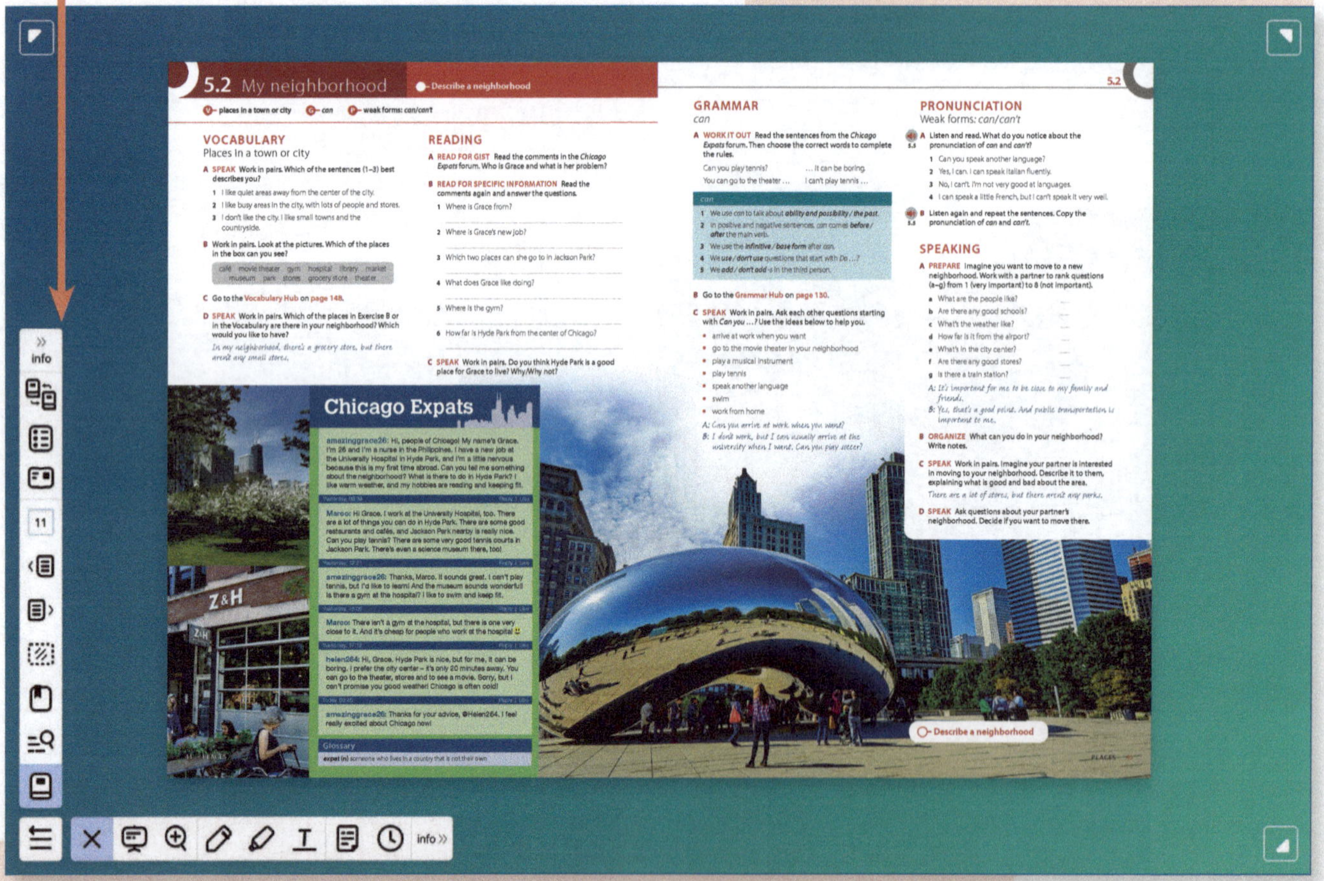

Preparation and Practice

Teachers can also configure student preparation and practice using the Teacher's App. Using the practice activities available, teachers can select and publish content to their students which they will receive through a push notification when they access their app. This enables teachers to personalize the amount and type of practice students do every week and to track their progress. Students can practice the grammar or vocabulary for the week before they go to class, allowing more time in the class for communication.

Test Generator

The Teacher's App also gives access to the Test Generator. In the Test Generator, teachers can create tests or use the pre-built tests for each level of the course and print these to assign to students. There are unit tests, mid- and end-of-course tests for each level, testing vocabulary, grammar and the four skills.

Student's App

Each Student's Book includes a code for the Student's App, to engage and encourage your students to practice their English on the move. Students can access grammar, vocabulary and pronunciation activities to prepare them for the lesson. Students are able to complete activities with varying levels of challenge and earn medals.

Preparation
Allows more time for communicative activities in the class by providing pre-lesson exposure to the language covered in the Student's Book.

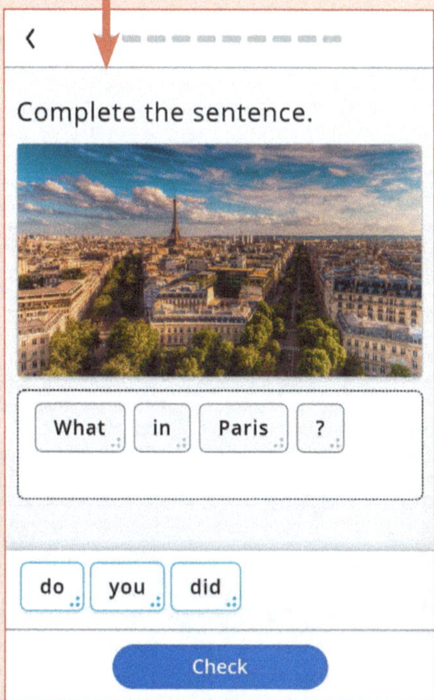

Practice
Provides additional practice to consolidate, revise and extend areas covered in the Student's Book.

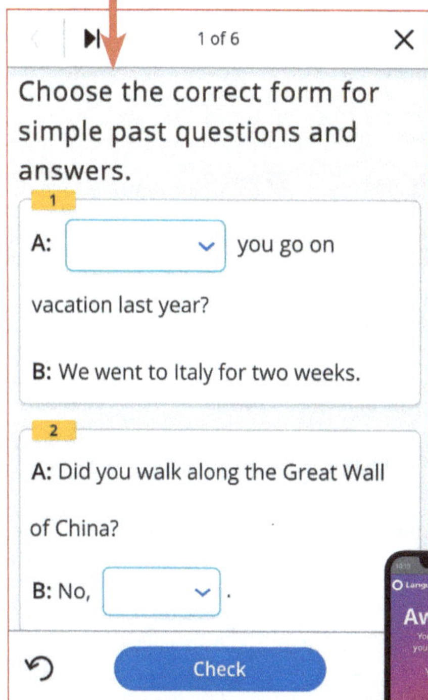

Rewards
A reward system helps to maintain student motivation.

Video

Two types of video are available with the course. Café Hub is a situation comedy which models functional language. Video Hub uses content from The Guardian as a resource for authentic English. All the videos from the course relate to the unit topics, and offer listening practice and scaffolding for speaking output.

Video Hub

Café Hub

Contents

Welcome

GREETINGS

A Read and listen to three conversations. Match conversations (1–3) with pictures (a–c).
0.1

1 c

Marc: Hi, Luca.

Luca: Hi, Marc. How are you?

Marc: Fine, thanks.

2 a

Emily: Good morning.

David: Hello. Nice to meet you.

Emily: You, too.

3 b

Gudrun: Bye, Clara.

Clara: Bye, Gudrun. See you later.

B Complete the table with the words and phrases in the box.

~~Bye.~~ ~~Fine, thanks.~~ ~~Good afternoon.~~ ~~How are you?~~ Good morning. Goodbye. Hi. Good night. I'm very well, thank you. Good evening. Not too bad. See you later.

Say hello	Ask a question	Answer	Say goodbye
Good afternoon. Good morning. Hi. Good evening.	*How are you?*	*Fine, thanks.* I'm very well thank you. Not too bad.	*Bye.* Goodbye. Good night. See you later.

C Complete the conversations with words from Exercise B.

1 A: How are you? B: Not too bad.

2 A: Goodbye. B: Good night.

3 A: How are you? B: I'm very well, thanks.

4 A: Bye. B: See you later.

NUMBERS 0–100

A Listen and repeat the numbers.
0.2

0 1 2 3 4 5 6 7 8 9 10 11 12 13 14 15 16 17 18 19 20 21
30 40 50 60 70 80 90 100

B Listen and write the numbers you hear.
0.3

a 9 c 77 e 24 g 60

b 16 d 53 f 81 h 11

DAYS OF THE WEEK

Write the days of the week in the correct order. Then listen and repeat.
0.4

Friday ~~Monday~~ Saturday Sunday Thursday Tuesday Wednesday

1 *Monday* 5 Friday

2 Tuesday 6 Saturday

3 Wednesday 7 Sunday

4 Thursday

THE ALPHABET

A Listen and repeat the letters of the alphabet.
0.5

a b c d e f g h i j k l m n o p q r s t u v w x y z

B Circle the letter in each group that has a different sound. Then listen and check.
0.6

1 b g m 2 a f k 3 j i y 4 l m r 5 i e t

C Listen and write the colors.
0.7

1 Green 4 Blue

2 Red 5 White

3 Yellow 6 Purple

D **SPEAK** Work in pairs. Spell these things for your partner to write.

- your first name
- your last name

CLASSROOM INSTRUCTIONS

Match questions (1–5) with replies (a–e). Then listen and check.
0.8

1 What does *book* mean?

2 What's *libro* in English?

3 I don't understand.

4 Could you repeat that, please?

5 Could you write it down, please?

a That's OK. I'll explain it again.

b Yes, sure.

c It means *libro*.

d It's *book*.

e Of course – *book*.

A traveler watching the sun rise over a new city.

Arrival (n) the time when someone arrives at a place from somewhere else
Synonyms: entry (n), homecoming (n)

Ask students to label the photo if you need time to set up the class.

A traveler watching the sun rise over a new city.

Socrates means no one is a stranger where there is the same sun, moon and stars.

Socrates (470–399 BC) was a classical Greek philosopher, one of the founders of Western philosophy.

OBJECTIVES

- talk about countries and nationalities
- ask and answer questions about a place
- talk about everyday items
- greet people and make introductions
- fill in a form with personal details

Work with a partner. Discuss the questions.

1 Where are you from?
2 Look at the picture. Which country is this?
3 What's your favorite city?

ARRIVALS 1

OBJECTIVES

Read the unit objectives to the class.

UNIT OPENER QUESTIONS

Write *Hi! My name's [your name]. I'm from [your country]* on the board with the sentence stems in one color and the name and country in another. Ask the class *Where am I from?* Write the answer on the board. Then put students into pairs to ask and answer *Where are you from?* For a big class, you could ask students to walk around the room and introduce themselves to everyone using the sentence stems on the board.

Then ask them to read Questions 2 and 3. Check that students understand the vocabulary. Write useful sentence stems on the board, e.g. *I think it's …*, *My favorite city is …* Ask students to discuss the questions with their partner.

If you have time, bring the class back together to discuss Questions 2 and 3 as a group.

WORKSHEETS

Lesson 1.1 People and places

Countries and nationalities (W1)

Simple present *be*: positive and negative (W2)

Lesson 1.2 Where are you?

Big numbers (W3)

Simple present *be*: questions (W4)

Lesson 1.3 What's in your bag?

Everyday items (W5)

a/an and plural nouns; *this, that, these, those* (W6)

1.1 People and places

Talk about countries and nationalities

V countries and nationalities P syllable stress G simple present *be*: positive and negative

LISTENING

1.1 **A LISTEN FOR GIST** Look at the picture and listen. Are the two women friends? No – they're meeting for the first time.

1.1 **B LISTEN FOR DETAIL** Choose the correct options to complete the boarding pass. Then listen again and check.

1.1 **C LISTEN FOR KEY WORDS** Listen again. Choose the correct words to complete the sentences.

Canadian Mexico Mexico City names

1. Helen likes Spanish ___names___.
2. Veronica is from ___Mexico___.
3. Helen is ___Canadian___.
4. Helen's company is in ___Mexico City___.

D SPEAK Work in pairs. Introduce yourself to your partner.

A: Hi. I'm Anton.

B: Nice to meet you, Anton. I'm Katie.

VOCABULARY
Countries and nationalities

A Work in pairs. Look at the flight map. Match the numbers on the screen (1–4) with the countries in the box.

_4_ Brazil _1_ Canada _3_ Mexico _2_ the US

B Go to the **Vocabulary Hub** on **page 146**.

PRONUNCIATION
Syllable stress

1.2 **A** A syllable is a word or a part of a word that has only one vowel sound. Listen and repeat the words.

One syllable words	Two-syllable words	Three-syllable words	Four-syllable words
France	Japan	Canada	Canadian
French	China	Mexico	American
Spain	Chinese	Mexican	
	Brazil	Japanese	
	Spanish	India	
		Indian	

1.3 **B** Add the words in the box to the table in Exercise A. Then listen, check and repeat.

Brazil American India Indian Spain Spanish

C Underline the stressed syllables in the table in Exercise A. Use the information box to help you.

Syllable stress

In words with multiple syllables, one syllable is stressed more than others.

●● Japan ●● China ●●● Indian

1.1 People and places

LEAD-IN

Ask students to close their books. Write the names of these famous people on the board and ask students where they come from. The answers are in parentheses.

Giorgio Armani (Italy)	*Lionel Messi (Argentina)*
Ryan Gosling (Canada)	*Steve Jobs (US)*
Frida Kahlo (Mexico)	*Lewis Hamilton (UK)*

LISTENING

1.1 **A** Focus students on the picture of two women talking on a plane. Ask the class if the women are friends. *Do they know each other?* Then play the audio. Check the answer as a class.

1.1 **B** Focus students on the picture of the boarding pass. Ask questions to check understanding, e.g. *Where do you get a boarding pass?* (at an airport) *Why do you need a boarding pass?* (to get on a plane) Highlight the information that students need to choose (i.e. *first name*, *destination* and *seat number*). In pairs, students try to remember any answers. Play the audio again.

1.1 **C** Allow time for students to read the sentences and predict the answers. Play the audio again. Then check answers as a class.

D Write the conversation on the board. Model the conversation using appropriate stress, pauses and intonation. Then model the conversation with a strong student using your own names. Next, put students into pairs and give them time to introduce themselves to their partner. Ask for one or two pairs to demonstrate to the rest of the class. Provide feedback on stress, pauses and intonation as necessary.

VOCABULARY

A Put students into pairs to match the numbers on the flight map to the countries in the box. As a class, check answers and model and practice the correct syllable stress for each country (*Bra<u>zil</u>*, *<u>Can</u>ada*, *<u>Mex</u>ico*, *A<u>mer</u>ica*).

B Direct students to the **Vocabulary Hub** (TB121). Give students time to complete exercises alone before checking with a partner. Give feedback as a class. Take the time to teach any additional countries/nationalities that are relevant to your class.

PRONUNCIATION

1.2 **A** Books closed. Draw a table with four columns on the board. Write *France* in one column and *Japan* in the other. Practice the correct pronunciation of the words. Elicit the number of syllables in each. Add 'One-syllable words' and 'Two-syllable words' as headings to your table. Next, add *Canada* and *Canadian* to the third and fourth columns. Again, practice the correct pronunciation, elicit the number of syllables and add headings to your table. Ask students to open their books, then listen and repeat the words in the table.

1.3 **B** Use *Brazil* as an example with the class, practicing the correct pronunciation and adding it to the second column of your table. Then give students time to add the remaining words in the box to their own tables, before listening to check and repeat. Since this is the first pronunciation section in the book, take the time to establish how you will practice new vocabulary. Remember to practice words both chorally and individually, and use gestures to clearly show what you expect of your students.

1.3 **C** Clear the board and write *Japan*, *China* and *Indian*. Practice the correct pronunciation for *Japan*, clearly indicating that the stress is on the second syllable. Mark the stressed and unstressed syllables using small and large circles (i.e. oO). Follow the same process for *China* (Oo) and *Indian* (Ooo). Then give students time to underline the stressed syllables in each word in the table in Exercise A, before giving feedback as a class. If necessary, play the audio again. Use the **Vocabulary Worksheet** W1 for extra practice.

Extra activity

To consolidate the countries vocabulary, set up a simple A-Z race. Put students into groups and give them 2-3 mins to brainstorm as many countries beginning with each letter of the alphabet as possible. When the time is up, give feedback as a class, awarding one point for each correct answer. Build up a list on the board, practicing the correct pronunciation of anything new. With particularly strong groups, you could also try to elicit sentences using the nationalities of the countries listed on the board (e.g. *Javier Bardem is a Spanish actor.*).

AUDIO SCRIPT

1.1

Listening, Exercise A
H = Helen V = Veronica P = Pilot

H: Excuse me, is this row 15?
Ex B Q3 **V:** Yes. I'm in seat 15A.
H: My seat is 15B. Hi, I'm Helen.
Ex A; Ex B Q1 **V:** Nice to meet you. I'm Veronica Martinez.
Ex C Q1 **H:** That's a nice name. I like Spanish names.
Ex C Q2 **V:** Thanks, but I'm not Spanish. I'm Mexican. I'm from Mexico. Where are you from?
Ex C Q3; Ex C Q4 **H:** I'm Canadian, but I live in Mexico. My company's office is in Mexico City.
P: Good morning, ladies and gentlemen. This is the 9:45
Ex B Q2 flight to Mexico City …

TEACHING IDEA by David Seymour and Maria Popova

Vocabulary: Knowledge race

Use this activity to review the vocabulary section. Say this to your students:

Work in groups of four and appoint one person to be the secretary. I'm going to name a country. You have one minute to write as many notes as you can about the people and the geography before I name the next country, e.g. *China – big, over a billion people, Great Wall, capital city Beijing.*

America, Sweden, India, Iceland, Spain, Russia, Brazil, Australia

You have five minutes to turn your notes into complete sentences, e.g. *China – It's a big country. There are over a billion people. The Great Wall is visible from space. The capital city is Beijing.* (Go around and help during this stage.)

Read out your sentences. You score one point for every sentence. You can challenge the other group's sentences on factual accuracy and claim their point.

GRAMMAR

1.1 **A** Get students to read the conversation and predict which contractions complete each blank. Give them time to compare answers with a partner, before playing the recording so they can listen and check. During class feedback, highlight the title of this section (*simple present be: positive and negative*), and tell them that the verbs in the conversation are all examples of the simple present of *be*.

B Give students time to complete the rules before checking answers as a class. To clarify understanding, elicit examples for each positive form of *be* and write them on the board. Use students' names and nationalities to provide personalized examples (e.g. *I'm from Germany. / Yuko's from Japan. / They're Italian.*). Elicit that these are positive sentences and write a '+' symbol above them. Next, follow the same process for the negative forms of *be*.

C Direct students to the **Grammar Hub** (see below).

1.4 **D** Stronger students may benefit from reading the introduction and predicting the answers individually or in pairs. Play the audio and ask students to complete the introduction individually. Check answers as a whole class.

Chloe: Hi, I'm Chloe. I'm from France. I often go to Germany to see my friend, Camille. We're old friends. Camille lives in Berlin, but she isn't German. She's French like me. Her boyfriend, Luc, is German, but his mother and father aren't. They're French.

E Read through the task instructions and the example with students. Then write sentences about yourself on the board (one should not be true). Ask them to guess which sentence isn't true. Add any useful language produced by the students to the board (e.g. *I don't think you're …, You're not …*) to support the discussion exercise. Students then write three similar sentences about themselves. Model and assist as required.

F Put students into pairs to read their sentences and guess which isn't true. For whole-class feedback, ask individual students to say their sentences and invite other students to guess which sentences aren't true. Use the **Grammar Worksheet** on W2 for extra practice.

SPEAKING

A Explain that students are going to imagine they are on a plane, and write a conversation. Ask them to also imagine they are from a different country. Ask them not to say anything at this point to other students.

B Ask two stronger students to read out the conversation. Elicit from students which parts of the conversation can be changed (for example, *14B, 14A, Frederic*, etc). Ask students to decide what information they will change.

C Give students time to practice their conversation. If time allows, challenge students to look up from the page to say their parts, until they have memorized each section. Students swap partners and practice their conversations with others.

GRAMMAR HUB

1.1 Simple present *be*: positive and negative

	Positive	Negative
I	**I am** in this class. **I'm** in this class.	**I am not** in this class. **I'm not** in this class.
he/she/it	**She is** South Korean. **She's** South Korean.	**He is not** South Korean. **He isn't** South Korean.
you/we/they	**They are** from Japan. **They're** from Japan.	**We are not** from Japan. **We aren't** from Japan.

- We use *be* to talk about states, facts and personal details, e.g. name, nationality, age or status.
- We use a noun or subject pronoun (*I, you*, etc) before the verb *be*.

He's South Korean. NOT ~~*Is South Korean.*~~

- We often use contractions when we speak.

I am 20 years old. → *I'm 20 years old.*

- In the negative contraction, we can also say: *You're not, He's not, She's not*, etc.

She isn't 24 years old. OR *She's not 24 years old.*

Be careful!

- We use *you* for one person and more than one person.

Tony, you're in this class.
Tony and Paola, you're in this class.

1.1 Simple present *be*: positive and negative

A Choose the correct form of *be* for each subject.

1 I am / is / are (**am**)
2 you am / is / are (**are**)
3 it am / is / are (**is**)
4 they am / is / are (**are**)
5 she am / is / are (**is**)
6 we am / is / are (**are**)

B Choose the correct form of *be* for each subject.

1 I __am__ Italian.
2 We __are / 're__ married.
3 She __is / 's__ my friend.
4 It __is / 's__ 20 years old.
5 You __are / 're__ in class 4A.
6 Asim and Akil __are__ Egyptian.

C Rewrite the sentences in the positive and negative. Use contractions.

		POSITIVE (+)	NEGATIVE (-)
1	He is sorry.	*He's sorry.*	*He isn't sorry.*
2	They are friends.	They're friends.	They aren't friends.
3	We are from Turkey.	We're from Turkey.	We aren't from Turkey.
4	You are famous!	You're famous!	You aren't famous!
5	It is Spanish.	It's Spanish.	It isn't Spanish.
6	She is in this class.	She's in this class.	She isn't in this class.

➤ Go back to page 3.

GRAMMAR

Simple present *be*: positive and negative

1.1 **A** Listen to the conversation between Helen and Veronica again. Complete the conversation with *'m*, *'s* or *'m not*.

Helen: Excuse me, is this row 15?

Veronica: Yes. I'm in seat 15A.

Helen: My seat is 15B. Hi, I [1] ___'m___ Helen.

Veronica: Nice to meet you. I'm Veronica Martinez.

Helen: That [2] ___'s___ a nice name. I like Spanish names.

Veronica: Thanks, but I [3] ___'m not___ Spanish. I'm Mexican. I'm from Mexico. Where are you from?

Helen: I [4] ___'m___ Canadian, but I live in Mexico. My company's office is in Mexico City.

Pilot: Good morning, ladies and gentlemen. This is the 9:45 flight to Mexico City …

B **WORK IT OUT** Choose the correct options to complete the rules. Use the conversation in Exercise A to help you.

Simple present *be*

1 We use *'m, 's* and *'re* to make ***positive*** / ***negative*** sentences with *be*.

2 We use *'m not, isn't* and *aren't* to make ***positive*** / ***negative*** sentences with *be*.

C Go to the **Grammar Hub** on **page 122**.

1.4 **D** Listen to Chloe introducing herself. Complete the introduction with the correct forms of *be*.

Hi, I [1] ___'m___ Chloe.
I [2] ___'m___ from France.
I often go to Germany to see my friend, Camille. We [3] ___'re___ old friends.
Camille lives in Berlin, but she [4] ___isn't___ German.
She [5] ___'s___ French like me. Her boyfriend,
Luc [6] ___is___ German, but his mother and father [7] ___aren't___.
They [8] ___'re___ French.

E Write three sentences about nationality – two true, and one false.

I'm Japanese. I'm not Chinese. My mother is Japanese.

F **SPEAK** Work in pairs. Read your sentences from Exercise E. Guess which sentence is false.

A: I'm Japanese. I'm not Chinese. My mother is Japanese.

B: You're Japanese. That's true. But your mother isn't Japanese. She's French!

SPEAKING

A **THINK** Imagine you are on an airplane. Choose the country you are from.

B **PLAN** You are going to introduce yourself to another passenger. Look at the model conversation and write notes on what you are going to say.

A: Hello, is this seat 14B?

B: Yes, it is. I'm in seat 14A. Hi, I'm Frederic by the way.

A: Nice to meet you, Frederic. I'm Sonia. I'm from Italy.

B: Nice to meet you, too, Sonia! I live in Italy, too. But I'm French. My wife is Italian.

A: Oh, great! I'm Italian, but my family isn't. They're Spanish.

C **SPEAK** Work in pairs. Practice your conversation.

Talk about countries and nationalities

1.2 Where are you?

Ask and answer questions about a place

V big numbers **P** similar numbers **G** simple present *be*: questions

READING

A Work with a partner. Look at the picture in the text message below. Where is it?

Carlos
Typing ...

Hi Carlos! Where am I?

Hi Lee. I don't know. Where are you?

Ex C 01 I'm 6,028 miles from home – that's 13 hours by plane.

Ex B
Ex C 02 I'm in Japan! It's amazing. The picture is from my hotel window. There are thousands of people everywhere. It's always busy.

Wow! Where are you in Japan? Is the food good? Is it hot there? Tell me more!!!

Ex B
Ex C 04 I'm in Tokyo. Yes, the food is really good. There are hundreds of great restaurants. Is it hot here? It's
Ex C 03 very HOT. It's 30 degrees every day. How are you? Is work busy?

Ex C 05 I'm fine. Work isn't busy – everyone is on vacation. Except me!

B READ FOR GIST Read the messages between Carlos and Lee. Where is Lee? Tokyo, Japan

C READ FOR DETAIL Read again. Are the sentences true (T) or false (F)? Correct the false sentences.

1 Japan is far from where Carlos and Lee live. (T) / F
2 The picture is from Carlos's work. T / (F)
The picture is from Lee's hotel window.
3 It isn't hot where Lee is. It's very hot. T / (F)
4 Lee likes Japanese food. (T) / F
5 Carlos is very busy at work. T / (F)
Work isn't busy - everyone's on vacation.

VOCABULARY

Big numbers

A Match numbers (1–5) with the words (a–e).

1 100 — e
2 1,000 — d
3 10,000 — b
4 100,000 — c
5 1,000,000 — a

a one million
b ten thousand
c one hundred thousand
d one thousand
e one hundred

B Listen and write the numbers you hear. 1.5

1 6,028 / six thousand and twenty-eight
2 628 / six hundred and twenty-eight
3 60,288 / sixty thousand, two hundred and eighty-eight

C SPEAK Work in pairs. How far is Lee from home? 6,028 miles

D SPEAK Work in pairs. Student A – say how far a city is from Paris. Student B – name the city. Then swap.

Paris → New York	3,625 miles
Paris → Melbourne	10,427 miles
Paris → Seoul	5,568 miles
Paris → Milan	529 miles
Paris → Cape Town	7,965 miles

A: This city is 5,568 miles from Paris.
B: It's Seoul. This city is …

PRONUNCIATION

Similar numbers

A Listen to part of a phone call between Carlos and Lee. Which number does Lee say? 1.6

a thirteen (13)
(b thirty (30))

B Listen and repeat. Underline the stressed syllables in the numbers in Exercise A. 1.7

C Listen and check (✓) the number you hear. 1.8

a 17 ☐	70 ✓	e 16 ✓	60 ☐
b 19 ☐	90 ✓	f 14 ☐	40 ✓
c 15 ✓	50 ☐	g 18 ✓	80 ☐
d 12 ☐	20 ✓	h 13 ✓	30 ☐

D Listen again and repeat the numbers. 1.8

1.2 Where are you?

LEAD-IN

Ask students to close their books. Write five numbers on the board that have significance to your life. For example, your apartment number, how many brothers or sisters you have, the year of your birth, an important date you need to remember, etc. Ask students to guess why the numbers are important to you. Then write the answers in a different order and ask students to match them. Then put students into pairs and ask them to replay the activity using their own five numbers. Has any student guessed all five numbers correctly?

READING

A Put students into pairs to discuss the picture, guessing where it is. Check answers with the whole class, and ask students to justify answers they give.

B Focus students on the text and ask students where they might see it (i.e. *a text messaging service or an application on a smartphone*). Give a time limit of one minute for students to read the text quickly. Check where Lee is (*Japan*), and ask students to give more information from the text, without looking back. Ask questions to prompt them (e.g. *What city is Lee in? How hot is it?*)

C Ask students to read the messages again in detail. Give them time to complete the exercise alone before checking their answers with a partner. Check answers as a class, asking students to explain their answers. If you have time, you could ask if anyone has been to Japan. Ask which city they visited, how hot/cold it was and their opinion of the food.

VOCABULARY

A Give students time to complete the exercise alone before they compare answers in pairs. In class feedback, practice pronunciation of the numbers.

1.5 **B** Play the recording and ask students to write the numbers that they hear. Encourage them to write numbers rather than words. Check answers, practicing the pronunciation of each number.

C Put students into pairs to answer the question. In class feedback, ask students to explain where in the text they found the answer (Lee's second text message – *I'm 6,028 miles from home …*).

D Explain that the table shows how far different cities are from Paris. Tell students that they are going to play a guessing game. Choose one of the cities from the table and say the following: *This city is [number] miles from Paris.* Elicit which city you're describing. Repeat a few times, before putting students into pairs to play the game themselves. Monitor and give feedback on students' pronunciation of big numbers. Use the **Vocabulary Worksheet** on W3 for extra practice.

PRONUNCIATION

1.6 **A** Play the audio. Students decide which number Lee says. Allow time for students to compare answers and play the audio again. Give feedback as a class.

Carlos: Is it hot there?
Lee: Yes, it is! It's 30 degrees every day!

1.7 **B** Play the audio again and give students time to underline the stressed syllable in each word. Give feedback, practicing the correct pronunciation of each word.

1.8 **C** Write the numbers *13* and *30* on the board. Say one of the numbers (repeating if necessary) and elicit which of the two numbers you said. Tell students that they're going to do the same thing for letters a–h, then play the audio. Give students time to compare answers, then play the audio again. In class feedback, write the pairs of numbers on the board. Play the audio one last time and ask students to identify the correct number. Circle the correct numbers on the board.

1.8 **D** Point out that a stressed syllable has a louder, longer, clearer vowel sound. Play the audio again and ask students to repeat the numbers.

a seventy *b ninety* *c fifteen* *d twenty* *e sixteen* *f forty* *g eighteen* *h thirteen*

TEACHING IDEA by David Seymour and Maria Popova

Vocabulary: Numbers quiz

Use this activity to review the vocabulary section. Say this to your students:

Here are the answers to some questions. (Write the answers in random order on the board.) Copy them as a list and practice saying them with a partner.

Join another pair and play as a team. I'll ask the questions and the first team to yell out the right answer gets a point.

1. How far is London from Tokyo? (9,562 km)
2. How far is New York from Buenos Aires? (8,454 km)
3. What temperature does water boil at? (100°C)
4. How many bones are there in the human body? (206)
5. What is 477 + 345? (822)
6. What is 1568 – 744? (824)
7. How much of the world's electricity is used by America? (33%)
8. How big is the Pacific Ocean? (179,679,000 km^2)
9. How high is Mount Kilimanjaro? (5,895 m)
10. What is the population of Australia? (19,888,000)

AUDIO SCRIPT

1.9

Listening, Exercise A
L = Lee C = Carlos

L: Hello?
C: Hi Lee, it's Carlos. Where are you? Are you still in Tokyo?
L: Oh, hi Carlos! No, I'm not. I'm 1,300 miles from Tokyo. I'm in China now. *(Ex A; Ex C 1+2)*
C: Wow! Where are you in China?
L: I'm in Beijing. *(Ex A; Ex C 3)*
C: Cool. What's it like there?
L: It's very busy in the center. There are lots of new buildings and long streets. It's a big city. *(Ex A; Ex C 4)*
C: Is the food good?
L: Yes, it is. I really like Chinese food. *(Ex C 5)*
C: What's your next destination?
L: I don't know. Maybe Shanghai, or maybe the countryside. *(Ex B 6)*
C: Sounds fun! Send me more photos!
L: I will!

1.2 Where are you?

GRAMMAR

A Work together to complete the first question in the table, asking students to tell you where they found the answer in the text. Then give students time to complete the table alone before comparing their answers with a partner. Check answers as a class. Elicit that all of the words they added to the table are different forms of the verb *be*.

B Give students time to complete the rules alone, before giving feedback. Use the examples in Exercise A to help clarify and explain each rule. Write new examples for each rule if necessary.

C Direct students to the **Grammar Hub** (see below). Read the examples and go through the rules with the class.

D Work together to match the first question with an answer. Highlight that *where* asks about a place, so *e* is the only possible answer. Give students time to complete the exercise alone before checking their answers with a partner. Check answers as a class.

E Write *Where/from?* on the board and elicit how to write a question from this (*Where are you from?*). Put students into pairs to complete the remaining questions with the correct form of *be*. Check answers as a class. Then put students into new pairs to ask and answer the questions. Monitor and assist as necessary. Use the **Grammar Worksheet** on W4 for extra practice.

LISTENING

1.9 **A** Focus students on the three photos, eliciting some of the differences between the images. Ask students where Lee is now, then play the audio. Check the answer.

1.9 **B** Explain that the questions are from the conversation but are in the wrong order.

C Put students into pairs to answer the questions in Exercise B. Give feedback encouraging students to tell you as much as they can remember from the recording.

SPEAKING

A Model the activity for students. Tell the class you are thinking of your home (or somewhere different, if they know your home). Elicit questions, based on the prompts given. Students ask you the questions. Give answers and ask students to guess which place you are thinking of.

B Students write questions based on the prompts in Exercise A. Monitor and assist as necessary.

C Students work in pairs to ask and answer the questions. They should guess where their partner is thinking of. Monitor and give positive feedback. Ask one or two pairs to ask and answer questions in front of the whole class, for everyone to guess where the place is.

GRAMMAR HUB

1.2 Simple present *be*: questions

Question	Positive short answer	Negative short answer
Am I in this class?	Yes, **you are**.	No, **you aren't**.
Are you married?	Yes, **I am**.	No, **I'm not**.
Is he/she/it French?	Yes, **he/she/it is**.	No, **he/she/it isn't**.
Are we in this class?	Yes, **you/we are**.	No, **you/we aren't**.
Are you married?	Yes, **we are**.	No, **we aren't**.
Are they friends?	Yes, **they are**.	No, **they aren't**.

- In questions, the subject pronoun (*I, you, he, she*) comes after the verb *be*.

  Am I in this class? NOT ~~*I am in this class?*~~

- In negative short answers we can also say: *No, you're not., No, he's not., No, she's not.*, etc.

Be careful!

- In positive short answers, we don't use contractions.

  Yes, she is. NOT ~~*Yes, she's.*~~

Question word + *be* + subject + ?	
Age	**How old are** you?
Place	**Where are** you from?
Thing	**What's** your name?

1.2 Simple present *be*: questions

A Use the prompts to write questions and short answers.

1 you / married
Are you married (?) *No, I'm not.* (-)

2 your hometown / nice
Is your hometown nice? (?) Yes, it is. (+)

3 they / your new shoes
Are they your new shoes? (?) Yes, they are. (+)

4 he / in a relationship
Is he in a relationship? (?) No, he isn't. (-)

5 you / Turkish
Are you Turkish? (?) No, I'm not. (-)

6 you / a student
Are you a student? (?) Yes, I am. (+)

B Write *be* in the simple present in each blank.

1 What *is* your favorite food?
2 Where are you from?
3 How old are you?
4 What is your flight number?
5 Where is Max from?
6 How old is Cara?

➤ Go back to page 5.

GRAMMAR

Simple present *be*: questions

A WORK IT OUT Look at the text conversation between Lee and Carlos again. Complete the table with words from the text.

Wh- questions	*Yes/No* questions
A: Where [1] are you? B: I [2] 'm in Tokyo.	A: [5] Is the food good? B: Yes, the food [6] is really good.
A: How [3] are you? B: I [4] 'm fine.	A: [7] Is it hot there? B: It [8] 's very hot.

B Look at the table in Exercise A and complete the rules.

Present simple *be*: questions

1. We put question words **before** / *after* *be*.
2. We put the subject *before* / **after** *be*.
3. When we answer *yes/no* questions, we put the subject **before** / *after* *be*.

C Go to the **Grammar Hub** on **page 122**.

D PRACTICE Match the questions (1–5) with the answers (a–e).

1 Where are you?
2 How far is Mumbai from there?
3 Is your city big?
4 Are you Egyptian?
5 What's your flight number?

a It's 10 hours by plane.
b It's J230.
c No, I'm not.
d Yes, it is.
e I'm at the hotel.

E SPEAK Work in pairs. Write questions, adding the correct form of *be*. Take turns asking and answering questions.

1 Where / from? Where are you from?
2 food good / your country? Is the food good in your country?
3 your hometown / big? Is your hometown big?
4 your hometown / hot or cold? Is your hometown hot or cold?
5 How far / your home / from here? How far is your home from here?

LISTENING

1.9 **A LISTEN FOR GIST** Listen to Carlos and Lee talking on the phone. Where is Lee now? Beijing

1.9 **B LISTEN FOR DETAIL** Listen again. Number Carlos's questions in the order you hear them (1–6).

2 Are you still in Tokyo?
5 Is the food good?
4 What's it like there?
6 What's your next destination?
3 Where are you in China?
1 Where are you?

C Work in pairs. Answer the questions in Exercise B for Lee.

SPEAKING

A PREPARE Choose a place. It could be your home or another place that you know. Imagine you are in that place. What is it like? Think about:

- far from here?
- busy/quiet?
- hot/cold at the moment?
- what kind of food?

B PLAN Use the prompts in Exercise A to make questions to ask your partner about the place he/she is in.

C SPEAK Work in pairs. Take turns asking and answering questions about your places. Guess where the place is.

Ex A - This is the correct picture.

Ask and answer questions about a place

1.3 What's in your bag?

● Talk about everyday items

V everyday items G *a/an* and plural nouns; *this, that, these, those* P vowel sounds: /ɪ/ /æ/ /iː/ /oʊ/ S reading for gist

What's in your **carry-on bag?**

Ex A **Three travel experts talk about the things in their carry-on bag when they go on a plane.**

Bruce I don't carry a lot of luggage when I go on a plane. Ex B Q1+2 My bag is very small. **I have a bottle of water and tissues.** That's it. I buy the water at the airport once I am through security. I usually sleep on a plane.

Wei I never use a suitcase. I put everything in my carry-on bag, so there's no need to wait at baggage claim. Ex B Q3 My carry-on bag is very heavy, but that's OK. Ex B Q4 **I have two watches.** I wear one and I put one in my bag, so I always know what time it is at home. **I travel to lots of countries.** I just want to get off the plane and leave the airport as soon as I can.

Elif I always have a laptop and my phone in my carry-on bag when I go on a plane. Ex B Q5 **I usually have an umbrella and my keys.** Flying is a good time to do my work. I can relax at home.

VOCABULARY
Everyday items

A Work in pairs. Look at the picture. Match the items in the picture (1–12) with the words in the box.

10 a bottle of water 1 a credit card 4 headphones 12 keys 9 a laptop 3 a magazine 8 a cell phone 5 a bag 7 tissues 6 an umbrella 2 a wallet 11 a watch

B SPEAK Work in pairs. Tell your partner what is in your bag.

A: What's in your bag?
B: My keys, a bottle of water and an umbrella.

READING

A READ FOR GIST Read *What's in your carry-on bag?* What is the text about? Things people …

a take to work.
b take to a party.
c take on a plane. (circled)

Reading for gist

When you read a text for the first time, it is important to get a general idea of what it is about. Think about:

- the title of the text and the pictures
- the general topic
- key words

B READ FOR DETAIL Read the text again. Are these sentences true (T) or false (F)? Correct the false sentences.

1 Bruce's bag is very big. Bruce's bag is very small. T / **F**
2 Bruce takes a bottle of water and tissues on the plane. **T** / F
3 Wei never uses a suitcase. **T** / F
4 Wei always has his watch and a wallet in his bag. T / **F**
Wei has a watch in his bag.
5 Elif likes to relax on the plane. T / **F**
Elif likes to work when she is flying. She relaxes at home.

GRAMMAR
a/an and plural nouns

A WORK IT OUT Look at the bold sentences in *What's in your carry-on bag?* Underline the nouns in each sentence.

B Look at the nouns you highlighted in Exercise A and complete the rules.

***a/an* and plural nouns**

1 We use *a/an* with ***plural / singular*** nouns.
2 We use *a* with singular nouns that begin with a ***consonant sound / vowel sound***.
3 We use *an* with singular nouns that begin with a ***consonant sound / vowel sound***.
4 We add ***-s / -es*** to most nouns to make a plural.
5 We add ***-s / -es*** to nouns that end in *-s* or *-ch* to make a plural.
6 For nouns that end in consonant + *-y*, we cut the *-y* and add ***-es / -ies***.

C Go to the **Grammar Hub** on **page 122**.

D SPEAK Work in pairs. Point to items in the picture in Vocabulary Exercise A. Your partner says what it is.

1.3 What's in your bag?

LEAD-IN

Before the class prepare your own bag with as many of the items as you can find that appear in the illustration. Perhaps include a child's soft toy and give it a cute name to add an element of fun to help students remember the activity. To start the lesson, silently pull out each item and elicit a response from the class. Teach the students about each item. Repeat and see if the class can remember each item.

VOCABULARY

A Put students into pairs to match the items in the picture to the words in the box. Give feedback, practicing the correct pronunciation of each word. Encourage students to connect the words in *a_bottle_of_water*, rather than saying each word individually. To review the items, you could (now or later in the lesson) produce these items from your own bag and ask students to say the word. This will help students to learn and remember the vocabulary.

B Model the conversation with a strong student. Prompt the student to ask you *What's in your bag?* Reply and show some items. Then ask the student *What's in your bag?* Support and assist the student as necessary. Then put students into pairs to talk about their own bags. Monitor and add any useful new vocabulary to the board. Use the **Vocabulary Worksheet** on W5 for extra practice.

READING

A Read through the *Reading for gist* box with the class. Elicit the title of the text (*What's in your carry-on bag?*) and ask for suggestions for key words (repeated important words), e.g. *carry-on bag, plane, bag*. Then give students time to read the text and complete the exercise before checking their answers in pairs. Check answers as a class, asking students to explain what information in the text helps them choose the correct option.

B Set a longer time limit for students to read through the text in detail and decide if the sentences are true or false. Students compare answers in pairs and correct the false sentences. Check answers as a class, asking students to explain where in the text they found the answers.

GRAMMAR

A Write the first bold sentence from the text on the board: *I have a bottle of water and tissues*. Elicit which words are nouns (*bottle, water, tissues*) and underline them. If necessary, explain that nouns are 'things' that we can name. Next, give students time to underline the nouns in the other sentences before checking answers as a class.

B Give students time to complete the rules before checking in pairs. In class feedback, ask students to identify the noun in the bold sentences which helped them to decide on the correct answer. Give new examples of each rule if necessary.

C Direct students to the **Grammar Hub** (see below and TB7). Read the examples and go through the rules with the class. Elicit that we use *an* before a vowel sound.

D Put students into pairs to practice saying the words. Monitor and encourage students to use complete sentences, rather than individual words (e.g. *It's a bottle of water*). Use the **Grammar Worksheet** on W6 for extra practice.

> **Extra activity**
> For a flexible stage in your lesson, focus on the phrases 'a bottle of', 'a bag of' and 'a box of'. Put students into groups to brainstorm ideas. Monitor and help with any vocabulary. Give feedback as a class, building up a mind map on the board. Give students new vocabulary for other containers if necessary.

GRAMMAR HUB

1.3 *a/an* and plural nouns; *this, that, these, those*

- We use *a/an* with singular nouns.
- We use *a* with nouns that begin with a consonant sound (e.g. *s, w*) and *an* with nouns with a vowel sound (*a, e, i, o, u*).

a	**a s**andwich **a w**allet
an	**an e**mail **an a**irport

- We don't use *a* or *an* with plural nouns.

	Singular	Plural
Add -s.	pen	pen**s**
Add -es to nouns that end -s or -ch.	addres**s** wat**ch**	address**es** watch**es**
Change -y after a consonant to -ies.	countr**y** nationalit**y**	countr**ies** nationalit**ies**
Some nouns are irregular.	man child person	men children people

	this	With a singular noun that's near	**This** is my bag here.
	that	With a singular noun that's far	**That** is Paola's bag over there.
	these	With a plural noun that's near	**These** are our bags here.
	those	With a plural noun that's far	**Those** are your bags over there.

- In questions, the verb *be* comes before *this, that, these* or *those*.
  Is that your bag over there? NOT ~~*That is your bag over there?*~~

1.3 What's in your bag?

LISTENING

A Check that students understand the meaning of *carry-on bag* (a small bag that you can carry onto a plane when you travel), and elicit ideas. Elicit the names for each item in Exercise A and write them on the board. Then put students into pairs to discuss which of the items can be taken on a plane.

1.10 **B** Read through the task and the questions. Play the audio and allow time for students to compare their ideas before checking answers as a class.

1.10 **C** Give students time to read through the conversations and try to remember or guess the missing words. Play the audio for students to confirm and complete the sentences.

PRONUNCIATION

1.11 **A** Play the audio and ask students to repeat the words. Highlight the different vowel sounds in each group of words.

B Put students into pairs to practice the conversations in the Listening section.

GRAMMAR

A Give students time to complete the exercise, before checking with a partner.

B Give students time to complete the rules before checking with a partner. Check answers as a class.

C Direct students to the **Grammar Hub** (see below and TB6). Read the examples and go through the rules.

SPEAKING HUB

A Model the activity by drawing six everyday items on the board. Ask students to guess what they are, before working in pairs to draw six of their own items.

B Students work alone to make a list of three items.

C Students play the game in pairs. Monitor, helping students with any new vocabulary if necessary. Focus on the accuracy of the students' grammar here, ensuring they're using *this/that* and *these/those* correctly.

AUDIO SCRIPT

1.10

Listening, Exercise B
N = Narrator G = Guard W = Woman M = Man

N: 1
Ex C Q1 **G:** Excuse me, ma'am. Is this your bag?
W: Yes, it is.
Ex B Q1 **G:** I need to look inside. Oh, is this a bottle of water?
W: Yes, it is.
G: Sorry – bottles aren't allowed.
W: Oh, of course. I'm sorry.
G: Is there a laptop or a phone in this bag?
Ex B Q1; **W:** No, there isn't.
Ex C Q2 **G:** OK. You can go. Oh, wait! Are these your keys?
W: Oh, yes, they are. Thank you so much!
N: 2
Ex C Q3 **G:** Excuse me, sir. Is that your bag?
M: Yes, it is.
G: Can you bring it here, please?
M: Sure.
Ex B Q2 **G:** Is your phone in this bag?
M: Yes, it is.
G: You need to take it out, please.
M: Oh, OK.
G: Thank you … One more thing …
M: Yes?
Ex C Q4 **G:** Are those your bags?
M: No, they aren't. I think they belong to that family over there.
G: I see. You can go.

GRAMMAR HUB

1.3 ***a/an*** **and plural nouns;** ***this, that, these, those***

A Complete the sentences with *a* or *an*.

1 MSU is ___a___ university in Moscow.
2 Take ___an___ umbrella – it's raining!
3 Tonya is ___a___ French student.
4 Send me ___an___ email later.
5 Mexico is ___a___ country in South America.
6 This is ___an___ example.

B Complete the sentences with the plural form of the nouns in bold.

1 Are these your ___keys___? **key**
2 There are two ___sandwiches___ for you. **sandwich**
3 Where are my ___headphones___? **headphone**
4 Harvard and Stanford are ___universities___ in the US. **university**
5 He has six different ___watches___! **watch**
6 Poland and Sweden are ___countries___ in Europe. **country**

C Look at pictures (1–6) and choose the correct words to complete the sentences.

1 Is *this / that / those* your wallet?

2 *Those / These / This* are my sunglasses.

3 *This / Those / These* are my sandwiches.

4 Are *these / those / that* bags yours?

5 *This / These / Those* suitcase is really heavy!

6 Is *those / that / this* your pen?

➤ Go back to page 7.

LISTENING

A SPEAK Work in pairs. Which of these items can you take in your carry-on bag?

B LISTEN FOR GIST Listen to two conversations at airport security. Which items from Exercise A does:

1.10

1 the woman have in her bag? a bottle of water; keys

2 the man have in his bag? a phone

C LISTEN FOR KEY WORDS Listen again. Complete the sentences with the correct words.

1.10

1 **A:** Excuse me, ma'am. Is this your ___bag___?
B: Yes, it is.

2 **A:** OK. You can go. Oh, wait! Are these your ___keys___?
B: Oh, yes, they are! Thank you so much!

3 **A:** Excuse me, sir. Is that your ___bag___?
B: Yes, it is.

4 **A:** Are those your ___bags___?
B: No, they aren't. I think they belong to that family over there.

PRONUNCIATION

Vowel sounds: /ɪ/ /æ/ /iː/ /oʊ/

A Listen carefully and notice the vowel sounds. Then listen again and repeat.

1.11

/ɪ/ this, kiss, sit
/æ/ that, hat, cat
/iː/ these, key, tree
/oʊ/ those, toes, nose

B SPEAK Work in pairs. Practice the conversations in Listening Exercise C.

GRAMMAR

this, that, these, those

A WORK IT OUT Look at the pictures. Match the situations (1–4) from Listening Exercise C with the pictures (a–d).

B Choose the correct words to complete the rules.

this, that, these, those

1 We use *this* / *that* to talk about a singular noun that's near.
2 We use *this* / *that* to talk about a singular noun that isn't near.
3 We use *these* / *those* to talk about a plural noun that is near.
4 We use *these* / *those* to talk about a plural noun that isn't near.

C Go to the **Grammar Hub** on **page 122**.

SPEAKING HUB

A Work in pairs. Imagine you are going on vacation. Draw six everyday items to take with you.

B PLAN Work alone. Choose three of the items in Exercise A to take in your carry-on bag.

C DISCUSS Imagine you are at airport security. Try to find out what is in your partner's carry-on bag. Follow these steps:

Student A – Point to a picture in Exercise A and ask a question with *Is this / Are these your …?*

Student B – Answer Student A's question.

Student A – Keep asking questions until you know which three items are in your partner's bag.

Talk about everyday items

Café Hub

1.4 Good morning

F – greet people and make introductions P – word stress

COMPREHENSION

A Watch the video. Complete the information about each person in the photo captions below.

B Write a question about each person in Exercise A.

1 How old is Sam?
2 Where is Gaby from?
3 Is Milly married?

C SPEAK Work in pairs. Close your books and ask each other your question from Exercise B.

A: How old is Sam?
B: He's 34.

FUNCTIONAL LANGUAGE

Greeting people and making introductions

A Complete the phrases with the words in the box.

bad fine ~~Hi~~ meet morning See too you

Say hello	Greet people + reply
Hello.	How are you?
[1] Hi .	Not too [3] bad .
Hey!	I'm [4] fine , thanks.
Good [2] morning .	Very well, thanks.
Good afternoon.	
Good evening.	

Introduce people + reply	Say goodbye
This is …	Bye.
This is my friend …	See [7] you .
It's nice to [5] meet you.	See you soon.
Nice to meet you, [6] too .	[8] See you later.

B Watch the first part of the video again. Check your answers to Exercise A.

Glossary

flat **(n) (British)** = apartment **(n) (American)**
pounds **(n) (British)** = dollars **(n) (American)**

MILLY

SAM

NEENA

ZAC

GABY

USEFUL PHRASES

A Match the useful phrases (1–3) with the replies (a–c).

1 What would you like?
2 That's £2, please.
3 Take a seat.

a Thanks.
b Can I have a croissant to go, please?
c Here you go.

B 00:24–01:14 Watch part of the video again and check your answers to Exercise A.

PRONUNCIATION

Word stress

A 00:24–01:14 Watch part of the video again and read the conversation. Notice that the underlined words are stressed.

Neena: Good morning. How are you Sam?
Sam: Not too bad. How are you?
Neena: I'm fine, thanks. This is my friend, Milly.
Sam: Hi Milly. Nice to meet you.
Milly: Nice to meet you, too.

B 00:24–01:14 Watch again and repeat the conversation. Copy the word stress.

C **SPEAK** Work in groups of three. Practice the conversation in Exercise A. Remember to use the correct stress.

SPEAKING

A **PREPARE** Walk around the class. Introduce yourself to your classmates.

A: Hello, I'm Andreas. It's nice to meet you.
B: It's nice to meet you, too.

B **DISCUSS** Work in pairs. Walk around the class. Greet the people you know and introduce your partner.

A: Hello, I'm Andreas. It's nice to meet you.
B: It's nice to meet you, too.
A: This is Nadia.

C **PLAN** You're going to record a 'selfie' presentation. Write notes about what you want to say. Then record it.

Introducing	
Hi! My name's …	I'm …
My friends call me …	I'm from …
I'm single/married …	I'm a …

D **PRESENT** Work in groups. Compare your presentations.

Greet people and make introductions

➤ Turn to page 160 to learn how to fill in a form with personal details.

1.4 Good morning

COMPREHENSION

A ▶ Read through the text and focus students on the photos. Ask students to predict which words or which kinds of words (e.g. *a noun, a number*, etc) are missing from each person's information. Play the video and allow time for students to compare and confirm answers.

B Look at the example questions with students. Highlight the form of *be* in each question and the word order. Students then work alone to write a question about each person in Exercise A. Monitor and assist as necessary.

C Put students into new pairs. Ask them to close their books and use their questions to test each other about the characters in the video. Monitor and assist as necessary.

FUNCTIONAL LANGUAGE

A ▶ Students work alone to complete the phrases. Allow time for students to compare answers in small groups.

B ▶ 00:00-01:14 Play the first part of the video again for students to check their answers to Exercise A. Give feedback, practicing the correct stress and intonation for any of the longer phrases.

USEFUL PHRASES

A Students match the useful phrases with the replies. Encourage them to think about the situations they could use each phrase in.

B ▶ 00:24-01:14 Play the next part of the video again for students to check their answers. Check answers as a class.

PRONUNCIATION

A ▶ 00:24-01:14 Go through the conversation with students. Elicit why some of the words are underlined (*they are stressed when we say them*). Ask why only the first part of *morning* is underlined (*it has two syllables and the first one is stressed*). Ask students to identify another similar word (*Milly*). Then play part of the video again so students can hear the stressed words in context.

B ▶ 00:24-01:14 Play the video and ask students to repeat the conversation, copying the word stress.

C Put students into groups of three to practice the conversation.

SPEAKING

A Model the conversation for students. Ask students to identify the word stress before practicing the correct intonation. Ask one or two pairs to model the conversation in front of the whole class. Then set a time limit and ask students to mingle and greet everyone in the class, including you.

B Ask students to identify the stressed syllables the word stress, before practicing the correct intonation. Model the conversation with another student, using natural clear stress, pauses and intonation. Then put students into pairs and ask them to mingle, introducing themselves and their partner to all of the other pairs in the class.

C Tell students that they're going to give a short presentation about themselves. Give them time to write notes about what they want to say, using the Useful language box for help.

D Students give their presentations in groups. Monitor and assist as necessary.

METHODOLOGY HUB by Jim Scrivener

Running a fluency activity

If the main goal is to get the students to speak, then one way to achieve that would be for you to reduce your own contributions. Probably the less you speak, the more space it will allow the students. It could be useful to aim to say nothing while the activity is underway, and save any contributions for before and after. In an activity mainly geared toward encouraging fluency, you are likely to monitor discreetly or vanish.

Ideas for correction work after a fluency activity:

- Write up a number of sentences used during the activity and discuss them with the students.
- Write a number of sentences on the board. Ask the students to come up to the board and correct the sentences.
- Invent and write out a story that includes a number of errors you overheard during the activity. Hand out the story the next day, and the students, in pairs or as a whole group, find the errors and correct them.

NOTE: The Glossary boxes on these pages point out differences between American English and British English, which is used in the video clips.

▶ VIDEO SCRIPT

S = Sam N = Neena G = Gaby Z = Zac

S: Hi! Good morning! My name's Sam. I'm 34 and this is my café. Ah! customers!
N: Good morning. How are you, Sam?
S: Not too bad. How are you?
N: I'm fine, thanks. This is my friend, Milly.
S: Hi Milly. Nice to meet you.
M: Nice to meet you, too.
S: What would you like?
M: Can I have a croissant to go, please?
S: Sure. That's £2, please.
M: Here you go.
S: Thanks Milly.
M: Thanks. See you later, Neena.
N: Bye, Milly. See you soon!
M: Bye, Sam.
S: Bye, Milly. What would you like Neena?
N: Can I have a black coffee, please?
S: No problem. Take a seat.
N: Thanks. So … My name's Neena, that's N-E-E-N-A. I'm a lawyer. I live in a flat and there are two free rooms. This is my ad. See you later.
Z: Hey! My name's Zac. I know Sam. He's a good friend. I love that guy. I'm American – I'm from Seattle, but I live here in London.
G: Hi! I'm Gabriela, but my friends call me Gaby. It's nice to meet you! I love London, but I'm not from here. I'm Spanish. I'm from a small town near Madrid.
M: Hello. I'm Milly, I'm 25 and I'm single. And this is my clothes store! I'm American. I love clothes and … I love music. Well … See you!

1 Writing

Fill in a form with personal details

W capital letters

A Look at the visitor card. Where would you fill in a card like this?

a At a university
b On a plane
c At work

B Complete the visitor card with the words in the box.

07713 8765543 1997 10 months Poland ~~Polish~~ student

Visitor card

Last name: Kowalska
First/middle name(s): Marta Irena
Nationality: Polish
Date of birth: month 0 3 day 1 0 year 1 9 9 7
Country of birth: Poland
Occupation: student
Passport number: ZS 0067389
Address in the UK: 24 Bridge Street, Leeds, LS5 7RT
Email: mkowalska23@polemail.com
Phone number: 07713 8765543
What is the main reason for your visit?
business / tourism / other
I am here to take a course at a university in Leeds.
Duration of visit: 10 months

C Complete the rules in the box with words from the visitor card in Exercise B.

Capital letters

You use capital letters for:

- the names of countries — Poland
- the names of towns and cities — Leeds
- nationalities — Polish
- people's names — Marta Irena Kowalska
- the personal pronoun 'I' — I am here to take a course at a university in Leeds.

D Look at the student registration form. Find and correct five mistakes with capital letters.

Student registration

Last name: ~~puente~~ Puente
First/middle name(s): Ricardo
Nationality: ~~mexican~~ Mexican
Date of birth: month 0 2 day 1 7 year 1 9 9 7
Country of birth: ~~us~~ US
Occupation: student
Address in the UK: 11 Lark Close, ~~london~~ London, SW5 9JT
Email: m.puente@hotmail.com
Phone number: 07665 456829
What is the main reason for studying English?
business / tourism / other
~~i~~ I want to study at a university in the UK.
Duration of visit: 2 weeks

WRITING

Imagine you are on a plane. Complete the visitor card. Remember to use capital letters correctly.

Visitor card

Last name:
First/middle name(s):
Nationality:
Date of birth: month day year
Country of birth:
Occupation:
Passport number:
Address in the UK:
Email:
Phone number:
What is the main reason for your visit?
business / tourism / other
I am here to take a course at Leeds University.
Duration of visit:

160 WRITING

Students can complete this card or write it out in their notebooks.

Refer students to this card as a model for the writing task.

Other rules you could mention are abbreviations like BBC or UN, languages like English and Spanish or the titles of books or movies.

WRITING

In this writing lesson, students will learn how to fill in a form with personal details and learn how to use capital letters for proper nouns and to begin a sentence.

A Focus students on the blue visitor's card that has already been filled in. Use this as a model for students to follow when they come to the final writing task. Ask students where they would see a card like this. Say it is given out on the plane or at a place of arrival like an airport, port or border crossing point. Elicit what data people need to use to complete the forms.

B Ask students to look at the numbers and words in the box. Ask students to read them out. Remind them that a '0' in a telephone number is pronounced 'zero' or 'oh' in American English. Then ask them to say what each word or number might be. Finally ask students to match the words to the blanks in the card.

C In pairs, students match the rules to the examples in the two model answers. You might need to point out that 'university' does not take a capital letter but as part of 'Leeds University', it is a proper noun and so it needs a capital letter.

D Students work alone to identify the five mistakes with capital letters before comparing answers in pairs. Ask them to look at the Capital letters rule box as required. Check answers as a class.

WRITING TASK

Ask students to write their own card either in the class or at home. If students are not sure how to do the task, point out that they should use the models on the page to copy. Otherwise, you could model one example as a whole class on the board using your own information first and elicit responses from the class. If students are unwilling to use their own data, say that they can invent data to fill in the form.

Unit 1 Review

VOCABULARY

A Complete the table with the correct countries and nationalities.

Country	Nationality
Brazil	1 Brazilian
2 China	Chinese
3 Egypt	Egyptian
India	4 Indian
Japan	5 Japanese
6 Portugal	Portuguese
Sweden	7 Swedish
The UK	8 British

B Correct the mistakes in each sentence.

1. Tokyo is the capital of Japanese. Tokyo is the capital of Japan.
2. IKEA is a Sweden company. IKEA is a Swedish company.
3. My father's from Hanoi in Vietnamese. My father's from Hanoi in Vietnam.
4. I'm from New York, in US. I'm from New York, in the US.
5. I love Switzerland chocolate! I love Swiss chocolate!

C Match the words (1–8) with the numbers (a–h).

1 one million	a 500,000
2 five hundred and ten	b 510
3 fifty-five thousand	c 5,002
4 one thousand two hundred	d 1,000,000
5 five hundred thousand	e 1,200
6 one hundred thousand	f 55,000
7 five thousand and two	g 250
8 two hundred and fifty	h 100,000

D Complete the everyday items with *a*, *e*, *i*, *o* or *u*.

1. headphones
2. a credit card
3. money
4. a cell phone
5. a bottle of water
6. a watch
7. a box of tissues
8. a laptop
9. a magazine
10. a wallet

E SPEAK Work in pairs. Discuss the questions.

1. Where are you from?
2. How old are you?
3. What nationality are your parents?
4. What's the capital of your country?
5. What's in your bag?

GRAMMAR

A Choose the correct words to complete the sentences.

1. I *'m* / *'s* from the US.
2. We *'s* / *'re* Russian.
3. They *isn't* / *aren't* married.
4. You *'s* / *'re* my friend.
5. She *isn't* / *aren't* American.
6. He *'m* / *'s* 36 years old.
7. I *isn't* / *'m not* from Sweden.

B Write questions and short answers.

1. you / Japanese
   Are you Japanese (?) Yes, I am. (+)
2. they / students
   Are they students (?) Yes, they are. (+)
3. he / German
   Is he German (?) No, he isn't. (-)
4. she / 18 years old
   Is she 18 years old (?) Yes, she is. (+)
5. you / married
   Are you married (?) No, I'm not. (-)

C Match the questions (1–4) with the answers (a–d).

1 What's your name?	a Oakland.
2 How old are you?	b It's in the US.
3 Where are you from?	c Susan.
4 Where's that?	d 26.

D Complete the text with *a*, *an* or – (no article).

This is my bag. I usually carry [1] an apple, [2] a cell phone and [3] — keys. Oh, and [4] a credit card!

E Choose the correct words to complete the sentences.

1. Is *this* / *these* your phone?
2. *That* / *Those* aren't my keys.
3. *That* / *Those* 's my book.
4. Are *this* / *these* your sunglasses?

FUNCTIONAL LANGUAGE

A Complete the conversation with the words in the box.

from Good Hi meet small Where

A: [1] Hi. I'm Andreas.
B: Nice to [2] meet you, Andreas. I'm Tia.
A: [3] Good to meet you, too, Tia.
B: [4] Where are you from, Andreas?
A: Switzerland. I live in a [5] small town near Zurich.
B: Really? I'm [6] from Chicago, but I live in Paris.

B Work in pairs. Practice the conversation in Exercise A. Use your own information.

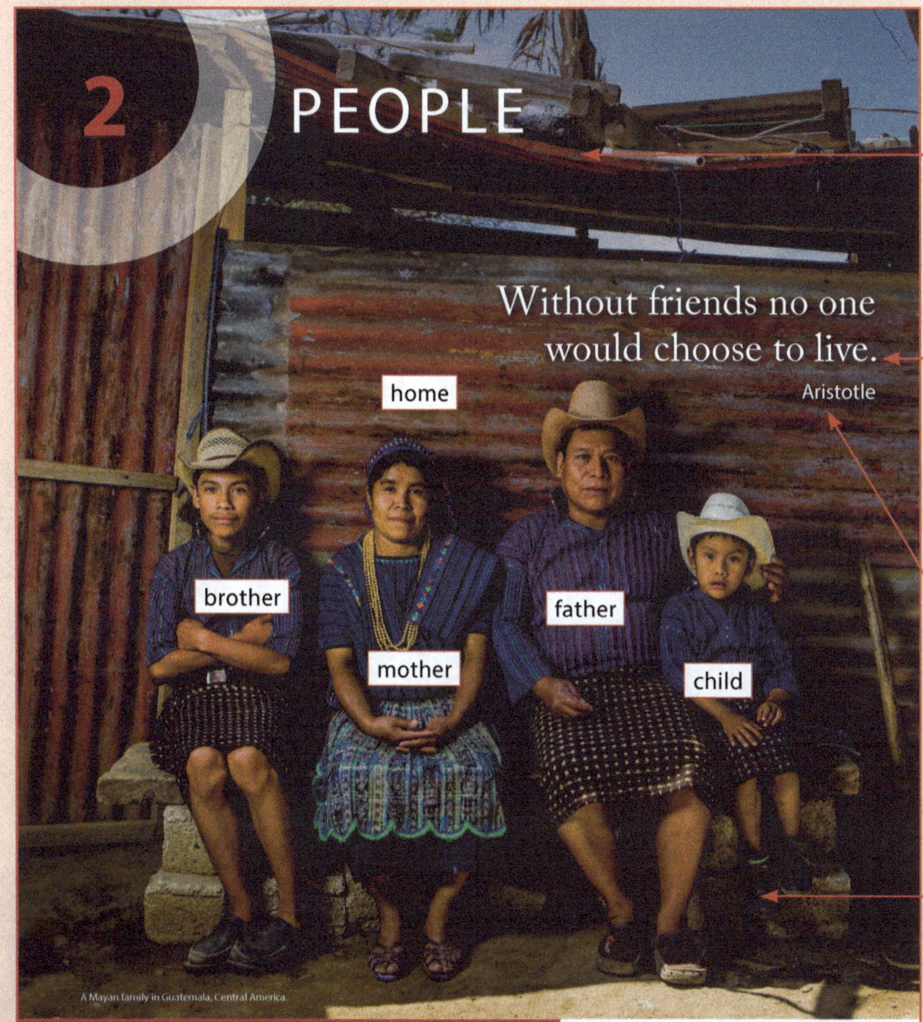

A Mayan family in Guatemala, Central America.

Ask students to label the photo if you need time to set up the class.

Aristotle means that having friendships is what is really important, rather than owning things, even if we are rich enough to own everything or anything in the world.

Aristotle (384–322 BC) was a Greek philosopher and scientist. He wrote on many subjects including physics, biology, poetry, music, psychology and linguistics.

A Mayan family in Guatemala, Central America.

OBJECTIVES

- talk about your family
- talk about appearance
- describe family members and friends
- make and respond to requests
- write an email to a friend

Work with a partner. Discuss the questions.

1 Do you have a big family?
2 Do you have any brothers or sisters?
3 What do you like doing with your friends?

PEOPLE 11

OBJECTIVES

Read the unit objectives to the class.

UNIT OPENER QUESTIONS

Ask students to look at the photo and describe the family. Use this as an opportunity to assess how well students can talk about family and appearances. Write *He has* and *She has* on the board. Point out that students can use these sentence stems to talk about the people's hair, clothes and skin color.

Write *Do you have a big family?* on the board. Tell students how many people are in your family and if you have any brothers and sisters. Put students into pairs to say how many people are in their families.

Then ask them to read Questions 2 and 3. Check that students understand the questions and write these sentence stems on the board: *I have [number] brother(s) and [number] sister(s)*. Point out that students can use *no brothers* or *no sisters* if they don't have any.

Students then discuss the questions in pairs. Monitor students and help with grammar and vocabulary when necessary.

If you have time, bring the class together and ask two or three students to share their answers with the class. Encourage students to listen to each other and to extend the discussion with further questions and ideas.

WORKSHEETS

Lesson 2.1 Family

Family (W7)

Possessive adjectives and apostrophes (W8)

Lesson 2.2 The same, but different

Describing appearance (W9)

have/has (W10)

Lesson 2.3 Friends

Personality adjectives (W11)

Using adjectives (W12)

2.1 Family

Talk about your family

V – family P – /ə/ 'schwa' G – possessive adjectives and apostrophes

READING

A Work in pairs. Look at the pictures in *Famous Families*. Why are these people famous?

B **READ FOR GIST** Read *Famous Families* and check your answers to Exercise A.

C Work in pairs. How many of the people do you know?

D **READ FOR DETAIL** Read *Famous Families* again. Are the sentences true (T) or false (F)? Correct the false sentences.

1 Sofia is a famous actress. T / (F)
She's a famous movie director.
2 Sofia's grandparents were Italian. (T) / F
3 Sofia's brother is named Francis Ford Coppola. T / (F)
Sofia's brother is named Roman.
4 Sofia's aunt was in the movie *Rocky*. (T) / F
5 Sofia and her husband, Thomas, live in Italy. T / (F)
They live in New York City.

E **SPEAK** Work in pairs. What other famous families do you know?

FAMOUS FAMILIES

This week, we continue our series on Hollywood families with a look at the Coppolas.

Sofia Coppola is an American screenwriter and director. She's famous for directing the movies *Marie Antoinette*, *Somewhere*, *The Bling Ring* and *The Beguiled*. Sofia's family is famous, too. There are famous movie directors, actors and musicians in her family. Ex B; Ex D Q1

Ex B; Ex D Q2 Her grandparents, Carmine Coppola and Italia Pennino, were musicians from Italy. Sofia's father is the movie director Francis Ford Coppola. He is the Ex B; Ex D Q3 director of the three *Godfather* movies. Sofia's brother, Roman Coppola, is also a movie director. Ex B; Ex D Q3

Ex B Sofia's aunt is Talia Shire. She's an actress, and she was Ex D Q4 in the *Godfather* and the *Rocky* movies. Talia's son is Ex B the actor Jason Schwartzman. Jason is Sofia's cousin. The actor Nicolas Cage is her cousin, too. Nicolas's father was August Coppola. He was Francis Ford Coppola's brother.

Ex B Sofia's husband is Thomas Mars, the singer of the Ex D Q5 rock band Phoenix. Sofia and Thomas live in New York City, and they have two daughters. Their daughters' names are Romy Mars and Cosima Mars.

Thomas Mars

Sofia Coppola

Francis Ford Coppola

Talia Shire

Jason Schwartzman

2.1 Family

LEAD-IN

Play 'Who am I?' with the class. Think of a famous person your students will be familiar with. Students ask you *yes/no* questions to discover your identity (e.g. *Are you an actor?*). Provide clues as needed using the target language of the unit (e.g. *He has black hair.*). When students guess your famous person, ask them to play the game in small groups.

READING

A Focus students on the photos of the famous people. In pairs, they say who the people are and why they are famous. Check answers as a class. If you have time, you could ask the class to say how the people's appearances are similar.

B Allow students one or two minutes to read through *Famous families*. Point out that they should only try to check their answers to Exercise A. Check answers as a class.

C Remind students to correct the false sentences. Allow students to compare answers in pairs, before checking as a class.

D Model the exercise by sharing your knowledge of a famous family. Show images, if possible, of the people. Try to use words for family relationships and adjectives for describing the people's appearance.

Extra activity
Put students into groups. Give them time to research other famous families (real or fictional). Monitor and encourage each group to choose one family. Then, ask groups to prepare a short presentation on the family they chose, using the *Famous families* text to help them. Finally, have groups give their presentations to the class. Focus on fluency here, rather than accuracy. Help with any challenging or new vocabulary.

GRAMMAR HUB

2.1 Possessive adjectives and apostrophes

Subject pronouns	Possessive adjectives
I	my
he	his
she	her
it	its
we	our
you	your
they	their

Be careful!

- We only add *'s* to the last name.
  Ivan and Hannah's family NOT ~~*Ivan's and Hannah's family*~~
- We don't put an apostrophe in *its* when it is a possessive adjective.
  *France is famous for **its** cheese.* NOT ~~*France is famous for it's cheese.*~~
- We only add 's to last name when the thing referred to belongs to both people. If you are talking about two different things (Ivan's blog and Hannah's blog - We read Ivan's and Hannah's blogs) both would get the apostrophe.

- We use possessive adjectives to show that something belongs to someone.
  *Ali lives with **her** parents.*
  *I live with Tom and **his** sister.*
- We use the same possessive adjectives for singular and plural nouns.
  *They're **her** friends.* NOT ~~*They're hers friends.*~~
- We use possessive apostrophes to show that something belongs to someone.
  She's married to Dave's brother.
- We use *'s* with singular nouns.
  My sister's children are named Tanya and Kyle.
- We use *s'* with plural nouns.
  My grandparents' names are Ed and Jilly.
- We use *'s* with irregular plural nouns.
  The children's names are Moya and Daryl.

2.1 Possessive adjectives and apostrophes

A Complete the sentences with a possessive adjective.

1. My cousin and his wife live in Paris. ___Their___ house is very big.
2. Sofia Coppola is a screenwriter and director. ___Her___ movies are famous.
3. Switzerland is famous for ___its___ chocolate.
4. We're French, but ___our___ children speak English at home.
5. Ken, is ___your___ last name 'Clark' or 'Clerk'?
6. That's Michael with ___his___ wife, Laura.
7. I'm British, but ___my___ parents are German.

B Choose the correct options to complete the sentences.

1. My ***husband's*** / *husbands'* family lives in Brazil.
2. Their ***daughter's*** / *daughters'* name is Lillie.
3. The ***children's*** / *childrens'* grandfather is an artist.
4. My *grandparent's* / ***grandparents'*** names are Mel and Bob.
5. What are the ***women's*** / *womens'* names?

C Choose the correct words to complete the text.

[1]***I*** / *My* am an actor, and so is my father. [2]*He* / ***His*** name is Juan. [3]***He's*** / *His* famous in South America. [4]*I* / ***My*** mother is famous too. [5]***She's*** / *Her* a singer. I also have two brothers. [6]***Their*** / *They* names are Miguel and Esteban. [7]*Their* / ***They're*** singers like [8]*we* / ***our*** mother.

➤ Go back to page 13.

2.1 Family

VOCABULARY

A Read through the sentence with students and ask them to find it in *Famous families*. Then ask students to find seven more words for family members. Allow students time to compare answers in pairs and then check answers as a class.

B Focus students on the family tree. Point out that there are some names missing. Tell students to complete the family tree with names from *Famous families*.

C Focus students on the table and ask them why *grandparents* is in the third column, under *Female or male*. Point out that a *grandparent* can be a man (a grandfather) or a woman (a grandmother). Students then complete the table with words from Exercise A. Check answers as a class, and write the table on the board.

D In pairs, students add the words to the table. Check answers by asking different students to come to the board to complete the table.

E Put students into pairs. Tell them that they are going to read about a famous person and ask and answer questions about their families. Direct students to the **Communication Hub**. Tell Student A to read about Bebel Gilberto. Tell Student B to read about Matthew Centrowitz Jr. and point out that *Jr.* is short for *Junior*. This means that his father has the same name but is called Matthew Centrowitz Sr. (short for *Senior*). Allow students up to two minutes to read about their person. Then tell them to ask each other their questions and write notes on the answers. Monitor and assist as required. Use the **Vocabulary Worksheet** on W7 for extra practice.

PRONUNCIATION

2.1 **A** Write *mother*, *brother* and *actor* on the board and say them naturally. Ask students how many syllables are in each word (*two*) and which one is stressed (*the first*). Then play the recording and ask students to repeat the words. Point out that the 'schwa' sound is very common in unstressed syllables (it is never heard in stressed syllables).

2.2 **B** Focus students on the words in the box. Ask them how many syllables are in each word (*two, except for television, which has four*). Then ask them which syllable is stressed in each word (*the first syllable, except for director which has the second syllable stressed*). Tell students to underline where they think the 'schwa' sound is in each word. Check answers as a class by playing the recording and asking students to practice saying the words.

GRAMMAR

A Read through the task instructions with students. Point out that they need to focus on the word in bold (not the underlined phrase). Check answer for Question 1 before students move on to Question 2.

B Focus students on the table and point out that the possessive adjectives from Exercise A (*their*, *her*) are already in the correct place in the table. Put students into pairs to complete the table with the words in the box. Check answers as a class by writing the table on the board.

C Read through the task instructions with students, highlighting that they need to review the sentences in Exercise A. Then allow time for students to complete the rules and compare answers in pairs, before checking as a class.

D Direct students to the **Grammar Hub** (see TB12). Read the examples and go through the rules with the class. Use the **Grammar Worksheet** on W8 for extra practice.

SPEAKING

A Draw your own family tree on the board. Keep it simple, showing only your parents, grandparents, children and brothers or sisters. Use it to tell the class about your family. Tell students to draw their own family tree. Monitor and assist as required.

B Put students into pairs and ask them to show each other their family trees. Students use them to tell their partner about their families. Monitor and make a note of effective language and phrases which can be reformulated. Give whole-class feedback on the language used.

TEACHING IDEA by David Seymour and Maria Popova

Grammar: Dictation

Use this activity to review the grammar section. Say this to your students:

I'm going to dictate a note for you to write down. I'll read the text twice.

Hi, how's it going? There's a party at Steve's place. Tom's going with his roommate, Tracey. She's a guitarist and she has a great voice. It's always good to go to Steve's house. It's always fun. He's cooking dinner and he has a lot of drinks, but let's take some drinks, too. There's a store near Steve's house. Let's meet there at seven. OK, see you later.

Compare your text with a partner. How many times did you write *'s*? There should be 12. Decide whether each *'s* is (a) an abbreviation of *is*, (b) an abbreviation of *has*, (c) an abbreviation of *us* or (d) a possessive *'s*.

TEACHING IDEA by David Seymour and Maria Popova

Vocabulary: My relatives

Use this activity to review family vocabulary. Say this to your students:

In small groups, tell each other the names of your relatives (e.g. *My dad's name is Alfred.*).

niece, father, sister, brother, aunt, mother, nephew, uncle, son, grandfather, daughter, grandmother, cousin

Tell each other what you think your relatives are doing right now (e.g. *My brother Dan is sitting at his office desk. My aunt Mary is doing the gardening.*).

VOCABULARY

Family

A Look at the word in **bold** in the sentence below. Find and underline seven other words for family members in *Famous families*.

*Her **grandparents**, Carmine Coppola and Italia Pennino, were musicians.*

B Read the text again. Complete the family tree.

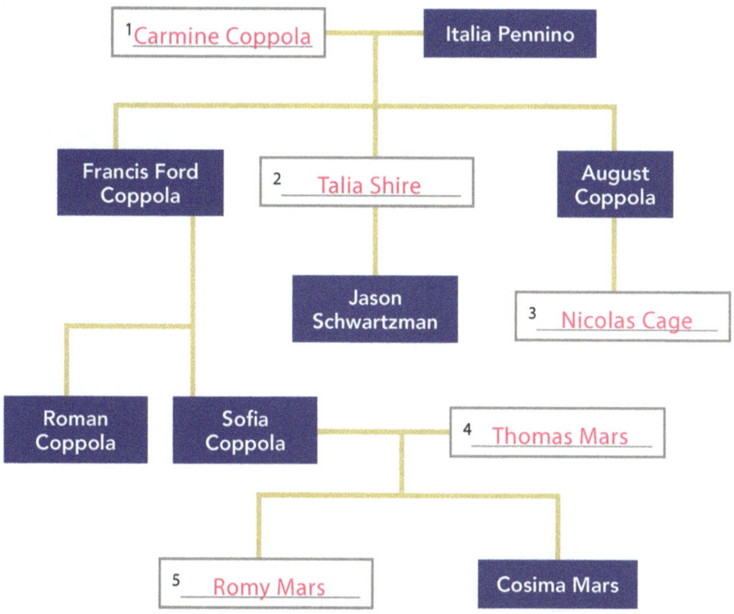

C Complete the table with the words you found in Exercise A.

Female	Male	Female or male
aunt	brother	*grandparents*
daughter	father	cousin
grandmother	husband	children
mother	son	parents
sister	grandfather	
wife	uncle	

D Add the words in the box to the table in Exercise C.

children grandfather grandmother mother parents sister uncle wife

E **SPEAK** Work in pairs. Student A – go to the **Communication Hub** on **page 156**. Student B – go to the **Communication Hub** on **page 158**.

PRONUNCIATION

/ə/ 'schwa'

2.1 **A** Listen and repeat. Notice how we say the underlined sounds.

/ə/ family, husband, famous

2.2 **B** Say these words with a partner. Underline the /ə/ sound in each word. Then listen, check and repeat.

actress family famous husband parents sister television woman

GRAMMAR

Possessive adjectives and apostrophes

A Look at the sentences from *Famous families*. Which name matches the word in **bold**? Choose a, b or c.

1 *Jason is Sofia's cousin. The actor Nicolas Cage is **her** cousin, too.*

a Jason (b) Sofia c Nicolas

2 *Sofia and Thomas live in New York City, and they have two daughters. **Their** daughters' names are Romy Mars and Cosima Mars.*

(a) Sofia and Thomas b Sofia c Thomas

B **WORK IT OUT** Complete the table with the words in the box.

his its my our your

Subject pronouns	Possessive adjectives
I	1 my
you	2 your
we	3 our
they	their
he	4 his
she	her
it	5 its

C **WORK IT OUT** Look at the underlined words in Exercise A. Then complete the rules.

Possessive apostrophe

1 We add ' / 's to regular singular nouns.
2 We add ' / 's to regular plural nouns.
3 We use the possessive apostrophe to show that something ***belongs to*** / ***doesn't belong to*** someone.
4 We add 's to show that something ***belongs to*** / ***doesn't belong to someone*** when their name ends with an s.

D Go to the **Grammar Hub** on **page 124**.

SPEAKING

A **PREPARE** Draw your family tree. Include any grandparents, uncles, aunts or cousins.

B **SPEAK** Work with a partner. Take turns telling each other about the people in your family tree.

My grandfather's name is Hiroyuki. He's 98 years old. My grandmother's name is Saya. She's …

Talk about your family

2.2 The same, but different

Talk about appearance

V describing appearance   G *have/has*   P *have/has*

VOCABULARY
Describing appearance

A Work in pairs. Match the people in the pictures (1–2) with the words in the box.

beard	blond hair	blue eyes	brown eyes	curly hair
gray hair	light skin	long hair	short hair	straight hair

B Go to the **Vocabulary Hub** on **page 146**.

TWO in a million

This is a picture of Bobby and Riley George on the day they were born. (Ex C Q1) They're twins. They have curly hair, brown eyes and light skin.

(Ex C Q2+3) This is Bobby and Riley three years later, and they look really different! Bobby looks like his mother. He has light skin, blond hair and blue eyes. Riley (Ex B) looks like his father. He has dark skin and brown eyes, and short, brown hair. The boys don't look the same, but do they have the same personality? (Ex C Q4) No, they don't. Bobby is very noisy and Riley is quiet. They really are one in a million!

READING

A Look at picture a in *Two in a million*. Choose three sentences that describe the babies.

1 They are the same age. (circled)
2 They look different.
3 They look like each other. (circled)
4 They have the same parents. (circled)
5 They have different parents.

B **READ FOR GIST** Read *Two in a million*. Check your answers to Exercise A. What is the name of the child on the left in picture b?
Riley

C **READ FOR DETAIL** Read again. Choose the correct words to complete the sentences.

1 Bobby and Riley's birthdays are on ***the same day*** / ***different days***.
2 Bobby and Riley look ***the same*** / ***different*** three years later.
3 Bobby and the twins' mother have ***the same*** / ***different*** skin color.
4 Riley and Bobby have ***the same*** / ***different*** personalities.

look like

The phrase *look like* means have the same appearance.

- I/You/We/They + *look like* + noun
  I look like my mother. I don't look like my father.
- He/She It + *looks like* + noun
  My sister doesn't look like me. She looks like our mom.

D **SPEAK** Work in pairs. Describe someone in your class to your partner. Can they guess who it is?

A: *He's tall. He has long, brown hair and brown eyes. He looks a little like Johnny Depp …*
B: *Is it Matteo?*

2.2 The same, but different

LEAD-IN

Show a picture containing a group of people. Describe one of them without saying who it is. Try to use some of the target words that students will be learning (*He has …*, *She has …* and words like *beard*, *blond hair*, *blue eyes*, *light skin*, etc). When a student guesses who you are describing, they should come to the front of the class to point to the person. If the student is right, he or she then gets to try describing one of the people. Help students by reformulating their vocabulary or grammar, if necessary.

VOCABULARY

A Put students into pairs to match the words in the box to Pictures 1 and 2. Point out that some words can be used more than once. Check answers as a class. Model the pronunciation of the words and phrases, and ask students to repeat.

B Direct students to the **Vocabulary Hub**. Do Exercise A as a class. Point out that *height* refers to how tall or short someone is. You could tell students your own height. Explain that *build* refers to the size and shape of a person's body. Model and practice the pronunciation of *mustache* and *bald*. Give them time to complete Exercise B alone before checking answers in pairs. Use the **Vocabulary Worksheet** on W9 for extra practice.

READING

A Focus students on the picture of the two babies in *Two in a million*. Then put them in pairs to complete the exercise. Don't give feedback yet.

B Give students time to read the text and answer the question. Give feedback as a class.

C Students read the text in detail and complete the sentences. Give them time to check their answers in pairs, before giving feedback as a class. If you have time, read through the *look like* box as a class and give examples (ideally using pictures on your phone). Then elicit examples from students. Read through the *look like* box with students. If you have time, you could show your own family photos. Write *Does [name] look like [name]?* on the board, and ask students for their opinions. Ask students to talk about their own family or people they know, using *look like* or *looks like*.

D Put students in pairs to describe people in the class. Monitor and assist as necessary.

Extra activity

Put students into groups. Ask them to write short descriptions of three famous people without mentioning their name. Then, ask groups to read their sentences to the class and try to guess who they're talking about.

METHODOLOGY HUB by Jim Scrivener

Presentation techniques for lexis

If you just want to quickly convey the meaning of one or more lexical items, there are a number of ways you could do that. The most common technique probably involves a presentation-practice route:

- Present: you first offer some cues, pictures or information about the target items and elicit the words from students or model them yourself. You will need to check that learners have understood how they are formed, what they mean and how they are used.
- Practice: you then get the students to practice, e.g. by repeating items, using them in short dialogues, etc.

Alternatively, there are many other ways to convey meaning. For each lexical item in the following random list, I've suggested a different way that you could help students begin to learn the meaning.

gloves Mime putting them on.

disgusting Mime (e.g. smelling old food) and make a facial expression.

café Draw a quick sketch on the board or show a flashcard or picture in a book.

often Draw a line. Mark *never* at one end and *always* at the other. Mark points along it: *usually*, *rarely*, etc.

chase Get two or three students to act it out.

frightened Tell a personal anecdote.

window sill Point to the object.

put up with Tell a short story that includes it.

put your foot down Act out a short conversation.

contact lens Students who know explain to those who don't.

reduction Draw a diagram or graph.

TEACHING IDEA by David Seymour and Maria Popova

Grammar: Celebrity *'s*

Use this activity to review the vocabulary section. Say this to your students:

Here are some words for describing people. In small groups, write pairs of sentences about famous people using the possessive *'s* and *be/have*, e.g. *Leonardo di Caprio's eyes are blue – Leonardo di Caprio has blue eyes.* (You may like to add a few features to this list for describing celebrities that are well known to your students.)

blue eyes, red hair, big teeth, long legs, curly hair, green eyes, big muscles, nice voice, bushy eyebrows

TEACHING IDEA by David Seymour and Maria Popova

Grammar: *Have/has and does/does not*

Use this activity to review the vocabulary section. Say this to your students:

In pairs, ask and answer questions using the correct form of have/has and does/does not and these words, e.g.

A: Do you have any CDs?

B: Yes, I do. / No, I don't.

A: What CDs do you have?

B: I have …

sisters, brothers, pets, children, books, toys, house plants, middle names, friends in New York, relatives in the UK, English books

(Allocate one thing to each student to mingle and find out who in class has the most certifications, pets, etc)

In pairs, tell each other about the rooms and features your house has, e.g. *My place has a large, sunny kitchen.* Do the same for your country, e.g. *My country has some of the most beautiful mountains in the world.*

2.2 The same, but different

GRAMMAR

A Focus students on the three sentences and ask them to go back to *Two in a million* to complete them. Highlight that they should use no more than three words for each sentence. Check answers as a class and write them on the board.

B In pairs, students complete the table. Check answers as a class by building up the table on the board.

C Direct students to the **Grammar Hub** (see below). Read the examples and go through the rules and exercises with the class.

D Focus the students on the picture and elicit a description of the woman. Then ask students to read the conversation and work together to complete it. Highlight that they should use the correct form of have/has and does/does not as well as contractions where possible (*she has or she doesn't have*). Allow time for students to practice the conversation. Encourage them to look up and say each line and not just read it from the page.

E Students ask their partners which family members they look like. Tell them to listen carefully to their partner. Students then change partners and report what their first partner said (e.g. *She looks like her … They both have …*). Use the **Grammar Worksheet** on W10 for extra practice.

PRONUNCIATION

2.3 **A** Play the recording for students to listen and repeat.

/v/ I have */z/ he has*

2.4 **B** Play the recording for students to listen and choose the correct sound. Give feedback as a class.

C Students work in pairs to complete the sentences. Monitor and practice natural pronunciation as necessary.

LISTENING

A In pairs, students describe the man in the picture. Check answers as a class by asking for descriptions from two or three students.

2.5 **B** Students listen and decide if they had the same ideas.

A: *My brother doesn't look like me. We both have long red hair, but everything else is different. He's short, and I'm not. I'm very slim, but he isn't. He has glasses. I don't. And he has a beard. I definitely don't have a beard.*

C Students work in pairs to describe family members. Monitor and assist as necessary.

SPEAKING

Students turn to the **Communication Hub**.

GRAMMAR HUB

2.2 have/has

	Positive	Negative
I/you/we/they	**I have** a roommate.	**I don't have** a roommate.
he/she/it	**He has** a big family.	**She doesn't have** a big family.

- We use *have/has* to talk about someone's appearance, family or possessions.

  I have a new phone.
- We use *Have/Has* + subject to make questions.
- We often use *any* before plural nouns in the question form.

  *Does she have **any** children?*

	Question	Short answers	
I/you/we/they	**Do you have** any brothers or sisters?	Yes, **I do.**	No, **I don't.**
he/she/it	**Does she have** long hair?	Yes, **she does.**	No, **she doesn't.**

Be careful!

Does she have any children? Yes, she does. NOT ~~Yes, she has.~~

2.2 have/has

A Complete the sentences using *have* or *has*.

1 They ___have___ a house in the countryside.
2 Georgiana and Stefania ___have___ long, blond hair.
3 Diane ___has___ a twin sister named Erin.
4 My sister ___has___ brown eyes, but I don't.
5 They ___have___ three children.

B Rewrite the sentences in Exercise A to make them negative. Use contractions where possible.

1 *They don't have a house in the countryside.*
2 Georgiana and Stefania don't have long, blond hair.
3 Diane doesn't have a twin sister named Erin.
4 My sister doesn't have brown eyes, but I do.
5 They don't have three children.

C Use the prompts to write questions and short answers.

1 your dad / a beard
Does your dad have a beard? (?) *No, he doesn't.* (-)
2 you / any lipstick
Do you have any lipstick? (?) Yes, I do. (+)
3 they / a car
Do they have a car? (?) Yes, they do. (+)
4 Maria / short hair
Does Maria have short hair? (?) Yes, she does. (+)
5 we / any shampoo
Do we have any shampoo? (?) Yes, we do. (+)
6 you / your glasses
Do you have your glasses? (?) No, I don't. (-)

➤ Go back to page 15.

GRAMMAR

have/has

A WORK IT OUT Look at *Two in a million* again. Complete the sentences with no more than three words from the text.

1 ____Riley has____ brown hair, brown eyes and dark skin.

2 ____Bobby has____ blond hair and blue eyes.

3 The boys don't look the same, but do they have the same personality? No, ____they don't____.

B WORK IT OUT Complete the table with the words from the box.

have have doesn't

	Positive (+) / Negative (-)		
1	I	___have___ / don't have	blue eyes.
2	He/She/It	has / ___doesn't___ have	
3	You/They/We	have / don't ___have___	

C Go to the **Grammar Hub** on **page 124**.

D PRACTICE Look at the picture. Complete the conversation about the woman with the correct form of *have/has* and *does/does not*. Use contractions.

A: Who do you look like?

B: My aunt. She's my dad's sister.

A: Does your aunt [1] ___have___ long hair?

B: No, she [2] ___doesn't___. She [3] ___has___ short, gray hair.

A: [4] ___Does___ she [5] ___have___ glasses?

B: Yes, she [6] ___does___.

A: What color eyes [7] ___does___ she have?

B: She [8] ___has___ blue eyes. We also have the same nose.

E SPEAK Find out who your partner looks like in their family.

I look like my mother. She has brown eyes, like me. And we both have curly hair.

PRONUNCIATION

have/has

2.3 **A** Listen and repeat the phrases with *have* and *has*. Notice the /v/ and /z/ sounds.

2.4 **B** Listen and choose the correct sound /v/ or /z/.

1 he has /v/ (/z/)
2 it has /v/ (/z/)
3 I have (/v/) /z/
4 she has /v/ (/z/)
5 they have (/v/) /z/
6 you have (/v/) /z/

C SPEAK Work in pairs. Complete the sentences about people in your class.

1 I have ...
2 You have ...
3 He/She has ...
4 We have ...
5 They have ...

LISTENING

A Work in pairs. Describe the man in the picture.

2.5 **B LISTEN FOR KEY WORDS** Listen to a description of the man in Exercise A. Does it match yours?

C SPEAK Work in pairs. Think of someone in your family. Tell your partner how you and this person are the same, and how you are different.

A: My dad doesn't look like me. He has gray hair and a beard. I have brown hair. I have glasses, but he doesn't.
B: My sister looks the same as me. We're twins!

SPEAKING

Work in pairs. Go to the **Communication Hub** on **page 154**.

Talk about appearance

2.3 Friends

Describe family members and friends

V personality adjectives **P** syllable stress: adjectives **G** using adjectives **S** reading for organization

VOCABULARY

Personality adjectives

A Complete the descriptions with the adjectives in the box.

friendly funny quiet sad neat

1 She's really ___funny___ – she always makes me laugh.
2 My uncle is a ___quiet___ person. He doesn't talk much; he just listens.
3 Hakim always puts things away after he uses them – he's very ___neat___.
4 My father's often ___sad___. He doesn't laugh or smile a lot anymore.
5 Reema is a very nice person – she's ___friendly___ to everyone.

B Match the adjectives (1–5) with their opposites (a–e).

1 friendly	a messy
2 funny	b unfriendly
3 quiet	c happy
4 sad	d noisy
5 neat	e serious

PRONUNCIATION

Syllable stress: adjectives

2.6 Work with a partner. Say the adjectives, and then add them to the table. Listen and check your answers.

~~friendly~~ funny happy messy noisy quiet sad serious neat unfriendly

●	●•	●••	•●•
sad neat	*friendly* funny messy noisy quiet happy	serious	unfriendly

LISTENING

A **LISTEN FOR GIST** Listen to the conversation. Match people (1–3) to the names below.
2.7

Zoe ___1___ Alice ___2___ Jody ___3___

B **LISTEN FOR DETAIL** Look at the questions and check (✓) the correct person or people. Listen again and check your answers.
2.7

	Keisha (speaker)	Zoe	Alice	Jody
1 Who's in the same study group?	✓	✓	✓	✓
2 Who's funny?		✓		
3 Who's neat?				✓
4 Who's quiet?			✓	
5 Who's serious?				✓
6 Who's messy?	✓			

C **SPEAK** Work in pairs. Are you like Keisha, Zoe, Alice or Jody? Give examples.

GRAMMAR

Using adjectives

A **WORK IT OUT** Look at the sentences from the conversation. Underline the adjectives.

1 They're all really <u>friendly</u>.
2 She's a very <u>funny</u> person.
3 She's fairly <u>quiet</u>, but I like her.

B Choose the correct words to complete the rules. Use the sentences in Exercise A to help you.

Using adjectives

1 We put adjectives *before* / *after* the verb *be*.
2 We put adjectives *before* / *after* nouns.

C Go to the **Grammar Hub** on **page 124**.

D **SPEAK** Work with a partner. Tell them about someone you know. Use *really*, *very* or *fairly* in your descriptions.

2.3 Friends

LEAD-IN

Write five adjectives on the board, three which describe you well and two that don't. Include some adjectives which describe physical appearance (e.g. *tall, short, blond*, etc) and one or two of the personality adjectives from this lesson (e.g. *serious, funny, neat*, etc). Ask students to work in pairs to decide which three adjectives describe you. Give feedback as a class, encouraging pairs to make statements using the adjectives they chose (e.g. *You're tall.*). Answer each statement with either *Yes, I am* or *No, I'm not.* Continue until the class has guessed all three adjectives correctly. If you have time, put students into groups to repeat the activity for themselves.

VOCABULARY

A In pairs, students complete the sentences using the adjectives in the box. Give feedback as a class, providing more examples for each adjective if necessary. Model and practice correct pronunciation.

B Students work alone to match the adjectives to their opposites before comparing their answers in pairs. Give feedback as a class, eliciting example sentences for the new adjectives. Use the **Vocabulary Worksheet** on W11 for extra practice.

PRONUNCIATION

2.6 **A** Write *friendly* on the board. Say the word and elicit that the stress is on the first syllable. Underline it on the board (*friendly*) and write the stress pattern *Oo* above it.

LISTENING

2.7 **A** Play the recording for students to match the people to the names. Check answers as a class.

2.7 **B** Focus students on the table, and tell them to try to apply check marks to the correct people. Play the recording again for students to check their answers.

C Put students into pairs to discuss the question. Monitor and encourage students to give examples or why they are or aren't like the people they heard about. Encourage them to use personality adjectives when giving examples.

GRAMMAR

A In pairs, students work to identify the adjective in each sentence. Point out that there is only one in each sentence. Check answers as a class.

B Allow time for students to complete the rules for using adjectives, before comparing answers in pairs. Check answers as a class.

C Direct students to the **Grammar Hub** (see below). Read the examples and go through the rules and exercises with the class.

D Read through the instructions with the class. Allow up to two minutes for students to think of adjectives they can use. Put students into pairs to describe the person to their partner. Monitor and assist as required, making sure that students are using *really*, *very* and *fairly* effectively. Use the **Grammar Worksheet** on W12 for extra practice.

GRAMMAR HUB

2.3 Using adjectives

- We use adjectives to describe things.
- Adjectives have one form for singular and plural.

  a kind woman

  two kind women NOT ~~two kinds women~~
- In sentences with a noun, the adjective comes before the noun.

  *She is a **good** friend.*
- The adjective comes after the verb *be* when we describe the subject of a sentence.

  *Frederica **is tall**.*

Be careful!

- We use *very* and *really* to make an adjective stronger.

  very tall
- We use *fairly* to mean 'a little but not very'.

  ***fairly** long*
- *Very, really* and *fairly* come before the adjective.

  *Her hair is **very/really/fairly** long.*

2.3 Using adjectives

A Reorder the words to make sentences.

1 busy / is / it / here / in

It's busy in here.

2 happy / today / Tim / is

Tim is happy today.

3 is / Al's / desk / really / messy

Al's desk is really messy.

4 house / really / is / big / this

This house is really big.

5 a / has / he / car / fast

He has a fast car.

6 really / sister's / funny / your

Your sister's really funny.

B Correct the mistakes in each sentence.

1 Toby is ~~a~~ fairly noisy.
2 Roxanna is ~~a~~ really friendly.
3 Marin is a big very man. Marin is a very big man.
4 Greg is serious really. Greg is really serious.
5 Magdalena has a very bedroom messy. Magdalena has a very messy bedroom.
6 Alicia and Georgina are quiet~~s~~ young women.
7 Wow! These paintings are beautiful~~s~~.
8 This café is quiet fairly. This cafe is fairly quiet.

➤ Go back to page 16.

2.3 Friends

READING

A Focus students on the photograph. Elicit ideas on where the people are and what they are doing, but don't confirm any answers at this point. Then read through the task instructions and questions. Give students a time limit of one minute to find the answers in the email.

B Read through the *Reading for organization* box with students. Point out that sentences usually connect to other sentences. Write the following sentences on the board: *There's a guy in my class named Erdem – he's from Turkey. He has long hair, a beard and he's really noisy …* Point out that the second sentence adds more information about Erdem. It doesn't repeat the word *Erdem* but uses *he* instead.

Go through the task instructions with students. Tell them to work alone to read the email again and to add Sentences 1 to 5 in the correct places. Then, students compare answers in pairs. Ask them to explain if each new sentence adds new information, explains something or changes the topic (*1 – adds more information; 2 – adds more information and explains something; 3 – adds more information; 4 – helps to change the topic; 5 – adds more information*). Check answers as a class.

SPEAKING HUB

A Ask the class to say what they remember about Yassir (e.g. *where he is and why he isn't happy*). Read through the task with students. Elicit the type of person Yassir would like to live with. Write any adjectives that students use on the board (e.g. *friendly, funny, happy, neat*). Ask students about the type of person Yassir would not like to live with. Again, write adjectives on the board, in a different section (e.g. *noisy, unfriendly, messy*).

B Students work in pairs to read through the information about the three different people. They should discuss and write notes on who would be the best roommate. Ask each group to share their final answer and to give reasons. Conduct whole-class feedback. If you have time, you could ask the class to vote on who would be the best roommate.

Extra activity

Put students into pairs to discuss their own roommates and what they like/dislike about them. If they live with their parents or alone, ask them to discuss their ideal roommates.

AUDIO SCRIPT

2.7

Listening, Exercise A

F = Fiona K = Keisha

F: I like this picture.

Ex B Q1 **K:** This is on our first day. These are the people in my study group.

F: Everyone looks so happy.

K: Yes. They're all really friendly and nice.

F: That's great! So, who is who?

Ex A; Ex B Q2 **K:** The girl with dark curly hair is Zoe. She's my best friend. She's a very funny person.

F: Are any of your roommates in this picture?

K: Yes. Jody is my roommate. She has long hair.

F: Does she have black hair?

Ex A; Ex B Q4; Ex A **K:** No, that's Alice. She's fairly quiet, but I like her. This is Jody – she has long, blond hair.

F: Is she neat? It's good to have neat roommates.

Ex B Q3 & 5; Ex B Q6 **K:** Yes, she is. She's fairly serious and very neat! I'm the messy one in our apartment!

METHODOLOGY HUB by Jim Scrivener

Approaches to speaking

Here are some suggestions for how to organize a speaking lesson.

- **Topic and cues**

At its simplest, you (or learners) would possibly bring to class a topic (e.g. 'banning smoking' or 'globalization'), as well as a cue (e.g. in the form of a short newspaper article or a provocative question) that will serve to help spark conversation. Most of the lesson would then be taken up with discussing this, stating and comparing views. There might be little or no explicit 'teaching' of grammatical or vocabulary points. In planning the lesson, it would be a good idea to prepare a number of further cues (e.g. a follow-up article or question).

- **Structuring talk**

Your main role will be to structure the talk, making sure that all learners get a chance to participate, trying to prevent it getting boring, occasionally adding to the discussion itself in order to keep it interesting. It is likely that you will generally want to reduce your own participation level; the more you talk, the less space there is for learners to say something.

- **Avoiding the talk–talk loop**

There is a danger of getting locked into a 'talk–talk loop', in which you say something, but because there is no response from the learners, you say something else, and again with no response you add something else, etc. It takes a little courage initially, but you will usually get far more conversation out of a class by asking one clear question and then shutting up – and patiently allowing even a fairly long silence, while learners formulate what they want to say. Repeatedly adding new comments or new questions can have the opposite effect to that intended, confusing the class and closing down people who were planning to speak.

- **Open questions**

A key technique will be to use 'open questions' (e.g. where, what, who, why, how, when questions that require a longer answer) rather than 'closed questions' (e.g. verb–subject questions that require nothing more than yes or no). For example, instead of 'Is noise pollution a bad thing?', you could ask 'What do you think about noise pollution?' Focusing on specific issues is even more likely to encourage reactions, for example, 'When they make that noise with the drill outside, how do you feel?'

- **Playing devil's advocate**

One useful intervention you can make is to sometimes play 'devil's advocate' (i.e. deliberately taking an opposing or contrasting viewpoint in order to spur on conversation).

READING

A READ FOR GIST Read Yassir's email. Where is he and who is he talking about? He's at college; he's talking about his classmates and roommates

RE: How're things?
Sent: Friday November 10, 2017, 2:19 pm
To: a.nadar@screen.nett
From: YassirAwad@logbox.com

Hi Ahmed,

I'm having a great time at college! [a]___ There are about 20 people in my class, and all of them are friendly. There's a guy in my class named Erdem – he's from Turkey. He has long hair, a beard and he's really noisy, but he's very funny! He's one of my close friends now. [b]___ I met a French guy named Nico at soccer practice. He's really friendly, but very different from Erdem. He's fairly quiet and serious.

[c]___ The bad news is about my roommate. [d]___ His name's Erik. He's quiet in the day and noisy in the middle of the night! He's so unfriendly – he never speaks to me. And he's really messy! [e]___ I want to live with a happy, friendly and neat person!

See you soon,
Yassir

B READ FOR ORGANIZATION Read again. Match the sentences (1–5) with the blanks in the email (a–e). Use the information in the box to help you.

Reading for organization

To help you understand how a text is organized, think about how one sentence connects to another. Does it add more information? Does it explain something? Does it change topic?

d **1** I only have one roommate.
a **2** There's a lot of work to do, but there are also a lot of fun things to do in my free time.
e **3** I want to find a new place to live.
c **4** That's the good news.
b **5** I always laugh a lot when I'm with Erdem.

SPEAKING HUB

A Imagine you can choose a new roommate for Yassir. Think about the type of person Yassir wants to live with.

B PLAN Read about these people. Write notes about who would be a good/bad roommate for Yassir.

Antonio
Italian
'I'm from Naples, and I love cooking and soccer. I like listening to music when I study. I have lots of friends and I like to cook for them.'

Cvetomir
Bulgarian
'I love watching soccer on TV, but I never play. I never cook at home because I hate cleaning the kitchen. I like to sleep a lot. I'm a good roommate – I'm very quiet.'

Jonas
Swedish
'I like to study a lot in the day and talk to friends in the evening. My friends say I'm really funny, but I think I can be serious, too. I like to play sports and relax with friends on the weekend.'

C SPEAK Work in groups. Discuss the different people. Who is the best roommate for Yassir?

Describe family members and friends

2.4 Café chaos

F– make and respond to requests   P– stress and intonation

COMPREHENSION

A **Look at the pictures. Then watch the video and check (✓) the things you see.**

a camera ☑

keys ☐

a croissant ☑

a laptop ☑

headphones ☑

an umbrella ☐

a skateboard ☑

a phone ☑

B **Work in pairs. Correct the wrong information in each sentence. Then watch the video again and check.**

1 It's the ~~afternoon~~. *It's the morning.*
2 ~~Gaby's~~ cappuccino and croissant is ~~£6.50~~. Gaby's cappuccino and croissant is £4.50.
3 ~~Gaby~~ has a skateboard. Zac has a skateboard.
4 Zac is from ~~Detroit~~. Zac is from Seattle.
5 Gaby is ~~Italian~~. Gaby is Spanish.
6 Gaby's ~~mum's~~ name is Maria. Gaby's sister's name is Maria.
7 Gaby ~~has a~~ flat. Gaby doesn't have a flat/apartment.
8 Zac ~~has a~~ flat. Zac doesn't have a flat/apartment.

FUNCTIONAL LANGUAGE

Making and responding to requests

2.8 **A** **Complete the phrases in the table with the words in the box. Then listen and check.**

afraid ahead cappuccino dollars sit that

Asking for things
Can/Could I have a [1] cappuccino, please?
Can/Could I [2] sit here?
Saying Yes/No
Sure, no problem.
Go [3] ahead.
Of course.
No, sorry. I'm [4] afraid not.
Asking for prices
How much is [5] that?
How much are they?
Giving prices
£4.50 / four pounds, fifty.
$2.20 / two [6] dollars and twenty cents.
€15.75 / fifteen euros, seventy-five.

Glossary

mum **(n) (British)** = mom **(n) (American)**
pounds = **(British)** currency

B **Work in pairs. Think of other ways of completing requests 1 and 2 in Exercise A. Practice saying them to each other.**

Can I have a pen, please?

2.9 **C** **How do you say the prices in the box? Practice with a partner, then listen and check.**

£5.25 $6.50 €13.30 $8.90 £14.40 €17.70

D **Work in pairs. Write down three different prices and say them to your partner. Write what you hear.**

MILLY

SAM

NEENA

ZAC

GABY

USEFUL PHRASES

A Complete the useful phrases with the words in the box.

funny idea sorry this way wrong

I am so ___sorry___.

No ___way___!

That's ___funny___!

What's ___wrong___?

I have a great ___idea___.

Let's do ___this___!

B ▶ 00.58–05:17 Watch the second part of the video again and check your ideas in Exercise A.

PRONUNCIATION

Stress and intonation

A ▶ 00:00–00:58 Watch the first part of the video again and read the conversation. Notice the stress and intonation.

Sam: Morning. What can I get you?
Gaby: Hi! Can I have a cappuccino please?
Sam: Sure. Anything to eat?
Gaby: Could I have a brownie?
Sam: No, sorry. I'm afraid not. There aren't any.
Gaby: OK. Erm. Can I have a croissant then?
Sam: No problem. Is that everything?
Gaby: Yes, thanks. How much is that?
Sam: Four pounds fifty. Take a seat.
Gaby: Thank you.

B ▶ 00:00–00:58 Work in pairs. Watch again and repeat the conversation. Copy the stress and intonation.

C **SPEAK** Work in pairs. Practice the conversation in Exercise A. Remember to use the correct stress and intonation.

SPEAKING

A **PREPARE** Work in groups of three. Write your own café conversation.

- Student A is the café owner. Students B and C are customers.
- Use the phrases in Functional Language to help you.
- Include all of the words in the box below.

afraid ahead sit can you could I
course here can we sorry sure

B **DISCUSS** Practice your conversation. Perform it for the rest of the class.

A: Hello! Can I help you?
B: Hi! Can I have a coffee, please?
A: Sure, no problem.
B: And could I have a croissant?

Make and respond to requests

➤ Turn to page 161 to learn how to write an email to a friend.

2.4 Café chaos

LEAD-IN

Play a guessing game with students. Tell them that you are thinking of an object (e.g. a croissant), but do not say what it is. Give them a clue as to what it is (e.g. *It's from France.*). Elicit guesses from the class, and give them more clues if required. If students do not know the word, add letters to the board to support their guesses (e.g. *cr______t*).

COMPREHENSION

A ▶ Focus students on the pictures. Then play the video for students to apply a check mark to the things they see. Allow time for students to compare their answers in pairs before checking answers as a class.

B ▶ Give students time to read through the sentences. Explain that every sentence has wrong information.

FUNCTIONAL LANGUAGE

2.8 **A** Focus students on the table and the column headings. Students complete the table with the words in the box. Then check answers by playing the recording. Spend some time modeling and practicing the phrases.

B Students work in pairs to practice asking and answering the requests (*Can/Could I have a cappuccino, please?* and *Can/Could I sit here?*). Tell them to use their own ideas. Monitor and give students praise for correct language use and pronunciation.

2.9 **C** Model the first price in the box for the class (*five pounds twenty-five*). Also model the words *euros* and *dollars*. Students work in pairs to practice saying the rest of the prices. They then listen and check.

D Students work in pairs to practice saying prices. Monitor and assist as necessary.

USEFUL PHRASES

A Give students time to complete the phrases alone, before checking their answers in pairs. Give feedback as a class.

B ▶ 00:58-05:17 Play the second part of the video again for students to check their answers.

PRONUNCIATION

A ▶ 00:00-00:58 With books closed, write the first line of the conversation on the board. Say the line naturally, using hand gestures to emphasize the rhythm, stress and pauses. Ask students to comment on the way you said it and to identify the stressed syllables. Underline the stressed syllables on the board and repeat the line. Allow time for students to read through the conversation in the book before playing the video again.

B ▶ 00:00-00:58 Play the video again for students to listen and then repeat the conversation in pairs.

C Put students into new pairs. Ask them to practice the conversation together. Encourage them to look up and say each line, rather than reading from the book. Monitor and provide positive feedback on good use of stress and intonation.

SPEAKING

A Put students into groups and explain that one is a café owner and the other two are customers. Students work together to write their dialogues.

B Give students time to practice their conversations, before performing them for the class. Make a note of any useful words or phrases that come up and add them to the board after each conversation.

▶ VIDEO SCRIPT

S = Sam **G** = Gaby **Z** = Zac

S: Morning. What can I get you?
G: Hi! Can I have a cappuccino, please?
S: Sure. Anything to eat?
G: Could I have a brownie?
S: No sorry. I'm afraid not. There aren't any.
G: OK. Um. Can I have a croissant then?
S: No problem. Is that everything?
G: Yes, thanks. How much is that?
S: £4.50. Take a seat.
G: Thank you.

Z: I am so sorry! Are you OK?
G: Yes. I'm sorry, too. Thank you.
Z: You're welcome! Here is your camera.
G: Here's your skateboard. Could I sit here?
Z: Sure. Go ahead.
G: I'm Gaby. What's your name?
Z: Zac.
G: Cool name.
Z: Thanks.
G: Are you … American?
Z: Yeah. I'm from Seattle – and you?
G: I'm Spanish from Madrid.
Z: Do you live in London?
G: Yeah. I live with my sister, Maria.
Z: No way! My sister's name is Maria, too.
G: That's funny!
Z: So … are you a photographer?
G: Yes … and a Spanish teacher. Miércoles. Miérrrrrrrrrrrrrrrrrrrrrrrrrrrrrrrr … How about you?
Z: I'm a programmer. I make video games.
G: Cool!

Z: Hi Gaby. Can I sit here?
G: Of course! Could I have the sugar, please?
Z: Yes. Here you are. Hey, what's wrong?
G: My sister has got a new job in Madrid, so I need a new flat. Can you help?
Z: No, sorry. I'm afraid not. I have a big apartment, but … I'm sorry. I need to answer this. Hi … OK … Right … Really? Next week! OK. Bye.
G: Who was that?
Z: My landlord.
G: What's wrong?
Z: I need a new apartment. Now!
G: I've got a great idea. Are you clean and tidy?
Z: Uh … Yeah?
G: Good. What about bathrooms?
Z: Uh … Yeah?
G: Are you a good cook?
Z: Yeah! I love food!
G: OK! Perfect!
Z: What's perfect?
G: My name is Gabriela García Martínez and I am … your future housemate!
Z: OK. Let's do this!

2 Writing — Write an email to a friend

W – *and, but* and *or*

A Read the email. Who is it to?

a a close friend **b an old friend** (circled) c a colleague

How's things?
Sent: Friday, November 10, 2017, 2:19 pm
To: jbloggs@screen.nett
From: Aiden_28@logbox.com

Hi Joe,
How are you? Long time no see!
How are things? I live in London now with my girlfriend. Do you still live here? How's your family?
Look forward to hearing your news!
Best wishes,
Aiden

B Check (✓) the topics you think Joe will write about in his reply. Then read and check.

- food ☐
- family ☑
- job / school ☐
- friends ☐
- home ☑
- clothes ☐

RE: How's things?
Sent: Friday, November 10, 2017, 4:37 pm
To: Aiden_28@logbox.com
From: jbloggs@screen.nett

Hi Aiden,
I'm very well, thanks. It's great to hear from you!
Yes, we are still in London, but we're not in the apartment anymore. We live in a house because … we have two beautiful children now!
We have a son, Ben, and a daughter, Maya. Ben is three and Maya is four - it's a noisy house! Ben looks like his mom (lucky him!) but he has my personality. He isn't neat or serious, but he's only three! Maya has blond hair and blue eyes like me. Here's a picture for you of all of us on vacation this year!
How about you, Aiden? How are things with you and your family?
Best wishes,
Joe

C Read the email in Exercise B again and underline examples of *and, but* and *or*.

D WORK IT OUT Choose the correct words to complete the rules.

and, but and or

1 We use ***and*** / *but* / *or* when we want to add more or similar information in positive statements.
2 We use *and* / *but* / ***or*** when we want to add more or similar information in negative statements.
3 We use *and* / ***but*** / *or* when we want to add different or unexpected information.

E Complete the sentences with *and, or,* or *but.*

1 I have two pets, a cat ___and___ a dog.
2 I don't have any children ___or___ pets!
3 I live in a house with my friends Amy ___and___ Emma.
4 I have a horrible roommate. She isn't friendly ___or___ neat!
5 My roommate loves soccer ___but___ I hate it.

F SPEAK Work in pairs. Look at the emails in Exercises A and B and answer the questions.

1 How do you start an email to a friend? Hi [name]
2 How do you end an email to a friend? Best wishes
3 Which phrases are useful when it's the first contact in many months or years? Long time no see! Looking forward to hearing your news! It's great to hear from you!

WRITING

A PLAN Imagine you are responding to the email in Exercise A. Write notes about:

How to start the email
How to answer the questions
How to finish the email.

B WRITE Write your email. Use the email in Exercise B to help you. Remember to:

Start and end your email appropriately
Answer the questions
Use *and, but* or *or* to join sentences together.

WRITING 161

Build up words and phrases on the board and give time for students to make a record of them in their notebooks.

Refer students to this email as a model for the writing task.

Students can do this in class or for homework.

WRITING

In this writing lesson, students will learn how to write an email to a friend and how to use the linking words *and*, *but* and *or* to add information.

A If possible, display the email on the board. Students read it and decide who it is to. Ask students to explain how they decided and which information they used.

B In pairs, students discuss the topics and apply check marks to the ones they think Joe will write about in his reply. Check answers as a class. Again, ask students to explain how they decided. Students then read the second email and check their answers.

C Read through the task with students. Students then identify and underline the examples of *and*, *but* and *or* in the email in Exercise B. If possible, check answers as a class with the email displayed on the board. Elicit the general idea that these words are used to connect ideas and add information.

D Students work alone to choose the correct words to complete the rules. Give time for students to compare answers in pairs. Check answers as a class.

E Students work alone to complete the sentences with *and*, *or* or *but*. Students compare and discuss answers in pairs before checking as a class.

F Students discuss the questions in pairs.

WRITING TASK

A Students write notes on the three points listed. Then they can compare their ideas with a partner.

B Students write their emails using the model in Exercise B. Make sure that they use *and*, *but* and *or* to make longer sentences. Monitor and assist as required.

Extra activity
Display the students' emails around the room. Then ask the class to walk around, read the emails and choose one to reply to for homework.

Unit 2 Review

VOCABULARY

A **Look at the family tree. Match the beginnings of sentences (1–8) with the ends of sentences (a–h).**

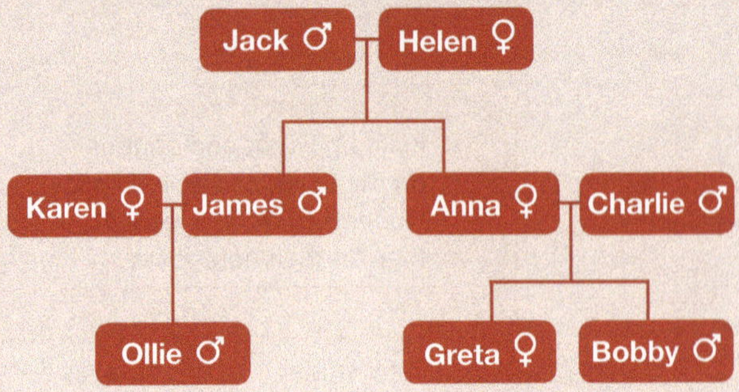

1	Anna is Greta's	a	granddaughter.
2	Greta is Bobby's	b	uncle.
3	Jack is Greta's	c	mother.
4	Helen is Jack's	d	grandfather.
5	Anna is Ollie's	e	cousin.
6	Greta is Helen's	f	wife.
7	Bobby is Ollie's	g	sister.
8	James is Bobby's	h	aunt.

B **SPEAK** **Work in pairs. Tell your partner about your family.**

C **Complete the descriptions (1–4) with the words in the box.**

beard curly light fat glasses long tall

1 Paolo has ___long___, straight hair, blue eyes and a big ___beard___.
2 Julia has ___light___ skin, brown eyes and blond, ___curly___ hair.
3 My grandfather is very ___tall___. He has gray hair and wears ___glasses___.
4 My baby brother is very ___fat___.

D **Complete sentences (1–6) with the words in the box.**

funny messy noisy quiet serious neat

1 Laurence is so ___noisy___! Why does she shout so much?
2 My brother is so ___messy___. His bedroom is full of dirty clothes and old pizza boxes.
3 Michael is really ___funny___. He always makes me laugh.
4 Your sister never smiles. Why is she so ___serious___ all the time?
5 Erin cleans the kitchen every day. She's a very ___neat___ person.
6 Why is he so ___quiet___? I can't hear anything he says!

E **Work in pairs. Describe:**

- your best friend
- your teacher
- someone you work or study with

GRAMMAR

A **Complete the text with pronouns or possessive adjectives.**

Hi! 1 ___I___'m Carrie. I'm Australian and I'm a doctor. 2 ___My___ parents are Mike and Jennifer. 3 ___They___'re actors. I have one sister. 4 ___Her___ name is Lula and 5 ___she___'s 18. I have two brothers. 6 ___Their___ names are Tom and Brad. 7 ___They___'re all from Brisbane.

B **Correct the sentences by adding *'s* or *s'*.**

1 Carrie's last name is Pinto.
2 Her sister's name is Lula.
3 Her brothers' names are Tom and Brad.
4 Jennifer's children's names are Carrie, Lula, Tom and Brad.
5 My brother's dog is named Rufus.
6 His parents' house is amazing!

C **Complete the text with the correct form of *have/has*.**

How many brothers and sisters 1 ___do___ you 2 ___have___? My family is small. It's just me, my brother, Eric and my mom. I look like my mom. She 3 ___has___ blond hair and blue eyes. Eric 4 ___has___ dark, curly hair, but I 5 ___have___ blond, straight hair. My eyes are blue, like Mom's, but Eric 6 ___has___ brown eyes.

D **Find and correct one mistake in each sentence.**

1 This is a ~~house~~ very big *house*.
2 My sisters are smalls.
3 I'm very quiet not. I'm not very quiet.
4 He's a unfriendly really person. He's a really unfriendly person.
5 Are you messy very? Are you very messy?
6 Erin's quiet fairly today. Erin's fairly quiet today.

FUNCTIONAL LANGUAGE

A **Reorder the words to make requests and offers.**

1 I / please / have / a / Could / sandwich, / ?
Could I have a sandwich, please?
2 I / open / window / the / Can / ?
Can I open the window?
3 use / Can / please / I / dictionary, / your / ?
Can I use your dictionary, please?
4 help / Would / me / you / like / to / ?
Would you like me to help?

B **Work in pairs. Take turns reading the situations and decide what to say. Make requests and offers.**

1 Your friend has a very big bag.
2 You are cold.
3 You don't have a pen.
4 You are thirsty.

3 DAYS

Yesterday's history, tomorrow's a mystery but today is a gift. That's why it's called the present.
Alice Morse Earle

People walking through the snow in Tokyo, Japan.

OBJECTIVES

- talk about daily routines
- discuss daily activities
- describe a special day
- make and respond to suggestions
- write a blog post about your day

Work with a partner. Discuss the questions.

1. What's your favorite day of the year?
2. Look at the picture. Where is it?
3. What do you do on the weekend?

DAYS 21

It's important to appreciate the moment we are in now. We cannot change the past and we cannot know for sure what the future holds. We should feel grateful for the present, rather than taking it for granted. The quote uses the dual meaning of *present* (*a gift* and also *the here and now*).

Alice Morse Earle (1851–1911) was an American writer and historian. She was very interested in the customs, traditions and history of the US.

Ask students to label the photo if you need time to set up the class.

People walking through the snow in Tokyo, Japan.

OBJECTIVES

Read the unit objectives to the class.

UNIT OPENER QUESTIONS

Focus students on the picture. Ask students what time of year they think it is. Write ***My favorite day of the year is*** …
Use this sentence stem to say what your favorite day is. Then, elicit students' ideas.

Ask students how similar or different the picture is to their own country, and give them time to expand on and explain their answers. Ask students if they think the picture shows people on a weekend or on a weekday. Elicit that it is probably a weekday, showing people going to work.

Ask students to read the questions at the bottom of the page. Check that students understand them. Put students into pairs or small groups to discuss them. Monitor students and help with grammar and vocabulary when necessary.

When students have finished the questions, ask one or two pairs or groups to share their ideas with the class. Encourage students to listen to each other and respond with their own ideas and opinions.

WORKSHEETS

Lesson 3.1 A typical day

Everyday activities (W13)

Simple present positive (W14)

Lesson 3.2 All day, every day

Adverbs of frequency (W15)

Prepositions of time (W16)

Lesson 3.3 A special day

Simple present negative (W17)

Big celebrations (W18)

3.1 A typical day

Talk about daily routines

V everyday activities **G** simple present positive **P** third person -s

LISTENING

A Read the information about a guest on the radio show *Two minutes*. Are the sentences true (T) or false (F)? Correct the false sentences.

1. Venus Mack works for a radio station. **T** / F
2. She's in her mid-thirties. She's in her mid-twenties. T / **F**
3. She starts and finishes work in the afternoon. She starts work at 10 pm and finishes at 6 am. T / **F**
4. She's American. **T** / F

3.1 **B LISTEN FOR KEY WORDS** Listen to the radio show *Two minutes*. Match the names (1–3) with the nouns (a–c).

1. Bowie — b
2. Reuben — c
3. Joel — a

a. Venus's producer
b. Venus's dog
c. a rock band

3.1 **C LISTEN FOR DETAIL** Listen to the interview again. Choose the correct time to complete the sentences.

1. I have breakfast at *4 pm* / ***6 pm***.
2. I get to work at ***8 pm*** / *9 pm*.
3. The show starts at *10 am* / ***10 pm***.
4. I have coffee with friends at ***6 am*** / *9 am*.
5. I go to bed at *2 am* / ***9 am***.

D SPEAK Work in pairs. Do you agree or disagree with these sentences? Why?

1. Venus's typical day is interesting.
2. Venus works long hours.
3. Venus has a lot of energy.

A: I agree. I think Venus's typical day is very exciting.
B: Why?
A: She meets a lot of musicians.

VOCABULARY

Everyday activities

A Look at the pictures of Tom's morning routine. Complete the phrases with the verbs in the box.

get | get up | ~~have~~ | leave | work

1

I get up at 7:00 am.

2

I *have* breakfast at 7:30 am.

3

I leave home at 7:45 am.

4

I get to work at 8:30 am.

5

I work at a desk all day.

B Go to the Vocabulary Hub on page 147.

C SPEAK Work in pairs. Take turns asking and answering questions with *What time do you …?* and an everyday activity.

A: What time do you get up?
B: Seven o'clock.
A: What time do you have breakfast?
B: Seven thirty.

3.1 A typical day

LEAD-IN

On the board, write a list of six things you do on a typical day and four things you don't (e.g. drink six cups of coffee, go to the gym for two hours). Try to make these as interesting as possible, yet also believable. Then ask students to guess which six things you do on a typical day and in which order. Give feedback as a class.

LISTENING

A Elicit where you might see this kind of information (e.g. on a website for a radio station). Then give students time to complete the exercise before checking in pairs. Give feedback as a class.

3.1 **B** Play the recording so students can complete the exercise alone. Give feedback as a class.

3.1 **C** Give students time to read through the sentences first, before playing the interview again. Give students time to compare answers in pairs before checking answers as a class.

D Put students into pairs to discuss the questions. Monitor, encouraging students to explain their reasoning.

VOCABULARY

A Focus on the verbs in the box. Write *at 7:00 am* on the board and ask which verb goes with this phrase (*get up*). Students then work in pairs to complete the other phrases. Check answers as a class.

B Write *What time do you …?* on the board. Then say an activity from Exercise A (e.g. *have breakfast*). Ask a stronger student to say the question (*What time do you have breakfast?*) and then ask another student to answer.
Put students into pairs to ask and answer questions using the verb phrases from Exercise A. Use the **Vocabulary Worksheet** on W13 for extra practice.

Extra activity

Do a 'Find someone who …' activity. Give students time to decide who they want to find (e.g. someone who gets up before 6:30 am) and to write questions to help them do so (e.g. *What time do you get up?*). They then mingle and ask their questions and make a note of anyone who fits what they were looking for. Students report back to the class on what they found (e.g. *No one gets up at 6:30.*).

AUDIO SCRIPT

3.1

Listening, Exercise B
T = Tom V = Venus

T: Hello and welcome to *Two minutes* with me, Tom Fenn. Our guest today is Venus Mack, who is
Ex A Q4 phoning in from California. Good morning, Venus.

V: Hey, Tom. Hey, UK. Good *evening* from Los Angeles.

T: You have two minutes to tell us about your typical day.

Ex A Q2 **V:** OK, well, my name's Venus Mack, I'm 25 years old
Ex A Q1 and I'm a late-night DJ for a radio station here in LA! I live in a small house, and – uh – a typical day? My day is unusual because I get up at four o'clock in the afternoon. That's right! 4 pm.
Ex B Q1 So, first, I go for a long run. My dog, Bowie, comes, too. Then, I go home, take a shower and have
Ex C Q1 breakfast – breakfast at 6 pm, right? – it's usually fruit and coffee. I leave home at around 6:30. I go to
Ex C Q2 work by car. Everyone drives here in LA! I get to work at 8 pm. I love my job! I meet a lot of musicians, and some of them are on my show.
Ex B Q2 This week it's a band – from the UK – called Reuben.
Ex A Q3; Ex C Q3 My show starts at 10 pm and ends at 2 am. After
Ex B Q3 the show, I work with my producer, Joel, and
Ex A Q3; Ex C Q4 prepare for the next show. I finish work at 6 am and then I go to a café and have coffee with friends and maybe some dinner, and then I go home to
Ex C Q5 give Bowie his breakfast. I go to bed at around 9 am.

T: Fantastic! Thanks, Venus.

METHODOLOGY HUB by Jim Scrivener

Eliciting

'Eliciting' means drawing out information, language, ideas, etc from the students. It is a technique based on the principles that:

- students probably know a lot more than we give them credit for;
- starting with what they know is a productive way to begin new work;
- involving people in a question-and-answer movement toward new discoveries is usually more effective than simply giving 'lectures'.

Eliciting enables me to start from where the learners are and then to work forward from there. The learners have a real effect on the outcome of the lessons in terms of ideas, language and pace. With constant learner involvement, I can work more at their speed rather than my own. I can find out where the real difficulties and problems are.

There are three steps to eliciting:

1 I convey a clear idea to the students, perhaps by using pictures, gestures or questions, etc.
2 They then supply the appropriate language, information or ideas.
3 I give them feedback.

I can elicit language, ideas, feelings, meanings, contexts, memories, etc. I can't elicit things they don't know.

3.1 A typical day

GRAMMAR

A Read through the task with students. Ask them to do it in two stages. First, check which words are verbs. Then, give students time to identify the incorrect rule in the box. Give feedback as a class, matching the examples.

B Students complete the table with the correct form of the verb 'live'. Draw the table on the board and ask students to tell you how to complete it.

C Direct students to the **Grammar Hub** (see below).

D Model the activity by describing the typical day of your best friend. Write three to four example sentences on the board. Then, put students into pairs to describe the typical day of someone they know. Monitor and make a note of any errors students make when using the simple present, especially when adding *-s* to verbs. Use these notes in whole-class feedback. Use the **Grammar Worksheet** on W14 for extra practice.

Extra activity
Write three simple present sentences about yourself on the board, two true and one false (e.g. *I play video games every night, I get up at 6:30 am on Saturdays.*). Encourage the class to guess which sentence is false, focusing on fluency at this stage, not accuracy. Next, give students time to write three sentences about themselves. Monitor, correcting grammatical errors as necessary. Finally, put them in pairs to guess which sentences are true and which are false.

PRONUNCIATION

3.2 **A** Read through the task instructions and Sentences 1–3. Model the sounds /s/, /z/ and /ɪz/ before playing the recording, so that students know what the symbols mean. Then play the recording and ask students to repeat the sentences.

3.3 **B** Play the recording and ask students to decide which sound they hear. Give time for students to compare answers in pairs. Then check answers as a class by playing the recording again.

3.3 **C** Play the recording again and ask students to repeat the sentences. Do this as a whole class, then practice with students individually, focusing on the target sounds.

SPEAKING

A In pairs, students make a list of jobs. Monitor and help with words as necessary. If you have time, you could allow students to look up and/or translate job titles using dictionaries. Elicit ideas from the whole class and build up a list on the board.

B Students work together, choosing a job and writing sentences about someone with that job. Monitor and assist as required. Make sure students are using the target vocabulary (everyday activities) and grammar (simple present positive) correctly.

C Put students into new pairs to complete the activity. Monitor, helping with any new challenging vocabulary. Correct any mistakes with the target language. Practice correct pronunciation of third person *-s* endings as appropriate, but try not to let this interfere with the flow of the activity.

GRAMMAR HUB

3.1 Simple present positive

I/you/we/they	**I finish** work at 5 pm.
he/she/it	**She finishes** work at 5 pm.

- We use the simple present to talk about habits and routines.
- We also use the simple present to talk about:
  - facts and things that are true.
    Paris is the capital of France.
  - likes and dislikes.
    Alessia likes her apartment.
  - possessions with *have* and *has*.
    He has a pet dog.
  - fixed times.
    The movie starts at 6 pm.

Spelling rules		
Add -s to most verbs.	love play	She love**s** music. He play**s** computer games.
Add -es to verbs that end -ss, -ch, -sh, -x, -o.	wat**ch** g**o**	She watch**es** TV. He go**es** for a run.
Change -y after a consonant to -ies.	stud**y**	She stud**ies** after dinner.

Be careful!
- The *he/she/it* form of *have* is *has*.
  She has a nice flat. NOT ~~She haves a nice flat.~~

3.1 Simple present positive

A Complete the sentences with the correct form of the verb in parentheses.

1 I ___live___ (live) in an apartment in Hong Kong.
2 My mother ___watches___ (watch) TV every day.
3 We ___listen___ (listen) to the same music.
4 She ___has___ (have) a gym class after work.
5 My dad ___goes___ (go) to work by train.
6 The store ___closes___ (close) at ten o'clock.

B Rewrite the sentences. Correct the mistakes in bold.

1 They **works** in an office. They work in an office.
2 She **study** every day. She studies every day.
3 He **gos** to school at eight o'clock. He goes to school at eight o'clock.
4 I **buys** sandwiches for lunch every day. I buy sandwiches for lunch every day.
5 Our dog **watch** TV with us. Our dog watches TV with us.
6 We **eats** dinner at seven o'clock. We eat dinner at seven o'clock.
7 She **live** in New York with her sister. She lives in New York with her sister.
8 The train **leave** at 10:30 am. The train leaves at 10:30 am.

➤ Go back to page 23.

GRAMMAR

Simple present positive

A WORK IT OUT Read the sentences from *Two minutes*. Underline the verbs. Then cross out the incorrect rule in the box.

I get up at four o'clock.

Bowie comes with me.

I go to work by car.

My show starts at 10 pm.

Simple present
1 We use the simple present to talk about everyday habits and routines.
2 ~~We use *be* + the main verb to make the simple present.~~
3 We add an *-s* (or *-es*) to verbs when the subject is *he*, *she* or *it*.

B Complete the table with the correct form of the verb *live*.

Simple present		
I/You/We/They	1 live	in a small house.
He/She/It	2 lives	

C Go to the **Grammar Hub** on **page 126**.

D SPEAK Work in pairs. Think about someone you know. Tell your partner about their typical day.

A: My sister gets up at six o'clock.

B: My friend Lukas plays video games every night.

PRONUNCIATION

third person *-s*

A (3.2) There are three different ways of pronouncing the endings of simple present verbs in the third person. Can you hear the difference? Listen and repeat.

1 /s/ She work**s** in an office.

2 /z/ He play**s** video games every night.

3 /ɪz/ He watch**es** the news every morning.

B (3.3) Listen to the sentences. Circle the correct pronunciation of the third person *-s* ending.

1 She leave**s** home at 8 am. /s/ (/z/) /ɪz/

2 He teach**es** French at the university. /s/ /z/ (/ɪz/)

3 She get**s** home at seven o'clock. (/s/) /z/ /ɪz/

4 He go**es** to bed late on the weekend. /s/ (/z/) /ɪz/

5 She wash**es** her hair twice a week. /s/ /z/ (/ɪz/)

6 He look**s** like Johnny Depp! (/s/) /z/ /ɪz/

C (3.3) Listen again and repeat the sentences. Be careful to pronounce the third person *-s* endings correctly.

SPEAKING

A PREPARE Work in pairs. Make a list of five interesting or exciting jobs.

B PLAN Choose one of the jobs in Exercise A. Write sentences to explain a typical day for someone with that job.

- She gets up at six in the morning.
- She goes to the studio at eight o'clock.
- She talks to the actors.

C SPEAK Work in new pairs. Read your sentences and try to guess the job.

A: She gets up at six o'clock in the morning. She goes to the studio at eight o'clock. She talks to the actors ...

B: She's a movie director!

A: Correct!

Talk about daily routines

3.2 All day, every day

Discuss daily activities

G adverbs of frequency P word stress V prepositions of time

READING

A Work in pairs. Look at the photos. Which of the activities do you do every day?

B READ FOR MAIN IDEA Read *Lifestyle online*. Choose the correct option to complete the definition of *essential*.

essential (adj.) = something you *learn* / *need*

C Read the comments on *Lifestyle online*. What four daily essentials do they write about that are not in the *Top 10 daily essentials* list? soccer on TV; music; Facebook; exercise (yoga)

D READ FOR DETAIL Read the comments again. Are the sentences true (T) or false (F)? Correct the false sentences.

1. Milos thinks breakfast is essential. (T) / F
2. Scotgirl eats breakfast every day. Scotgirl sometimes eats breakfast. T / (F)
3. Topdog44 isn't a soccer fan. (T) / F
4. Lisab needs to exercise every day. (T) / F
5. Celine drinks black coffee every night. Celine drinks black coffee every morning. T / (F)

E SPEAK Work with a partner. Make a list of your top ten daily essentials.

Lifestyle *online*

What do you use every day? What couldn't you live without? We asked 100 people for their top 10 daily essentials. Here's what they said … Ex B

Top 10 daily essentials

1	the internet	6	a cell phone
2	a shower or bath	7	a good friend
3	TV	8	a cup of coffee or tea
4	laptop or tablet	9	breakfast
5	a car	10	a pet

Milos
For me, I need a good breakfast and soccer on TV. Ex D Q1 Ex C

Scotgirl
LOL @Milos! I sometimes eat breakfast, but not every day. For me, it's music. I always listen to music on my way to work. Ex D Q2 Ex C

Topdog44
I never watch soccer on TV. I think it's really boring. I need my cell phone. It's an essential – no question. Ex D Q3

Fumi
For me, Facebook is essential. I travel a lot for work, so I'm often away from my friends and family. I use Facebook to talk to friends and send pictures of the places I travel to. Ex C

Lisab
Hmm … interesting question! For me, it's exercise. I usually do yoga for an hour before work. Ex C; Ex D Q4

Celine
Haha! I rarely exercise, @Lisab! Coffee is my daily essential. I always start my day with a cup of strong, black coffee. I couldn't live without it. Ex D Q5

GRAMMAR

Adverbs of frequency

A Complete the sentences with adverbs from the text.

1. I ___sometimes___ eat breakfast, but not every day.
2. I ___never___ watch soccer on TV.
3. I'm ___often___ away from my friends and family.
4. I ___rarely___ exercise, @Lisab!

B WORK IT OUT Read the sentences in Exercise A and complete the rules.

Adverbs of frequency

1. We put adverbs of frequency ***before*** / *after* main verbs.
2. We put adverbs of frequency *before* / ***after*** the verb *be*.

C Go to the **Grammar Hub** on **page 126**.

D SPEAK Work in pairs. Write five sentences about yourself using adverbs of frequency. Tell your partner.

A: I rarely watch TV.
B: Really? I watch TV every day.

3.2 All day, every day

LEAD-IN

Write these activities on the board: *have breakfast, meet friends, use my phone, listen to music, exercise.* Include the activities in the photos on page 24, to pre-teach them. Tell students that you do all of them every day except for one and that they have to guess which one. Write *Do you … ?* on the board, and invite them to guess.

Students can then play the same game in small groups. Give time for students to prepare by writing a short list of activities, using dictionaries if required. Then monitor as each group plays the game, making a note of useful emergent vocabulary to teach later on.

READING

A In pairs, students say which activities they do every day.

B Give students time to read the first part of *Lifestyle online* (not including the comments) and complete the definition. Give feedback as a class.

C Read through the task carefully with students. Highlight that students need to find the activities which are not listed in the Top 10. Allow time for students to compare answers in pairs before checking as a class.

D Give students time to complete the exercise alone before checking their answers with a partner. Give feedback as a class.

E In pairs, students make a list of their top ten daily essentials. If you have time, put pairs into small groups to try and agree on a top five list of essentials. Give feedback as a class, encouraging discussion as appropriate.

GRAMMAR

A Work through the first example on the board. Point out where the sentences are in the comments section of the text. Students then work alone to complete the sentences with adverbs. Check answers as a class and build up a list of adverbs on the board.

B Students read the sentences and complete the rules. Check answers as a class by writing an example sentence for each rule on the board (e.g. 1 *I sometimes eat breakfast …*; 3 *I'm often away from my friends and family.*).

C Direct students to the **Grammar Hub** (see below). Read the examples and go through the rules and exercises with the class.

D Go through the task instructions and the example with students. Give students up to five minutes to write sentences about themselves. Monitor and check students' sentences for use of adverbs of frequency correctly. Then put students into pairs to discuss their sentences. Use the **Grammar Worksheet** on W15 for extra practice.

Extra activity

Write three sentences about yourself on the board using adverbs of frequency (e.g. *I always get up at 5 am.*). One sentence should not be true. Ask students to identify the false sentence and then correct it by changing the adverb (e.g. *I never get up at 5 am. – I always get up at 7 am.*). Students then do the same in pairs. Monitor and make a note of how students use adverbs of frequency, and use this in class feedback.

GRAMMAR HUB

3.2 Adverbs of frequency

0% ←――――――――――――――――――――→ 100%

never | rarely | sometimes | often | usually | always

- We use adverbs of frequency to talk about how regularly we do things.
- Adverbs of frequency go after *be* and *can*.

  *It's **usually** busy on a Saturday.*

  *I **can never** find my keys in the morning.*

- Adverbs of frequency go before other verbs.

  *I **sometimes play** soccer on Saturdays.*

- Look at where the adverbs go in questions.

  *How **often do** you play soccer?*

  *What time **do you usually eat** dinner?*

3.2 Adverbs of frequency

A Reorder the words to make sentences.

1 by train / go to work / I / never
I never go to work by train.

2 play / we / video games / often
We often play video games.

3 always / the radio / they / in the car / listen to
They always listen to the radio in the car.

4 home / he / rarely / before seven / is
He is rarely home before seven.

5 busy / is / usually / Andrea / on the weekend / ?
Is Andrea usually busy on the weekend?

6 work late / you / do / sometimes / ?
Do you sometimes work late?

B Rewrite the sentences using the adverbs in parentheses.

1 I go to the gym. (never)
I never go to the gym.

2 I read in bed. (often)
I often read in bed.

3 Eleni plays soccer on Sundays. (usually)
Eleni usually plays soccer on Sundays.

4 Dan's late for his English class. (sometimes)
Dan's sometimes late for his English class.

5 I eat sushi. (rarely)
I rarely eat sushi.

6 Lin goes to bed at 11 pm. (always)
Lin always goes to bed at 11 pm.

➤ Go back to page 24.

3.2 All day, every day

LISTENING

A Write *screen-free week* on the board and ask students to discuss what it means in pairs. Focus students on the search result text, and give them one minute to check their ideas. Check answer as a class.

3.4 **B** Read through the task with students. Play the recording for students to answer the question about Ali. Give feedback as a class, encouraging students to explain their answers using information from the conversation.

No, he doesn't. He needs his phone.

3.4 **C** Allow time for students to read through the sentences and try and guess the answers. Play the recording again for students to decide which sentences are true and to correct the false sentences. Check answers as a class.

D Put students into pairs to discuss the questions. Then put pairs into groups to extend the discussion. In feedback, ask groups to share the main points of their discussion. Ask for a show of hands as to who wants to have a screen-free week and why. Encourage students who would not like a screen-free week to say why.

PRONUNCIATION

3.5 **A** Focus students on the table and the underlined parts of the words. Point out that these syllables are stressed. Play the recording for students to hear the four different stress patterns and practice saying the words.

3.6 **B** Play the recording for students to listen and add the words to the table. Encourage them to also underline the stressed syllable in each word. If students are having trouble hearing the stressed syllable, model the word with the wrong syllable stressed. This usually makes the correct stress pattern clearer.

3.6 **C** Play the recording again, pausing after each word for students to repeat. Then, practice the words with the class.

VOCABULARY

A Give students time to read through the phrases from the conversation, focusing on the prepositions in bold. They then complete the rules with the correct preposition.

B Write the following prepositions on the board: *at, in, on*. Go through the exercise with the class, eliciting the correct preposition for each word or phrase. Use the **Vocabulary Worksheet** on W16 for extra practice.

SPEAKING

A In pairs, students make a list of ten activities people can do in a screen-free week. Monitor and assist with vocabulary as required, and encourage students to look up words in dictionaries.

B Ask students to put the activities in order. They can do this individually or in pairs.

C Put students into new pairs to share their lists, and decide on the five most essential activities.

TEACHING IDEA by David Seymour and Maria Popova

Vocabulary: Personal time

Use this activity to review the vocabulary section: Say this to your students:

In pairs, ask and answer questions about these things. (If students have children, they can talk about them instead.)

the day you were born, the time of day you were born, the month you were born, the season you were born, the year you were born, the decade you were born

In pairs, ask and answer questions using this table.

What do you do	in the morning on	Sundays?
	in the afternoon	Wednesdays?
	at night	Saturdays?
		Christmas Day?

Take a survey of the rest of the class. Choose one of these subjects and find out how long each student spends doing it each day. Make a list, with those who spend the most time at the top and those who spend the least at the bottom.

watching TV, sleeping, eating, sitting on public transportation, exercising, talking on the phone, cooking, walking, relaxing, reading, drinking tea or coffee, studying, using a computer

Report your findings to the class, highlighting the most extreme examples (e.g. the person who spends the most time watching TV, the person who spends the least time studying, etc).

AUDIO SCRIPT

3.4

Listening, Exercise B
I = Ian A = Ali

I: So, are you ready for screen-free week, Ali?
A: Screen what?
I: Screen-free week. No internet, no cell phone, no TV for a week.
A: What? You're joking!
I: Ali, how many hours a day are you on your phone?
A: How many hours a day? I don't know. About nine?
Ex C Q1 From early in the morning to late at night.
Ex C Q2 **I:** You look at it when you wake up?
A: Yeah, my phone is my alarm clock! Then, I look at the news and read my texts and emails.
I: What about during the day, at work?
Ex C Q3 **A:** Well, I use maps on my phone all the time for my work. I have an app. It's great. It tells me if there are problems on the roads.
I: What about after work?
A: Yeah, I use my phone a lot in the evening – I talk
Ex C Q4 to my friends – well, text my friends or play games
Ex C Q5 with them online. On the weekend, we watch soccer on TV, and we chat online – we have a group chat – about the games. On Saturday and Sunday, it's non-stop soccer! I love soccer!
I: So, what about screen-free week?
Ex B **A:** No way! Impossible! I need my phone!

LISTENING

A PREDICT What is a 'screen-free week'? Discuss your ideas with a partner. Then read the search result and check.

What's going on?

Screen-free week

November 7, 2017 Most people these days spend at least 15 hours every week online or on their phones. Well, May 2–8, join us and other people around the world in screen-free week – a week when people take a break from screens and the internet. No cell phone, no internet and no TV. There is life beyond the screen!

Ex A

3.4 **B LISTEN FOR GIST** Listen to a conversation between Ali and Ian. Does Ali want to do screen-free week? Why/Why not? No, he doesn't. He needs his phone.

3.4 **C LISTEN FOR DETAIL** Listen again. Are the sentences true (T) or false (F)? Correct the false sentences.

1 Ali spends nine hours a week on his phone. T / (F) Ali spends all day on his phone.
2 He looks at his phone when he wakes up. (T) / F
3 He uses his phone at work. (T) / F
4 He plays games online with his friends. (T) / F
5 He never watches soccer on TV. He watches soccer on the weekend. T / (F)

D SPEAK Work in pairs. Answer the questions.

1 How often do you check your phone?
2 Do you think you need a screen-free week? Why/Why not?

PRONUNCIATION

Word stress

3.5 **A** Listen and repeat. Stress the underlined syllables.

Oo	oO	Ooo	oOo
morning	online	internet	computer
open	begin	Saturday	umbrella
chocolate	before	serious	essential
laptop	relax	usually	unfriendly
rarely	routine	grandmother	

3.6 **B** Add the words in the box to the table in Exercise A. Then listen and check your answers.

before chocolate essential grandmother laptop rarely relax routine serious unfriendly usually

3.6 **C** Listen again and repeat the words.

VOCABULARY

Prepositions of time

A Look at the phrases from the conversation between Ali and Ian. Then complete the rules with the correct preposition, *in*, *on* or *at*.

1 *... from early **in** the morning to late **at** night.*
2 ***On** Saturday and Sunday, it's non-stop soccer!*
3 ***On** the weekend, we watch soccer on TV.*

Prepositions of time

1 We use __in__ with a time period (the morning, the afternoon, the summer, 1990, etc).
2 We use __on__ with the day of the week (Monday, Tuesday, etc) and dates.
3 We use __at__ with exact times (6 pm, noon, etc).

B Write the correct preposition of time next to the words.

1 __on__ Sunday
2 __at__ three o'clock
3 __on__ March 6
4 __in__ the evening
5 __in__ June
6 __on__ my birthday

SPEAKING

A PLAN Work in pairs. Think of ten activities to do during screen-free week.

B PREPARE Make a top ten list. Put the most essential activity at number 1.

C Work in pairs. Discuss your lists from Exercise A. Agree on the top five essentials.

A: I think 'go for a run' is the most essential. I need to do lots of exercise.
B: Really? I'm not sure. What about 'spend time with friends' as number one?

Discuss daily activities

3.3 A special day

Describe a special day

G simple present negative P sentence stress V big celebrations S listening for detail

READING

A Work in pairs. Look at the pictures in *A birthday to remember* and answer the questions.

1 What can you see in the pictures? Mooncake, paper lanterns, dancers in colorful costumes performing traditional dances.
2 Which country are these things from? China.

B **SCAN** Read *A birthday to remember* quickly to check your answers to Exercise A.

C **READ FOR GIST** Read *A birthday to remember* again and answer the questions.

1 Why is Katie in China? She's on vacation.
2 Which festival does she write about? The Moon Festival/ Mid-Autumn Festival.
3 Is she enjoying her birthday? Yes - 'So far, this birthday is one of the best ever'.

D **READ FOR DETAIL** Read *A birthday to remember* again. Find and correct five more mistakes in the summary.

Katie sometimes celebrates her birthday with ~~friends~~ her mom. This year, she is on vacation in China, and it is the time of the Moon Festival. The festival happens on ~~the same day every September~~ a different day every year, and it is ~~150~~ 3000 years old. People ~~wear~~ don't wear traditional clothes. They eat mooncakes and watch dancers in ~~modern~~ colorful costumes. They light lanterns to say thank you ~~to their grandparents~~ for children. Katie loves Moon Festival. She thinks this a good birthday.

Compass Travel

A birthday to remember

July 7 | Leave a comment

I don't usually celebrate my birthday. I sometimes go out for a birthday lunch with my mom, Ex D but I usually just take it easy. My best friend doesn't understand, but for me, my birthday is no big deal. But this year, my birthday is a little different. I'm on Ex C Q1 vacation in China at the moment, and my birthday is Ex D on the same day as the Moon Festival. It's really cool. Ex C Q2

Moon Festival is also called Mid-Autumn Festival, and people in China celebrate it every September or October. It's on a different day every year, but there's Ex D always a full moon. The festival is more than 3,000 Ex D years old. It's amazing, and really colorful – I love it! The people don't wear traditional clothes, but they Ex D eat traditional food, like mooncakes. They are small, round cakes and they're delicious! You can see dancers in colorful costumes perform traditional dances. There are also lots of paper lanterns with bright patterns. People light them to say thank you for children, who Ex D make everyone so happy – most of the time! So far, this birthday is one of the best ever! Ex C Q3

GRAMMAR

Simple present negative

A **WORK IT OUT** Look at the sentences from *A birthday to remember* and complete the table with *don't* or *doesn't*.

I ***don't*** *usually celebrate my birthday.*

My best friend ***doesn't*** *understand, …*

The people ***don't*** *wear traditional clothes, …*

Simple present negative		
I/You/We/They	1 don't	eat special food.
He/She/It	2 doesn't	

B Go to the **Grammar Hub** on **page 126**.

C **SPEAK** Work in pairs. Write three negative simple present sentences – two true, one false. Then read them to your partner. Guess which sentence is false.

A: I don't speak French. I don't watch TV. I don't eat meat.
B: The second one is false. You always watch TV!

PRONUNCIATION

Sentence stress

3.7 **A** Listen and repeat. Then underline the stressed words.

1 I like festivals. 2 I don't like festivals.

B Look at the underlined words in Exercise A. Complete the rules.

Sentence stress in simple present
1 In short simple present positive sentences, we usually stress the *main verb* / *noun*.
2 In short simple present negative sentences, we usually stress the *auxiliary verb (don't/doesn't)* / *main verb*.

1 decorations

2 special food

3.3 A special day

LEAD-IN

Write *Special Days* on the board, and describe a special day without mentioning the name of the actual day (e.g. a birthday, graduation, a national holiday, etc). Ask if students know the word for the day. Write the word on the board. Ask students if they celebrate this day and, if so, how. Then as a class, brainstorm other special days that people celebrate. Add them to the board.

READING

A Focus students on the pictures in the blog post. Put them into pairs to discuss the questions. Do not check answers at this point.

B Give students a short time limit to read the blog post and check their answers to Exercise A.

C Ask students to read through the questions and identify the key words in each one. Check answers as a class.

D Tell students that they need to find five more mistakes in the summary and correct them. Point out that the mistakes are factual ones, not grammatical ones.

GRAMMAR

A Give students time to complete the exercise alone. Then check answers as a class by building up the table on the board.

B Direct students to the **Grammar Hub** (see below). Read the examples and go through the rules and exercises with the class.

C Put students into pairs to continue the activity. Use the **Grammar Worksheet** on W17 for extra practice.

PRONUNCIATION

3.7 **A** Play the recording and ask the students to listen and underline the stressed words. For whole-class feedback, write the sentences and the underlined words on the board.

B Ask students to read through the rules and choose the correct words to complete them. Check answers as a class.

3.8 **C** Students read through the conversation and predict the stressed words.

D In pairs, students practice the conversation.

GRAMMAR HUB

3.3 Simple present negative

	do/does not + base form
I/you/we/they	**I don't cook** every evening.
he/she/it	**She doesn't cook** every evening.

Be careful!

With *he/she/it* forms, we don't add *-s* to the verb.

It doesn't start at 8 o'clock. NOT ~~*It doesn't starts at 8 o'clock.*~~

- We use the simple present negative to talk about habits and routines.
  I do not exercise on the weekend.
- We also use the simple present negative to talk about:
  - facts and things that are true.
    I don't live in London.
  - dislikes.
    Sarah doesn't like sushi.
  - possessions with *have* and *has*.
    They don't have any children.
  - fixed times.
    The store doesn't open until 6 pm.
- We use the contraction *don't* (*do not*) and *doesn't* (*does not*).

3.3 Simple present negative

A Complete the sentences with the correct form of the verb in parentheses.

1 He *doesn't have* (not have) coffee with breakfast.
2 I don't like (not like) jazz music.
3 You don't need (not need) a coat – it's really hot outside!
4 We don't have (not have) children.
5 Amy doesn't go (not go) to the movie theater very often.
6 Zach doesn't work (not work) in an office.
7 My parents don't work (not work) anymore. They're retired.

B Rewrite the sentences in the negative.

1 Sam likes parties.
Sam doesn't like parties.
2 We usually have lunch in the kitchen.
We don't usually have lunch in the kitchen.
3 Eleni speaks Arabic.
Eleni doesn't speak Arabic.
4 They have a big house.
They don't have a big house.
5 I listen to music on the train.
I don't listen to music on the train.
6 Lin watches TV in the morning.
Lin doesn't watch TV in the morning.

➤ Go back to page 26.

VOCABULARY

A Students match the words in the box to the pictures. Allow time for students to discuss their choices with a partner before checking as a class.

B Ask students to identify the type of word in the box (verbs). Students then work alone to complete the questions. Check answers as a class.

C In pairs, students ask and answer the questions from Exercise B. Model the first question by asking a stronger student. Ask a follow-up question to encourage the student to expand on the answer. Point out that students should ask follow-up questions like this when working in pairs. Monitor and encourage students as they discuss the questions.

For whole-class feedback, ask two or three students to share the most interesting information they heard. Use the **Vocabulary Worksheet** on W18 for extra practice.

LISTENING

3.9 **A** Play the recording. Give feedback as a class, encouraging students to try and remember how the words were used in the conversation.

3.9 **B** Read through the *Listening for detail* box as a class. Then, tell students to close their books. Ask students to recall the three things they should do when listening for detail.

Give students time to read through Sentences 1–5, underlining the key words. Play the recording again for students to choose the correct options.

SPEAKING HUB

A Explain to students that they are going to compare special days in a group and that you will give them some time to prepare individually for this. Focus students on the list of special days and ask them to choose one or think of their own.

B Model the planning stage for students by writing your own special day on the board, and then talking through each of the points listed in Exercise B. You could add key words to the board in a mind map. Give time for students to write notes. Encourage them to make a mind map of key words.

C In groups, students work to describe their special days. Encourage students to ask follow-up questions, rather than just listen.

For whole-class feedback, ask groups to report back on the most interesting or unusual festival they talked about.

TEACHING IDEA by David Seymour and Maria Popova

Vocabulary: Important dates

Use this activity to review dates and words from the Vocabulary section. Say this to your students:

Work in small groups. Tell each other about some important dates in your country's history.

When are these celebrations?

Christmas Day (December 25)
St. Patrick's Day (March 17)
April Fool's Day (April 1)
Valentine's Day (February 14)
Independence Day in the US (July 4)
New Year's Eve (December 31)
Thanksgiving Day in the US (4th Thursday in November)
Halloween (October 31)

Compare your answers with another group.

Work in small groups. Write down these dates as a list on the left of your paper. (Dictate the dates in parentheses below.)

Listen to these historic events, and write them next to the correct dates. (Read them aloud in random order.)

The first man to walk on the moon. (July 20, 1969)

The first telephone call. (March 10, 1876)

The Wright brothers made the first powered flight. (December 17, 1903)

The first man in space. (April 12, 1961)

The end of the Soviet Union. (December 25, 1991)

Compare your answers with another group.

AUDIO SCRIPT

3.9

Listening, Exercise A
C = Carlos M = Moira

C: Moira, are you free tomorrow night?
M: I don't know. Why?
Ex B Q1 **C:** Well, tomorrow is September 16th – Independence Day in my country – and there's a party at my friend's Ex A house. Do you want to come?
M: Oh, that sounds like fun! I'd love to come. We have Independence Day in my country, too. How do you celebrate it in Mexico?
Ex B Q2 **C:** All the stores and banks close and everyone takes a day off because it's party time! There are parties everywhere. People play music in the streets. Everybody dances and sings.
M: Oh, it's the same in Madagascar. We all dance and sing in the streets, too. There's usually a big parade in Ex A town – and we eat special food!
C: In Mexico, there's a big parade in Mexico City, and in
Ex A; Ex B Q3 the evening, we go and watch the fireworks! It's really noisy!
M: Oh, I love fireworks!
Ex A; Ex B Q4 **C:** And we put up red, white and green decorations. That's the color of our flag.
M: Madagascar's flag is red, white and green, too! We don't put up decorations, but we wear traditional clothes and we dance.
Ex A; Ex B Q5 **C:** We don't wear traditional clothes, but we shout 'Viva Mexico!' and we dance!
M: I want to go to Mexico next September!
C: Well, come to the party tomorrow and it will be just like Mexico!

3 party

6 parade

7 traditional clothes

4 present

5 fireworks

C Read the conversations. Underline the stressed words. Then listen and check. 3.8

1 **Katia:** Do you like mooncakes?
Bian: Yes, but I don't eat them often.

2 **Amelia:** Do you like New Year's Eve?
Lizzie: Uh, yes. I like the fireworks.

D SPEAK Work in pairs. Practice the conversations in Exercise C. Be careful to stress the words correctly.

VOCABULARY
Big celebrations

A Match the pictures (1–7) with the words in the box.

decorations fireworks parade party present special food traditional clothes

B Complete the questions with the words in the box.

eat give have put up wear

1 Do you usually ___have___ a party on your birthday?
2 When do you ___put up___ decorations?
3 Do you ___eat___ special food on New Year's Day?
4 When do people ___wear___ traditional clothes in your country?
5 When do you ___give___ presents in your country?

C SPEAK Work in pairs. Answer the questions in Exercise B.

LISTENING

A LISTEN FOR KEY WORDS Listen to a conversation about big celebrations. Which words from Vocabulary Exercise A do they talk about? They mention all of them except presents. 3.9

B LISTEN FOR DETAIL Listen to the conversation again and choose the correct options to complete the sentences. Use the information in the box to help you. 3.9

Listening for detail

Sometimes we need to listen for specific information (e.g. what time something opens, etc). Use these ideas to help you listen for detail:

- Read the questions carefully.
- Underline key words.
- Listen carefully for the key words that you underlined.

1 Mexico celebrates Independence Day in *September* / *December*.
2 All of the stores and banks *open* / *close* for the party.
3 In the evening, people go to watch *a big parade* / *the fireworks*.
4 At home, people put up red, white and *green* / *blue* decorations.
5 Carlos *wears* / *doesn't wear* traditional clothes to dance in.

SPEAKING HUB

A PREPARE Think of a special day. It could be:

- a birthday
- a national holiday
- a religious day
- a festival

B PLAN Write notes. Think about:

- the food you eat
- the clothes you wear
- the songs you sing
- the music you listen to
- the presents you give
- the people you see

C DISCUSS Work in groups. Describe your day. Compare your festivals.

In Japan, families often eat KFC together on Christmas!

Really? We eat together, but we don't eat fried chicken!

Describe a special day

3.4 Finding Neena

F– make and respond to suggestions   P– stress and intonation

COMPREHENSION

A ▶ Watch the video and answer the questions.

1 Who lives in the flat? ___Neena___
2 Who wants to live in the flat? ___Zac and Gaby___
3 When do they agree to move in? ___Next week___
4 How many bathrooms are there? ___One___
5 What time does Zac start work? ___11 am___
6 What time does Neena get up? ___6 am___

B Look at the pictures. Which flat (a–c) is the one in the video? Flat/Apartment C

C ▶ 00:29–01:30 Work in pairs. Complete the advertisement. Then watch part of the video again and check your answers.

D ▶ 02:40–03:25 Put Zac's morning routine in the correct order (1–7). Then watch part of the video again and check your answers.

_4_ have a shower
_6_ start work
_1_ wake up
_5_ have a coffee
_7_ finish work
_3_ brush teeth
_2_ have breakfast

E **SPEAK** Work in pairs. Compare your morning routine to Zac's.

A: I wake up at 8 am, not 9. What about you?
B: I wake up at 6 am! When do you start work?

FUNCTIONAL LANGUAGE

Making and responding to suggestions

Complete the phrases with the words in the box. There are two words you do not need.

about don't getting up let's moving in not sounds sure

Make suggestions	Say *yes*
What/How [1] ___about___ this apartment?	[5] ___Sounds___ good/great.
What/How about [2] ___moving in___ next week?	Looks good/great!
Why [3] ___don't___ we email her/go now?	Great!
[4] ___Let's___ call her.	Awesome!
	Say *no*
	I'm not [6] ___sure___.

a
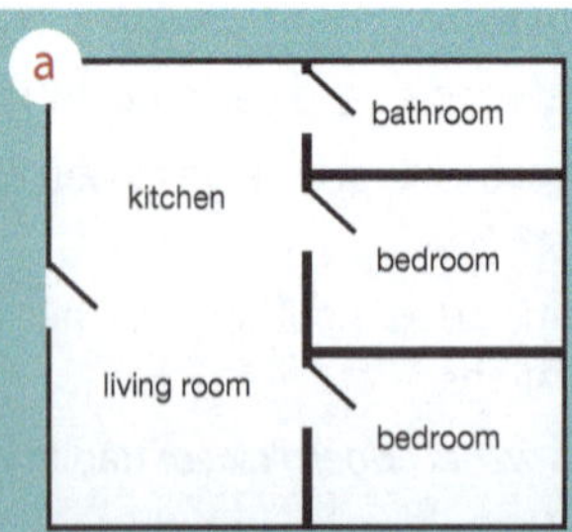

b
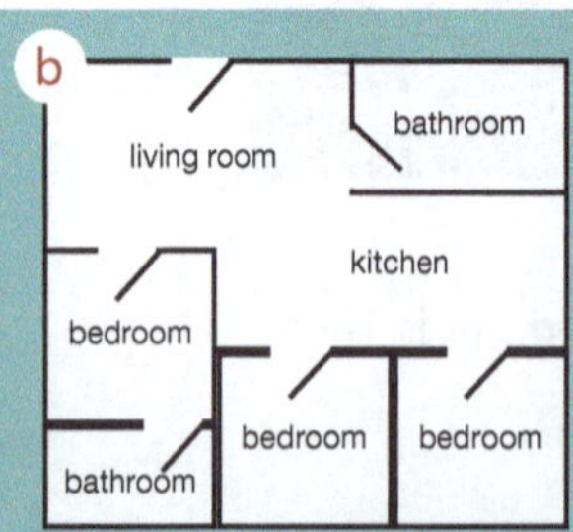

c
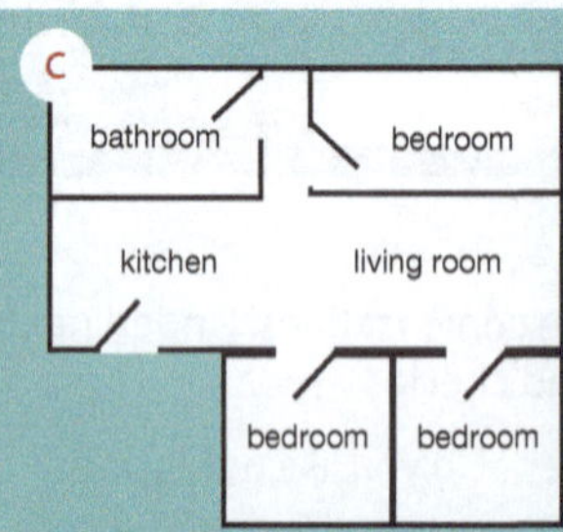

Beautiful flat | £190 pw
Single room(s) | Clapham Common (SW4)

Hi. I'm [1] ___Neena___. I need [2] ___2___ lovely new housemates. I live in a [3] ___3___ bedroom flat on Park [4] ___Road___. I'm [5] ___27___. I like [6] ___coffee___, [7] ___languages___ and playing [8] ___video___ games.

Please call
0770 090 [9] ___0926___.

Glossary

housemates **(n) (British)** = roommates **(n) (American)**
lovely **(adj) (British)** = nice **(adj) (American)**
flat **(n) (British)** = apartment **(n) (American)**
have a shower **(British)** = take a shower **(American)**

MILLY

SAM

NEENA

ZAC

GABY

USEFUL PHRASES

Choose the correct definition of each useful phrase.

1 Any luck?
  a Are you lucky? (b) Were you successful?

2 Cool!
  (a) Great! b It's cold!

3 Of course.
  (a) Yes. b No.

4 Actually, …
  a At the moment, (b) In fact, …

5 It's not far.
  (a) It's near here. b It isn't near here.

6 Lucky you!
  (a) I want to do that! b I don't want to do that!

PRONUNCIATION

Stress and intonation

A ▶ 00:00–02:20 Watch the first part of the video again. Complete the conversations (A–C).

A

Gaby: Hey, [1] _What about_ this [2] _flat_? It's nice.

Zac: Hmmm … [3] _I'm not_ sure. It's very small.

B

Gaby: [4] _Sounds_ good. [5] _Why don't we_ email [6] _her_?

Zac: No, [7] _let's_ call [8] _her_!

C

Zac: Can we see the apartment today?

Neena: Of course. Actually, it's not far. [9] _Why don't we go_ now?

Zac: [10] _Sounds_ great!

Gaby: Brilliant! Let's go!

B ▶ 00:00–02:20 Watch again and repeat the conversations. Copy the stress and intonation.

C **SPEAK** Work in pairs. Practice the conversations in Exercise A. Remember to use the correct stress and intonation.

SPEAKING

A **PREPARE** Work in pairs. Complete the suggestions for what to do after school. Use the ideas in parentheses.

- What about going to ______ (*a place*)?
- Let's eat ______ (*food*).
- Why don't we watch ______ (*a movie*)?
- How about listening to ______ (*a band / music*)?
- Let's play ______ (*a game*).

B **DISCUSS** Go around the class and make suggestions to your classmates. Reply using the Functional language phrases.

A: How about going to a concert?
B: Awesome!

Make and respond to suggestions

➤ Turn to page 162 to learn how to write a blog post about your day.

3.4 Finding Neena

LEAD-IN

Describe your home to the class. Draw a simple plan of your home on the board as you do so, with some key words (e.g. *kitchen*). When the plan is complete, ask a student to use it to describe your home. Students then work in pairs, with one student describing their home and the other drawing a plan of it.

COMPREHENSION

A ▶ Give students time to read through the questions before watching the video. Then play the video for students to answer the questions. They should compare answers in pairs before checking as a class.

B In pairs, students discuss the floor plans to decide which one matches the flat/apartment in the video. For whole-class feedback, ask students to explain their answers.

C ▶ 0:29-01:30 Focus students on the advertisement and elicit where they would see it (e.g. on a property search website). In pairs, students try to complete the ad. Play the first part of the video again for students to check.

D ▶ 02:40-03:25 Read through the task with students and check their understanding of the daily activities. Students discuss the order of the activities. Then play the second part of the video again for students to check.

E Model the activity for students by comparing your morning routine to Zac's. Then put students into pairs to compare their routines with each other and Zac. Monitor and make a note of effective language being used and also phrases which need reformulating. When students have finished, provide feedback on the use of the simple present.

FUNCTIONAL LANGUAGE

Focus students on the table. Point out that there are phrases for making suggestions in the first column and phrases for positive or negative replies in the next two columns. If necessary, write *suggestions* on the board, and explain that these are ideas that we give other people for them to think about.

USEFUL PHRASES

Go through the first useful phrase and definition together. In pairs, students complete the activity. Check answers as a class.

PRONUNCIATION

A ▶ 00:00-02:20 Play the first part of the video again. Students complete the conversation. Give students time to compare answers in pairs before checking answers as a class.

B ▶ 00:00-02:20 Play the first part of the video again and ask students to say the conversations at the same time, focusing on the stress and intonation.

C In pairs, students practice the conversations. Monitor and provide positive feedback on correct stress and intonation.

SPEAKING

A In pairs, students complete the suggestions with things they can do after school. Make sure that they understand that they need to write down the name of a place, a type of food, a movie, a band or type of music and a game.

B Focus students on the table in the *Functional Language* section and on the responses. Students can also check the useful phrases again.

▶ VIDEO SCRIPT

G = Gaby S = Sam Z = Zac N = Neena

G: Hey, what about this flat? It's nice.
Z: Hmm … I'm not sure. It's very small.
S: Any luck?
G: Not yet.
Z: Oooh … Gaby, how about this one?
G: It looks good!
Z: 'Hi. I'm Neena and I need two lovely new housemates. I live in a three-bedroom flat on Park Road. I'm 27. I like coffee …'
G: We like coffee!
Z: 'I like languages …'
G: Spanish teacher!
Z: And … playing video games!'
G: Sounds good. Why don't we email her?
Z: No. Let's call her.
G: What's the number?
Z: It's … 07700 900926.
N: Hello?
G: Hello?
Z: Hello!
N: Hello!
Z: Are you … Neena?
N: Yes.
G: Neena with the flat?
N: Yes. Neena with the flat. Is that my ad?
Z and G: Yes.
G: We are lovely people!
N: Haha! Well, that's good to know.
G: And I love coffee and languages!
Z: And I … make video games.
N: Cool! I love video games.
Z: Can we see the apartment today?
N: Of course. Actually, it's not far. Why don't we go now?
Z: Sounds great!
G: Brilliant! Let's go!
N: And this is the living room. So, what do you think?
G: We love it!
N: So, how about moving in next week?
G: That sounds great!
Z: Awesome.
N: OK. There's only one bathroom, so what time do you usually get up?
Z: I always wake up at 9 am. I have breakfast at 9:15. I brush my teeth at 9:45. I have a shower at 10 am. At 10:30, I have a coffee. Sometimes I play guitar, and then I start work at 11 am. And then I work all day until 7 pm.
N: You start work at 11 am?
Z: Yeah.
N: Lucky you! I wake up at 6 and start work at 8 every day! How about you, Gaby?
G: I wake up at about 8.
N: Ok, cool. Showers. Check. Next, cleaning?

3 Writing — Write a blog post about your day

W– sequencing words

A Work in pairs. Look at the photo in the blog post. Guess the answers to the questions. Explain your ideas.

1. Where's she from? She's from Ireland.
2. What's her job? She's an athlete.
3. Why is she famous? She's famous because she's the Irish 800m champion.

A DAY in the LIFE of…

about | archive | contact

Ciara Everard Irish 800m champion

January 7, 2017 | Leave a comment

I'm an athlete. On weekdays, I always get up at 8 am. First, I go for a run. I'm usually out for 30 minutes – not long. Then I go home, take a shower and have breakfast – banana pancakes and a cup of tea. I'm not a morning person, so I usually need some coffee, too!

From 10 am to lunchtime, I'm in the gym. I don't like it, but I know it's good for me! After that, I go home and make lunch. I usually have an omelette, some fish and toast. In the afternoon, I'm always really tired, so I sleep for about 30 minutes. At 3 pm, I get up, read my emails and do some work.

At 5 pm, I go for my evening run. Then I exercise and take an ice-bath. At 7 pm, I go home and make dinner. I usually prepare my meals on the weekend so I don't need to cook every night.

In the evening, I relax and watch TV. Finally, I have a snack and go to bed at 11 pm.

162 WRITING

B Read the blog post and check your answers to Exercise A.

C Read the blog post again. Complete Ciara's diary.

Day	Time	What?
Mon 26th	8:00 am	get up and go for a run
	8:30 am	take a shower and have breakfast
	10:00 am	go to the gym
	1:00 pm	go home and make lunch
	2:30 pm	sleep
	5:00 pm	go for a run
	7:00 pm	go home and make dinner
	11:00 pm	have a snack and go to bed

Refer students to this blog as a model for the writing task.

D Work in pairs. Would you like a life like Ciara's? Why/Why not?

E Read the first sentence in the box. Then find and underline five sequencing words in the blog post about Ciara Everard.

Sequencing words

We use sequencing words (*first, after that, then* and *finally*) to help the reader understand the order of things in a text.

- We use [1] first to say what we do first.
- We use [2] after that or [3] then to say what we do after another thing.
- We use [4] finally to say what we do last.

You could mention that *after that* and *then* both mean the same as *next*.

F Complete the rules in the box with the sequencing words you underlined in Exercise E.

WRITING

A PREPARE You are going to write a blog post about your day. Write a diary like Ciara's. Include 6–10 activities you do in a normal day and the times you do them.

B WRITE Use your diary to write a short blog post about your day. Add details and use sequencing words (*first, after that, then* and *finally*) to explain the order.

Students can do this in class or for homework.

C REVIEW Work in pairs. Compare your blog posts.

WRITING

In this writing lesson, students will learn how to write a blog post about their day and how to use sequencing words like *first, after that, then* and *finally* to say when things happen.

A Focus students on the blog post, and ask them where they can see this type of text and if they read any blogs. Then focus on the photo. Ask the questions and elicit students' ideas. Encourage students to explain their ideas.

B Tell students to read the blog post and check their answers. Check answers as a class.

C Focus students on the diary, highlighting that the diary is completed in note form, rather than complete sentences. Students then read the blog post again in more detail and complete the diary with notes.

D In pairs, students discuss the questions. Then open up the discussion to the whole class. Add your own ideas and opinions to help extend the discussion.

E Read through the first sentence in the *Sequencing words* box with students, and focus students on the sequencing words. Students then look back at the blog and underline five sequencing words in the text. Check answers as a class.

F Students work alone to complete the rules in the *Sequencing words* box. Students use the words they underlined in the text in Exercise E to do this.

WRITING TASK

A Go through the task with students. Explain that they will write a blog post about a normal day, explaining the activities they do and the times they do them.

B Ask a stronger student to write the start of their diary on the board. It should include two times and notes about two activities from a normal day. Demonstrate to the whole class how to build these into sentences using sequencing words (e.g. *I always get up at 6:30 am. First, I …*). Tell students to use their diaries to write a blog post.

C Put students into pairs and ask them to read each other's blog posts.

Unit 3 Review

VOCABULARY

A Complete the sentences with the words in the box.

get to get up have leave work

1. I work in a large office in King's Cross.
2. I usually have toast and coffee for breakfast.
3. I get up at 6:30 every morning.
4. I try to leave home before seven o'clock.
5. I get to work between nine and nine thirty.

B Match the verbs (1–8) with the words (a–h) to make phrases describing everyday activities.

1 have	a to music / to the radio
2 get	b in a house / in an apartment
3 listen	c a book / a magazine
4 watch	d to work / to bed / for a run
5 live	e up early / home from work
6 read	f for a bank / in Spain
7 work	g breakfast / lunch
8 go	h a movie / TV

C Complete the sentences with the correct prepositions.

1. I usually watch the news in the afternoon.
2. I sometimes listen to music at night.
3. I sometimes go for a walk on the weekend.
4. I have an English class on Tuesday.
5. I read the newspaper in the morning.
6. I rarely work on Fridays.

D Complete the sentences with the words in the box.

decorations fireworks parade party presents special food traditional clothes

1. What are you doing on Saturday? Do you want to come to a party?
2. It's sad, but many people don't wear traditional clothes at the festival anymore.
3. My mom spends three days cooking so we can have special food on the big day.
4. My family doesn't put up decorations until December 24th.
5. We usually open all of the presents after breakfast.
6. There's a big parade through the streets with giant balloons, dancers and people wearing costumes.
7. We don't have fireworks on New Year's Eve anymore because they scare the dog.

GRAMMAR

A Complete the paragraph with the correct form of the verbs in the box.

get (x2) go (x3) have leave live work (x2) take

Luke Timms 1 works six days a week and his days are usually the same. He 2 lives in a small apartment in Milan. He 3 gets up early every day and 4 takes a shower. He 5 has breakfast and then 6 leaves the apartment at around eight. He 7 goes to work by motorcycle. He 8 works for a television station in the city center. He finishes work at 6:30 pm. He 9 gets home around 7 pm and 10 goes for a long run. He usually 11 goes to bed at around midnight.

B Rewrite the sentences with the adverbs in parentheses.

1. I get up at 6 am. (usually)
   I usually get up at 6 am.
2. I go for a walk in the park. (often)
   I often go for a walk in the park.
3. I watch TV. (sometimes)
   I sometimes watch TV.
4. I am late for my English class. (never)
   I am never late for my English class.
5. I have breakfast at 7 am. (always)
   I always have breakfast at 7 am.
6. I am late for work. (rarely)
   I am rarely late for work.

C Rewrite the sentences to make them negative.

1. We go to work.
   We don't go to work.
2. People eat special food.
   People don't eat special food.
3. We dance.
   We don't dance.
4. People wear special clothes.
   People don't wear special clothes.
5. People stay at home.
   People don't stay at home.

FUNCTIONAL LANGUAGE

Complete the phrases with the words in the box.

~~about~~ how idea let's sounds why

1. What *about* going out for a meal?
2. Sounds good, but I'm not hungry.
3. How about watching a movie?
4. Why don't we stay in?
5. That's a great idea!
6. Let's have a nice cup of tea!

4 WORK AND EDUCATION

Choose a job you love and you'll never have to work a day in your life.
Confucius

Firefighters at work in London, UK.

OBJECTIVES
- talk about jobs
- talk about the perfect job
- talk about adult education and career development
- ask for someone and leave a message
- write an email asking for information

Work with a partner. Discuss the questions.

1 Do you like your job?
2 Look at the picture. Do you think this is an easy job? Why/Why not?
3 Would you like to do this job?

WORK AND EDUCATION 31

Education (n) someone's experience of learning or being taught
Synonyms: training (n), tuition (n)

Ask students to label the photo if you need time to set up the class.

Firefighters at work in London, UK.

This quote suggests that when we find a job that we love, it doesn't feel like work.

Confucius (551–479 BC) was a Chinese philosopher, teacher and politician. He believed in the power of learning and argued that individuals can create their own selves and futures through self-improvement.

OBJECTIVES

Read the unit objectives to the class.

UNIT OPENER QUESTIONS

Ask students to look at the picture on the page and describe what they see. Ask students what job this is (*firefighter*) and ask for suggestions of other tasks these people may have to do in their working day. Elicit any personal experience of this job (e.g. if a student is or has a friend or family member who is a firefighter). Then ask what jobs the students, their families and their close friends have, and write a list of job titles on the board in a column.

Ask students to read the questions at the bottom of the page. Check that students understand the questions and write these sentence stems on the board to help them: *I like / don't like my job because … ; I would / wouldn't like to do this job because …*

Put students into pairs or small groups to discuss the questions. Monitor to help with grammar and vocabulary if required. Encourage students to listen to each other and to extend the discussion with follow-up questions. For whole-class feedback, ask two or three students to share their ideas with the class.

WORKSHEETS

Lesson 4.1 What do you do?

Work and jobs (W19)

Simple present *yes/no* questions; short answers (W19)

Lesson 4.2 Good job!

have to / don't have to (W20)

Time expressions (W21)

Lesson 4.3 Learn something new

Question words (W22)

Education collocations (W23)

4.1 What do you do?

Talk about jobs

V work and jobs **G** simple present *yes/no* questions; short answers **P** linking sounds: *do/does*

VOCABULARY
Work and jobs

A Match the pictures (1–4) with the words in the box.

4 doctor 1 engineer 3 pilot 2 teacher

B Go to the **Vocabulary Hub** on **page 147**.

C Complete the sentences with the words in the box.

computer home meet meetings office travel (x2) wear (x2)

1 I sometimes ___travel___ for my job, but I usually work in an ___office___. I go to ___meetings___ and I meet a lot of different people.

2 I like my job because I ___meet___ new people every day. I ___wear___ a uniform. I don't work in an office – I work in a hospital.

3 I always ___travel___ for my job, but I usually work with the same people. I ___wear___ a uniform and I go to a lot of different places.

4 I usually work from ___home___. I sometimes go out to meet people. I spend a lot of time on my ___computer___.

D SPEAK Work in pairs. Talk about your job or the job of someone you know. Use the words and phrases in Exercise C to help you.

A: I'm a designer. I don't work in an office. I work from home.

B: My sister is a businessperson. She travels a lot for her work. She always goes to different places.

READING

A READ FOR GIST Read the interview. Are the sentences true (T) or false (F)? Correct the false sentences.

1 He's a nurse. He's an engineer. T / (F)

2 He works in an office. (T) / F

3 He sometimes works from home. He never works from home. T / (F)

4 He loves his job. (T) / F

B READ FOR DETAIL Read the interview again. Find and correct mistakes in the summary.

Matheus is an engineer. He works in an office, but he also goes to meetings and he visits ~~hospitals~~ factories. He doesn't work from home because he ~~never~~ always needs to talk to other people. He works for a ~~small~~ large company in the ~~US~~ Brazil. He ~~never~~ often visits other countries. He says his job is ~~easy~~ difficult, but he loves it because it's ~~unusual~~. interesting and exciting

C SPEAK Talk to your partner. Do you think Matheus has an interesting job? Why/Why not?

Working Week – Out for lunch

Every week, we catch someone on their lunch break and ask them five quick questions about their job.

This week: Matheus Oliveira, 32

What's your job?

I'm an engineer, like my brother. Ex A Q1

Does your brother work for the same company as you?

No, he doesn't. He works for a big company in the US.

Do you work in an office?

Yes, I do. I also spend a lot of time out of the office. Ex A Q2 I go to meetings and I visit factories. Ex B

Do you work from home sometimes?

No, I don't. I always need to talk to other people, so Ex A Q3 I don't stay at home.

Do you travel for work?

Yes, sometimes. I work for a large company in Brazil, but I often go to the US, China and Japan. Ex B

Do you like your job?

Yes, I love it. It's difficult, but it's also Ex A Q4 interesting and exciting. I'm very lucky. Ex B

4.1 What do you do?

LEAD-IN

Play an alphabet game. Write the letter 'A' on the board and elicit jobs beginning with that letter (e.g. *artist, accountant, etc*). Repeat the process with the letter 'B'. Next, put students into small groups and tell them you're going to play an alphabet game. Give them up to five minutes to think of as many jobs as they can for each letter of the alphabet. They should use the first half of the time without any help. For whole-class feedback, elicit students' ideas, writing the jobs on the board and correcting them if necessary. Award points to the group with the most jobs.

VOCABULARY

A Students match the words in the box with the pictures. Check answers as a class. Elicit some ideas on what each of these people does at work (e.g. a pilot flies a plane) to get an idea of the students' language level in this area.

B Direct students to the **Vocabulary Hub**. Give them time to complete the exercise alone before checking answers in pairs. Give feedback as a class.

C Give students time to complete the exercise alone, before checking in pairs. Give feedback as a class.

D Model the activity by talking about your job using the language in Exercise C. Then, put students into pairs to talk about their jobs or the jobs of someone they know. Monitor and assist as required. Use the **Vocabulary Worksheet** on W19 for extra practice.

READING

A Focus students on the text, and elicit what type of text it is (*an interview*) and how students know this (*there are questions followed by answers, and the name and age of the person being interviewed is shown*). Students then read the interview and answer the four questions. Allow a short time limit for this, to encourage students to move through the text quickly. Check answers as a class.

B Read through the task instructions with students, highlighting that they need to read the interview more carefully now and check the summary to find the seven mistakes. You could pre-teach the words *factory* (a building where goods are produced) and *engineer* (someone who builds or designs things like bridges, roads or machines). Next, give students time to complete the exercise alone before checking their answers with a partner. Give feedback as a class.

C Students discuss the question in pairs. Monitor, helping with any new or challenging vocabulary. Give feedback, encouraging class-wide discussion. Add any useful emergent language to the board.

Extra activity

Play 'back to the board' to review jobs vocabulary. Put students into two groups. Ask one group to stand up, facing the board. Then nominate one student from the group to stand with their back to the board. Write a job on the board and ask the other students in the group to mime it. Award one point for every correctly guessed job.

TEACHING IDEA by David Seymour and Maria Popova

Vocabulary: Picture board

Use this activity to practice jobs vocabulary. Say this to your students:

Work in two teams. Take turns coming up to the board. I'm going to give you a job. (Write it on a piece of paper or whisper it.) You have 60 seconds to draw pictures to help your team guess the job. You must not write any letters, or speak.

waiter, doctor, gardener, bricklayer, policeman, carpenter, artist, receptionist, chef, surgeon, farmer, vet, nurse

TEACHING IDEA by David Seymour and Maria Popova

Vocabulary: Job clap

Use this activity to review the vocabulary section. Say this to your students:

Stand in a circle. Take turns naming a job, then the workplace for that job, and then another job, and so on, e.g. A – pilot. B – plane. C – baker. Clap your hands to this rhythm (demonstrate) and give your answer on every fourth beat. If you miss the beat, you are out.

METHODOLOGY HUB by Jim Scrivener

Deciding on your role while students do an activity

Let's distinguish two steps.

Step 1: The first 30 seconds: are they doing the task set?

Immediately after you have given the instructions for a task and students start doing it, there is usually an immediate need to check to make sure that students are doing the activity that you asked them to do and have understood the basic mechanics of the activity.

You could do this by quietly and relatively inconspicuously wandering around the room, listening briefly to parts of the discussion from many groups and assuring yourself that students are doing what they are supposed to. We could call this 'monitoring to check the mechanics'.

Step 2: The task itself

In many activities, the prime aim is for learners to get a chance to work on their own, speaking fluently and trying out things without too much interference and correction. If they are doing the task correctly, then possibly they don't need you any more once the task is under way. Your presence might actually be an interference. If you are around and very visible, they might look to you for language items and help whenever they hit a problem, whereas it might be more useful for them to struggle a little and learn to make use of their own resources. So once an activity is safely under way, your options usually boil down to the following choices: monitor discretely or vanish.

In some tasks – especially those in which students might not move forward quickly but need ongoing advice, support, input and encouragement – you may find that some kind of more active role is called for. In these cases, your best options are probably to monitor actively or participate.

4.1 What do you do?

GRAMMAR

A Write the first question and short answer on the board. Underline the main verb in the question (*work*). Then go through the task instructions with the class. Elicit the point that each question starts with the auxiliary verb *do*. Highlight the short answer and focus students on the fact that the auxiliary *do* is repeated, rather than the main verb. Then, put students into pairs to complete the rest of the task.

B Students work alone to complete the rules. Allow time for students to compare answers in pairs before checking as a class.

C Go through the task instructions and highlight that there is a mistake in either the question or the short answer. Do the first one together on the board. Point out that the question is correct, but the short answer isn't. Students then work alone to complete the exercise. Display the questions and answers on the board, and ask individual students to come to the board to identify and correct the mistakes.

D Go through the example with students. Allow them time to complete the exercise individually and compare answers with a partner. For whole-class feedback, invite students to come to the board to write their answers.

E Direct students to the **Grammar Hub** (see below). Read the examples and go through the rules with the class.

F Model the exercise by having a student ask you the questions. Reply to each question with a short answer and then follow up with further information.

Use the **Grammar Worksheet** on W19 for extra practice.

PRONUNCIATION

4.1 **A** Go through the task instructions. Focus students on what they need to listen for (the link between *do/does* and *you/he/she*, marked by the linking line).

4.2 **B** Play the recording again for students to listen and repeat.

C In pairs, students complete the questions. They then practice the questions together, making sure they produce the linking sounds.

SPEAKING

A Go through the task instructions with students and then put them into groups of three or four. Monitor and assist as required while the groups write their list of *yes/no* questions.

B Go through the steps with students, then model the exercise. Think of a job and tell students to ask you their questions. Answer with only *Yes, I do* or *No, I don't*. Take questions from the different groups in the class, but only allow students ten questions. If they haven't guessed by that point, then they lose the game.

C Students change roles and continue.

GRAMMAR HUB

4.1 Simple present *yes/no* questions; short answers

	Question	Short answers	
I/you/we/they	**Do I have** a meeting today?	Yes, **you do**.	No, **you don't**.
he/she/it	**Does it have** a good camera?	Yes, **it does**.	No, **it doesn't**.

- We use simple present *yes/no* questions to ask about habits and routines.
- We use *Do/Does* + subject + base form to make questions.

Be careful!

Does she like tea? NOT ~~*Does she likes tea?*~~
Yes, she does. NOT ~~*Yes, she likes.*~~

4.1 Simple present *yes/no* questions; short answers

A Complete the questions with *Do* or *Does*.

1 ___Do___ you work in an office?
2 ___Do___ they work from home?
3 ___Does___ she work with animals?
4 ___Does___ he like his job?
5 ___Do___ we wear a uniform?
6 ___Does___ it have a name?
7 ___Does___ it get busy on the weekend?
8 ___Do___ your sisters work in London?

B Use the prompts to write questions and short answers.

1 you / work / part time
___Do you work part time?___ (?) ___Yes, I do.___ (+)
2 they / live / in the city center
Do ___they live in the city center?___ (?) ___No, they don't.___ (-)
3 she / wear / a uniform
___Does she wear a uniform?___ (?) ___Yes, she does.___ (+)
4 he / travel / for his job
___Does he travel for his job?___ (?) ___No, he doesn't.___ (-)
5 you / speak / French
___Do you speak French?___ (?) ___Yes, I do.___ (+)

➤ Go back to page 33.

GRAMMAR

Simple present *yes/no* questions; short answers

A Work in pairs. Look at the questions and short answers from the interview. Underline the main verbs in the questions. What is at the beginning of each question?

Do/Does is at the beginning of each question.

1 Do you work in an office? Yes, I do.

2 Do you work from home sometimes? No, I don't.

3 Do you travel for work? Yes, sometimes.

4 Does your brother work for the same company as you? No, he doesn't.

B Complete the rules with the words in the box.

do/does (x2) *don't/doesn't* the main verb

Simple present – *yes/no* questions; short answers

- To form questions in the simple present, we use [1] *Do/Does* + subject + [2] the main verb.
- In affirmative short answers, we use [3] *do/does*.
- In negative short answers, we use [4] *don't/doesn't*.

C Correct the mistakes in the questions and answers.

1 A: Do you go to meetings? B: Yes, ~~do I~~. I do

2 A: Do they work in the same office? B: ~~Yes~~, they don't. No

3 A: ~~Does~~ you work from home? Do B: Yes, sometimes.

4 A: ~~Do~~ she have lunch in a café? Does B: Yes, she does.

5 A: Do you meet a lot of new people? B: Yes, I ~~meet~~. do

D Use the prompts to write simple present questions.

1 you / work in an office?
Do you work in an office?

2 you / wear a uniform?
Do you wear a uniform?

3 you / travel for your job?
Do you travel for your job?

4 you / work with people?
Do you work with people?

5 you / like your job?
Do you like your job?

6 anyone in your family / have an interesting job?
Does anyone in your family have an interesting job?

E Go to the **Grammar Hub** on **page 128**.

F SPEAK Ask and answer the questions in Exercise D. Use information about yourself, or imagine you are someone else.

A: Do you work in an office?
B: Yes, I do. It's in the city center.
A: Does anyone in your family have an interesting job?
B: Yes, my brother does! He's a police officer.

PRONUNCIATION

Linking sounds: *do/does*

A 4.1 Listen to the questions and answers. Notice how some sounds link together.

/ʤʊ/	Do‿you like your job?	Yes, I do.
	Do‿you work from home?	No, I don't.
/dʌziː/	Does‿he travel for his job?	Yes, he does.
/dʌzʃiː/	Does‿she work long hours?	No, she doesn't.

B 4.2 Listen to the questions again and repeat. Link the sounds together.

C SPEAK Complete the questions with your own ideas, and then ask and answer with a partner. Remember to link sounds together.

1 Do you …
2 Do you …
3 Does he …
4 Does she …

SPEAKING

A PREPARE Work in groups. Write ten *yes/no* questions that will help you guess someone's job.

1 Do you work in an office?
2 Do you wear a uniform?
3 Do you work with other people?

B SPEAK Follow the steps below to play the game.

Student 1: Choose a job. Don't tell the other students.

Other students: Ask Student 1 the questions. You must guess the job in ten questions (or fewer).

Student 1: Answer the questions. You can only say *Yes, I do.* or *No, I don't.*

A: Do you work outside?
B: No, I don't.
A: Do you work with people?
B: Yes, I do.

C SPEAK Change roles and repeat.

Talk about jobs

4.2 Good job!

Talk about the perfect job

G *have to / don't have to* **P** connected speech: *have to* **V** time expressions

Good job / Bad job

Everyone wants to have a good job, but what exactly does a 'good job' mean? Is it the money, the location or the hours? What about the company culture? We speak to two people with very different jobs to find out more.

Jie Chen

Ex B I work for a small company, and the office is near my house, so I don't have to take the subway or drive my car. Ex B; Ex C Q2 I walk to work every day, and it only takes five minutes!

I really like the office. It's a nice space, and it's very quiet and relaxing. Also, there's an outside space, Ex C Q5 so we don't have to stay indoors on sunny days – we can work outside!

Ex B; Ex C Q1 My salary isn't great, but it's okay. My favorite thing about my job is that I can choose my own hours. I don't have to work nine to five! Ex B; Ex C Q4 I usually work from seven in the morning until three in the afternoon. Ex C Q3 I'm a morning person, so I'm very happy that I can work early, and get home early, too.

Glossary

nine to five (n phrase) the hours of a typical working day in many countries

salary (n) the fixed amount of money that you get for your job

self-employed (adj) working for yourself, not for one company

Mike Carlstrom

I like my job sometimes, but it isn't easy. I'm very busy every day and I have to make a lot of important decisions. Ex C Q6

The good thing about my job is the money – I'm very well paid. I don't have any free time. Ex B; Ex C Q1

I have to work long hours. I usually get to the office at 8:30 am, and I often leave at around 9 pm. Ex B; Ex C Q4 My office is in the center of the city, and the drive from my home takes over an hour. Ex B; Ex C Q2

Also, I often have to work on the weekend, so I don't see my family much. I want to work from home and spend more time with my children, so my plan is to become self-employed soon.

READING

A Work in pairs. Rank the things in the box in order of importance for a job (1 = very important, 4 = not important).

__ colleagues/boss __ money __ hours __ location

B **READ FOR GIST** Read an article about jobs. Which of the things in Exercise A do the two people talk about? hours; location / trip to work; money

C **READ FOR DETAIL** Read the article again. Are the sentences true (T) or false (F)? Correct the false sentences.

1 Both Jie and Mike make a lot of money. Jie's salary isn't great. Mike is very well paid. T / (F)

2 Jie and Mike travel to work in different ways. (T) / F

3 Jie likes working in the evening. Jie is a morning person. T / (F)

4 Jie and Mike work the same hours. Jie: 7 am–3 pm. Mike: 8:30 am–9 pm. T / (F)

5 Jie can work outside sometimes. (T) / F

6 Both Jie and Mike's jobs are quiet and relaxing. T / (F)
Mike's job is not easy; he's busy and he has to make important decisions.

D **SPEAK** Work with a partner. Discuss Jie and Mike's jobs. Talk about:

- the good things about their jobs
- the bad things about their jobs

A: Mike has a good salary. *B: Yes, but the hours are long.*

GRAMMAR

have to / don't have to

A Complete the sentences with verbs from the article.

1 I don't have to ___take___ the subway or ___drive___ my car.

2 I don't have to ___work___ nine to five!

3 I have to ___make___ a lot of important decisions.

4 I often have to ___work___ on the weekend.

B Look at the sentences in Exercise A. Choose the correct option to complete the rule.

have to / don't have to

We use *have* or *has to* to talk about rules and things we *need / don't need* to do.

C Go to the **Grammar Hub** on **page 128**.

4.2 Good job!

LEAD-IN

Elicit the name of your job and write it on the board. Ask students if they think it is a good job or not and why. Write their ideas on the board, putting the positives on the left and any negatives on the right. Add or elicit your own ideas, too. Then put students in groups and ask them to discuss the positives and negatives of three of the jobs from the previous lesson.

READING

A Focus students on the *Good job / Bad job* article. Point out the separate sections for the introduction and for Jie and Mike. Tell students to read the introduction and decide which thing (*colleagues / boss*, etc) is most important, second most important and so on. Then put students into small groups to discuss their opinions and find out if they agree or not.

B Go through the task and give students a short time limit of one minute, to encourage them to read quickly.

C Give students a longer time limit to read the article in more detail. Then put students into pairs to compare answers, making sure they correct any false sentences.

D Focus students on the example answer and the use of *Yes, but …* to introduce a different opinion. In pairs, students discuss Jie and Mike's jobs. For whole-class feedback, ask a few students to say what the good things and the bad things about the jobs are.

GRAMMAR

A Go through the task instructions with students, and ask them to find the first sentence in the article (in Jie's section). Tell students to identify the missing verbs.

B Students read and complete the rule in pairs before checking as a whole class.

C Direct students to the **Grammar Hub** (see below). Use the **Grammar Worksheet** on W20 for extra practice.

GRAMMAR HUB

4.2 *have to / don't have to*

	Positive	Negative
I/you/we/they	**I have to work** on the weekend.	**I don't have to work** on the weekend.
he/she/it	**She has to wear** a uniform.	She **doesn't have to wear** a uniform.

	Question	Short answers	
I/you/we/they	**Do I have to** start at 9 am?	Yes, **you do**.	No, **you don't**.
he/she/it	**Does she have to** travel a lot for work?	Yes, **she does**.	No, **she doesn't**.

- We use *have to* + base form without *to* to talk about rules and things we need to do.
- We use *don't/doesn't have to* to talk about things we don't need to do.
- We use *Do/Does* + subject + *have to* + base form to make questions.

Be careful!

I don't have to work long hours. NOT ~~*I haven't to work long hours.*~~
Do I have to work long hours? NOT ~~*Have I to work long hours?*~~
No, you don't. NOT ~~*No, you haven't.*~~

4.2 *have to / don't have to*

A Choose the correct options to complete the sentences.

1. You *has to / have to* take your shoes off first.
2. You *haven't to / don't have to* wear a uniform.
3. She *don't / doesn't* have to pay the hotel bill.
4. *You do / Do you* have to get up early?
5. *Has he to / Does he have to* work nine to five?
6. A: Do I have to pay for training?
   B: Yes, you *don't / do*.

B Complete the sentences with the correct form of *have to*.

1. Doctors have to work long hours.
2. I don't have to go to bed early. It's a weekend.
3. He doesn't have to wear a tie. He's a chef.
4. You have to study hard to learn a language.
5. Sally has to study. She has an exam tomorrow.

C Complete the conversations with the correct form of *have to* and short answers.

1. A: Do you have to pay (you / pay) for food at work?
   B: Yes, I do.
2. A: Do I have to wear (I / wear) a uniform?
   B: Yes, you do.
3. A: Does she have to finish (she / finish) it today?
   B: No, she doesn't.
4. A: Do they have to take (they / take) a course?
   B: Yes, they do.
5. A: Does he have to study (he study) tonight?
   B: Yes, he does.
6. A: Do we have to pay (we pay) for training?
   B: No, you/we don't.

➤ Go back to page 34.

4.2 Good job!

PRONUNCIATION

4.3 **A** Go through the instructions before playing the recording. Give feedback as a class, highlighting that *have* and *to* link together to sound like /ˈ**hæf**tə/. Model and practice the two example sentences, correcting any student that leaves a noticeable pause between *have* and *to* and/or uses a strong form of *to*.

4.4 **B** Play the recording, pausing after each question for students to listen and repeat. Make sure that they are saying /ˈ**hæf**tə/, rather than leaving a clear pause between *have* and *to*, or using the strong form of *to*. If this is a particularly strong group, you could review that *Do you* is pronounced as /**dʒʊ**/. So in Questions 1, 2, 3 and 4, the most natural pronunciation of *Do you have to* is /**dʒʊ**ˈhæftə/.

C Students work alone to write four questions with *have to*. Monitor and check the grammar as they do this. Then model the activity for the class by inviting individual students to ask you one or two questions. Reply with a short answer and then add further information using *have to*. Students then work in pairs to ask and answer the questions. Monitor and encourage correct pronunciation.

LISTENING

4.5 **A** Focus students on the two pictures and ask them to describe what they can see in each one. Ask them how the pictures are different.

Play the recording. Students listen to the conversation and decide which picture shows where Hussam works. Explain that *take it easy* means to relax and not do something that makes you tired. *Noon* means 'the middle of the day' or 12:00 pm.

4.5 **B** Play the recording again. Ask students to complete the sentences by writing one word in each blank. Students compare answers in pairs. Check answers as a class by playing the recording again.

C In pairs, students discuss the questions. Monitor and encourage students to ask follow-up questions with *Why/ Why not?*. For whole-class feedback, ask students to share their ideas together.

VOCABULARY

A Remind students that *noon* means 'the middle of the day'. Students then match the other time expressions with the times. Check answers as a class.

B Students work alone to complete the sentences and compare answers in pairs. Check answers as a class.

C Write *Do you have to work from nine to five?* on the board. Ask students to identify the main verb in the question (*work*). Practice the question, making sure students pronounce *have to* as /ˈ**hæf**tə/.

In pairs, students write five more questions. Then put them into different pairs to ask and answer their questions. Use the **Vocabulary Worksheet** on W21 for extra practice.

SPEAKING

A Go through the instructions. You could have a brief class discussion about what things make a good job. Elicit ideas and write them on the board. Then, ask students to work alone to write a list of five things which they think are important.

B Put students into groups of three or four. Students compare their lists and together decide on a final list of five things. Encourage them to put them in order, deciding which is most important, which is second most important and so on.

C Ask each group to share their list with the class. Encourage them to explain their choices and what was top of their list. Finally, if you have time, you could conduct a class vote on what the class thinks is the most important thing for a good job.

TEACHING IDEA by David Seymour and Maria Popova

Vocabulary: What time do you …?

Use this activity to practice time expressions:

When you hear these words, quickly make a question about what time I do the thing, e.g. train – *What time do you catch the train to work?* Make a note of my answers. (Answer two questions with lies and the rest truthfully.)

work/class, get up, lunch break, home, bed, breakfast, bus/train

Two of my answers were lies. In pairs, decide which ones.

In pairs, ask each other questions in the same way, e.g. A – *What time do you get up?* B – *I get up at 11.*

TEACHING IDEA by David Seymour and Maria Popova

Vocabulary: Workplaces

Use this activity to develop work place vocabulary and to practice simple present questions with *have to*:

Work in pairs. Imagine you have a job in one of these places. Your partner will ask you yes/no questions to discover your job, e.g. A – *I work in a hospital.* B – *Do you operate on people?* A – *No. I'm not a surgeon.* B – *Do you clean the floors?* A – *No. I'm not a housekeeper.* A – *Do you have to wear a uniform?* B – *No. I don't work in a hotel.*

a hospital, Disneyland, an airport, an office, a hotel, an ESL school

AUDIO SCRIPT

4.5

Listening, Exercise A, page 173
S = Salah H = Hussam

S: How's your new job?
H: It's great. I don't have to work nine to five. I can choose my own hours.
S: That's great, so when do you work?
Ex B Q1 **H:** I usually start work at noon. Why? When do you start?
S: I start really early in the morning. Sometimes before six!
Ex B Q2 **H:** Ugh! I couldn't do that!! I usually take it easy in the morning, because I don't go to bed until midnight or later.
S: When do you have lunch?
Ex B Q3 **H:** I have lunch any time I feel like it. Some days, I have lunch at 1 pm; other days I eat late in the afternoon.
S: What time do you usually finish work?
Ex B Q4 **H:** I finish when I want to. I don't have to ask my boss. It's my decision.
S: That's amazing. So you can leave whenever you like?
H: No, I don't leave. I stay where I am.
S: I don't understand.
Ex A / Ex B Q5 **H:** I don't work in an office. I'm self-employed now. I work from home.

PRONUNCIATION
Connected speech: *have to*

A Listen to the questions. Is there a pause between 'have' and 'to'? No, there isn't. In natural English, *have to* links together to sound like /'hæftə/.
4.3

1 Do you have‿to work long hours?
2 Do employees have‿to eat in the company restaurant?

B Listen and repeat the questions.
4.4

1 Do you have to wear a uniform?
2 Does he have to go to a lot of meetings?
3 Do they have to organize a lot of trips?
4 Do you have to ask your boss for a vacation?

C SPEAK Write four questions using *have to*. Work with a partner and ask your questions.

A: Do you have to work on weekends?
B: No I don't! I only have to work nine to five, Monday to Friday.

LISTENING

A LISTEN FOR GIST Listen to the conversation between Hussam and Salah. Which picture is Hussam's work? 1
4.5

B LISTEN FOR DETAIL Listen again and complete each sentence with one word.
4.5

1 Hussan usually starts ___work___ at noon.
2 He usually takes it easy in the ___morning___.
3 He sometimes has ___lunch___ at 1pm.
4 He can decide when to ___finish___ work.
5 He is self-employed so he works from ___home___.

C SPEAK Work with a partner. Do you want a job like Hussam's? Why/Why not?

VOCABULARY
Time expressions

A Read the sentences from the conversation. Match the time expressions in **bold** with the times (1–5).

I don't have to work ***nine to five****.*
I usually start work at ***noon****.*
I have to start really ***early in the morning****.*
I don't go to bed until ***midnight*** *or later.*
...other days, I eat ***late in the afternoon****.*

1 12 pm ___noon___
2 4 pm – 6 pm ___late in the afternoon___
3 9 am – 5 pm ___nine to five___
4 12 am ___midnight___
5 5 am – 9 am ___early in the morning___

B Complete the sentences with the time expressions from Exercise A.

1 I work better at night. Sometimes I study late in the evenings, until ___midnight___ or later.
2 I don't have to work from ___nine to five___, like my friends in offices. It's great!
3 I have lunch at ___noon___ every day. I start early in the morning, so I'm always hungry by then.
4 I find it difficult to think ___late in the afternoon___. I just want to go home and relax.
5 I like to go for a run ___early in the morning___ before I go to work.

C SPEAK Work with a partner. Write five questions using the words and phrases from Exercise A. Ask and answer the questions with your partner.

A: Do you have to work from nine to five?
B: No, I can choose my own hours.

SPEAKING

A PLAN Make a list of five things that make a good job.

1 A big salary!
2 The people you work with.

B SPEAK Work in small groups. Compare your ideas from Exercise A. Together, decide on a top five list.

C PRESENT Read your list to the class. Explain your ideas.

1

2
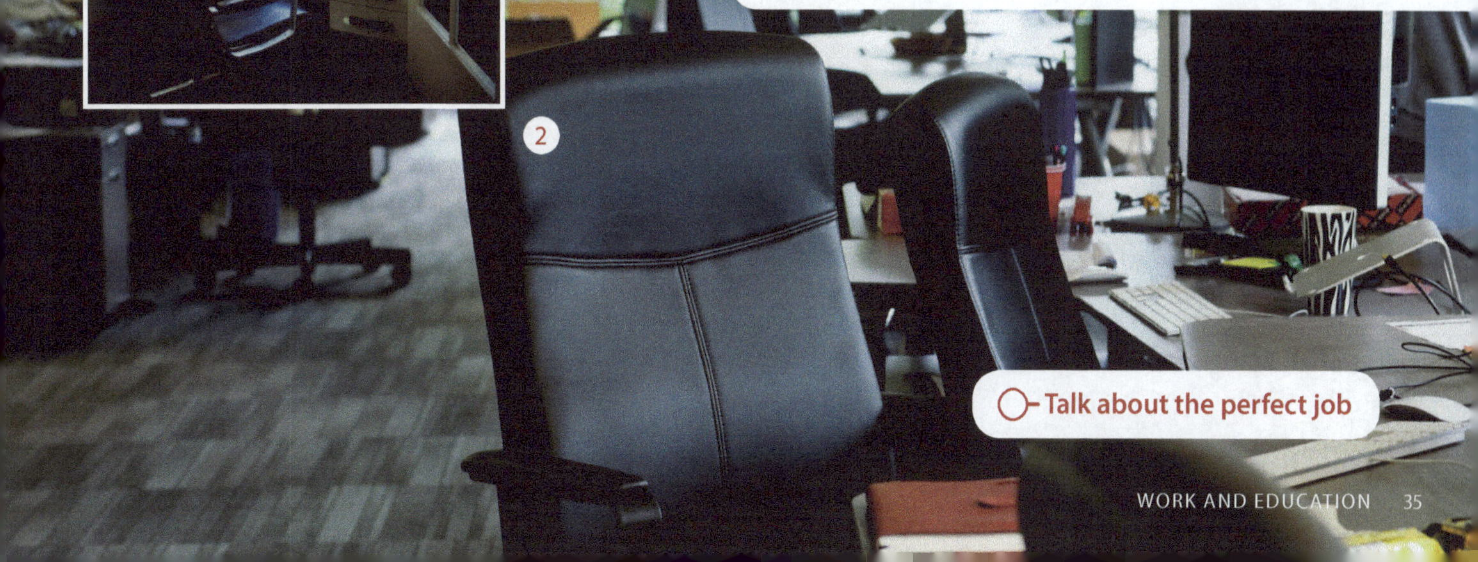

Talk about the perfect job

4.3 Learn something new

Talk about adult education and career development

G question words P word stress: questions V education collocations S listening for gist

The Open University

It's never too late to learn something new. The Open University is the largest university in the UK, with almost 174,000 students in 2015/2016 alone. It is a distance learning university, and it's for anyone who wants to study and learn a new skill. Ex D Q1 Ex C Q1

FAQs

Who are the courses for? Ex D Q2
Open University degree courses are open for anyone. Many people who have jobs or cannot go to a normal university on weekdays choose to study with us. As a distance learning university, it's perfect for anyone who wants to study from home. Ex B

How much does it cost?
The cost of full-time study is almost half that of other universities in the UK.

What subjects do you teach?
There are nearly 500 courses to choose from. Ex C Q2

When do students go to classes?
Students don't 'go' to classes. All of the classes and resources are available online or through print and video sources, so students can access them when they need to. Ex D Q3

Where do students meet their teachers?
They don't. Students usually send homework to their teachers. The teachers reply by email. Ex D Q4

How long does an average degree course take?
It takes an average of six years for most students to finish their degrees. Ex C Q3

Why do people take distance learning courses?
A lot of people work during the day and study in their free time. The Open University is flexible. You can study anywhere, anytime. Ex D Q5

Glossary

course (n) a series of lessons in one subject
degree (n) a certification you get after you complete a university course
resources (n) things you can use to help you to study
skill (n) the ability to do something well
university (n) a place where adults study

READING

A Work with a partner. Discuss the questions.

1 Why do people with a job study in their free time?
2 What kinds of things do they study?

B READ FOR GIST Read the webpage about the Open University. How is it different from a typical university?
It's a distance learning university. People study from home.

C READ FOR DETAIL Read the webpage again. Work in pairs. What do these numbers refer to?

1 174,000 students 2 500 courses 3 6 years

D Read the webpage again. Are the sentences true (T) or false (F)? Correct the false sentences.

1 The Open University is the largest university in ~~Europe.~~ the UK T / (F)
2 It's only for British people. It's for anyone. T / (F)
3 You study when you want to. (T) / F
4 Students don't usually meet their teachers. (T) / F
5 A lot of people study during the day. A lot of people work during the day and study in their free time. T / (F)

GRAMMAR

Question words

A Look at the questions on the webpage. Complete the rules with the question words in the box.

How long How much What When Where Who ~~Why~~

Question words

1 __Why__ to ask for a reason.
2 __What__ to ask a question about a thing.
3 __Where__ to ask a question about a place.
4 __Who__ to ask a question about a person.
5 __How much__ to ask a question about quantity.
6 __How long__ to ask about a length of time.
7 __When__ to ask a question about a time.

B Go to the **Grammar Hub** on **page 128**.

C Complete the questions with words from Exercise A.

1 __What__ subjects are popular in your country?
2 __Why__ are they so popular?
3 __Where__ can you get information about courses?
4 __How much__ does it cost to go to this university?
5 __When__ do people usually start and finish classes?
6 __How long__ do people usually study for (e.g. three years, four years, etc)?
7 __Who__ is your favorite teacher? Why?

D SPEAK Ask and answer the questions in Exercise C.

4.3 Learn something new

LEAD-IN

Show students a picture of someone working in a café. Tell them that this is your friend X (give them a name appropriate to the image). Elicit their job (i.e. a *waiter/waitress*). Write this word on the board, adding the phonemes (/ˈweɪtər/ or /ˈweɪtrəs/) and practicing good pronunciation. Tell students that your friend loves being a waitress, but really wants to be a designer. Ask the class what your friend should do. Write any good ideas on the board. Next put students into groups. Ask them to discuss if they know anyone in a similar position to your friend. Monitor, helping with any challenging grammar/vocabulary.

READING

A In pairs, students discuss the questions. Ask them to share their ideas with the whole class and add them to the board in two columns: *Reasons* and *What people study*.

B Give students a short time limit to read the webpage and identify how the Open University is different from other universities. Check answers as a class.

C Ask students to scan the text quickly to find the numbers and check what they refer to. Allow them up to two minutes to do this. Check answers as a class.

D Allow students a longer time limit to read the text again in more detail. Then ask students to compare answers in pairs and correct the false sentences. Then check answers as a class.

1 F (It is the largest university in the UK.); 2 F (It is for anyone.); 3 T; 4 T; 5 F (A lot of people work during the day and study in their free time.).

GRAMMAR

A Elicit how many questions are in the text about the Open University (*seven*) to ensure students understand the organization of the text. Students then use the questions in the text to help them to complete the rules with the question words. Check answers as a class.

B Direct students to the **Grammar Hub** (see below). Read the examples and go through the rules and exercises with the class.

C Students work alone to complete the questions. Point out that they need to read the rest of the question carefully to understand what the question is about. Check answers as a class.

D Put students into pairs to ask and answer the questions. Use the **Grammar Worksheet** on W22 for extra practice.

Extra activity

Tell students they are going to interview their classmates. Give them time to write simple present questions with each of the question words in the Grammar section. Monitor and assist as necessary, encouraging students to avoid anything too personal. Next, put students into pairs to ask and answer their questions. If you have the space, you could extend this activity by rearranging the seats in the classroom into two even rows of students facing each other. Students then have a minute to ask and answer as many of their questions as possible. When the minute is up, ask one row of students to stand up and move one seat to the left to sit across from a new partner. Repeat this process until everyone has worked with each other.

GRAMMAR HUB

4.3 Question words

Why	To ask for a reason	**Why** are you late?
What	To ask about a thing	**What** does it do?
Where	To ask about a place	**Where** do you work?
Who	To ask about a person	**Who** is your boss?
How much	To ask about a quantity	**How much** does it cost?
How long	To ask about a length of time	**How long** does the movie last?
When	To ask about a time	**When** does the meeting start?

- We use question word + auxiliary verb + subject + main verb to make *Wh-* questions.

  Where do you live? NOT ~~*Where you live?*~~

  How much does it cost? NOT ~~*How much it costs?*~~

4.3 Question words

A Complete the sentences with the question words in the box.

how what when where who why

1 Where do most college students live?
2 Who is your teacher?
3 How long is the course?
4 What class do you have now?
5 Why do you want to work there?
6 When does your course start?

B Reorder the words to make questions.

1 do / where / you / study
Where do you study?
2 much / it / how / does / cost
How much does it cost?
3 long / last / how / it / does
How long does it last?
4 the / when / course / does / start
When does the course start?
5 course / study / what / you / do
What course do you study?

➤ Go back to page 36.

4.3 Learn something new

PRONUNCIATION

4.6 **A** Write *Where do you work?* on the board and model the pronunciation. Use hand gestures to emphasize the rhythm and stress of the question, and then underline the stressed words (*where/work*). Point out that the other words in the question are not stressed. This means that they become shorter and weaker. Also point out that in words of more than one syllable, only one syllable will carry the main stress. Play the recording, pausing after each question. Give students time to underline the stressed words. Then play the recording again for students to listen and repeat the questions. Encourage students to pronounce *do you* as /dʒʊ/.

LISTENING

4.7 **A** Read through the *Listening for gist* box with students. Point out that key words are usually stressed when we speak English. These are usually the words that carry the most important information.

Play the recording. Students listen to the conversation and choose the correct summary. Ask students to compare answers with a partner before checking answers as a class.

Remind students of the *Listening for gist* box. Ask them what key words helped them to decide.

4.7 **B** Tell students that they will now listen for more detail. Allow time for students to read through the beginnings and ends of sentences before listening, and then play the recording again. Check answers as a class.

C In pairs, students discuss the questions. If they are from different countries, it would be good to open the discussion to the whole class.

VOCABULARY

A Focus students on the first sentence and elicit the correct answer (*take*). Then write *take a course* on the board. Ask students if they can think of any words that are usually used with *take* (e.g. *take* ***classes***, *take* ***lessons***, *take* ***tests***) and write any good examples on the board. Explain that words that are usually used together are called 'collocations'. Elicit that the examples covered in this exercise are verb + noun collocations. Tell students that collocations are not necessarily the same in different languages and that their English will sound more natural when they use collocations correctly.

B Do this as a whole class. Ask students to identify each collocation. Then write each one on the board. If you have time, you could ask students to test each other in pairs. One student says a noun (e.g. *a course*) and the other students should say a verb (e.g. *take*). Use the **Vocabulary Worksheet** on W23 for extra practice.

SPEAKING HUB

A Go through the instructions with students. Point out that they should think about adults, rather than young people, and that they should focus on people *re*training (i.e. people who have done other jobs before). Put students into groups of three or four and ask them to follow the two steps.

B Give a time limit for the groups to work through the six questions. Monitor and encourage discussion within the groups.

C If you have time, include a practice section. Ask students to record themselves using their phones before they present anything to the class.

D Finish the lesson by taking a class vote to decide which course is the most popular.

TEACHING IDEA by David Seymour and Maria Popova

GRAMMAR: Interviews

Use this activity to practice question forms:

In pairs, ask questions to help you fill in this form with information about your partner, e.g. *What's your name?*

Name	Age
Address	Nationality
Marital status	Children
Telephone number	Job

Keep your notes and swap partners. Ask and answer questions about the person on your partner's form, e.g. *What's her name?*

AUDIO SCRIPT

4.7

Listening, Exercise A
T = Tom L = Lily

T: Hello. Can I help you?
Ex A L: Hi. Yes, please. I work in an office, but I want to change jobs. I'd like to take a course.
Ex B Q2 T: Well, you've come to the right place. We offer over 800 courses. My name's Tom. Come and sit down.
L: Thank you. I'm Lily.
T: Nice to meet you, Lily. Now, what subject do you want to study?
L: I want to train to be a teacher.
T: Ah, an excellent job! We have a very good teacher training course. I'm a teacher myself.
L: Oh?
T: Yes, I teach an art history course and …
Ex A L: I want to teach art history!
T: That's great. I can definitely help you.
L: Do I have to go to a university?
T: Yes, you do.
L: That's a problem. I have to stay at work while I study. I need the money.
Ex B Q1 & 4 T: I recommend online classes. You study when you want. You work from home and you send your
Ex B Q3 homework to us by email.
L: That sounds good. I want to get a certification. Does this course offer one?
Ex B Q5 T: Yes, of course! This is a degree course. You pay for access to our online materials and we provide you with your own teacher. The teacher of this art history course is … um, well … me actually.
L: Oh! OK!
T: At the end of each course, you take an exam. You can pay for one year at first and see how you like it. Then, after two more years, you can get a degree.
L: That sounds great. Now, how much …

PRONUNCIATION
Word stress: questions

4.6 Listen and repeat the questions. Underline the stressed words.

1 Where do you work?
2 Why do you study history?
3 When do you start work?
4 What do you do?
5 How much does your course cost?

LISTENING

4.7 **A LISTEN FOR GIST** Listen to a conversation. Choose the correct summary (1–3).

Listening for gist

Gist is the main idea. When you listen for gist, you don't need to understand every word. Listen for key words, which help you to understand the main idea(s) and summarize what you heard.

1 Lily is a teacher. She wants to teach art history to Tom.
2 Lily works in an office. She wants to teach art history like Tom.
3 Lily wants to study art history at a university so she can work in an office.

4.7 **B LISTEN FOR DETAIL** Listen again. Match the beginnings of sentences (1–5) with the ends of sentences (a–e).

1 I recommend online
2 We offer over
3 You send your homework to us
4 You study when
5 You pay for access to our online

a by email.
b materials.
c classes.
d 800 courses.
e you want.

C SPEAK Work in groups. Discuss the questions.

1 How long do you have to study to become a teacher in your country?
2 Who pays for it?

VOCABULARY
Education collocations

A Choose the correct verbs to complete the sentences.

1 I want to *take* / *get* a course in my free time.
2 I don't want to *study* / *train* a subject I don't like!
3 I want to *train* / *do* to be a teacher.
4 I want to *go* / *study* to a university.
5 I have to *take* / *get* a lot of exams.
6 Then, after two more years, I can *study* / *get* a degree.
7 My company says I have to *take* / *get* a certification.

B Underline the verb–noun collocations in Exercise A.

SPEAKING HUB

A PLAN Work in small groups. Imagine you are planning a new course for adults who want to retrain.

- Think about the types of jobs that adults retrain for in your country.
- Choose the type of course (for example, English, science, business).

B PREPARE Plan the course. Decide on your answers to these questions:

- When will the course happen? (weekdays, weekends, any time)
- Where? (in a college, at a university, online)
- How long will it take?
- How much will it cost?
- What exams do students have to take?
- What certifications do they get?

C DISCUSS Imagine you are at a career fair.

- Present your course to the rest of the class.
- Be prepared to answer questions.
- Watch the other groups' presentations. Ask them questions about their courses.

D THINK ABOUT IT Take a class vote. Find out how many people are interested in each course.

— Talk about adult education and career development

Café Hub

4.4 Busy day

F – ask for someone and leave a message   P – stress and intonation

COMPREHENSION

A ▶ **Watch the video. Are the sentences true (T) or false (F)? Correct the false sentences.**

1 Neena works in an office. (T)/ F
2 Richard Sharp is busy. (T)/ F
3 Neena's surname is Patel. (T)/ F
4 She has to finish the Smith account today. (T)/ F
5 She meets her mum for dinner. T /(F) She doesn't meet her mum/mom for dinner.
6 She usually finishes work at 10 pm. T /(F) She usually finishes work at 6 pm.
7 Neena wants a new job. (T)/ F
8 She tells her mum about her new housemates. (T)/ F

B ▶ **Number the events in the order they happen. Then watch the video again and check.**

Neena leaves a message for Richard Sharp.

Neena gets more work.

Neena gets started.

Lunchtime?

Neena speaks to her mum.

Finished?

FUNCTIONAL LANGUAGE

Asking for someone and leaving a message

A ▶ 00:00–01:37 **Complete Neena's conversation with the receptionist. Then watch the first part of the video again and check.**

Neena / **Receptionist**

Receptionist: Good [1] ___morning___. This is Morgan and Wise. Can I help?

Neena: Hello. [2] ___Could___ I speak to Richard Sharp, please?

Receptionist: Who's [3] ___calling___, please?

Neena: [4] ___It's___ Neena Patel.

Receptionist: Hold on a [5] ___moment___, please.

Receptionist: … I'm [6] ___afraid___ he's not available at the moment. Would you like to [7] ___leave___ a message?

Neena: Yes, please. Can he call me [8] ___back___?

Receptionist: Yes, what's your number?

Neena: It's 0207 946 0865.

B **Work in pairs. Practice the conversation using your own name. Copy the stress and intonation.**

MILLY

SAM

NEENA

ZAC

GABY

USEFUL PHRASES

Match the phrases (1–5) with their uses (a–e).

1	Hi, [mum]. It's me.	a	To change the subject.
2	Right then,	b	To react to bad news.
3	Oh, dear.	c	To start a voicemail to someone you know.
4	Look,	d	To make someone listen/understand.
5	Anyway,	e	To begin a big or difficult job.

PRONUNCIATION

Stress and intonation

A 00:59–01:27 Watch part of Neena's conversation with the receptionist again. Notice the stress and intonation.

Neena:	Yes, please. Can he call me back?
Receptionist:	Yes, what's your number?
Neena:	It's 0207 946 0865.
Receptionist:	So, that's 0207 946 0865.
Neena:	Yes, that's right.

B 00:59–01:27 Watch again and repeat the conversation. Copy the stress and intonation.

Saying '0'

In British English, we usually say 'oh'.

In American English, we say 'oh' or 'zero'.

C Work in pairs. Practice the conversation in Exercise A, but change the phone number. Remember to use the correct stress and intonation.

Glossary

mum **(n) (British)** = mom **(n) (American)**
surname **(n) (British)** = last name **(n) (American)**

SPEAKING

A PLAN Work in pairs. Write a telephone conversation between yourself and a receptionist. Include these stages:

- You want to speak to a famous person.
- The famous person isn't available.
- You leave your name and number.

B PRACTICE Practice your conversation. Be careful with your stress and intonation.

C PRESENT Perform your conversation for the class.

A: Hello. Could I speak to Adele, please?
B: Who's speaking, please?

Ask for someone and leave a message

➤ Turn to **page 163** to learn how to write an email asking for information.

4.4 Busy day

LEAD-IN

Use this activity to review numbers in the context of telephone numbers. Say a phone number (you can use *207-946-0865*) and ask students to write it down. Ask a student to repeat it back to you, and write it on the board. Show how the numbers are grouped and pauses are used when saying the number. Explain that we can say *zero* or *oh*.

Ask the class to stand up and mingle. Students ask each other *What's your number?* and write down the phone number of each student they talk to. Students can invent numbers if they don't want to give their real ones.

COMPREHENSION

A Allow time for students to read through the sentences. Play the video for students to decide if the sentences are true or false. Students then compare answers in pairs and correct the false sentences. Check answers as a class.

1 T; 2 T;3 T; 4 T; 5 F (She doesn't meet her mum/mom for dinner.); 6 F (She usually finishes work at 6 pm.); 7 T; 8 T.

B Focus students on the photos. Ask them to put them in order. Then play the video again for them to check answers.

FUNCTIONAL LANGUAGE

A 00:00-01:37 In pairs, students complete the conversation. Monitor and assist as required, reminding students that the conversation is the same as in the video. Play the video again for students to check their answers.

B Put students into pairs to pratice the conversation. Monitor and encourage correct stress and intonation.

USEFUL PHRASES

Give students time to complete the exercise alone before giving feedback as a class. Give examples to clarify meaning if necessary.

PRONUNCIATION

A 00:59-01:27 Read through the task and the conversation with students. Play the video for students to watch the conversation.

B 00:59-01:27 Read through the box about saying '0' with students. Highlight that people will understand both versions, but we should be consistent and not say 'oh' and then 'zero', for example, in the same number.

C Put students into pairs to practice the conversation from Exercise A. Monitor and practice correct pronunciation as appropriate.

SPEAKING

A Read through the task instructions and highlight the three stages to include, and the students need to decide which famous person they are trying to speak to. In pairs, students write a conversation between the two people. Monitor and assist as required.

B Tell students to practice their conversations. Encourage them to repeat this stage two or three times, until they are able to go through the conversation with appropriate stress and intonation.

C Ask students to perform their conversations to the class. Make a note of any useful emergent vocabulary or structures to teach after each conversation.

VIDEO SCRIPT

FC = Female Colleague N = Neena
R = Receptionist M = Neena's mum

FC: It's the Morgan account. Do you have time for this today?
N: Yes, no problem.
R: Good morning. This is Morgan and Wise. Can I help?
N: Hello. Could I speak to Richard Sharp, please?
R: Who's calling, please?
N: It's Neena Patel.
R: Hold on a moment, please. … I'm afraid he's not available at the moment. Would you like to leave a message?
N: Yes, please. Can he call me back?
R: Yes, what's your number?
N: It's 0207 946 0865.
R: So, that's 0207 946 0865.
N: Yes, that's right.
R: And your name is Neena …
N: Patel.
R: Patel … OK.
N: OK, thanks. Bye.
R: Goodbye.
N: OK then, let's go! Finished!
FC: The Smith account – we have to finish this today.
N: Sure.
M: Hello! I'm not here at the moment. Please leave a message after the tone.
N: Hi, Mum. It's me. Can you call me back? It's about dinner tonight. Great.
FC: Sorry Neena!
N: Right then … Hi Mum.
M: Hi Neena. Are you ready? I'm hungry. Where are you?
N: I'm still at work. I have to work late tonight.
M: What time do you finish?
N: Well … 6 pm usually but tonight 10 pm.
M: Oh dear. That's OK.
N: I'm sorry about dinner.
M: Let's have dinner next week. You work too hard!
N: I have to.
M: You don't have to.
N: Look. I know Mum. I know … I need a new job … Anyway, good news! I've got some new housemates. They're really nice.
M: That's good.
N: I need to finish work now. I'll call you tomorrow.
M: OK darling. I love you.
N: I love you too, Mum. Bye.

4 Writing

Write an email asking for information

W– punctuation: question marks, commas and periods

A Work in pairs. Complete the advertisements with the words in the box.

weekend company ten-week course

Start up your own ¹ company

One-day training course with experienced business teacher
Contact Trevor East: teast@ivory.nett

² **Ten-week** language courses

Are you interested in languages?
Learn with us.
Don't wait – call now to get started.
Alena Chin: alenac@onthewall.com

Summer computer skills ³ course

Do you want to learn computer skills?
Classes every day.
Contact Ed Soames: edso@screen.nett

⁴ Weekend **résumé writing course**

Five-week course (Saturdays and Sundays only)
Perfect for graduates or people who want to change jobs
Contact Anne Roberts: anne@roberts.nett

B Read the email. Which advertisement is it for?
The 'Summer computer skills course' advertisement.

Inquiry about your course
Sent: Friday, November 10, 2017, 2:19 pm
To: edso@screen.nett
From: SKhan@logbox.com

Dear Mr. Soames,
I am writing to ask about your summer computer skills course.
First, what are the dates of the course? I am free in May, June and July and the first part of August. Second, when do the classes start – are they in the morning or in the afternoon?
And finally, how much does the course cost?
I look forward to hearing from you.
Regards,
Samira Khan

C Look at the email in Exercise B again. Circle question marks, commas and periods.

D Look at the question marks, commas and periods that you circled in the email. Choose the correct options to complete the rules.

Punctuation: question marks, commas and full stops

We use *question marks / commas / periods* at the end of sentences.
We use *question marks / commas / periods* at the end of questions.
We use *question marks / commas / periods* to separate words in a list or after sequencing words.

> It's also a good idea to remind students about using capital letters for people's names, months and for starting sentences.

E Number the stages of the email in Exercise B.

3 Asking about when the course starts and ends
1 Greeting and name of the person you're writing to
6 Standard 'end of letter' phrase
2 Reason for writing
4 Asking about the times of classes
7 Salutation and name of writer
5 Asking about the cost of the course

F Complete the table with the phrases in the box.

All the best Best wishes Dear Monica Dear Mr. Ikeda ~~Dear Mrs. Bennett~~ Kind regards ~~Sincerely yours~~

Starting an email	Finishing an email
Dear Mrs. Bennett	*Sincerely yours*
Dear Mr. Ikeda	Kind regards
Dear Monica	Best wishes
	All the best

> Refer students to this email as a model for the writing task.

G Order the two groups of phrases in Exercise F from most formal to least formal.

> Tell students that it's important to know who your target reader is and to decide whether to write in a formal or informal style.

WRITING

A PREPARE Imagine you want to apply to one of the courses in Exercise A. Choose a course and write three questions to ask in an email.

B WRITE Write an email asking for information. Use the email in Exercise B to help you.

C REVIEW Work in pairs. Check your partner's email for:

- spelling and punctuation
- grammar
- organization

WRITING 163

WRITING

In this writing lesson, students will learn how to write an email asking for information, paying attention to correct use of punctuation (question marks, commas and periods).

A Focus students on the ad. Elicit where students might see them (*on a website or a bulletin board*). Students then work in pairs to complete the ad. Check answers as a class. Point out the collocation *start up a company*, which means to create a new company.

B Allow students one minute to read the email and decide which ad it relates to. Check answer as a class and encourage students to explain their choice.

C Write *punctuation* on the board along with the first two sentences of the email from Exercise B. Ask students to identify the punctuation in the sentences and to name each type. Circle the punctuation as the students identify it. Then focus students on the complete email in Exercise B and circle the punctuation. Check answers as a class, displaying the email on the board if possible.

D Students complete the rules in the box. Check answers as a class.

E Focus students on the example. Elicit what the actual greeting is in the email (*Dear …*). Students then work alone to put the other stages in order. Point out that a *salutation* can be a way of saying goodbye.

F Students complete the table with the phrases from the box. Check answers as a class by building up the table on the board.

G In pairs, students discuss the phrases. Check answers as a class.

WRITING TASK

A Students work alone to choose the course they want to take. They then think of three questions to ask about the course and make a note of these.

B Allow time for students to review the email in Exercise B and the stages of an email in Exercise E. Students then write their email.

C Put students into pairs and ask them to look at each other's work.

Unit 4 Review

VOCABULARY

A Complete the definitions with the jobs in the box.

dentist designer doctor hairdresser
journalist mechanic pilot sales clerk

1 doctor (n) a person that helps sick people
2 hairdresser (n) a person that cuts people's hair
3 mechanic (n) a person that fixes cars
4 pilot (n) a person that flies planes
5 dentist (n) a person that fixes your teeth
6 sales clerk (n) a person that works in a store
7 designer (n) a person that decides how something looks or works
8 journalist (n) a person that reports the news

B Choose the correct words to complete the sentences.

1 In my country, teachers earn a good ***money* / *salary***.
2 My sister works ***full time* / *part time***. She's in the office three days a week.
3 I work for an electronics ***company* / *boss***.
4 My father's an actor. He's ***salary* / *self-employed***.
5 There are 200 ***colleagues* / *employees*** in the company.
6 My brother is a nurse. He works ***long hours* / *nine to five*** at night.

C Complete the sentences with the time expressions in the box.

early in the morning late in the afternoon
noon midnight nine to five

1 The restaurant closes at 11 pm, so I usually don't get home until after midnight.
2 I have a normal office job. I work from nine to five.
3 My wife starts work at 6 am, so she has to get up really early in the morning
4 I have a meeting at noon. Maybe we could go for lunch after that?
5 I work all night, so I sleep for most of the day. I usually don't get up until late in the afternoon

D Complete the text with the words in the box.

course degree exam study train college

At the moment, I'm in my last year of school, but after that I want to go to [1] college. I want to [2] study medicine, then [3] train to be a doctor. I need to take an [4] exam at the end of this year before I can go to college and start my [5] degree. It takes five years to complete the [6] course, and it's a lot of work – but it's my dream!

E SPEAK Work in pairs. Discuss the questions.

1 Do you have a degree? Do you want one?
2 Does anyone in your family go to college? Where? What do they study?
3 What would you like to take a course in?
4 How do you feel before an exam?

GRAMMAR

A Use the prompts to write *yes/no* questions then write short answers that are true for you.

1 you / work / outside?
Do you work outside? Yes, I do.
2 your colleagues / work / full time?
Do your colleagues work full time?
3 your company / make computers?
Does your company make computers?
4 your boss / earn / a good salary?
Does your boss earn a good salary?
5 you / like / your job?
Do you like your job?

B Complete the text with the correct form of *have to* and the verbs in parentheses.

My sister's a police officer in our hometown. She [1] has to work (*work*) long hours, sometimes 10 or 12 hours a day, and she often [2] has to get up (*get up*) early, at 4 am. She [3] has to wear (*wear*) a blue uniform when she works outside, but when she's in the office, she [4] doesn't have to wear (*wear*) special clothes – she can wear her normal clothes. She and her colleagues often [5] have to help (*help*) people in dangerous situations.

C Write questions to match the answers.

1 A: Where do you live?
B: I live in a small apartment in the city center.
2 A: Who is your teacher? / What's your teacher's name?
B: My teacher is Ms. Magnabosco.
3 A: When do you do your homework? / What do you do on the weekend?
B: I do my homework on the weekend.
4 A: How long is your English course?
B: My English course is two years.

FUNCTIONAL LANGUAGE

Complete the conversation with the words in the box.

call hang here message number speak that's

A: Hello?
B: Hi, it's Joe. Can I [1] speak to Maria, please?
A: She's not [2] here at the moment.
B: Oh, right. Can I leave a [3] message?
A: [4] Hang on a minute. I don't have a pen …
OK, I'm ready.
B: Can she [5] call me back? My [6] number is 800-555-0199.
A: OK, so [7] that's 800-555-0199.
B: That's right. Thanks!

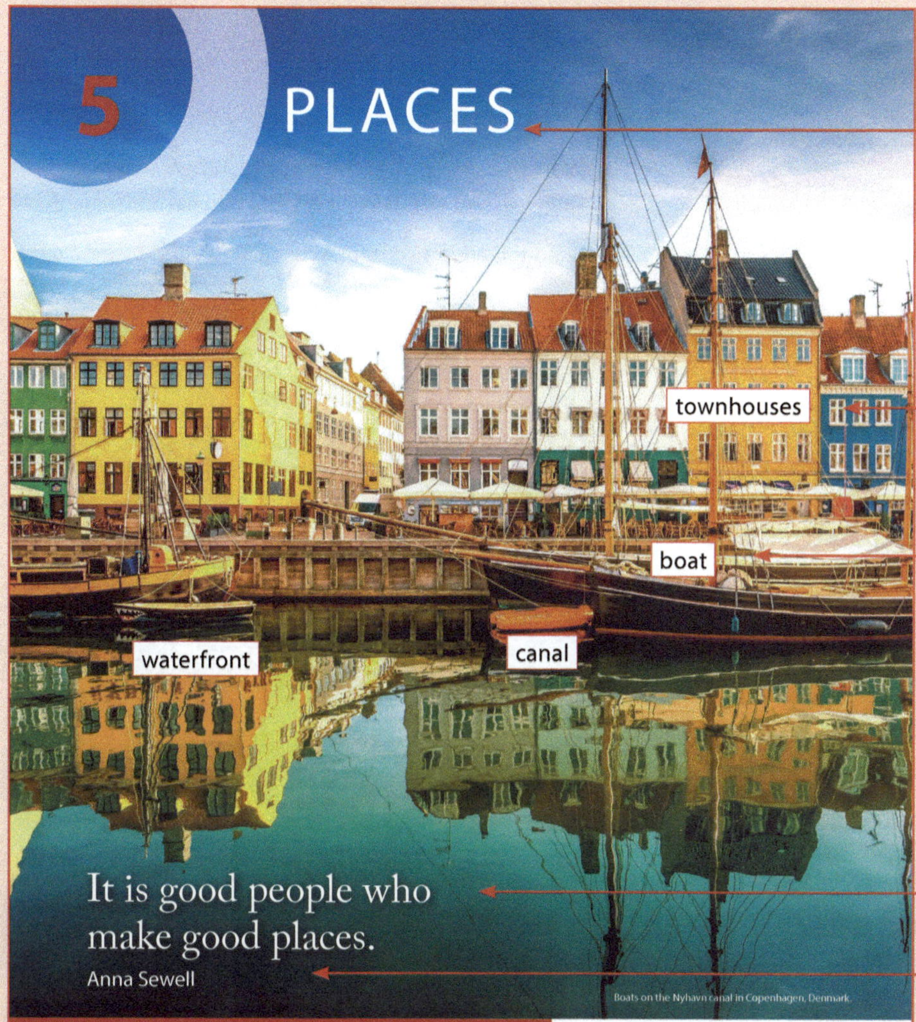

Boats on the Nyhavn canal in Copenhagen, Denmark.

Place (n) an area, location or a particular town, country or building
Synonyms: location (n), neighborhood (n)

Ask students to label the photo if you need time to set up the class.

Boats on the Nyhavn canal in Copenhagen, Denmark.

The quote suggests that the feelings we have about places depend on the people that are there, not how the place looks. For example, the office you work in might be modern and look great, but if the people that work there aren't friendly, you won't like that place. The same is true of cities, houses, etc.

Anna Sewell (1820–1878) was a British author of the well-known children's book about a horse, *Black Beauty*. Sewell made it her goal to write about horses to help people see how this animal should be treated with kindness and respect.

OBJECTIVES

- describe a home
- describe a neighborhood
- describe an interesting building
- ask for and give directions
- write a description of a place

Work with a partner. Discuss the questions.

1 Where do you live?
2 Look at the picture. Would you like to live there? Why/Why not?
3 What's your favorite city?

PLACES 41

OBJECTIVES

Read the unit objectives to the class.

UNIT OPENER QUESTIONS

Ask students to look at the picture on the page and describe what they see. Ask students where they think the place might be and why. Ask what they think the buildings might be used for (e.g. *cafés, offices*, etc). Ask students to share any experiences they have of visiting or living in an area like this. Elicit how the place is different from where the students live.

Ask students to read the questions at the bottom of the page. Check that students understand the questions and write the following sentence stems on the board for students to use as prompts: *I live in … ; I would / wouldn't like to live here because … ; My favorite city is … because …* Model the prompts by giving your own answers to the questions.

Students then discuss the three questions in pairs or small groups. Monitor and help with grammar and vocabulary as required. Encourage students to listen and ask follow-up questions to find out more. For whole-class feedback, ask two or three students to share their ideas.

WORKSHEETS

Lesson 5.1 There's no place like home

Rooms and furniture: prepositions of place (W24)

there is/are (W25)

Lesson 5.2 My neighborhood

Places in a town or city (W26)

can (W27)

Lesson 5.3 Amazing buildings

Adjectives to describe the appearance of things (W28)

Imperatives (W29)

5.1 There's no place like home

Describe a home

V – rooms and furniture; prepositions of place P – /b/, /d/ and /g/ G – *there is/are*

VOCABULARY
Rooms and furniture

A Work in pairs and discuss the questions.

1. Do you live in a house or an apartment?
2. Who do you live with?
3. How many rooms are there?
4. Where do you spend most of your time?

B Go to the **Vocabulary Hub** on **page 148**.

C **SPEAK** Work in pairs. Student A – imagine you are in a room in your house or apartment. Describe what you can see. Student B – guess which room your partner is talking about.

A: I can see a TV and a lamp.
B: You're in the living room!
A: No, I'm in the bedroom!

PRONUNCIATION
/b/, /d/ and /g/

5.1 **A** The words below all begin with /b/, /d/ or /g/ sounds. Listen and repeat.

/b/	/d/	/g/
bedroom	dining	garden
bathroom	don't	go
brother	day	grow
because	do	give
ball	doctor	game
business	daughter	got

5.2 **B** Listen and write the words in the correct place in Exercise A.

5.3 **C** Listen, check and repeat.

LISTENING

A Work in pairs. Look at the pictures. Where would you prefer to stay when on vacation? Why?

B Read the advertisement. What is it for? It's an advertisement for a caravan on a beach in California which is available for a house swap.

Houseswap

Laguna Beach, California, US
Caravan on private beach near Los Angeles.
Great home right on the Pacific Ocean. Sleeps four.
Close to Disneyland.
My dream swap: Italy, Greece, France, UK
Contact Luke Westman at 1-213-509-6995

5.4 **C** **LISTEN FOR GIST** Listen to Sadie talking to Luke about his house. Which sentence (1–3) best describes their conversation?

1. Sadie doesn't like the house.
2. Sadie and Luke agree to swap houses.
3. Sadie doesn't understand the house swap rules.

5.4 **D** **LISTEN FOR KEY WORDS** Listen again. Choose the correct words to complete the sentences.

1. Sadie is from the south of *France* / *England*.
2. Luke's caravan has *two* / *three* beds.
3. Luke's caravan *has* / *doesn't have* a swimming pool.
4. Luke's caravan *has four* / *doesn't have any* chairs.
5. Sadie *has* / *doesn't have* a house.

E **SPEAK** Work in pairs. What do you like about Luke's home? What don't you like?

5.1 There's no place like home

LEAD-IN

Show students a picture of your living room (or find a picture and pretend – maybe even a picture of somewhere large and expensive looking!). Elicit what kind of room it is (adding a label to the image) and what kind of things you do there (e.g. *watch TV, read books, play video games,* etc). Next, ask students what they can see in the room. Label any furniture that you elicit, adding the phonemes and practicing good pronunciation.

VOCABULARY

A Model the activity for students. Tell a student to ask you Questions 1–4. Reply and give extra information. Ask the student to repeat back what you said, using full sentences. In pairs, students then discuss the questions. For whole-class feedback, ask individual students to report back on what their partners said (e.g. *She lives in an apartment. She …*).

B Direct students to the **Vocabulary Hub**. Give them time to complete Exercises A–B alone before checking answers in pairs.

C Go through the model with students. Then give your own example and encourage students to guess the room you are describing. In pairs, students play the game. Use the **Vocabulary Worksheet** on W24 for extra practice.

PRONUNCIATION

5.1 **A** Go through the task instructions. Elicit the sound of the phonemic symbols listed in the column headings. Point out that the **/b/** sound is made by making a sound with the lips touching. Play the recording and ask students to repeat the words.

5.2 **B** Read through the task instructions. Play the recording for students to write the words in the correct columns. Play the recording again if required.

because, do, ball, give, doctor, game, business, daughter, got

5.3 **C** Play the recording for students to listen and check. Play the recording again, pausing after each section, for them to repeat the words.

LISTENING

A Focus students on the three pictures at the bottom of the page. Tell the class which place you would prefer to stay on vacation and why. Students then tell each other where they would prefer to stay. For whole-class feedback, take a vote on the best place.

B Students read through the ad for the house swap. Elicit the type of home in the picture (*a caravan or camper*). Ask students if they have ever stayed in a caravan or camper on vacation. Explain that a *house swap* is when two people live in each other's homes for a short time.

5.4 **C** Go through the instructions and the three sentences with students. Play the recording for students to choose the best sentence. Check answers as a class.

5.4 **D** Allow time for students to read through the five sentences and recall or predict the answers in pairs. Play the recording for students to listen and check.

E Put students into pairs to discuss the questions. Monitor, helping with new vocabulary as appropriate. Give feedback as a class, encouraging students to explain their answers.

AUDIO SCRIPT

5.4

Listening, Exercise C
S = Sadie L = Luke

S: Hello? Is this Luke Westman?
L: This is Luke speaking.
S: My name's Sadie Parfitt. I'm calling about your beach house.
L: Sure! Where are you from?
Ex D Q1 **S:** I'm from the south of England.
L: OK, that's great.
S: Uh … yes. So, are there any beds in your house?
Ex D Q2 **L:** Beds? Yes, there are. There are two beds. There's a bed in the bedroom and another bed across from the kitchen.
S: Very good. And is there an oven?
L: Yes, there's an oven. It's in the kitchen. There's a fridge, a coffee machine and a dishwasher, too.
S: I see. Is there a swimming pool?
L: Yeah, sure there is. It's huge … It's called the Pacific Ocean!
S: Sorry? There *is* a swimming pool?
Ex D Q3 **L:** No, ma'am. It's a joke. It's the ocean. No, there isn't a swimming pool.
S: Oh! Yes, a joke. Great. So, is there a yard?
L: A yard? No, there isn't a yard – there's a beach. It's a caravan by the beach.
S: A caravan? The advertisement said a 'wonderful home' …
L: It IS a wonderful home!
S: OK … Well, are there any chairs in the dining room?
Ex D Q4 **L:** No, there aren't any chairs. It's a dining area, not a dining room. There's a table, and four people can sit at the table, but there aren't any chairs.
S: I see.
L: So, tell me about your house. How many bedrooms are there?
Ex D Q5 **S:** My house? Oh, I don't have a house.
Ex C **L:** But … this is a house swap. We swap houses. You stay in my house and I stay in your house …
S: No, sorry, I don't have a house. So when can I stay in your caravan?
L: OK, ma'am. Thank you for calling. Goodbye now. Thanks.

5.1 There's no place like home

GRAMMAR

A Ask students to read the three parts of Luke and Sadie's conversation. Highlight that these are from the recording which students have just listened to. Students then complete the table with *is* or *are*. Check answers as a class by writing the complete sentences on the board.

B Direct students to the **Grammar Hub** (see below). Read the examples and go through the rules and Exercises A and B with the class.

C In pairs, students discuss their homes using the vocabulary in the box. Monitor and assist as required. Use the **Grammar Worksheet** on W25 for extra practice.

VOCABULARY

Model the exercise by asking *Where's the coffee machine?* Elicit the answer (*5 It's next to the kitchen sink.*) Point out that *next to* is a preposition of place. We use prepositions of place to say where things are.

Give students time to complete the exercise alone before checking with a partner. Give feedback as a class.

SPEAKING

A Show images of different vacation homes around the world. Ask students to guess which your favorite is. Then ask students to imagine where their perfect vacation home would be.

B Give example answers for each question in the planning stage by talking about your imaginary vacation home from Exercise A. Students then work through the steps individually taking notes on their answers.

C Students prepare an advertisement for a house swap. Refer students to the example ad on page 42, and highlight the type of layout and language used.

D Put students into groups. Ask them to read each other's ad and ask follow-up questions about the house (e.g. *Is it near a city?*). Students then decide who they would like to swap with. For whole-class feedback, ask each group to share their decisions with the rest of the class.

Extra activity
Ask students to write house swap ads for their own homes. Monitor and help with any challenging language. Then, display the ads around the class and ask students to choose one house to stay in.

GRAMMAR HUB

5.1 *there is/are*

	Positive	Negative
Singular	**There's** a dishwasher in the kitchen.	**There isn't** a TV in the living room.
Plural	**There are** four chairs in the dining room.	**There aren't** any cushions on the couch.

	Question	Short answers	
Singular	**Is there** a microwave in the kitchen?	Yes, **there is**.	No, **there isn't**.
Plural	**Are there** any tomatoes in the fridge?	Yes, **there are**.	No, **there aren't**.

- We use *there is / there are* to say that something exists and talk about position.
  There's a coffee machine in the kitchen.
  There are more plates in the cupboard.
- We use *any* in negative sentences and questions with plural nouns and uncountable nouns.
  There aren't any plates in the cupboard.
  Is there any milk in the fridge?

Be careful!
- In a list of nouns, we use *there is* when the first is singular.
  There is a coffee maker, two cups and three plates on the table.
- In a list of nouns, we use *there are* when the first is plural.
  There are two cups, three plates and a coffee maker on the table.

5.1 *there is/are*

A Complete the sentences with *is* or *are*.

1 ___Is___ there a microwave in the kitchen?
2 There ___is / 's___ a mirror in the bathroom.
3 There ___are / 're___ some eggs in the fridge.
4 There ___are / 're___ some people here to see you.
5 ___Are___ there any bedrooms upstairs?
6 ___Is___ there a coffee machine?

B Use the prompts to write questions and short answers.

1 plates / in the cupboard
Are there any plates in the cupboard? (?) *No, there aren't.* (-)
2 dishwasher / in the kitchen
Is there a dishwasher in the kitchen? (?) Yes, there is. (+)
3 swimming pool / in the yard
Is there a swimming pool in the yard? (?) No, there isn't. (-)
4 tomatoes / in the fridge
Are there any tomatoes in the fridge? (?) No, there aren't. (-)
5 TV / in the bedroom
Is there a TV in the bedroom? (?) No, there isn't. (-)
6 socks / in that drawer
Are there any socks in that drawer? (?) Yes, there are. (+)

➤ Go back to page 43.

GRAMMAR

there is/are

A WORK IT OUT Read three parts of Luke and Sadie's conversation. Complete the table using the conversation as an example.

1

Sadie: Uh … yes. So, are there any beds in your house?

Luke: Beds? Yes, there are. There are two beds. There's a bed in the bedroom and another bed across from the kitchen.

2

Sadie: I see. Is there a swimming pool?

Luke: … No, there isn't a swimming pool.

3

Sadie: OK … Well, are there any chairs in the dining room?

Luke: No, there aren't any chairs.

there is/are		
	Singular	Plural
Positive +	There[1] __'s__ a dining room.	There [2] __are__ two bathrooms.
Negative -	There [3] __isn't__ a TV.	There [4] __aren't__ any plants.
Questions ?	[5]__Is there__ a dishwasher?	[6] __Are there__ any chairs?

some* and *any

We use *some* in positive sentences with plural nouns.

We use *any* in questions and negative sentences with plural nouns.

A: ***Are there any armchairs?***

B: ***No, there aren't any armchairs, but there are some chairs.***

B Go to the **Grammar Hub** on **page 130**.

C SPEAK Work in pairs. Ask your partner about their home using some of the words in the box.

armchair bathtub coffee machine cupboard fridge lamp plant shower sink couch table TV dishwasher window

A: Are there any lamps in your living room?
B: No, there aren't. But there is a lamp in the bedroom. Is there a dishwasher in your kitchen?
A: Yes, there is.

VOCABULARY

Prepositions of place

Look at the pictures of Luke's caravan. Match sentences (1–5) to objects (a–e).

d **1** They're **in** the small cupboard **near** the coffee machine.
c **2** They're **behind** the lamp.
b **3** It's **under** the window, **between** the plant and the wall.
e **4** They're **on** the small table, **across from** the couch.
a **5** It's **next to** the kitchen sink.

a coffee machine
b bed
c books
d keys
e TV and DVD player

SPEAKING

A Imagine you have a vacation home. Where is it?

B PLAN Write notes about your vacation home. Think about these questions:

- What type of home is it?
- How many rooms are there?
- Does it have a big or small kitchen?
- Is there a yard or swimming pool?

C PREPARE Write an advertisement for a house swap.

D SPEAK Work in groups. Read each other's ads. Ask questions and decide who you want to swap with.

Describe a home

5.2 My neighborhood

Describe a neighborhood

V places in a town or city **G** *can* **P** weak forms: *can/can't*

VOCABULARY

Places in a town or city

A SPEAK Work in pairs. Which of the sentences (1–3) best describes you?

1 I like quiet areas away from the center of the city.
2 I like busy areas in the city, with lots of people and stores.
3 I don't like the city. I like small towns and the countryside.

B Work in pairs. Look at the pictures. Which of the places in the box can you see?

café movie theater gym hospital library market museum park stores grocery store theater

Suggested answers: park; café/restaurant; museum/stores

C Go to the **Vocabulary Hub** on **page 148**.

D SPEAK Work in pairs. Which of the places in Exercise B or in the Vocabulary are there in your neighborhood? Which would you like to have?

In my neighborhood, there's a grocery store, but there aren't any small stores.

READING

A READ FOR GIST Read the comments in the *Chicago Expats* forum. Who is Grace and what is her problem?

B READ FOR SPECIFIC INFORMATION Read the comments again and answer the questions.

1 Where is Grace from?
She's from the Philippines.
2 Where is Grace's new job?
Her new job is in the University Hospital in Hyde Park, Chicago.
3 Which two places can she go to in Jackson Park?
She can go to the tennis courts and the science museum.
4 What does Grace like doing?
She likes reading and keeping fit.
5 Where is the gym?
The gym is near the hospital.
6 How far is Hyde Park from the center of Chicago?
Hyde Park is 20 minutes from the center of Chicago.

C SPEAK Work in pairs. Do you think Hyde Park is a good place for Grace to live? Why/Why not?

Chicago Expats

amazinggrace26: Hi, people of Chicago! My name's Grace. I'm 26 and I'm a nurse in the Philippines. I have a new job at the University Hospital in Hyde Park, and I'm a little nervous because this is my first time abroad. Can you tell me something about the neighborhood? What is there to do in Hyde Park? I like warm weather, and my hobbies are reading and keeping fit. Ex B Q1 Ex A; Ex B Q2 Ex B Q4

Yesterday, 08:39 Reply | Like

Marco: Hi Grace. I work at the University Hospital, too. There are a lot of things you can do in Hyde Park. There are some good restaurants and cafés, and Jackson Park nearby is really nice. Can you play tennis? There are some very good tennis courts in Jackson Park. There's even a science museum there, too! Ex B Q3

Yesterday, 12:21 Reply | Like

amazinggrace26: Thanks, Marco. It sounds great. I can't play tennis, but I'd like to learn! And the museum sounds wonderful! Is there a gym at the hospital? I like to swim and keep fit.

Yesterday, 15:05 Reply | Like

Marco: There isn't a gym at the hospital, but there is one very close to it. And it's cheap for people who work at the hospital 🙂 Ex B Q5

Yesterday, 17:12 Reply | Like

helen264: Hi, Grace. Hyde Park is nice, but for me, it can be boring. I prefer the city center – it's only 20 minutes away. You can go to the theater, stores and to see a movie. Sorry, but I can't promise you good weather! Chicago is often cold! Ex B Q6

Today, 09:45 Reply | Like

amazinggrace26: Thanks for your advice, @Helen264. I feel really excited about Chicago now!

Glossary

expat (n) someone who lives in a country that is not their own

5.2 My neighborhood

LEAD-IN

Show a picture of a busy city. Ask students to name what they can see and list the type of things found in a city. Build up a list on the board. Ask students to work in small groups to decide on the three most important things for a city to have (e.g. *good public transportation, a movie theater, a lot of stores and cafés*).

VOCABULARY

A In pairs, students read through the sentences and decide which one best describes them. Check answers as a class.

B If you did the Lead-in, ask students to also think about the words you listed on the board. Students then say which places they can see in the photos. If possible, display the photos to the whole class. Check the pronunciation of the words, practicing and repeating as required. Make sure students stress the correct syllable of each word (e.g. *grocery store, hospital, library, market, movie theater, museum, theater*). Point out the correct pronunciation of *gym* /dʒɪm/.

C Direct students to the **Vocabulary Hub**. Give them time to complete the exercise alone before checking answers in pairs. As a class, model and practice the correct word stress for each place.

D Go through the task and example answer with students. Then give your own model answer for students to hear. Ask students to repeat back what you have in your neighborhood, what you don't have and what you would like. In pairs, students discuss the questions. For whole-class feedback, ask students to report back what they discussed. Use the **Vocabulary Worksheet** on W26 for extra practice.

READING

A Focus students on the forum. Explain that a *forum* is a type of website where different people can post ideas and opinions. Ask students if they use a forum, and what kind of ideas they can see there. Give students one minute to read the comments and find out who Grace is, and what her problem is. Check answer as a class.

She's a nurse from the Philippines. She's nervous about moving to a new country.

B Give students time to read Questions 1–6. Then give them up to three minutes to read the comments in more detail and answer the questions. Allow students to compare answers in pairs before checking answers as a class.

C In pairs, students discuss the questions. For whole-class feedback, ask students to share their opinions.

Extra activity

Put students into pairs. Ask them to think of a list of things they like and don't like about the area your school is in. Next, put the pairs into small groups. Tell them they need to agree on three changes they would make to the area. Monitor and help with any new or challenging vocabulary. Give feedback as a class, encouraging students to explain their ideas. Focus on communication of ideas, rather than accuracy here.

METHODOLOGY HUB by Jim Scrivener

Reading around the class

Readers can be read outside class or can be used in 'quiet reading' class time. Some teachers use them in class for reading aloud, with different students reading short sections one after the other. This reading aloud 'around the class' is something many of us recall from our school days. Why might this popular technique not be effective?

Obviously a fluent reader with the ability to inject life and feeling into the reading is a wonderful bonus. Most students, however, do not fit this description, and around-the-class reading tends to be a slow, tedious turn off rather than an arouser of enthusiasm.

Here are some alternatives to try:

- You read;
- You read narrative, but students read character dialogue;
- You (having read the chapter yourself before class) tell the story in your own words, without notes, in the most spell-binding way you can; later, you get students to do the same with other parts;
- Students read to each other in small groups or pairs, stopping, changing, discussing and helping each other whenever they want to;
- Students read silently, then, without discussion, act out, improvising a scene based on what happened;
- Students silently speed read a chapter (say in two minutes) then report back, discussing, comparing, etc before silently reading it more carefully.

TEACHING IDEA by David Seymour and Maria Popova

Vocabulary: City streets

Use this activity to review the vocabulary section on page 44. Say this to your students:

I have a list of 19 things you can see on a city street. In two teams, take turns guessing the things on my list and score a point every time you get one correct.

bicycle, bus stop, car, dog, graffiti, lamppost, library, mailbox, motorcycle, movie theater, pigeon, signpost, taxi, traffic lights, trash, trash can, tree, truck

TEACHING IDEA by David Seymour and Maria Popova

Vocabulary: My neighborhood

Use this activity to practice prepositions of place and the vocabulary from this lesson:

In pairs, find out who has the best access to stores, amenities and transportation links where they live, e.g. *There's a café on the corner of my street. Around the corner there's a post office. It's about a two-minute walk to the nearest bus stop …*

While students are talking, draw a simple map on the board with at least five different places or buildings (e.g. a grocery store, park, etc). Include street names.

In pairs, decide where to put these places.
bakery, bus stop, café, corner store, newsstand, parking lot, pharmacy, restaurant,
Form a group with another pair. Don't show them your map. Ask and answer questions about your maps to find any similarities.

5.2 My neighborhood

GRAMMAR

A Write the sentences on the board. Read through them with the class. Then ask students to complete the rules. Allow time for students to compare answers in pairs. Then check answers as a class.

B Direct students to the **Grammar Hub** (see below). Read the examples and go through the rules with the class.

C Go through the task. Model the example with a stronger student, with the student asking you the question. Point out the use of *but* to extend the response and the use of another question to give the other person a chance to speak. Put students into pairs to ask and answer the questions about what they can do. For whole-class feedback, find out how many students in the class can do each of the things listed. Use the **Grammar Worksheet** on W26 for extra practice.

PRONUNCIATION

5.5 **A** Play the recording, pausing after each sentence. Put students in pairs and give them time to say what they noticed about the pronunciation of *can* and *can't*, before checking answers as a class.

The pronunciation of can changes. Can in questions and positive sentences is usually weak. We say /**kən**/. *Can in short answers is strong. We say* /**kæn**/. *Can't doesn't change. We say* /**kænt**/.

5.5 **B** Play the recording again for students to repeat the sentences. Note that in British English, there is a clear change in vowel sound between *can* and *can't*. However, in both British and US English, there is a clear difference in stress between positive and negative sentences (e.g. *I can swim* vs *I can't swim*). If you have a particularly strong class, you can also highlight that weak forms of *can* usually link with the pronoun before it (i.e. *I_can* sounds like /ˈ**aɪkən**/, *She_can* sounds like /ˈ**ʃiːkən**/, *He_can* sounds like /ˈ**hiːkən**/, *You_can* sounds like /**juːkən**/, *They_can* sounds like /**ðeɪkən**/, *We_can* sounds like /**wiːkən**/).

SPEAKING

A Go through the instructions with students. Allow time for them to read the questions alone, numbering them in order of importance. Students then compare their ideas in pairs. Encourage them to explain their answers. Monitor and encourage students to ask follow-up questions such as *Why?* and *Why not?*.

B Students write notes individually on what people can do in their neighborhoods.

C Put students into pairs with someone they haven't yet worked with in this lesson. Ask them to describe their own area to their partner.

D In pairs, students ask and answer questions to find out more about each other's neighborhoods. For whole-class feedback, ask students to say if they want to move to their partner's neighborhood and to explain why.

GRAMMAR HUB

5.2 *can*

	Positive	Negative
I/you/he/she/it/we/they	She **can swim**.	She **can't swim**.

- We use *can* to talk about ability and what is possible.
- In the negative, we can also say *cannot*.

She can't swim. OR She cannot swim.

	Question	Short answers	
I/you/he/she/it/we/they	**Can we go** to the movie theater?	Yes, you **can**.	No, you **can't**.

Be careful!

He can sing. NOT ~~He cans sing.~~ NOT ~~He can to sing.~~

5.2 *can*

A Complete the sentences with *can* or *can't*.

1. I'm sorry. I ___can't___ come on Saturday, I have to work.
2. ___Can___ you open the window, please? It's very hot in here.
3. She's not here I'm afraid. ___Can___ I take a message?
4. She ___can't___ come out tonight, because she doesn't have any money.
5. I ___can___ speak Japanese, but not write it.
6. We ___can't___ buy it now. The store is closed.

B Use the prompts to write sentences with *can*.

1. I / play / the guitar
   I can play the guitar.
2. they / leave / work / whenever they want
   They can leave work whenever they want.
3. she / speak / Arabic / ?
   Can she speak Arabic?
4. where / I / buy / laundry detergent / ?
   Where can I buy laundry detergent?
5. I / stay / at your house / tonight / ?
   Can I stay at yours tonight?

➤ Go back to page 45.

GRAMMAR

can

A WORK IT OUT Read the sentences from the *Chicago Expats* forum. Then choose the correct words to complete the rules.

Can you play tennis? ... it can be boring.

You can go to the theater ... I can't play tennis ...

can

1. We use *can* to talk about ***ability and possibility*** / ***the past***.
2. In positive and negative sentences, *can* comes ***before*** / ***after*** the main verb.
3. We use the ***infinitive*** / ***base form*** after *can*.
4. We ***use*** / ***don't use*** questions that start with *Do ...?*
5. We ***add*** / ***don't add*** *-s* in the third person.

B Go to the **Grammar Hub** on **page 130**.

C SPEAK Work in pairs. Ask each other questions starting with *Can you ...?* Use the ideas below to help you.

- arrive at work when you want
- go to the movie theater in your neighborhood
- play a musical instrument
- play tennis
- speak another language
- swim
- work from home

A: *Can you arrive at work when you want?*

B: *I don't work, but I can usually arrive at the university when I want. Can you play soccer?*

PRONUNCIATION

Weak forms: *can/can't*

A Listen and read. What do you notice about the pronunciation of *can* and *can't*? 5.5

1. Can you speak another language?
   Can in questions and positive sentences is usually weak.We say /kən/.
2. Yes, I can. I can speak Italian fluently.
   The pronunciation of *can* changes.
3. No, I can't. I'm not very good at languages.
   Can't in short answers is strong. We say /kænt/.
4. I can speak a little French, but I can't speak it very well.
   Can't doesn't change. We still say /kænt/.

B Listen again and repeat the sentences. Copy the pronunciation of *can* and *can't*. 5.5

SPEAKING

A PREPARE Imagine you want to move to a new neighborhood. Work with a partner to rank questions (a–g) from 1 (very important) to 8 (not important).

a. What are the people like? ___
b. Are there any good schools? ___
c. What's the weather like? ___
d. How far is it from the airport? ___
e. What's in the city center? ___
f. Are there any good stores? ___
g. Is there a train station? ___

A: *It's important for me to be close to my family and friends.*

B: *Yes, that's a good point. And public transportation is important to me.*

B ORGANIZE What can you do in your neighborhood? Write notes.

C SPEAK Work in pairs. Imagine your partner is interested in moving to your neighborhood. Describe it to them, explaining what is good and bad about the area.

There are a lot of stores, but there aren't any parks.

D SPEAK Ask questions about your partner's neighborhood. Decide if you want to move there.

Describe a neighborhood

5.3 Amazing buildings

Describe an interesting building

G – imperatives V – adjectives to describe the appearance of things P – word stress: adjectives
S – reading for specific information

READING

A Look at the famous buildings (1–5) in *The world's most interesting buildings*. What do you know about them? Do you know where they are?

B READ FOR GIST Read *The world's most interesting buildings*. Match pictures (1–5) with paragraphs (a–d). There is one picture you do not need.

C Read the article again. In which building(s) can you do these things? Use the information in the box to help you.

Reading for specific information

- Read the text quickly and look for keywords that help you find the information you're looking for.
- For example, if you want to know about prices or times, look for numbers. Then read around them to find the information.

1 have lunch Dancing House
2 see art Niteroi Contemporary Art Museum
3 swim Casa do Penedo or 'Stone House'
4 work Dancing House
5 live Piet Blom's Cube Houses

D SPEAK Work in pairs. Which building is your favorite? Which building don't you like? Why?

1

The world's *most interesting buildings*

What happens when you mix buildings and art? Read on and find out! This week's topic in *Architecture Online* is the world's most **interesting** and original buildings. These are our favorite buildings. Tell us which ones you like.

a This **strange** building isn't falling down! It's the Dancing House, in Prague, Czech Republic. It's **funny**! There are offices in the building, and there's a restaurant on the top floor. Look at how many windows there are! Some people don't like the Dancing House because it's next to a lot of old buildings in a historic part of the city on a busy road. They think it's **terrible**. 3
(Ex C Q4, Ex C Q1)

b These yellow and white buildings that look like trees are Piet Blom's Cube Houses in Rotterdam, the Netherlands. They are **tall** and **beautiful**. The living rooms are downstairs and the bedrooms are on the top floor. Some houses have a yard on the roof. 4
(Ex C Q5)

c This **amazing** house looks very **old**, but it isn't. In fact, it's only 40 years old. It's *Casa do Penedo*, or 'Stone House' in Portugal. The **small** house sits between four **big** rocks. There's a swimming pool in one of the rocks. You can visit the house because it's a local history museum. 2
(Ex C Q3)

d This is the Niterói Contemporary Art Museum in Rio de Janeiro, Brazil. It's an art gallery and a museum. The building is next to a beach and has views of Rio and the Sugarloaf Mountain. The museum is very popular with tourists. We think this **modern** building is **cool**. 5
(Ex C Q2)

2

3

5.3 Amazing buildings

LEAD-IN

Show images of interesting buildings in your local area, city or country. Ask students questions about each one (e.g. *Where is it? Do you know it? Do you like it? Why? / Why not?*). Hold a class vote on the students' favorite building.

READING

A If possible, display the images of the buildings to the whole class. Ask students what they can see in each picture. Find out what they know about the buildings and where they are. Do not confirm answers at this point.

B Go through the task with students. Give students up to two minutes to look through *The world's most interesting buildings* and match pictures with the paragraphs. Highlight that there are five pictures, but only four paragraphs, so there is one extra picture. Check answers as a class.

1 no matching paragraph

C Write *have lunch* on the board. Put students into pairs to quickly look at the pictures and predict which buildings they can have lunch in. Do not confirm any answers at this point. Then go through the box on reading for specific information. Ask students what words or phrases to look for, connected with lunch. Elicit ideas such as *food, restaurants*, etc.

Tell students that they need to scan the article, looking for words related to the idea of having lunch. This means that they don't need to read every word. Instead, they should be looking quickly through the article, until they find the specific information they need.

Give students one minute to find the paragraph which has information about having lunch. Check answer as a class. Explain that the information is in *Paragraph a*, and the answer is *the Dancing House*. Elicit what information helped them to decide (*... there's a restaurant on the top floor*).

Give students up to three minutes to complete the rest of the activity. Students compare answers in pairs. Check answers as a class.

D Put students into pairs to discuss the questions. For whole-class feedback, find out which building is students' favorite.

> **Extra activity**
> Put students into groups and give them time to research other interesting buildings around the world. Ask them to write notes about what the building is called, what it's used for and why they think it's interesting. Next, ask groups to report back to the class, adding any new or interesting vocabulary to the board.

TEACHING IDEA by David Seymour and Maria Popova

Vocabulary: People and places

Use this activity to review the vocabulary section on page 47:

Work in two groups, A and B. I'm going to say some nouns. Group A, yell out a positive adjective for each one. Group B, yell out a negative one, e.g. *rock star*. A – *famous*. B – *rude*.

house, baby, shirt, river, dog, tree, hair, shopping mall, car, shoe, girl, flower, park, street, town, trash

In pairs, think of a place you both know. Student A, write a positive description of the place. Student B, write a negative one. Compare your descriptions.

METHODOLOGY HUB by Jim Scrivener

Approaches to reading

Reading to oneself (as opposed to reading aloud) is, like listening, a 'receptive' skill, and similar teaching procedures can be used to help learners.

The most obvious differences are to do with the fact that people read at different speeds and in different ways. Whereas a recording takes a definite length of time to play through, in a reading activity, individuals can control the speed they work at and what they're looking at.

Difficulties when reading a foreign language

What are your own main problems when trying to read a text in a language you don't know very well?

Maybe:

I don't know enough vocabulary.

I need the dictionary all the time.

It's very slow – it takes a long time just to get through a few sentences.

I usually get to the stage where I understand all the individual words, but the whole thing eludes me completely.

Because it's slow, the pleasure or interest in the subject matter is soon lost.

Many learners approach reading texts expecting to read them thoroughly and to stop only when they have understood every word. Clearly, there is value in this way of improving their vocabulary and their understanding of grammar, but, as with listening, this kind of approach does not necessarily make them into better readers, because this plodding, word-by-word approach is not the way that we most often do our reading in real life. In order to make students better readers, we need first of all to raise their awareness that it's not always essential to understand every word and that practicing some different reading techniques in English may be very useful to them. And if their basic strategy is to read solely and ponderously, then a good first strategy could be to help them learn to read fast; not worrying about understanding every word; not, perhaps, even understanding most words; but still achieving a specific and useful goal.

5.3 Amazing buildings

GRAMMAR

A Give students instructions using imperatives (e.g. *stand up, sit down, open your books, look over there,* etc). Ask students to read the examples in Exercise A and complete the first rule together. Then put students into pairs and give them time to complete the rules before checking together as a class.

B Give students one minute to scan the article and find another example of the imperative. Check answer as a whole class.

C Direct students to the **Grammar Hub** on page 130 (see below). Read the examples and go through the rules with the class. If you didn't do so earlier, point out that we don't use a subject with imperatives (i.e. we don't use *you*).

D Check the meaning of the verbs in the box. Students then work in pairs to make imperative sentences. The person listening should respond by completing the requested action. Have whole-class feedback with students instructing you with their imperative sentences and you responding by completing the actions. Use the **Grammar Worksheet** on W28 for extra practice.

VOCABULARY

A Read through the task with students and do the first example together (*interesting*). Make sure students understand the meaning of positive and negative by writing plus (+) and minus (–) symbols on the board. Explain that *neutral* means that a word has no positive or negative feeling.

Students work alone to complete the task and then compare their ideas with a partner. Check answers as a class by writing the words on the board in the form of a table.

B Students match the adjectives with their opposites. Again, write the answers on the board in the table you have drawn.

C Model the example answer and ask students to identify the adjectives (*new, big, modern*). Ask if the description is positive, negative or neutral (*positive*).

If you did the Lead-in at the start of the lesson, show one of the buildings again and describe it using some of the adjectives from Exercises A and B. Again, ask students what adjectives you used and if the description was positive, negative or neutral.

In pairs, students describe buildings they know. Monitor, assist and encourage as appropriate. Use the **Vocabulary Worksheet** on W29 for extra practice.

PRONUNCIATION

5.6 **A** Play the recording. Students repeat the words. Focus students on the stress patterns in the table, and explain that stressed syllables tend to be a little longer and louder than unstressed syllables.

5.7 **B** In pairs, students complete the table. Encourage them to say the words out loud so that they can identify the number of syllables and the stress pattern. Play the recording for students to check their answers. Play it again if necessary.

5.7 **C** Play the recording again. Students listen and repeat the words, focusing on producing the correct word stress.

SPEAKING HUB

A Direct students to the **Communication Hub** for further practice of describing buildings.

B In pairs, students discuss the questions. Monitor and encourage students to ask follow-up questions to find out more.

C For whole-class feedback on the discussion, hold a short class debate, and then a vote, on the most interesting building.

GRAMMAR HUB

5.3 Imperatives

- We use imperatives to tell someone to do something.

  Call me later.
  Look at this website.
  Give me your phone.
  Open your books to page 23.
- We can use *please* to make imperatives more polite.

  Please ask at the front desk.
- We use *don't* to tell someone not to do something.

  Don't walk in the park at night.

Be careful!

Give me your phone. NOT ~~*To give me your phone.*~~

5.3 Imperatives

A Complete the sentences with the verbs in the box.

close drink drive play talk read sit

1 Don't ___play___ soccer on the grass.
2 ___Close___ the door behind you.
3 ___Drive___ on the right.
4 Don't ___talk___ in the library.
5 Don't ___drink___ the water.
6 ___Read___ this – it's really interesting!
7 Please ___sit___ down!

B Match the verbs (1–6) with the phrases (a–f) to make imperative sentences.

1 Go — a me more about amazing buildings.
2 Tell — b the window. It's hot.
3 Learn — c the rooftop gardens.
4 Look at — d your shoes off, please.
5 Open — e some Portuguese words before you go.
6 Take — f away.

➤ Go back to page 47.

GRAMMAR

Imperatives

A **WORK IT OUT** Look at the sentences from *The world's most interesting buildings*. Then choose the correct words to complete the rules.

Read on and **find** out!

Tell us which ones you like.

Imperatives

1. We use imperatives when we want to *<u>tell someone to do something</u> / talk about the future*.
2. We use the *infinitive / <u>base form</u>* to make imperatives.
3. We *<u>can</u> / can't* use *please* with imperatives.

B Find and <u>underline</u> one more imperative in *The world's most interesting buildings*.

Look at how many windows there are! (Paragraph a)

C Go to the **Grammar Hub** on **page 130**

D **SPEAK** Work in pairs. Use the verbs in the box to make imperative sentences. Remember to say *please*.

give lend sit down spell stand up tell write

Stand up, please.

VOCABULARY

Adjectives to describe the appearance of things

A Look at the adjectives in **bold** in *The world's most interesting buildings*. Which are positive? Which are negative? Which are neutral?

Positive: amazing, beautiful, cool, interesting, funny

Negative: strange, terrible

Neutral: tall, big, small, modern, old

B Match adjectives (1–5) with their opposites (a–e).

1. beautiful — e ugly
2. interesting — a boring
3. amazing — d terrible
4. big — c small
5. modern — b old

1 beautiful	a boring
2 interesting	b old
3 amazing	c small
4 big	d terrible
5 modern	e ugly

C **SPEAK** Work in pairs. Describe an interesting building in your neighborhood using adjectives from Exercise B.

There's a new shopping center in the middle of town. It's a big, modern building with lots of windows.

PRONUNCIATION

Word stress: adjectives

5.6 **A** Listen and repeat. Copy the word stress.

●•	●••
boring	*beautiful*
building	gallery
funny	interesting
modern	popular
ugly	terrible

5.7 **B** Complete the table in Exercise A with the words in the box. Then listen and check.

~~beautiful~~ ~~boring~~ building funny gallery interesting modern popular terrible ugly

5.7 **C** Listen again and repeat the words. Copy the word stress.

SPEAKING HUB

A **SPEAK** Work in pairs. Go to the **Communication Hub** on **page 154**.

B **DISCUSS** Work in groups. Discuss the questions.

1. Which of the buildings in the Communication Hub is your favorite? Why?
2. What's your favorite building in your country? Why do you like it?
3. Do you think it's important for buildings to look interesting? Why/Why not?

C Take a class vote on the most interesting building.

Describe an interesting building

Café Hub

5.4 Moving in

F– ask for and give directions   P– stress and intonation

COMPREHENSION

A Watch the video without sound. Check (✓) the items you see.

☑ café	☐ library
☑ chair	☑ park
☐ cinema	☑ plant
☑ fridge	☑ sofa
☐ gym	☑ supermarket
☑ house	☑ table
☑ lamp	☐ theater

B SPEAK Work in pairs. Ask questions to check your answers to Exercise A.

A: Is there a gym?
B: No, there isn't. Is there a café?
A: I'm not sure …

C Watch the video with sound and choose the correct option to complete the sentences.

1. Gaby *gets* / *doesn't get* cash.
2. Gaby *loses* / *doesn't lose* her phone.
3. Gaby *has to* / *doesn't have to* ask for directions twice.
4. Gaby *can* / *can't* find her door key.
5. Gaby *spends* / *doesn't spend* the evening with Neena.

FUNCTIONAL LANGUAGE

Asking for and giving directions

A Label pictures (1–4) with the directions in the box.

Go straight ahead   Turn right   Turn right at the café   Turn left

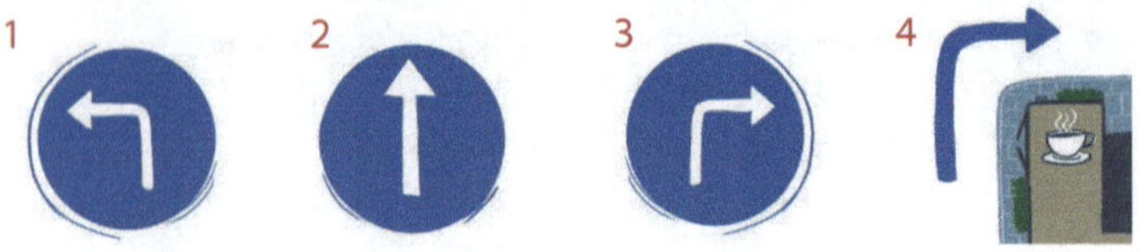

1 Turn left
2 Go straight ahead
3 Turn right
4 Turn right at the café

B Match the directions in the box to images (1–4).

Asking for directions	Excuse me, is there a cash machine near here? Excuse me, can you tell me the way to Park Road?
Giving directions	2 Go straight ahead to the end of the road. 4 Go past the stores. 1 Take the third turn on the left. 3 The cash machine is next to the supermarket.

C SPEAK Work in pairs. Take turns giving directions from your school to:

- a cash machine
- a train station
- a coffee shop

Glossary
cinema **(n) (British)** = movie theater **(n) (American)**
sofa **(n) (British)** = couch **(n) (American)**
door key **(n) (British)** = house key **(n) (American)**

MILLY

SAM

NEENA

ZAC

GABY

PRONUNCIATION

Stress and intonation

A ▶ 00:00–00:47 Watch the first part of the video again. Listen to the conversation between Gaby and the passer-by. Notice the stress and intonation.

Gaby: Excuse me, is there a cash machine near here?

Passer-by: Sure. Go straight on to the end of the road. Turn right at the café. And the cash machine is next to the supermarket.

B ▶ 00:00–00:47 Watch again and repeat the conversation. Copy the stress and intonation.

C **SPEAK** Work in pairs. Practice the conversation in Exercise A. Remember to use the correct stress and intonation.

SPEAKING

DISCUSS Work in pairs. Ask for and give directions using the map. Use some of the Functional language and the prepositions in the box to help you.

behind | between | near | next to | on

A: Excuse me. Is there a school near here?

B: Sure, take the second turn on the left.

Ask for and give directions

➤ Turn to page 164 to learn how to write a description of a place.

5.4 Moving in

LEAD-IN

Focus students on the photo. Elicit the character's name (*Gaby*) and ask students to guess what's happening in the photo. Encourage students to explain their reasoning, before confirming/explaining that Gaby is moving into a new apartment. Put students into groups. Ask them to discuss the following questions: *1 Do you like moving? Why/Why not? 2 Who usually helps you when you move? 3 Do you have a lot of stuff? Would it be easy for you to move?*

COMPREHENSION

A ▶ Focus students on the list of words. Check that students understand the meaning of *fridge* and *plant* by drawing these two objects on the board. Play the video with no sound. Students apply a check mark to the items they can see.

B Model the example for students. Highlight that they should use questions like this to check their answers in pairs. Check answers as a class by asking and answering the questions around the room.

C ▶ Give time for students to read through the sentences and predict or recall the answers. Play the video with sound for students to complete the sentences. Check answers as a class.

FUNCTIONAL LANGUAGE

A Go through the task with students. Focus students on the pictures and the words in the box. Students then work alone to complete the exercise. Allow time for students to compare answers in pairs before checking as a class. Explain that we usually use imperatives to give directions (*Go …* , *Turn …* , etc).

B Focus students on the first illustration. Ask whether this is a right or left turn. Write the imperative *Turn left* on the board. Elicit that this isn't a good instruction because there are three roads on the left. Ask students to look at the instructions in the *Giving directions* box and elicit the direction that matches the first picture (*Take the third turn on the left.*). Give students time to match the remaining pictures to directions, before going through the answers together as a class.

C Model the exercise for students by saying where you can find the nearest grocery store or café and how to get there. As you give the directions, draw simple maps on the board to match the instructions. Students then work in pairs to give each other directions.

PRONUNCIATION

A ▶ 00:00-00:47 Ask students to focus on the stress and intonation of the people in the video. Play the first part of the video again.

B ▶ 00:00-00:47 Play the video again. Students read the conversation as they watch. You could ask them to draw arrows on the conversation, to mark where the speakers' intonation goes up or down. Then, put them into pairs to practice saying the conversation, copying the underlined stressed words and intonation.

C In pairs, students practice saying the conversation. Monitor and assist as required, encouraging the students to look up and say the conversation naturally, rather than reading from the page.

SPEAKING

A Elicit the meaning of the prepositions in the box, reminding students that they saw the words earlier in the unit. You can do this by asking where things are in the classroom.

Focus students on the map. Model the exercise with a student, asking for and giving directions to places on the map. Stress key words, and use appropriate intonation. Then ask students to recall the content of the conversation when you finish (e.g. the places and the imperatives used).

Put students into pairs to ask for and give directions using the map. Monitor and encourage, making a note of good language use, as well as phrases to be reformulated. Use this in whole-class feedback at the end of the activity.

> **Extra activity**
> Ask students to make a list of five places in the local area (e.g. the train station, a popular restaurant, a bookstore, etc). Next, ask students to stand up and walk around the class, asking each other for directions to the places on their list. You can walk around too, helping with directions if students get stuck.

▶ VIDEO SCRIPT

G = Gaby PB = Passerby P = Pedestrian N = Neena

G: No. I don't need to get a taxi … Yes! I can look at the map on my phone … Sure, I can get some cash. See you later. Bye, Zac. Excuse me, is there a cash machine near here?
PB: Sure. Go straight on to the end of the road. Turn right at the cafe. And the cash machine is next to the supermarket.
G: Thank you.
I can't do this. I can do this! Argh! Where's my phone? Excuse me, can you tell me the way to Park Road?
P: Park Road … Park Road?
G: Yes. Do you know it?
P: Oh yes. Lovely road. Lovely road. Beautiful trees. Beautiful trees …
G: … Uh …
P: Ah, yes! You go straight on. Straight on. Go past the shops, past the shops. Then, take the third turning on the left. That's the third turning on the left.
G: OK. So straight on, past the shops and take the third turning on the left?
P: That's right. You are right! Because … Park road is next to the park. Hahaha. You see? Hahahaha.
G: Thank you. Now, where's my key? Oh! Hi, Neena.
N: Hi, Gaby. Where are you?
G: Outside. I can't find my key.
N: Your key's in the kitchen. I'll open the door.
G: Thanks.
N: I like that! It's really interesting.
G: Thanks. I think it's beautiful. It's from Barcelona.
N: Oh. I'd love to visit Barcelona.
G: Why don't you go? Barcelona is amazing! Anyway, I have to go to the shop for Zac. Do you want anything?
N: No, thanks.
G: Thanks. I'll be back soon.

5 Writing

Write a description of a place

W using adjectives

A Work in pairs. Look at the picture in the review. Answer the questions.

1 What can you see? Describe the building.
2 What do you think this building is?
3 Where do you think it is?

B Read the online review. Check your answers to questions 2 and 3 in Exercise A.

It's the Borghese Gallery in Rome.

C Read the review again. Choose the correct answers a, b or c.

1 What is the Villa Borghese?
 a a museum
 b a park
 c a café
2 What can you see in the museum?
 a paintings and furniture
 b cars and transportation
 c furniture and clothes
3 Why does the writer like the café?
 a because it's warm inside
 b because it's popular
 c because the food is good

D Read again. Underline the adjectives that the writer uses to describe these things:

- the park — famous, big, beautiful, great
- the paintings — amazing
- the museum building — interesting, old, white
- the rooms in the museum — beautiful
- the sandwiches — delicious

Using adjectives

When you write, use a variety of adjectives to make your writing more interesting.

*Villa Borghese is a **famous** park in Rome. It's very **big** and it's **beautiful**.*

Ex C Q1 Villa Borghese is a famous park in Rome. It's very big and it's beautiful. It's a great place to spend a couple of hours.

Ex C Q2 There's a museum in the park, the Borghese Gallery. There are some amazing paintings in the museum. The building is very interesting, too. It's an old, white house with a lot of windows. Inside the house, the

Ex C Q2 rooms are beautiful. They have some old furniture in them.

Ex C Q3 There's a café inside the gallery, but I like the café in the park. It's very popular. You can sit outside and have lunch under the trees. The sandwiches are delicious!

Share Like Comment

E Read about the Eiffel Tower. Change the adjectives *nice* and *good* for more interesting adjectives.

The Eiffel Tower is a nice tower in Paris, France. It's very popular with tourists. It's a nice place to spend an hour. It's tall and it's a very nice shape. There aren't any windows, and there aren't any walls. It's gray. I think it's really nice. You can go to the top of the Eiffel Tower. The views of the city are good. There's a restaurant on the first floor. The food is good.

Refer students to this description as a model for the writing task.

WRITING

A PREPARE Choose a building, place or landmark in your city (or in a city that you know well). Think about these questions:

1 What is the building?
2 Where is it?
3 What does it look like?
4 What is your opinion of it?
5 What can you see and do there?
6 Can you eat or drink anything there?

Remind students to think about the person who is reading the description. What do they want the reader to think or feel?

B PLAN Think about your answers in Exercise A. What adjectives can you use to describe topics 1–6 in Exercise A?

C WRITE Write your description. Use a variety of adjectives to make your writing more interesting.

Remind students that they can also use adjectives to make a review sound positive or negative.

164 WRITING

WRITING

In this writing lesson, students will learn how to write a description of a place, paying attention to using adjectives to make their writing more interesting.

A If possible, display the picture to the whole class. In pairs, students discuss the questions. Check ideas as a class but don't confirm answers at this point.

B Give students one or two minutes to check their answers in the online review.

C Go through Questions 1–3 with the class. Then give students three minutes to look at the review more carefully and choose the correct option.

D Read through the box on using adjectives. Ask students to identify the adjectives in the example sentence in the box (*famous, big, beautiful*). Ask whether these adjectives sound positive or negative (*positive*). Point out that without adjectives, the sentence would not sound very interesting (*Villa Borghese is a park in Rome.*).

Students then read the online review again and underline the adjectives used to describe the five different things. Students compare answers in pairs before checking as a class.

E Focus students on the description of the Eiffel Tower. Point out that it uses the positive adjectives *nice* and *good* too many times, and the description doesn't sound interesting.

In pairs, students try to change *nice* and *good* for more interesting adjectives. Students share ideas as a class.

WRITING

A Ask students to think of a building, place or landmark that they would like to write about. Tell them to write notes, and decide whether they have a positive or a negative opinion about the place.

B Students review their notes and add adjectives they can use to describe the place in an interesting way.

C Students write the description. Monitor and assist as required, encouraging students to include interesting adjectives which show their opinion.

Unit 5 Review

GRAMMAR

A Match the beginnings of sentences (1–5) with the ends of sentences (a–e).

1 There's — a a table in the kitchen?
2 There aren't — b some cupboards in the bathroom.
3 Are there — c a shower in the bathroom.
4 Is there — d any lamps in the sitting room?
5 There are — e any chairs in the dining room.

(Answers: 1–c, 2–e, 3–d, 4–a, 5–b)

B Complete the conversation with the correct form of *can*.

Simon: 1 ___Can___ you ride a motorcycle?

Patrick: No, I 2 ___can't___, but I 3 ___can___ drive a car. Do you want a ride?

Simon: 4 ___Can___ we walk to the park from here?

Patrick: Well, we 5 ___can___, but it takes a long time.

C Choose the correct words to complete the sentences.

1 ***Tell*** / *To tell* me more about the Colosseum in Rome.
2 ***Look*** / *Looking* at the tourists.
3 ***Please give*** / *Give please* me more information.
4 ***Ask*** / *To Ask* at the front desk for more information.
5 ***Write*** / *Wrote* about your favorite building.

VOCABULARY

A Complete the furniture and rooms with *a, e, i, o* or *u*.

1 We have a sh_o_w_e_r, but we don't have a b_a_tht_u_b in our b_a_thr_o_ _o_m.
2 We have a modern _o_v_e_n and fr_i_dg_e_ in our k_i_tch_e_n.
3 There's a TV, a big c_u_pb_o_ _a_rd, a c_o_ _u_ch and two _a_rmch_a_ _i_rs in our sitting room.
4 There's a l_a_mp on the t_a_bl_e_ by my bed in my b_e_dr_o_ _o_m.

B Look at the picture. Choose the correct prepositions to complete the sentences.

1 The coffee machine is ***between*** / *next to* the oven and the sink.
2 The house keys are hanging ***on*** / *in* the wall.
3 The dishwasher is ***next to*** / *behind* the oven.
4 The note is ***above*** / *under* the window.

C Complete the sentences with the places in the box.

airport	gym	~~hospital~~	library	market

1 You see a doctor at the ___hospital___.
2 You take a plane at the ___airport___.
3 You borrow a book from the ___library___.
4 You buy fresh food at a ___market___.
5 You exercise at the ___gym___.

D Complete the text with the correct adjectives.

My favorite building is Habitat 67, in Montréal, Quebec. It's 1 a_m_a_z_i_n_g – it's 2 b_i_g and looks very 3 m_o_d_e_r_n, even though it's 50 years old. It isn't one building, it's about 150 4 s_m_a_l_l houses on top of each other. Some people think it looks 5 s_t_r_a_n_g_e, but I think it's 6 b_e_a_u_t_i_f_u_l. You can see the sky through it, which is 7 c_o_o_l.

FUNCTIONAL LANGUAGE

A Complete the conversation with the words in the box.

down	~~excuse~~	here	how	on	tell	turn (x2)

A: 1 ___Excuse___ me.
B: Yes?
A: Can you 2 ___tell___ me the way to New Street?
B: Sorry?
A: Is New Street near 3 ___here___?
B: Excuse me?
A: 4 ___How___ do I get to New Street?
B: Oh, yes. Go 5 ___down___ College Road. 6 ___Turn___ right onto High Street and Moon Street is 7 ___on___ your right.
A: Moon Street? I want New Street.
B: New Street? No, no. New Street is near here. Take the second 8 ___turn___ on the right.
A: Oh, thanks.

B SPEAK Work in pairs. Give each other directions from your school to:

- a bookstore
- a train station
- a museum

An actor on stage in the Théâtre du Châtelet in Paris, France.

OBJECTIVES

- talk about likes and dislikes
- talk about entertainment in the present and the past
- talk about your life
- ask for and give opinions
- review an event

Work with a partner. Discuss the questions.

1. What's your favorite kind of music?
2. Look at the picture. What's he doing?
3. How often do you go to the movie theater?

THAT'S ENTERTAINMENT 51

Entertainment (n) TV shows, movies, concerts, etc used to entertain people Synonyms: enjoyment (n), recreation (n)

Ask students to label the photo if you need time to set up the class.

An actor on stage in the Theatre du Chatelet in Paris, France.

This quote is from Shakespeare's play *Twelfth Night*. The character who says it is Orsino, and he is frustrated in love. He wonders if by listening to music, he will be able to forget the love problems he is having.

William Shakespeare (1564–1616) was an English playwright and poet. He is said by many people to be the greatest writer of all time. He wrote around 40 plays and over 150 poems. His works have been translated into every major language, and he is the best-selling author ever.

OBJECTIVES

Read the unit objectives to the class.

UNIT OPENER QUESTIONS

Ask students to look at the picture on the page and describe what they see. Point out that this is a scene from a play in the theater. Ask the students to describe the last time they were at the theater or the movies and what they saw. Ask what types of entertainment the students like and dislike. This is a good opportunity to test the level of knowledge of the target language for the unit that students already have.

Ask students to read the questions at the bottom of the page. Check that students understand the questions. You could give your own answers as a model for students.

Put them into pairs to discuss the three questions. Monitor and help with grammar and vocabulary as required. Encourage students to listen to each other and ask follow-up questions to find out more. For whole-class feedback, ask two or three students to share their opinions with the rest of the class.

WORKSHEETS

Lesson 6.1 Let's go out

Entertainment (W30)

Likes and dislikes (W31)

Lesson 6.2 It was fun

was/were (W31)

Past time expressions (W32)

Lesson 6.3 Life stories

Simple past regular and irregular verbs (W32)

Life events (W33)

6.1 Let's go out

Talk about likes and dislikes

V entertainment   P word stress: noun patterns   G likes and dislikes

VOCABULARY
Entertainment

A Match pictures (1–6) with the places and events (a–f).

a	a comedy show	5	**d**	a concert	1
b	an exhibit	4	**e**	a festival	6
c	a movie theater	2	**f**	a theater	3

B **SPEAK** Work with a partner. How often do you go to the places and events in Exercise A?

PRONUNCIATION
Word stress: noun patterns

6.1 **A** Listen and repeat the words. Copy the word stress.

movie comedy concert exhibit festival internet magazine

6.2 **B** Complete the table with the words from Exercise A. Then listen, check and repeat.

Oo	Ooo	ooO	oOo
concert movie	comedy festival internet	magazine	exhibit

READING

A Read the *City Guide*. Check (✓) the information you can get from it.

- [x] the date of an event
- [ ] how much an event costs
- [x] what time the events start/finish
- [ ] how often the event happens
- [ ] how to get to an event
- [x] where an event is
- [x] the writer's opinion of an event
- [ ] things to do in October

City Guide

What's going on?

Today | **This week** | This weekend

Things to do this week (August 10 – 16)
No plans this week? Well, not anymore. We're here to help! From movies to festivals, here's your guide to the next seven days. Let's go out!

Star Wars ★★★★★
Watch the first three *Star Wars* movies, a different movie each evening over three nights. Saturday is a special family day when you can wear costumes.
Langley Outdoor Movie Theater, 6 pm, from Thursday, August 13 Ex B Q3

Cow ★★★
Californian rock band, Cow, often play in strange locations. This Friday, their concert is in an old Ex B Q4 swimming pool. Enjoy some old favorites and songs from their new album.
The Old Baths, 9 pm, Friday, August 14

Comedy Underground ★★★★
For one night, comedians Lily O'Connor and Josh Peet take their new show underground. That's right – two hours of free comedy as you travel on the subway!
City Line, 8 pm – 10 pm, Thursday, August 13

Kwame Abraham ★★★★★
This exhibit of Kwame Abraham's photographs shows people from his country, Ghana, during the 1960s. His images tell amazing stories.
The Hayforth Gallery, 10 am – 9:30 pm, Wednesday, August 12 – Sunday, September 6 Ex B Q1

Glossary

comedian (n) someone who tells jokes and stories to make people laugh
free (adj) something that doesn't cost anything
costume (n) clothes that performers wear in a play, movie, etc
location (n) where something is or where something happens
silent (adj) not making any noise

6.1 Let's go out

LEAD-IN

Tell students about a place you went to recently for entertainment (e.g. *the movie theater*, *a theater*, etc).

Write the name of the place on the board and add any key vocabulary. Tell students what you liked and didn't like about the experience. Put students into pairs and ask them to do the same. Encourage them to ask follow-up questions to extend their answers. Make this a focus on communication of ideas rather than accuracy at this point, and observe the level of knowledge of the target language of the unit.

VOCABULARY

A Make sure students know what an *event* is (a planned activity that several people take part in). In pairs, students match the photos with the places and events. For whole-class feedback, highlight that all the words are stressed on the first syllable (*comedy*, *concert*, etc) except *exhibit*.

B With books closed, ask students to recall the names of the places and events, and write them on the board. Ask them to spell the words for you as you write them up. Then talk through each one, giving information about how regularly you do or go to these things. Encourage students to ask you follow-up questions to find out more information. Then, put students into pairs and ask them to open their books. Tell them to discuss each place or event.

Use the **Vocabulary Worksheet** on W30 for extra practice.

PRONUNCIATION

6.1 **A** Play the recording and ask students to repeat the words. If they have difficulty hearing the correct stress, model the incorrect stress. This usually helps to highlight the correct version (e.g. compare *COmedy* with *coMEdy*).

6.2 **B** Give students time to complete the table alone. If they find the activity difficult, put them into pairs and encourage them to say the words aloud. Next, play the recording for students to listen and check. Practice correct word stress for anything students are struggling with.

READING

A Ask students to look at the *City Guide*. Elicit what it is and have students predict the type of information it contains. Ask students if they use websites like this to find out information.

Read through the types of information and double check that students understand everything. Then, allow them up to three minutes to skim the City Guide and apply a check mark to the information it includes. Give feedback as a class, encouraging students to explain where in the text they found the answers.

GRAMMAR HUB

6.1 Likes and dislikes

	verb + *-ing*	verb + noun
☺☺	I **love going** to concerts. She **loves going** to concerts.	I **love photography**. He **loves photography**.
☺	I **like watching** TV. He **likes watching** TV.	I **like rock music**. She **likes rock music**.
☹	I **don't like visiting** exhibits. She **doesn't like visiting** exhibits.	I **don't like pizza**. He **doesn't like pizza**.
☹☹	I **hate doing** the dishes. She **hates doing** the dishes.	I **hate cold weather**. He **hates cold weather**.

6.1 Likes and dislikes

A Complete the sentences with the words in the box.

doesn't going like loves singing

1 My dad ___loves___ Elvis. He has all his albums.
2 I like ___singing___ in the shower.
3 She ___doesn't___ like horror movies. She gets scared.
4 You don't ___like___ cheese, do you?
5 Bill hates ___going___ to art galleries.

B Correct the mistakes in each sentence.

1 She likes ~~to~~ rock music.
2 I don't ~~liking~~ photography. I don't like photography.
3 They love ~~stay~~ in on Friday nights. They love staying in on Friday nights.
4 We love ~~to~~ sitting outside.
5 How can you ~~hating~~ the *Star Wars* movies? How can you hate the Star Wars movies?
6 He ~~not~~ like sushi. He doesn't like sushi.

C Use the prompts to write sentences with *love, like, don't like* and *hate*.

1 Sheila / ☺☺ / go to the theater.
Sheila loves going to the theater.
2 Owen / ☹ / visit / his grandparents.
Owen doesn't like visiting his grandparents.
3 We / ☺ / watch / *Game of Thrones*.
We like watching *Game of Thrones*.
4 I / ☹☹ / clean / the bathroom.
I hate cleaning the bathroom.
5 I / ☺☺ / dance.
I love dancing.
6 They / ☹ / clean / their bedroom.
They don't like cleaning their bedroom.

➤ Go back to page 53.

B Go through the task instructions, and make sure students understand that they can write one, two or three words in each blank, but no more. Allow them time to look through the sentences. If you have time, you could put students into pairs to decide what information is missing from each blank, before they read.

Give students up to five minutes to read the article again in more detail and complete the blanks. Give them another two minutes to check their answers. They should make sure the words are spelled correctly and the completed sentences make sense. Check answers as a class.

C Explain what *recommend* means (say to someone else that something is good). Students check which events are recommended by the guide. Check answers as a class.

The What's going on? guide uses a star rating system to show what they recommend; four-star ratings = Comedy Underground, Silent Disco and Lost in the Forest festival; five-star ratings = Star Wars and Kwame Abraham.

D Put students into pairs. Ask them how they find out about events in their area. Elicit some ideas and write them on the board (e.g. *look in a magazine, search the internet, use an app, use a city guide*, etc). Check answers as a class.

GRAMMAR

6.3 **A** Go through the task with students. Give them time to review the events in the guide. Then play the recording. Students write notes of the events mentioned and what Dan and Lucy decide to do. Give students time to compare answers in pairs. Play the recording again if required.

They talk about the Cow concert, the Star Wars movies, the photography exhibit and the music festival. They decide to stay in and watch TV.

6.3 **B** Students complete the extracts from the conversation. Give students time to compare answers in pairs before playing the recording again to check.

C Students work alone to complete the rules. Check answers as a class.

D Direct students to the **Grammar Hub** (see TB52). Read the examples and go through the rules with the class.

E Put students into groups to discuss the questions. Monitor and encourage students to ask follow-up questions to find out more. Write notes on errors students make with talking about likes and dislikes. For whole-class feedback, go over these errors and ask students to correct them. Use the **Grammar Worksheet** on W31 for extra practice.

Extra activity

Ask students to write four sentences about something they like, love, don't like and hate. Explain that three sentences should be true and one should be false. Put students into pairs and ask them to read out their sentences. Students then try to guess which of their partner's sentences is false.

SPEAKING

A Students review the guide and then discuss what they *like, love, don't like* and *hate*. Monitor and encourage, asking follow-up questions to help students extend their answers.

B Direct students to the **Communication Hub** for further practice talking about likes and dislikes.

C Put students into pairs. Focus them on the *What's going on?* guide and ask them to plan an activity they would both like to do on the weekend. Go through the model conversation, and encourage students to use phrases like *Let's go …*, *Good idea* and *Sorry …* in their discussion. Students discuss the different events and give reasons for their choice.

D For whole-class feedback, ask students to vote on the event they would most like to go to.

Extra activity

Give students time to make a list of five real events currently going on in your area. If possible, bring in real *What's going on* or similar guides to help or direct students to a relevant website. Next, put students into small groups and ask them to decide on three events to go to as a group. Give feedback as a class, encouraging students to explain why they chose each event.

AUDIO SCRIPT

6.3

Grammar, Exercise A
D = Dan L = Lucy

D: I'm bored.
L: Me, too. Let's watch TV.
D: There's nothing on. Anyway, it's Friday! I hate staying in on Friday night. Let's go out.
L: Hmmm … maybe … what's going on?
D: Uh, let's see … Oh, there's a concert at the Old Baths tonight. It's that rock band from California, Cow. I like their music.
L: Oh, right. Hmm. Sorry, I don't really like them. I don't like rock music.
D: Oh, OK. Well … Oh, wow! *Star Wars* is on at the outdoor movie theater.
L: I don't like outdoor movie theaters. I don't like sitting outside. It's too cold.
D: Oh, OK. Well, how about this – an exhibit! You love photography, don't you?
L: No, I don't like photography! I like paintings.
D: Oh, right. Hey! How about this? There's a music festival this weekend. In Coney Forest. What do you think?
L: Oh, let's see. That sounds fun. $165 per person. That's not bad.
D: Really? 165 dollars? Per person?
L: Yeah, it's three days: Friday, Saturday and Sunday. And it includes camping.
D: Uh … OK. Right. 165 dollars. Camping. Great. Uh …, Lucy?
L: Yes?
D: I'm tired. Let's stay in. What's on TV?

B READ FOR SPECIFIC INFORMATION Read the guide again. Complete the sentences with no more than three words from the text.

1 The Kwame Abraham exhibit finishes on ___Sunday, September 6___.
2 The music festival lasts for ___three___ days.
3 The Star Wars event starts at ___6 pm___ on Thursday August 13.
4 Cow's performance is in a ___swimming pool___ in The Old Baths.
5 James Cave is ___Romeo___ in the performance of *Romeo and Juliet*.

Search

Silent disco ★★★★
The silent disco craze continues! Put on your headphones, choose any kind of music and dance to your favorite tunes.
Nanette's, 10 pm – 5 am, Saturday, August 15

Lost in the Forest Festival ★★★★
A three-day music festival with great food and dancing under the tall, green trees of Coney Forest. Ex B Q2
Coney Forest, Friday – Sunday, August 14 – 16

Shakespeare in the park ★★★
Tonight's play is *Romeo and Juliet*, Shakespeare's famous love story. With James Cave as Romeo and Ameera Hussain as Juliet. Bring warm clothes and a picnic. Ex B Q5
Linkside Park, 6 pm, Tuesday, August 11

C How do you know which events the *What's going on?* guide recommends? Which events have four- (★★★★) or five-star (★★★★★) ratings?

D SPEAK Work in pairs. How do you find events?

online apps newspaper magazine friends family social media

I find events on an app on my phone. I go to pop-up events all the time.

GRAMMAR
Likes and dislikes

A (6.3) Listen to Dan and Lucy planning a night out. Which events in the *What's going on?* guide do they talk about? What do they decide to do?

B (6.3) Complete the sentences from the conversation with the words in the box. Then listen again and check your answers.

don't like (x2) hate like love

1 **Dan:** I ___hate___ staying in on Friday night. Let's go out.
2 **Dan:** It's that rock band from California, Cow. I ___like___ their music.
3 **Lucy:** Sorry, I don't really like them. I ___don't like___ rock music.
4 **Lucy:** I ___don't like___ sitting outside. It's too cold.
5 **Dan:** You ___love___ photography, don't you?

C WORK IT OUT Look at the sentences in Exercise B. Complete the rules with *noun* or *verb*.

Likes and dislikes

1 We use *like*, *love*, *don't like* and *hate* + ___noun___
2 We use *like*, *love*, *don't like* and *hate* + ___verb___ + *-ing*.

D Go to the Grammar Hub on page 132.

E SPEAK Work in small groups. Discuss the questions.

1 What do you like doing in your free time?
2 What kind of events do you love? Which do you hate? Why?
3 What do you like doing on your birthday?
4 Do you like going to outdoor events (e.g. festivals, outdoor movie theaters, etc)? Why/Why not?

SPEAKING

A PREPARE Work in pairs and discuss what you *like*, *love*, *don't like* and *hate* in the *What's going on?* guide.

B SPEAK Go to the Communication Hub on page 154.

Talk about likes and dislikes

6.2 It was fun

Talk about entertainment in the present and the past

G *was/were* P weak forms: *was/were* V past time expressions

LISTENING

A Work in pairs. Label the pictures (1–4) with the time periods in the box.

1930s 1950s 1980s 2000s

6.4 **B LISTEN FOR KEY WORDS** Listen to Carrie and her grandfather talking about TV. Check (✓) the things that they talk about.

TV channels	✓	laptops and tablets	✓
movie night	☐	TV dinners	☐
TV on demand	✓	an old TV show	✓

6.4 **C LISTEN FOR DETAIL** Listen to the conversation again. Are the sentences true (T) or false (F)? Correct the false sentences.

1. Carrie can't watch the nature show. (T) / F
2. Carrie watches her favorite TV show on demand. (T) / F
3. Carrie's grandfather's favorite TV show was on once a week. (T) / F
4. When Carrie's grandfather was young, there were a lot of TV channels. There were three TV channels. T / (F)
5. TVs weren't expensive in the 1950s. TVs were expensive in the 1950s. T / (F)
6. Carrie's grandfather thinks families today don't do things together. (T) / F

D SPEAK Work in pairs. Answer the questions.

1. What are your favorite TV shows?
2. Do you watch them with friends and family or alone?
3. How often do you watch shows on demand?

GRAMMAR

was/were

A Read the sentences from the conversation between Carrie and her grandpa. Underline the verbs.

1. They were expensive.
2. There weren't many TV channels.
3. Was that nice, Grandpa?
4. I wasn't lonely.
5. It was fun.

B WORK IT OUT Look at Exercise A. Complete the rules with *was*, *wasn't*, *were* or *weren't*.

was/were

1. Was is the past form of *is*.
   Were is the past form of *are*.
2. Wasn't is the past form of *isn't*.
   Weren't is the past form of *aren't*.
3. We make *yes/no* questions with was or were + subject.

C Go to the **Grammar Hub** on **page 132**.

D SPEAK Ask *Where were you …?* using the times below.

- at 11 pm last night
- at 10 am on Saturday morning
- at 6 pm on Friday
- at 2 pm yesterday
- at 8 am this morning

Where were you at 11 pm last night?

6.2 It was fun

LEAD-IN

Tell students how you watch movies and TV shows (e.g. *on a tablet, phone* or *TV*), where you watch (e.g. *in the kitchen, bedroom, on the bus, in a café*) and who you watch with (e.g. *alone, friends, family*). Ask students to do the same in small groups. Monitor and assist, focussing more on the communication of ideas at this point rather than accuracy of language. Make a note of any useful emergent language to teach later on (especially anything related to the themes of entertainment, TV and movies).

LISTENING

A In pairs, students match the time periods in the box to the four pictures. Check answers as a class.

6.4 **B** Go through the task with students. Check understanding of *TV on demand* (TV you can watch when you want) and *TV dinners* (a meal you eat in front of the TV). Play the recording. Students apply a check mark to the things that are mentioned. Check answers as a class.

6.4 **C** Play the recording again. Give students time to check their answers in pairs before giving feedback as a class.

1 F (She wants to watch it on her tablet after dinner.); 2 T; 3 T; 4 F (When Carrie's grandad was young, there were three TV channels.); 5 F (TVs were expensive in the 1950s.); 6 T

D Students discuss the questions in pairs. Monitor and assist as necessary.

GRAMMAR

A Elicit the answer to Q1 before giving students time to complete the exercise alone. Give feedback as a class.

B Allow time for students to complete the rules individually.

C Direct students to the **Grammar Hub** (see below and TB55). Read the examples and go through the rules with the class.

D Put students into pairs or small groups to discuss the questions. Use the **Grammar Worksheet** on W31 for extra practice.

AUDIO SCRIPT

6.4

Listening, Exercise B, page 174
G = Grandad C = Carrie

G: Hey, Carrie. Let's watch that new nature show on TV. It starts in five minutes.

Ex C Q1 **C:** Oh, I can't, Grandpa. Mom says I have to do my homework. But we can watch it later.

G: Later? It ends at seven.

Ex B **C:** I can get it on demand. We can watch it on my tablet.

G: On demand?

C: Yeah. You know, you don't have to watch TV shows at a specific time on TV any more. You can watch them online, whenever you like.

G: So, can I watch the soccer game yesterday?

C: Yes! You know, most people watch TV on demand now. Last night, I watched three episodes of my

Ex C Q2 favorite TV show.

G: Amazing. When I was young, my favorite TV

Ex C Q3 show was on once a week. On Tuesday nights. It was a music show.

Ex B **C:** How many TV channels were there?

Ex C Q4 **G:** Hmm. There weren't many TV channels. Three, I think.

C: Three? Now there are hundreds. Was it boring?

G: No, it wasn't.

C: Were TVs cheap back then?

Ex C Q5 **G:** No, they weren't. They were expensive. TV wasn't an everyday thing. We were the first family in our street to get one. It was in 1951, when I was ten. That's nearly 70 years ago! TV was special in the 1950s. We all watched TV together – the whole family. It was the same in every home in the country.

C: Everyone at the same time? That's funny. Were they happy?

G: Yes, they were. It was normal!

Ex B **C:** Mom and Dad often watch TV on their laptops and Susan has a tablet. We all watch TV alone.

Ex C Q6 **G:** People today spend more time alone. It was very different when I was young. Parents, children, grandparents were all together more. TV was a shared experience.

C: Was that nice, Grandpa?

G: Yes, it was. I wasn't lonely. People did things together. It was fun.

GRAMMAR HUB

6.2 *was/were*

	Positive	Negative
I/he/she/it	**I was** at the theater.	**I was not** at the theater. **I wasn't** at the theater.
you/we/they	**They were** at the movie theater.	**They were not** at the movie theater. **They weren't** at the movie theater.

- We use *was/were* to talk about things that happened in the past.
- We often use these time expressions with *was/were*.

I was there two hours ***ago****.* *It was my birthday* ***on Sunday****.* *We were out* ***yesterday****.*
They were here ***last night****.* *I was busy* ***on the weekend****.*

	Question	Short answers	
I/he/she/it	**Was it** interesting?	Yes, **it was**.	No, **it wasn't**.
you/we/they	**Were they** out last night?	Yes, **they were**.	No, **they weren't**.

6.2 It was fun

PRONUNCIATION

6.5 **A** Play the recording. Elicit ideas from the class before confirming/ telling them that the pronunciation of *was/were* changes.

6.5 **B** Explain that there are two different ways to pronounce *was* – a strong from (/wʌz/) and a weak form (/wəz/), writing the phonemes on the board. Next, write a personal example using *was* on the board (e.g. *When I was a child, my favorite TV show was X*), modeling natural pronunciation of *was* (i.e. a weak form). Elicit that in this sentence, *was* is pronounced with a weak form, and write /wəz/ under both instances of *was* in the example sentence. Next, explain that *were* also has a strong and a weak form (/wɜːr/ and /wər/). Write an example using *were* on the board (e.g. *What did you watch on TV when you were young?*). Elicit that in this sentence, *were* is pronounced with a weak form and write /wər/ under *were* in the example sentence. Then put students into pairs and ask them to read the sentences in Exercise A out loud and to underline all weak forms of *was* and *were*. Play the recording again for students to listen and check. Elicit/explain that in positive sentences and questions, *was* and *were* are said in their *weak form*. We say /wəz/ and /wər/. In short answers, *was* and *were* are said in their *strong form*. We say /wʌz/ and /wɜːr/. The pronunciation of *wasn't* and *weren't* doesn't change.

C In pairs, students practice the sentences, focusing on pronouncing the correct form of *was* and *were*. Monitor and encourage as appropriate.

VOCABULARY

A In pairs, students complete the quiz. Alternatively, with books closed, you could run it as a whole class team quiz. Check answers as a class and ask the students what was the most surprising fact from the quiz.

B Draw the table on the board and add the word *June* to it. It should go in the *in* column, as well as the *last* column. Do this to demonstrate that some time expressions can go in more than one place. Students then work in pairs to complete the table. Check answers by building up the table on the board.

C Students work alone to complete the sentences. Check answers as a class.

D Model the exercise by asking one or two questions around the class. Students then work in pairs to ask and answer the questions. Use the **Vocabulary Worksheet** on W32 for extra practice.

Extra activity

Extend the exercise into a 'Find someone who' activity with students completing a list (e.g. *Find someone who was at home yesterday / in the UK last month*, etc). Students then go around the class asking the questions (e.g. *Were you at home yesterday?*) until they find someone for each question.

SPEAKING

A Go through the task with students. Students then write five of their own questions about entertainment now and in the past. Monitor and check the questions for accuracy. If students work in pairs for this, put them into different pairs for the next exercise.

B Students ask and answer their questions. For whole-class feedback, ask someone from each pair to tell the class the most surprising thing they found out.

GRAMMAR HUB

6.2 *was/were*

A Complete the sentences with *was* or *were*.

1 Wow! That show __was__ amazing!
2 TVs __were__ really expensive in the 1950s.
3 __Was__ Yuki there on Saturday?
4 There __were__ a lot of people at the party.
5 Where __were__ you last night?
6 The tickets __were__ really expensive.

B Complete the text messages with *was, were, wasn't* and *weren't*.

Hi Malc! I __was__ at an exhibit on Saturday. My friends Roma and Pete [1] __were__ there, too. There [2] __weren't__ any good paintings – we hated them all ☹! How [3] __was__ your weekend?

Hal and I were at a comedy show. It was fun! [4] __Were__ you out on Sunday?

Yeah. We [5] __were__ at the big soccer game. And you?

I was at home studying. [6] __Was__ the soccer game good?

It was great.

➤ Go back to page 54.

PRONUNCIATION
Weak forms: *was/were*

6.5 **A** Listen and read. What do you notice about the pronunciation of *was* and *were*?

1 When I was young, my favorite TV show was on once a week.
2 How many TV channels were there?
3 Yes, they were.
4 Was that nice, Grandpa?
5 Yes, it was. I wasn't lonely. People did things together. It was fun.

6.5 **B** Underline the weak forms of *was* and *were* in Exercise A. Then listen again and check.

C Work in pairs. Practice saying the sentences in Exercise A. Remember to use the correct forms of *was* and *were*.

VOCABULARY
Past time expressions

A Work in pairs to complete the *Big screen, small screen* quiz.

B Use the words in the box to make a table of past time expressions. Some words can go in more than one place.

10 minutes 1952 Friday June month six weeks two years weekend winter year

in	ago	last
1952	10 minutes	Friday
June	six weeks	June
winter	two years	month
		weekend
		winter
		year

C Complete the sentences with *in*, *ago*, *last* or *yesterday*.

1 I was in Mexico ___last___ year.
2 Our exams were exactly one year ___ago___.
3 I wasn't at home ___in/last___ July. I was on vacation.
4 I was a student two months ___ago___. Now I have a job!
5 My parents were students ___in___ 1982.
6 I was at home with my family ___yesterday___.

D SPEAK Work in pairs. Ask and answer questions beginning with *Where were you ...?* Use the table in Exercise B to help you.

A: Where were you last month?
B: I was in Istanbul last month. Where were you at this time yesterday?
A: I was in this class!

SPEAKING

A PREPARE Write five questions about entertainment now and in the past. Use time expressions in your questions.

What's your favorite TV show?
What was your favorite movie ten years ago?

B SPEAK Work in pairs. Ask and answer the questions in Exercise A.

five/ten/twenty years ago in the 80s/90s last year

A: What were your favorite TV shows ten years ago?
B: My favorite TV show 10 years ago was ...

BIG SCREEN, SMALL SCREEN

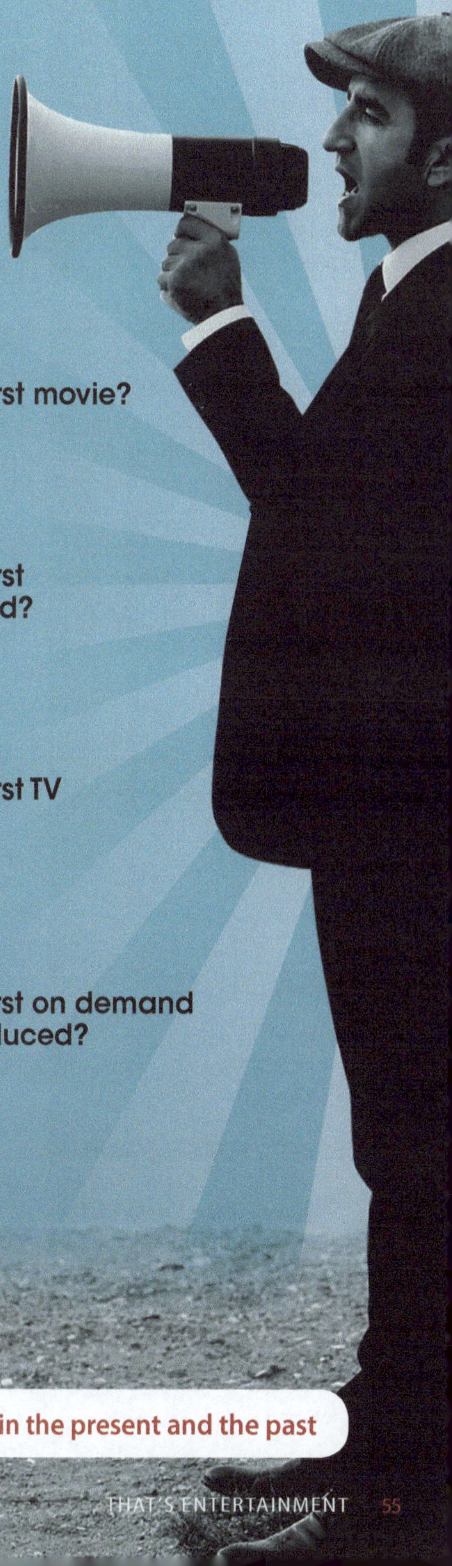

1 When was the first movie?
a in the 1850s
b in the 1880s
c in the 1900s

2 When was the first movie with sound?
a in the 1910s
b in the 1920s
c in the 1930s

3 When was the first TV introduced?
a 90 years ago
b 70 years ago
c 50 years ago

4 When was the first on demand TV service introduced?
a last year
b this century
c last century

Talk about entertainment in the present and the past

6.3 Life stories

Talk about your life

G – simple past regular and irregular verbs P – simple past regular endings V – life events S – scanning for names

Entertainer Magazine
Inspiring stories

Carlos Acosta
by Helena Nowak

Carlos Acosta was born into a large, poor family in Havana, Cuba, in 1973. When he was nine years old, his father, Pedros Acosta, **sent** him to dance school. (Ex C Q5) At first, he hated it – he just wanted to play soccer with his friends. But he worked hard and, eventually, **became** a talented dancer. He **studied** at the National Ballet School of Cuba. He won the gold medal at the Prix de Lausanne. (Ex C Q7)

Between 1989 and 1991, he performed around the world. He was a principal dancer at the Houston Ballet from 1993 to 1998, and then he **started** a new job at London's Royal Ballet. He met his wife, Charlotte Holland, in 2004. (Ex C Q2) They **got** married eight years later. They have three children. He **went** back to Cuba in 2011 to start a foundation to help young dancers. Acosta is also an actor. He appeared in the movies *New York, I Love You* (2008) and *Our Kind of Traitor* (2016). (Ex C Q3)

Venus Williams
by Nao Yamauchi

Venus Williams was born in Lynwood, near Compton in Los Angeles, in 1980. There was a lot of crime in the local area and her father, Richard Williams, thought tennis was a chance for Venus and her younger sister Serena to be rich and successful. (Ex C Q1)

The Williams sisters **played** tennis on old courts. They **practiced** with tennis balls from nearby country clubs. Their father was their coach, and their mother, Oracene Price, **gave** them school lessons at home. (Ex C Q8) When she was ten, Venus **moved** to Florida (Ex C Q4) where she went to Rick Macci's tennis academy. Before she was a teenager, she won 63 matches without losing one.

In February 2002, Venus Williams became the first African American to be the world's number one tennis player. (Ex C Q6) In July of the same year, Venus played Serena in the Wimbledon final, and Serena won and became world number one. These sisters, from a poor neighborhood in Los Angeles, are now recognized as two of the greatest female tennis players in the world.

Glossary

inspiring (adj) making you feel excited about something

READING

A Work in pairs. Look at the pictures in the article. What do you know about these people?

B **READ FOR GIST** Work in pairs. Student A – read about Carlos Acosta. Student B – read about Venus Williams. Tell your partner about your person.

C **READ FOR DETAIL** Read the article again and complete the sentences with names from the text. Use the information in the box to help you.

Scanning for names

- When scanning for names of people or places, look for CAPITAL LETTERS.
- When scanning for names of movies, albums and books, look for *italics*.

1 Richard Williams wanted Venus and Serena to learn tennis.
2 Carlos got married to Charlotte Holland.
3 In 2008, Carlos was in a movie called *New York, I Love You*.
4 Venus moved to Florida in 1990.
5 Pedros Acosta sent Carlos to dance school for the first time.
6 Serena became world number one in July 2002.
7 Carlos got a gold medal from the Prix de Lausanne.
8 Oracene Price helped Venus with school lessons at home.

D **SPEAK** Work in pairs. Which person inspires you? Why?

A: I like Carlos Acosta because he helps young dancers.
B: I think Venus is more inspiring. She was the first African American to be the world's number one tennis player.

6.3 Life stories

LEAD-IN

Tell students about someone that inspired you to do something (e.g. maybe you studied history in college because you had an amazing teacher in high school). Emphasize that this person made you feel that you wanted to do something or that something was possible/you could do it. Write a sentence about this person on the board using the word *inspiring*. Elicit that *inspiring* is an adjective, write the phonemes (/ɪn'spaɪərɪŋ/) and practice the correct pronunciation. Ask students to share examples of people who inspire them, explaining why. These could be famous people, friends or family members.

READING

A Focus students on the photos. Put students in pairs to say what they know about the people. If they don't know who the people are, they could say what the people's jobs are. Point out that the man is Carlos Acosta – a dancer. The woman is Venus Williams – a tennis player.

B Divide the class into As and Bs. Student A reads about Carlos Acosta and Student B reads about Venus Williams. Give students two minutes to read their part of the text. Then put students into A/B pairs. Students then tell their partner about the person they read about. Make sure students speak to each other rather than read each other's texts.

C Go through the *Scanning for names* box. Then focus students on Sentences 1–8. Ask them to underline all the names. Point out that this will make it easier for them to scan for the information they need.

Give students up to five minutes to read both texts and complete the sentences. Give them another minute to make sure they have spelled the names correctly and have used capital letters appropriately. Check answers as a class.

D In pairs, students discuss which of the two people from the text inspires them the most. Monitor and encourage students to ask each other follow-up questions to find out more.

TEACHING IDEA by David Seymour and Maria Popova

Grammar: The first time

Use this activity to review the grammar section on page 57.
Say this to your students:

In pairs, tell each other about your first: *bicycle, pet, job, friend, home, toys, swim, vacation, memory, day at school, word (as a baby), car, flight in a plane.*

GRAMMAR HUB

6.3 Simple past regular and irregular verbs

Regular verbs		
Base form	**Simple past**	
ask	ask**ed**	**I asked** for help.
like	lik**ed**	**She liked** the comedy show.
stop	stopp**ed**	**You stopped** the car.
study	stud**ied**	**We studied** English last night.
Irregular verbs		
Base form	**Simple past**	
become	became	**He became** a singer.
go	went	**They went** shopping.
have	had	**We had** very little money.
send	sent	**They sent** you an email.
write	wrote	**I wrote** you a letter.
win	won	**She won** the game.

Spelling rules	Base form	Simple past
Add **-ed**.	join	join**ed**
Add **-d** to verbs ending **-e**.	lik**e**	lik**ed**
Change **-y** after a consonant to **-ied**.	stud**y**	stud**ied**
Double the consonant and add **-ed** with verbs ending in vowel + consonant.	sto**p**	sto**pped**

6.3 Life stories

GRAMMAR

A Focus students on the table. Depending on students' level of knowledge, they could complete the table with the verbs they know. Then ask them to read *Inspiring stories* again and complete the table with the verbs in bold. Check answers as a class by building up the table on the board.

B In pairs, students discuss the rules and decide which are true. Check answers as a class.

C Point out that there are many irregular verbs in English. Write *go* on the board and elicit the simple past form (*went*). Point out that there are no clear rules for the spelling of irregular simple past verbs. Direct students to **Irregular Verbs** on page 121.

D Direct students to the **Grammar Hub** (see below and TB56). Read the examples and go through the rules and exercises with the class.

E Go through the example answers and ask students to identify the simple past verbs (*went, bought, passed, joined, met, started*). Ask which verbs are irregular *(went, bought, met)*.

Model the exercise for students by telling them three things you did last year. Ask students to repeat back to you what you did. Then put students into pairs. They tell their partner three things they did. For whole-class feedback, ask students to tell the class what their partner did last year. Use the **Grammar Worksheet** on W32 for extra practice.

PRONUNCIATION

6.6 **A** Go through the task instructions. Then play the recording and ask students to repeat the verbs. Highlight that the difference between /d/ and /t/ is that the first sound is voiced. If students touch their throat, they should feel something when they say /d/, but not when they say /t/. Also highlight that /ɪd/ adds an extra syllable to the verb.

6.7 **B** Play the recording. Students add the verbs from the box to the table.

6.7 **C** Students listen again to the verbs from Exercise B and repeat. Ask students to listen to each other and check for correct pronunciation.

VOCABULARY

A In pairs, students complete the phrases. Explain that they can refer to *Inspiring stories* for help but highlight that in the text the examples are all written in the simple past. Check answers as a class.

B Students put the phrases in order. Point out that there are no right or wrong answers here. Then put students into pairs to compare answers and give reasons. If you have time, you could ask students to think of other important life events. Add these to the board. Use the **Vocabulary Worksheet** on W33 for extra practice.

SPEAKING HUB

A Students work alone to complete the sentence stems. Ask students to choose as many as they can, depending on which ones are relevant to them.

B Ask students to select the five most important events and write each one on a separate piece of paper.

C Put students into groups and then put all that group's sentences in the center. They take turns to read a sentence. The rest of the group guesses who it belongs to.

D Put students into new groups. Ask them to report the information they found out about their group members. For whole-class feedback, ask students what were the most interesting facts they found out about their classmates' lives.

Extra activity

Give students time to research the life of a famous person that they admire. Ask them to write notes about:

- the person's name and why they're famous
- the key events in their life
- why they admire them

If you don't have Internet access in your area, you could print some short biographies of people you think the students might know. Next, put students into pairs to explain what they found out. Monitor and focus on their use of simple past.

GRAMMAR HUB

6.3 Simple past regular and irregular verbs

A Complete the sentences with the simple past form of the verbs in the box.

ask like play stay stop study

1 I can't believe I failed. I __studied__ all night for that test!
2 I really __liked__ Michael Jackson when I was younger.
3 They __stopped__ work to have lunch.
4 I think he __played__ for the university rugby team.
5 She __asked__ Rob to come, but he was busy.
6 We __stayed__ at home and watched *The Walking Dead* last night.

B Complete the sentences in the simple past with the verbs in parentheses.

1 David Bowie __died__ (die) in 2016.
2 John Lennon __left__ (leave) the Beatles in 1970.
3 Chris Brown __wrote__ (write) the hit song 'Disturbia'.
4 The movie *La La Land* __won__ (win) six Academy Awards.
5 Before he was an actor, Sylvester Stallone __taught__ (teach) gymnastics.
6 Bob Dylan __took__ (take) his stage name from the poet Dylan Thomas.

C Correct the mistakes in each sentence.

1 Real Madrid ~~winned~~ won the game 2–0.
2 He ~~teached~~ taught history for twenty years.
3 She ~~writed~~ wrote nine books in her lifetime.
4 We ~~taked~~ took a taxi to the restaurant.
5 She ~~leaved~~ left work early last night.
6 You ~~sended~~ sent the letter two weeks ago!

➤ Go back to page 57.

GRAMMAR

Simple past regular and irregular verbs

A WORK IT OUT Read *Inspiring stories* again. Complete the table with past verbs from the article.

Simple past regular and irregular verbs			
Regular		**Irregular**	
move	moved	become	became
play	played	get	got
practice	practiced	go	went
start	started	give	gave
study	studied	send	sent

B Look at the rules about simple past regular verbs. Check (✓) the rules that are true.

Simple past regular verbs

1 ✓ We add *-ed* to most verbs.
2 ✓ We add *-d* to verbs ending in *-e*.
3 ☐ We add *-s* to the third person.
4 ✓ With verbs ending in *-y*, we drop the *-y* and add ***-ied***.

C See the **Irregular verbs** list on **page 121**.

D Go to the **Grammar Hub** on **page 132**.

E SPEAK Work in pairs. Tell your partner three things you did last year.

A: I went to Greece, I bought a new laptop and I passed my English exam! What about you?

B: Good job! I joined a gym, I met my best friend and I started college.

PRONUNCIATION

Simple past regular endings

6.6 **A** There are three different ways of pronouncing the endings of simple past regular verbs. Can you hear the difference? Listen and repeat.

/d/	/t/	/ɪd/
died	liked	waited
moved	asked	decided
studied	stopped	wanted
	worked	

6.7 **B** Listen and add the verbs in the box to the table in Exercise A.

asked decided moved stopped studied wanted worked

6.7 **C** Listen again and repeat the verbs.

VOCABULARY

Life events

A Complete the phrases with the verbs in the box. Use the words in bold in *Inspiring stories* to help you.

be become get go have move start study

1 get married
2 become a dancer/musician/singer
3 go to school/college
4 start work
5 study art / a language
6 be born
7 have children
8 move to a different city/house

B SPEAK Put the life events in Exercise A in the order that you think they happen. Then work in pairs. Are your life events in the same order? Can you think of any other life events?

A: What about learning to drive? That's a big life event for most people.

B: That's true. I learned to drive when I was 17. It really changed my life!

SPEAKING HUB

A PREPARE You are going to write about your life. Think about how to complete the sentences.

- I was born in …
- I went …
- I studied …
- I started …
- I moved …
- I got married to …
- I had …
- I lived in …
- I worked in …

B PLAN Choose the five most important events in your life. Write each one on a separate piece of paper and then fold it in half.

C ORGANIZE Work in groups. Put all of your sentences in the middle. Take turns reading sentences aloud and guessing who wrote them. Award one point for every correct guess.

I graduated from Bologna University.

It's Francesca's sentence!

D DISCUSS Work in groups. Try to remember the events of other people's lives.

Sayeed studied English in Australia.

Yes, and Ana got married last month!

Talk about your life

Café Hub

6.4 Love hate

F – ask for and give opinions   P – stress and intonation

COMPREHENSION

A 00:00–00:56 **SPEAK** Work in pairs. Watch the first part of the video. What is Zac's big news? He wants to make a house playlist.

B 00:56–03:57 Watch the second part of the video and complete the table. Draw ☺ if the housemates like the song or ☹ if they don't like it.

Song	Zac	Gaby	Neena	Me
The river	☺	☺	☹	
Move	☺	☹	☺	
Chimes	☹	☺	☺	
Check it out	☺	☺	☺	

C **SPEAK** What do you think of the songs? Complete the *Me* column of the table with ☺ or ☹.

FUNCTIONAL LANGUAGE

Asking for and giving opinions

A Complete the table with the phrases in the box.

I hate it. I like it. I love it! I really hate it. It's good. I think it's awful. I'm not sure. It's awesome! It's great! It isn't great.

Asking for opinions	What do you think of it/this?
	How about you?
Giving opinions	☺☺☺ It's awesome!
	☺☺ It's great!
	I love it!
	☺ I like it.
	It's good.
	☹ I'm not sure.
	It isn't great.
	☹☹ I hate it.
	☹☹☹ I really hate it; I think it's awful.

B Rank the adjectives below from ☺☺☺ (very positive) to ☹☹☹ (very negative). Then, compare your answers with a partner.

1 great ☺☺
2 amazing ☺☺☺
3 bad ☹
4 awful ☹☹☹
5 happy ☺☺
6 sad ☹☹
7 terrible ☹☹☹
8 good ☺

MILLY SAM NEENA ZAC GABY

USEFUL PHRASES

A Match the beginnings (1–7) and the endings (a–g) of the useful phrases.

1	That's	a	sorry.	G
2	OK	b	one then.	N
3	I'm	c	it?	N
4	It makes me	d	go!	N
5	OK. Not that	e	Let's add it to the playlist.	Z
6	My	f	then.	N
7	Finally!	g	feel sad.	Z

B Watch the video again. Check your answers to Exercise A. Who says it? Write G (Gaby), N (Neena) or Z (Zac) next to each useful phrase.

PRONUNCIATION
Stress and intonation

6.8 **A** Listen and repeat. Copy the stress and intonation.

B Work in pairs. Student A – name a song, a singer or a band. Student B – give your opinion. Take turns.

A: Ed Sheeran.
B: He's OK. How about Haim?
A: I love them!

SPEAKING

A PREPARE Imagine you are going on a road trip. Make a list of your five favorite songs.

B SPEAK Work in small groups. Agree on a playlist of ten songs for your road trip. Use phrases from the Functional language section to help you.

C PRESENT Work in pairs. Compare your playlist. Do you like the same music?

Glossary

My go! **(British)** = My turn! **(American)**

Ask for and give opinions

➤ Turn to **page 165** to learn how to write a review of an event

6.4 Love hate

LEAD-IN

Write the names of three songs you enjoy listening to on the board (try to choose songs you think students will know). If appropriate, you could play the songs. Ask students what they think about them. Take a vote on which is the class favorite.

COMPREHENSION

A ▶ 00:00-00:56 Go through the instructions. Then play the first part of the video. Check answers as a class.

B ▶ 00:56-03:57 Focus students on the table. Play the second part of the video. Students complete the table with the smiley or sad faces. Students compare answers in pairs. Check answers as a class by building up the table on the board.

C Students complete the final column of the table with their own opinion. Put students into small groups to compare opinions. Encourage them to explain why.

FUNCTIONAL LANGUAGE

A Focus on the questions in the table. Students then complete the second column with the phrases in the box. Check answers as a class.

B Students work alone to rank the adjectives. They then compare their answers in pairs. Build up the ranked list on the board for a whole class check.

USEFUL PHRASES

A In pairs, students match the beginnings and endings of the phrases.

B ▶ Before playing the video again, point out that while watching, students need to check their answers and also check who says each useful phrase. Play the video again. Check answers as a class.

PRONUNCIATION

A 6.8 Play the recording, pausing after each sentence for students to listen and repeat, copying the intonation and stress.

It's OK.	***I'm not sure.***
I like it.	***It isn't great.***
It's great!	***It's terrible!***
I love it!	***I hate it!***
It's amazing!	***It's awful!***

B Go through the task and example with students. In pairs, students name a song, a singer or a band and share their opinions about it. (If it's more appropriate for your class, ask students to talk about movies, shows or books instead.)

SPEAKING

A Go through the task with students. Give students time, individually, to write a playlist of five songs and also to review the *Functional Language* phrases from earlier in the lesson.

B Put students into groups. Ask them to share their lists and discuss their opinions of each song. Monitor and encourage students to use the *Functional Language* phrases, with appropriate intonation. Ask students to agree on ten songs in a single list. Make sure that each student writes this list down.

C Put students into new pairs. Ask them to share their lists with each other.

Extra activity

Take this opportunity to teach different types of music. Elicit a few examples (e.g. *rock*, *jazz*, etc) and add them to a mind map on the board. Then put students into groups to brainstorm more. Give feedback as a class, adding new language to the board and eliciting examples for each.

▶ VIDEO SCRIPT

N = Neena G = Gaby Z = Zac

N: Morning.
G: Hi, Neena.
N: Coffee?
G: Sure. Zac? ZAC? Coffee!
Z: Guys, guys, guys. Big News!
N: What?
Z: We need to make a house playlist.
G: That's it?
N: THAT's the big news?
Z: Yeah! This is very important! We need to find music that we all like.
N: OK, then. Play something.
Z: Listen … to … this. Hi computer. Play the song: *The River* by Tobias. Ah … The River. I listened to this song all the time when I was young. So, what do you think of it?
G: I like it!
N: I'm sorry. I think it's awful. It makes me feel sad.
Z: OK. Not that one then.
N: My go. Ummm … OK … I heard this song last week: Hi computer. Play *Move* by The Tempo.
G: I think it's … OK …
N: Wait … wait for the chorus!
Z: It's great!
G: It's not great. Hi computer. Play the song *Chimes* by Lalala.
Z: I'm not sure about this one. This is so hard! Hi computer. Play:
N: I love it! How about you?
G: I'm not sure …
Z: It's awesome!
N: I hate it!
Z: I really hate it!
G: I love it.
Z: It's good.
N: I love it.
Z: Finally! Let's add it to the playlist.
N: I love it.
Z: I love it.
G: I love it! Add it!
Z: Computer: stop playing. OK… This next song is … awesome. I liked it the first time I heard it, years ago when I was in college. And I love this band. I went to their concert last month. I hope you like it.
G: I really hope I like it …
N: Please be good …
Z: Hi computer. Play the song: *Check it out* by Big Top.

6 Writing

Write a review of an event

W – using narrative sequencers

A Work in pairs. Look at the picture. What do you think happens at this event?

B Read the review. Check your answer to Exercise A.

C Choose the correct words to complete the sentences.

According to the review, …

1. the tour leader was *funny* / *serious*.
2. the tourists *learned* / *didn't learn* about Melbourne.
3. it lasted for *30 minutes* / *60 minutes*.
4. the weather was *good* / *bad*.
5. it was *cheap* / *expensive*.
6. it was a *good* / *bad* experience.

D Read the review again. Number the topics 1–6 in the order they are written about.

4 The weather	5 The writer's opinion
2 The location	6 The cost of the event
1 The type of event	3 Details of the event

E Look back at the review. Underline the narrative sequencers. Use the information in the box to help you.

Using narrative sequencers

- To begin the story, we use *first* or *to start with*.
  First, *we met in the city center.*
  To start with, *we got some headphones.*
- To continue the story, we use *then*, *next* and *after that*.
  Then, *we went to Main Street.*
  Next, *we learned about the city.*
  After that, *we had lunch.*
- To end the story, we use *finally* or *in the end*.
  Finally, *the concert ended.*
  In the end, *we called a taxi.*

F Complete the story with narrative sequencers. Use the information in the box to help you.

Last weekend was really busy. Saturday evening was Comedy Night at The Old Fire Station. 1 First / To start with we watched a comedian – I can't remember his name. 2 Then / Next, we saw the famous Ali Wong. She was great. We laughed a lot! 3 After that, there was a band for about 45 minutes. 4 Finally, the evening ended with a routine by Kyle Kinane. He was very funny, too. It was a great evening's entertainment and excellent value – it cost $30 each.

WRITING

A PREPARE You're going to write a review for an event you went to. Think about the event and write notes under the headings in Exercise D.

B WRITE Use your notes to write your review. Use narrative sequencers to help you organize your ideas.

Guru Dudu Silent Disco Walking Tour

★★★★

goodreviews, January 18, 2018

I went to my first disco 20 years ago. I went to my first silent disco last week. Well, my first silent disco walking tour!

The tour started outside the Federation Square in Melbourne. First, we each got some wireless headphones and followed Guru Dudu, our tour leader and DJ, through the streets of the city. Then, we met some local people who talked about the history of the city. (Ex C Q2) After that, we walked, danced and laughed as Guru Dudu played dance music and made jokes through our headphones. (Ex C Q1) It was a great way to see the city. It was warm and sunny, and everyone had fun. (Ex C Q4) Finally, the tour ended back where it started. The whole thing lasted an hour. (Ex C Q3) It really was the best city tour ever! (Ex C Q6) And it was a great value at just $24 a ticket. I really recommend it! (Ex C Q5)

Reviewed by Tom

WRITING 165

Answer

It's a silent disco walking tour. People can learn about a city as they walk around it. There is a group of people following a leader, who takes them through the city. They wear headphones. The leader plays music and speaks to them. Other people in the city can't hear the music or commentary.

Tell students that sequencers like these help make their writing clearer to readers.

Refer students to this review as a model for the writing task.

You could ask students to read each other's reviews and say if they would like to go to a similar event.

WRITING

In this writing lesson, students will learn how to write a review of an event, paying attention to how to make the order of events clear with narrative sequencers.

A Display the picture to the whole class if possible. Encourage students to share their ideas as to what the event is and what people can do there.

B Ask students to check their answers to Exercise A. You could also ask if the review is positive or negative about the event (*positive*). Ask students if they would like to attend this event.

C Students work alone to complete the sentences. Check answers as a class.

D Students read the review again and number the topics in the order they are written about. Give students time to compare answers in pairs before checking as a class.

E Read through the *Using narrative sequencers* box with students, highlighting the sequencers in bold. Students then underline the sequencers in the review. If possible, display the review to the whole class and ask students to identify the sequencers.

F Students work alone to complete the story. Monitor and assist as required. Put fast finishers together in pairs to compare their answers.

WRITING TASK

A Students decide what event they would like to write about. Refer students to the topics in Exercise D and ask them to write notes in relation to each one.

B Students use their notes to write a review of the event. Monitor and encourage students to focus on accurate punctuation, interesting adjectives and the use of narrative sequencers.

Unit 6 Review

GRAMMAR

A Write sentences about what Kyle likes and dislikes.

love — like — don't like — hate

1 play soccer ♥ *Kyle loves playing soccer.*
2 dance ☹ Kyle doesn't like dancing.
3 go clothes shopping Kyle hates going clothes shopping.
4 Wes Anderson movies ☺ Kyle likes Wes Anderson movies.
5 watch basketball ☺ Kyle likes watching basketball.
6 listen to jazz music Kyle hates listening to jazz music.
7 play video games ♥ Kyle loves playing video games.
8 Japanese food ☹ Kyle doesn't like Japanese food.

B Complete the conversation with *was*, *were*, *wasn't* or *weren't*.

A: [1] *Were* you at home last night?
B: No, I [2] wasn't . I [3] was at a comedy show.
A: Where [4] were your roommates?
B: They [5] were out, too.
A: [6] Were they at the concert?
B: No, they [7] weren't .

C Complete the text with the simple past form of the verbs in parentheses.

In 2016, Elvis Presley [1] *was* (*be*) on the Forbes list of highest-paid dead entertainers. He [2] earned (*earn*) $27 million! Other musicians on the list [3] included (*include*) Prince and David Bowie, who both [4] died (*die*) in 2016. David Bowie [5] made (*make*) his last album *Blackstar* in 2016. He [6] got (*get*) $10.5 million. Prince [7] sold (*sell*) more than 2.5 million albums last year.

VOCABULARY

A Complete the conversation with the words in the box.

concert exhibit festival movie play

Luis: Do you like Picasso? There's an [1] exhibit of his paintings.
Manu: I don't like looking at paintings.
Luis: OK. Well, how about going to see a [2] movie at the movie theater.
Manu: Hmm. I'm not sure.
Luis: There's a [3] play at the theater.
Manu: That's boring. I want to listen to some music. There's a rock [4] concert on tonight.
Luis: But I hate rock music.
Manu: Oh, right. There's a jazz music [5] festival this weekend. It's in the park. It starts at 2 pm.

B Complete the sentences with *in*, *last*, *ago* and *yesterday*.

1 I went to my first concert *in* 2010.
2 We saw that band two weeks ago .
3 The exhibit opened yesterday .
4 I met my best friend last year.
5 The first 3D movies were in the 1920s.
6 I went to the movie theater yesterday afternoon.

C Complete the sentences with the verbs in the box.

became got had moved started studied was went

1 My grandmother was born in 1959.
2 I became an English teacher in 2015.
3 My parents got married on a beach in Hawaii.
4 My brother went to Oxford University to study law.
5 Sarah had a baby a few months ago.
6 My sister moved to a new house last summer.
7 Beth started her new job two days ago.
8 I studied history in college.

D SPEAK Work in pairs. Tell your partner about five important events in your life.

A: A really important event in my life was getting married. I got married in 2016. It was sunny. I was very happy. What about you?
B: That sounds amazing! An important event in my life was starting college. I met lots of interesting people on my first day.

FUNCTIONAL LANGUAGE

A Choose the correct words to complete the sentences.

1 What do you *think* / *know* about the singer Katy Perry? I think she's great.
2 Listen to this! I *think* / *sure* Foals are great.
3 How *about* / *think* you?
4 I'm not *sure* / *know* about that.
5 I *love* / *loving* them!
6 I really *awful* / *hate* them!
7 This exhibit is boring. It isn't *great* / *sure*.

B SPEAK Work in pairs. Take turns asking and answering about these things. Use the sentences in Exercise A to help you.

- a band you like / don't like
- a famous singer
- a popular movie
- a movie you like

A: I love the new Jennifer Lawrence movie.
B: Me too! She's a great actress.

Goats cross the Zojila Pass in Kashmir, India.

Travel (v) to go on a long journey or visit different places
Transportation (n) a way of moving people and things from one place to another
Synonyms: explore (v), move (v)

Ask students to label the photo if you need time to set up the class.

Goats cross the Zojila Pass in Kashmir, India.

The quote suggests that in order to enjoy the world in full, we need to travel. If we don't, all we will know is our own lives.

Augustine of Hippo (AD 354–430) was a philosopher who greatly influenced Western thinking. He was from an area located in modern-day Algeria. He is a Christian saint and is the patron saint of many things, including printers and sore eyes.

OBJECTIVES

- talk about transportation in a city
- talk about a journey
- talk about a vacation
- check in and out of a hotel
- write a short article about a travel experience

Work with a partner. Discuss the questions.

1 Where did you go on vacation last year?
2 Look at the picture. Would you like to drive here? Why/Why not?
3 Which countries would you like to visit?

TRAVEL AND TRANSPORTATION 61

OBJECTIVES

Read the unit objectives to the class.

UNIT OPENER QUESTIONS

Ask students to look at the picture on the page and describe what they see. Ask students to say what they find interesting or surprising about it, and what is the same or different from where they are from.

Ask students to read the questions at the bottom of the page. Check that students understand the questions.

Put them into pairs to discuss the three questions. Monitor and help with grammar and vocabulary as required. Encourage students to listen to each other and ask follow-up questions to find out more. For whole-class feedback, ask two or three students to share their opinions with the rest of the class.

WORKSHEETS

Lesson 7.1 Getting around

Transportation (W34)

could (W35)

Lesson 7.2 A love of adventure

Simple past negative (W35)

Travel phrases (W36)

Lesson 7.3 A trip to remember

Simple past questions (W37)

Verb phrases (W38)

7.1 Getting around

Talk about transportation in a city

V – transportation P – /eɪ/ and /oʊ/ G – *could*

VOCABULARY
Transportation

A Look at the pictures in *Where in the world are they?* What types of transportation can you see? What other types of transportation can you think of?

B Go to the **Vocabulary Hub** on **page 149**.

C SPEAK Work in pairs. Think about a time you were in a different country or city. Answer the questions.

1 What types of transportation did you use?
2 Were they difficult to use? Why?
3 Were they cheap or expensive?

When I was in Vietnam last year, I took a motorcycle taxi. It was cheap and easy to organize.

PRONUNCIATION
/eɪ/ and /oʊ/

7.1 **A** Listen and repeat the transportation words in the box.

boat coach motorcycle plane train

7.2 **B** Listen to the vowel sound /oʊ/ in boat. Then underline the words in the box in Exercise A that have the same vowel sound. What letters can make the /oʊ/ sound?
The letters 'oa' usually make the /oʊ/ sound.

7.3 **C** Listen to the vowel sound /eɪ/ in plane. Then circle the words in the box in Exercise A that have the same vowel sound. What letters can make the /eɪ/ sound?
The letters 'ane' or 'ai' usually make the /eɪ/ sound.

D SPEAK Work in pairs. Practice saying the transportation words. Listen and check your partner's pronunciation. Be careful to pronounce the words correctly.

READING

A READ FOR GIST Read *Where in the world are they?* What is it about?

1 buildings 2 countries 3 transportation

B SPEAK Work in pairs. Complete the quiz.

C SCAN Read *Six quick facts*. Match facts (a–f) with pictures (1–6) in the quiz.

D READ FOR DETAIL Read *Six quick facts* again. Answer the questions.

1 How old are the buses in Mumbai?
80 years old
2 How many San Francisco trolleys are there today?
about 40
3 How many subway stations are there in Moscow?
206
4 What two types of transportation can you take from Amsterdam station? train and bus
5 Where does the Star Ferry go between?
Hong Kong Island and Kowloon
6 What are three popular types of transportation in Hanoi?
scooters, motorcycles, bicycles

E SPEAK Work in pairs. Think about the cities in the quiz. Which do you think are difficult to travel around? Why?

A: I think it's easy to travel around Hong Kong. It's a fairly small place. What do you think?
B: Yes, I agree.

Where in the world are they?

Do you know what color the taxis are in New York? And which Italian city has no cars? If you answered *yellow* and *Venice*, take our quiz!

Look at the pictures 1–6. Where are they? Choose a, b, or c.

1 a Mumbai b Hong Kong c London
2 a Lisbon b San Francisco c Mexico City
3 a Hanoi b Bangkok c Manila
4 a Budapest b Moscow c Kiev
5 a Shanghai b Sydney c Hong Kong
6 a Berlin b Amsterdam c Rio de Janeiro

Answers: 1 a, 2 b, 3 a, 4 b, 5 c, 6 b

7.1 Getting around

LEAD-IN

Bring pictures of five different types of transportation to class. Show the pictures one by one, eliciting the name and writing the new vocabulary on the board. Next, put students into pairs and ask them to brainstorm any transportation words they know in English. Give feedback, adding new words to the board.

VOCABULARY

A If possible, display the images on pages 62–63 to the whole class. Ask students what types of transportation they can see. Add the words to the board.

1 taxis, cars, buses; 2 trolleys; 3 motorcycles / mopeds / scooters; 4 trains / subway; 5 ferry / boat; 6 subway.

B Direct students to the **Vocabulary Hub**. Give them time to complete the exercise alone before checking answers in pairs. If you have time, you could ask students to test each other in pairs. One student takes turns saying a word, and the other student points to the correct picture.

C Students discuss the questions in pairs. Monitor and assist with any new or challenging vocabulary. Use the **Vocabulary Worksheet** on W34 for extra practice.

PRONUNCIATION

7.1 **A** Play the recording. Students listen and repeat the words in the box.

7.2 **B** Write the word *boat* on the board and underline the letters *oa*. Point out that in this word, the letters are said as one sound. Play the recording and ask students to repeat the word *boat*. Show the shape your mouth makes when making the /oʊ/ sound.

/oʊ/ *boat*

Students then underline the words in Exercise A which have the same sound. Add the answers to the board and elicit which vowel combinations make the sound.

7.3 **C** Write the word *plane* on the board and underline the letter *a*. Play the recording and repeat the word.

/eɪ/ *plane*

Ask students to circle the words in Exercise A that have the same vowel sound. Again, add the answers to the board and elicit which vowel combinations make the sound.

D In pairs, students practice saying the transportation words. Students listen to each other and help to correct as required. Monitor and assist as appropriate.

READING

A Go through the task with students, highlighting that they should not answer the questions at this point. Then give students one minute to skim the text and answer the question. Check answer as a class.

B Ask students to cover the answers at the bottom of page 62. Students then read the quiz and decide where each picture shows. Give students time to compare and discuss answers in small groups. If students need help, they can search online to find out which country each city is in.

This could be turned into a team quiz, with points given for correct answers.

C Give students up to three minutes to do this task. Students scan the quick facts and match them with the pictures. Before starting, highlight that students should look for key words (in this case, the transportation type and the place name) in order to match quickly. Check answers as a class.

D Give students up to five minutes to read the six facts again in more detail and answer the questions. They should provide short answers. Students compare answers with a partner, reviewing the text if necessary. Then check answers as a class.

E In pairs, students discuss the question. If you have time, put students into different pairs to repeat the activity, and also explain what their first partner said.

TEACHING IDEA by David Seymour and Maria Popova

Vocabulary: Personal time

Use this activity to review the vocabulary section. Say this to your students:

In pairs, ask and answer questions about these things. (If students have children, they can talk about them instead.)

the day you were born, the time of day you were born, the month you were born, the season you were born, the year you were born, the decade you were born

In pairs, ask and answer questions using this table. Carry out a survey of the rest of the class. Choose one of these subjects and find out how long each student spends doing it each day. Make a list, with those who spend the most time at the top and those who spend the least at the bottom.

watching TV, sleeping, eating, sitting on public transportation, exercising, talking on the phone, cooking, walking, relaxing, reading, drinking tea or coffee, studying, using a computer

Report some of your results to the class. (Elicit the extremes.)

METHODOLOGY HUB by Jim Scrivener

Phonemes

Simple variations on well known games are helpful in familiarizing students with phonemic symbols:

- **Phoneme bingo:** Hand out bingo cards with phonemes instead of numbers; call out sounds rather than numbers (see the *Phoneme bingo cards* resource on the DVD).
- **Anagrams:** Get students to work out anagrams of words using phonemes rather than normal alphabetic letters, e.g. /**kbʊ**/ (= *book*).
- **Category words:** Choose five or six categories – such as 'Food', 'Sports', 'Animals', 'Household objects', 'Clothing', etc – which students should copy down. Students work in small teams. When you call out (and write up) a phoneme, the teams must attempt to find a word containing that phoneme for each category. So, for example, if the phoneme is /iː/, a team could choose *cheese, skiing, sheep, teapot* and *jeans*. The teams then compare words and points are awarded.

7.1 Getting around

GRAMMAR

A Go through the task with students. If possible during feedback, display *Six quick facts* to the whole class and show where *could* and *couldn't* appear.

B Students work alone to complete the rules. Check answers as a class.

C Direct students to the **Grammar Hub** (see below). Read the examples and go through the rules with the class.

D Go through the task and example answers with students. Then provide model answers about yourself and your experience. Students then tell their partners things they *could* or *couldn't* do five or ten years ago. Monitor and encourage students to give as much information as possible and to use past time expressions. Make a note of successful examples of use of the target grammar and also of phrases which need reformulating. For whole-class feedback, use these as the basis for whole-class error correction. Use the **Grammar Worksheet** on W35 for extra practice.

SPEAKING

A Ask students if they use public transportation a lot in their town or city. Ask them if they like using it, or have any problems with it. Then, ask them to think of a city they know well. It shouldn't be the one they are currently in. Point out that it doesn't need to be a city they have visited. It could be a city they know from movies or TV.

B Students write questions about the transportation, using the prompts. Students could work in pairs at this point and then change partner for the next exercise. Monitor and assist with question formation as required. Check answers as a class, making sure that each student has formed the questions correctly.

C In pairs, students ask and answer questions about transportation about each other's city, and try to guess what city their partner is talking about.

GRAMMAR HUB

7.1 *could*

	Positive	Negative
I/you/he/she/it/we/they	A hundred years ago, **you could see** a lot of trolleys in San Francisco.	**I couldn't get** to work because of the traffic jam.

	Question	Short answers	
I/you/he/she/it/we/they	**Could you run** fast when you were younger?	Yes, **I could**.	No, **I couldn't**.

- We use *could* to talk about general abilities in the past.
- In the negative, we can also say *could not*.

  I couldn't drive. OR *I could not drive.*

Be careful!

He could drive. NOT ~~*He could to drive.*~~ NOT ~~*He could drove.*~~

7.1 *could*

A Use the prompts to write sentences with *could*.

Eighty years ago …

1. ✓ ride / a horse / into town
   You could ride a horse into town.
2. ✗ take / a bullet train / across Japan
   You couldn't take a bullet train across Japan.
3. ✓ find / trolleys / in San Francisco
   You could find trolleys in San Francisco.
4. ✓ see / red double-deckers / in Mumbai
   You could see red double-deckers in Mumbai.
5. ✗ fly / quickly / across Europe
   You couldn't fly quickly across Europe.
6. ✗ be / stuck / in a traffic jam
   You couldn't be stuck in a traffic jam.

B Complete the paragraph using *could* or *couldn't*.

Two hundred years ago you [1] couldn't travel around London on public transportation because … there wasn't any! In 1800, the city was still fairly small with only about one million people and most people [2] could walk from their home to their place of work. If you wanted to travel farther, you [3] could take a carriage pulled by horses, but only the very rich [4] could have their own private carriage. People [5] could cross the River Thames by taking a boat called a 'wherry'. Londoners [6] couldn't take the subway until 1863 when the first station opened.

➤ Go back to page 63.

GRAMMAR

could

A WORK IT OUT Scan *Six quick facts* again. Underline sentences with *could* or *couldn't*.

B Look at the sentences you underlined in Exercise A and complete the rules.

could
1 We use *could* to talk about abilities in the ***past*** / ***present***.
2 We use *could* ***before*** / ***after*** the main verb.
3 We use the ***infinitive*** / ***base form*** after *could*.
4 The ***negative*** / ***future*** form of *could* is *couldn't*.

C Go to the **Grammar Hub** on **page 134**.

D SPEAK Work in pairs. Tell your partner some things you *could* and *couldn't* do or see five or ten years ago.

A: Five years ago, I couldn't drive a car.

B: Ten years ago, you could see a lot of bicycles in my town.

SPEAKING

A PREPARE Think about the transportation in a city you know well.

B Write some questions to ask your partner about the transportation in their city. Use the ideas below to help you.

1 what / color / buses? *What color are the buses?*
2 is / river? Is there a river?
3 is / ferry? Is there a ferry?
4 where / ferry / go / between? Where does the ferry go between?
5 how many / train stations? How many train stations are there?
6 are / many / traffic jams? Are there many traffic jams?
7 bicycles / popular? Are bicycles popular?

C SPEAK Work in pairs. Ask questions and guess your partner's city. Then answer questions about your city.

A: What color are the taxis?
B: They're yellow.
A: Is there a ferry?
B: Yes, there is.
A: Where does the ferry go between?
B: The main ferry goes between Queens and Manhattan.

Six quick facts

a 3 Scooters and motorcycles are the most common type of transportation in Hanoi, Vietnam. There are also lots of bicycles. Twenty years ago, you couldn't see so many scooters and motorcycles on Hanoi's streets, but you could see a lot of bicycles. Ex D Q6

b 6 Every day, 250,000 people go through Amsterdam Central Station. It's the city's main train and bus station. Ex D Q4

c 5 The famous Star Ferry in Hong Kong carries over 70,000 passengers a day between Hong Kong Island and Kowloon. That's 26 million passengers a year! Ex D Q5

d 1 No, this isn't London – it's Mumbai! These Indian buses are 80 years old. The design and color is the same as London buses. Ex D Q1

e 2 Take a trolley in San Francisco for a traditional experience. But there aren't many these days. One hundred years ago, you could see hundreds of trolleys in San Francisco. Today, there are only about 40. Ex D Q2

f 4 Opened in 1935, there are now 206 subway stations in Moscow. Many of the stations are very beautiful. Each one is like an art gallery. Ex D Q3

Talk about transportation in a city

7.2 A love of adventure

Talk about a journey

G– simple past negative V– travel phrases P– word stress: cities

READING

A Work in pairs. Look at the routes around the world. Which route would you take? Why?

B **READ FOR GIST** Read *The Nellie Bly route*. Which route in Exercise A matches the one Nellie Bly took? Route 2

TRADITIONAL TRAVEL ADVENTURES

We travel the traditional way: by boat, train and bus.

Route 1: London, Reykjavík, St. Petersburg, Tokyo, Sydney, Cape Town, Rio de Janeiro

Route 2: New York, London, Paris, Brindisi, Port Said, Singapore, Hong Kong, Tokyo, San Francisco

Route 3: Miami, Cancún, Lima, Melbourne, Nairobi, Munich

SPECIAL OFFER!
This week, choose our Nellie Bly Adventure and get 30 percent off your vacation.

THE NELLIE BLY ROUTE

Ex C b In 1872, Jules Verne wrote about Phileas Fogg, an adventurer who traveled around the world in 80 days. But Fogg wasn't a real person, and nobody knew if this was actually possible.

In 1889, Nellie Bly, a 25-year-old American journalist, followed Phileas
Ex C d Fogg's route around the world. She went alone. She didn't take much luggage. She just took a large coat and a small suitcase. Her newspaper, the *New York World*, paid for her trip and told her story.

But a magazine, *Cosmopolitan*, sent their journalist, Elizabeth Bisland, to race against Nellie. Bisland left New York on the same day, but Nellie didn't know about it!

Car and plane travel didn't exist at the time, so Nellie traveled by bus, train and ship. She had many adventures, just like Phileas Fogg, and she sent her stories back home from every place.

Ex D Q1 Nellie crossed the Atlantic to London by ship. From there she traveled
Ex D Q2 by train and ferry to northern France, where she met Jules Verne. She
then continued by train to Brindisi, in Italy, where she took a ship to
Ex C a Egypt. She visited Port Said, in Egypt, where she rode on a donkey. Her
ship then went to Singapore (where she bought a monkey), Hong Kong Ex C c
Ex D Q3 and Tokyo. Finally, the ship crossed the Pacific Ocean to San Francisco, Ex D Q4
where she took the train to New York. This took four days. She arrived
Ex C e in New York 72 days after her journey began. It was a new world
record! Her story was in the newspapers.

And Elizabeth Bisland? She didn't join the celebrations. She missed her boat and returned to New York four days later.

Glossary

adventurer (n) someone who goes to exciting, unusual and sometimes dangerous places

route (n) a way that buses, trains, ships or planes travel regularly

7.2 A love of adventure

LEAD-IN

Display a map of the world on the board. Mark places that you have visited and talk about them using the simple past (e.g. *I visited Russia two years ago.*). You could also talk about places you regularly visit using the simple present (e.g. *I go to the UK every summer.*). Invite students to come to the board to mark places relevant to them. When students are all seated again, point to the places and elicit where it is and who went (or goes) there.

READING

A Focus students on the map at the top of page 64. Ask what the lines show, and elicit the word *routes* (the road or path you take to get from one place to another). You could also ask what countries the routes cross or stop in.

Focus students on Routes 1–3 at the top of the article. Ask students which route they would take, and why. Put them into pairs to read the routes and discuss the question. Encourage students to ask follow-up questions to extend the discussion.

For whole-class feedback, ask students for the main ideas from their discussion. Finish the exercise by saying which route you would take and why.

B Focus students on the photo of the woman. Tell them that her name was Nellie Bly. Ask students to predict who she was and when she lived. You could point out that she was a *journalist* and *adventurer* (someone who goes to exciting, unusual and sometimes dangerous places), who lived over 100 years ago. Ask students how people could travel around the world in Nellie Bly's time.

Give two minutes for students to quickly read *The Nellie Bly Route* to find out which route (1–3) she took. Check answer as a class.

Extra activity
Put students into pairs. Ask them to label the countries marked on the three routes on the map. Give feedback as a class, encouraging students to explain which countries they've visited using the simple past. Then ask which of the three routes they would most like to take and why.

TEACHING IDEA by David Seymour and Maria Popova

Vocabulary: Flying words

Use this activity to review the vocabulary section on page 65. Say this to your students:

In small groups, brainstorm words and phrases under these three headings: 1) *Before takeoff*, e.g. *check-in*. 2) *During the flight*, e.g. *in-flight entertainment*. 3) *After landing*, e.g. *baggage claim*.

Using as many of the words as you can, tell each other about your last flight, and ask each other questions, e.g. *A – Did you watch the movie? B – No. I'm always asleep when the movie is shown.*

TEACHING IDEA by David Seymour and Maria Popova

Grammar: Reactions

Use this activity to review the simple past. Say this to your students:

I'm going to dictate six pairs of short sentences. Write them down, leaving a space after each pair.

1 She reads the letter. She throws it in the trash can.
2 The shark appears. They panic.
3 He looks in the cupboard. He sees a mouse.
4 The mouse sees him. It runs away.
5 The bell rings. They run out into the playground.
6 They try my curry. Everyone starts choking.

Join each pair of sentences to make one sentence in the past, beginning with when, e.g. *When she heard the baby cry, she went to feed him.*

On your own, write a few pairs of sentences about things you have done in the last few days. Write at least one negative sentence. Swap your pairs of sentences with a partner. Join the ones you receive in the same way and pass them back.

METHODOLOGY HUB by Jim Scrivener

Top-down reading

As with listening lessons, many reading lessons move from 'big' to 'small', i.e. 'top-down' – from overview to details. Here are some specific ideas for reading tasks

- Put these illustrations of the text in the correct order.
- Put these cut-up paragraphs in the correct order.
- Find words in the text that mean the same as the words in this list.
- Read the text and find the mistakes in this illustration (or draw your own).
- Read the text and make a list of particular items (e.g. jobs that need doing, the author's proposals, advantages and disadvantages, etc).
- Give a headline to each section of the article (or match given headlines with the sections).
- Find appropriate places in the text to reinsert some sentences that have previously been separated from the text.
- Write a reply.
- Look at the title and the illustrations (but not the text). Predict which of the following list of words you will find in the text.
- Solve the problem.
- Discuss (or write) the missing last paragraph of the text.
- Discuss interpretations of, reactions to, feelings about the text.
- Write notes under the following headings: …
- Before you read this text, write notes about what you already know about the subject.
- Act out the dialogue, story, episode, etc.
- Put this list of events in the correct order.

C Give students up to three minutes to read the article again and number the pictures in the order they are written about. Check answers as a class.

D Give students a longer time limit of up to five minutes to complete the exercise alone. Then, ask them to check their answers in pairs before giving feedback as a class.

E Students discuss the questions in pairs. For whole-class feedback, ask students to share their opinions.

GRAMMAR

A Point out that there are two words missing from each sentence. Tell students to find the missing information in the article. Check answers as a class.

B Students use the sentences in Exercise A to help them complete the rule. Give feedback as a class.

C Direct students to the **Grammar Hub** (see below). Read the examples and go through the rules with the class.

D In pairs, students ask and answer the questions. For whole-class feedback, ask students to say which forms of transportation were most popular. Use the **Grammar Worksheet** on W35 for extra practice.

VOCABULARY

A In pairs, students match the verbs to the definitions. Point out the syllable stress in *arrive* and *return* when checking answers as a class.

B Direct students to the **Vocabulary Hub** on page 149. Give students time to complete the exercise alone before checking answers in pairs. Use the **Vocabulary Worksheet** on W36 for extra practice.

PRONUNCIATION

7.4 **A** Play the recording for students to listen and repeat the names of the cities. Point out that they should pay attention to the word stress. Explain that these are how the cities are pronounced in English, although they might have different pronunciations in other languages. Remind students, if necessary, that words with more than one syllable in English have the main stress on one syllable, with the other syllables being shorter and with less clear vowel sounds.

Ankara; Berlin; Cairo; Dubai; London; Miami; Nairobi; Paris; Reykjavik; Singapore; Tokyo

7.5 **B** In pairs, students add the cities to the table. Before starting, focus students on the two examples, highlighting how the circle patterns relate to the stress of each word. After students have completed the table, play the recording for them to check their answers. Play it again for students to repeat the words.

SPEAKING

Direct students to the **Communication Hub**. Put students into pairs and explain the game. Students will need dice and something to use as counters. If you don't have dice, students could use their phones to search for virtual dice online. Each student starts on the *START* square and takes turns rolling the dice, moving to another square. The square either contains an instruction or a sentence which students have to change using simple past verbs.

As an example, write *I (go) to China last year*. Elicit that the verb should be changed to *went*.

As students play the game, monitor and help them and confirm their answers. The winner is the student who reaches the *FINISH* square first.

GRAMMAR HUB

7.2 Simple past negative

	didn't + base form
I/you/he/she/it/we/they	**We didn't take** the trolley.

- We use the simple past negative to talk about things that did not happen in the past.
- We can also say *did not*.

*We **didn't** take the trolley. OR We **did not** take the trolley.*

Be careful!

We didn't wait at the traffic lights. NOT ~~*We didn't waited at the traffic lights.*~~

7.2 Simple past negative

A Complete the sentences with the simple past form of the verbs in parentheses. Use contractions.

1 It's OK. They *didn't miss* (not miss) their flight.
2 I didn't arrive (not arrive) home until midnight last night.
3 He didn't like (not like) the food on the plane.
4 We didn't take (not take) the train because it was very expensive.
5 Sarah didn't feel (not feel) well on the ship.
6 The children didn't enjoy (not enjoy) the journey. They were so bored!

B Complete the sentences with the negative form of the verbs in the box.

meet pay take travel ~~read~~ write

1 We *didn't read* *Journey to the Center of the Earth* at school.
2 Jules Verne didn't write about a real person.
3 Nellie Bly didn't travel to India.
4 She didn't take a lot of luggage with her.
5 She didn't pay for the trip. The *New York World* paid.
6 Nellie didn't meet Elizabeth Bisland on her journey.

➤ Go back to page 65.

C READ FOR DETAIL Read the article again. Number the pictures in the order they are written about.

a 3

b 1

c 4

d 2

e 5

D READ FOR SPECIFIC INFORMATION Read the article again. Write down how Nellie traveled at each stage.

1 New York to London by ship
2 London to France by train and ferry
3 Tokyo to San Francisco by ship
4 San Francisco to New York by train

E SPEAK Work in pairs. Answer the questions.

1 Do you know any of the places Nellie visited?
2 Do you know about any other famous journeys?

GRAMMAR

Simple past negative

A WORK IT OUT Complete the sentences with words from the text.

1 She didn't take much luggage.
2 Nellie didn't know about it.
3 Car and plane travel didn't exist at the time.
4 She didn't join the celebrations.

B Read the sentences in Exercise A. Choose the correct options to complete the rule.

Simple past negative

To make the simple past negative we use *did* / *didn't* + *infinitive* / *base form*.

C Go to the **Grammar Hub** on **page 134**.

D SPEAK Work in pairs. Which forms of transportation did you use last year? Which didn't you use?

VOCABULARY

Travel phrases

A Complete the definitions with the words in the box.

arrive leave miss return take

1 miss (v) to be too late for a train, bus
2 take (v) to use a particular type of transportation
3 return (v) to go somewhere and come back
4 leave (v) to go away from a place
5 arrive (v) to get to a place

B Go to the **Vocabulary Hub** on **page 149**.

PRONUNCIATION

Word stress: cities

7.4 **A** Listen and repeat the cities. Copy the word stress.

7.5 **B** Work in pairs. Add the cities in the box to the table. Then listen, check and repeat.

~~Ankara~~ Berlin ~~Cairo~~ Dubai London Miami Nairobi Paris Reykjavík Singapore Tokyo

Oo	oO	Ooo	oOo
Cairo	Berlin	Ankara	Miami
London	Dubai	Reykjavík	Nairobi
Paris		Singapore	
		Tokyo	

SPEAKING

SPEAK Work in pairs. Go to the **Communication Hub** on **page 155**.

Talk about a journey

7.3 A trip to remember

Talk about a vacation

G simple past questions **P** connected speech **V** verb phrases **S** guessing the meaning of unknown words

LISTENING

A Work in pairs. Look at the pictures. What country do you think it is? Why?

7.6 **B LISTEN FOR GIST** Listen to Emma talking to a colleague about a trip. What was unusual about it?

Emma used a 'mystery vacation' company. She didn't know anything about the trip before she arrived at the airport.

7.6 **C LISTEN FOR DETAIL** Listen to the conversation again. Check (✓) the things Emma did.

1 She decided to go to China. ☐
2 She went to Beijing. ✓
3 She saw pandas. ✓
4 She went sightseeing. ✓
5 She stayed with friends. ☐
6 She visited the Great Wall. ✓

7.7 **D** Listen to part of the conversation from Exercise B. Choose the correct meaning of the words. Use the information in the box to help you.

Guessing the meaning of unknown words

- When you don't know a word, listen for other words that you do know to help you understand.
- Think about: *What is the main idea? What is before and after the word that I don't understand?*

1 budget
  a the amount of money a person has (circled)
  b the amount of time a person has
2 destination
  a the place where someone is going (circled)
  b the place where someone is
3 surprise
  a something that we don't know about (circled)
  b something that we do know about

E SPEAK Work in pairs. Would you like to go on a mystery vacation? Why/Why not?

GRAMMAR

Simple past questions

A WORK IT OUT Look at the simple past questions from the conversation. Then choose the correct words to complete the rules.

Where did you go?

Did you visit the Great Wall?

Did you know the vacation was in China?

Simple past questions

1 To make *Yes/No* questions in the simple past we use ***do / did*** + subject + ***infinitive / base form***.
2 To make *Wh-* questions in the simple past we use question word + ***do / did*** + subject + ***infinitive / base form***.

B Go to the **Grammar Hub** on **page 134**.

C PRACTICE Reorder the words to write simple past questions.

1 to / Emma / China / did / fly / ?
Did Emma fly to China? Yes, she did.
2 a lot of / visit / she / cities / did / ?
Did she visit a lot of cities? Yes, she did.
3 she / on / boat / a / sleep / did / ?
Did she sleep on a boat? No, she didn't.
4 do / she / did / Beijing / what / in / ?
What did she do in Beijing? She went sightseeing.
5 go on / mystery / vacation / a / did / she / why / ?
Why did she go on a mystery vacation? She wanted (to have) an adventure.

D SPEAK Work in pairs. Ask and answer the questions in Exercise C.

7.3 A trip to remember

LEAD-IN

Show pictures from a vacation you went on. Ask students to guess where you went and encourage them to explain their reasoning. Next, elicit what they can see in each picture before explaining what you did using simple past sentences. Try to give as much detail as possible (e.g. who you went with, how much things cost, etc). Next, put students into pairs to discuss their own vacations.

LISTENING

A Students discuss the questions in pairs. Monitor and assist as required.

7.6 **B** Play the recording. Give students time to check their answers in pairs before giving feedback as a class.

7.6 **C** Give students time to read through the sentences. Then play the recording again for students to apply a check mark to the answers. Check answers as a class.

7.7 **D** Read through the box together before playing the recording. Give feedback as a class, making sure that students know the correct pronunciation of *budget* /ˈbʌdʒɪt/.

E In pairs or small groups, students discuss the questions.

GRAMMAR

A Focus students on the simple past questions from the conversation.

B Direct students to the **Grammar Hub** (see below and TB67). Read the examples and go through the rules with the class.

C Focus students on the example.

D In pairs, students ask and answer the questions. Use the **Grammar Worksheet** on W37 for extra practice.

AUDIO SCRIPT

7.6

Listening, Exercise B
C = Colleague E = Emma

C: Hi, Emma. Did you have a good vacation?
E: Yeah! It was amazing, thank you!
C: Where did you go?
E: To China.
C: China? Wow! That's interesting. What did you do? Did you visit the Great Wall?
Ex C Q6 **E:** Yes, I did. It was … well, great! Do you want to see some photos?
C: Sure … So, why did you choose China?
Ex B **E:** Well, I didn't choose it, actually. I went on a 'mystery vacation'.
C: What do you mean, a 'mystery vacation'?
E: I used a company that organizes your vacation for you. But they don't tell you anything about it until you get to the airport.
C: Huh? So how did it work?
E: I told them about my interests, how long I wanted to
Ex D Q1 go for, and my budget – I said I could spend about $1500 – then they chose the hotels and activities … and basically created a vacation for me.
Ex D Q2 **C:** So, did you know your destination? Did you know the vacation was in China?
Ex D Q3 **E:** No, I didn't. I didn't know anything except the date and the airport. When I arrived at the check-in desk, I got a letter with the details. I found out that I was
Ex C Q2; Ex D Q3 on a flight to Beijing. It was a complete surprise!
C: That's so cool! Was it cheap?
E: No, it wasn't. It was very expensive, actually. But they organized the flights, hotels, transportation, entertainment – they did everything!
C: So where did you stay?
E: In hotels, but I also stayed with a Chinese family in Shanghai. And I slept on a train, too – the overnight train to Shanghai.
C: Did the company organize that?
E: Yes, but I didn't know anything about it before. When I was in Beijing, I got an email about my next destination. Then in Shanghai, I got another email, and so on.
C: What else did you do?
Ex C Q4 **E:** I went sightseeing in Beijing, went on a boat trip on a river and climbed mountains in the forest.
C: Did you see any pandas?
Ex C Q3 **E:** Yes, I did. Hold on … Here's some pandas that I went to see in Chengdu.
C: Wow. I love pandas! You did so much. But why did you decide to do a mystery vacation?
E: Well, I wanted an adventure. Every day was a surprise and different. It felt new and exciting. And I didn't have to organize a thing!
C: It sounds great! I want to try a mystery vacation, too!

GRAMMAR HUB

7.3 Simple past questions

	Question	Short answers	
I/you/he/she/it/we/they	**Did they travel** to Beijing last year?	Yes, **they did**.	No, **they didn't**.

- We use simple past questions to ask about things that happened in the past.
- We can use question words with the simple past. These come before *did*.

Where did they go?
When did she leave?

- The verb *be* forms questions in a different way to other verbs.

Was it expensive? NOT ~~Did it be expensive?~~

See **the Grammar Hub 6.2** on **page 132** for more information.

7.3 A trip to remember

PRONUNCIATION

7.8 **A** Play the recording. Give feedback, confirming that in natural English, words usually link together. In the examples, this is shown by the (‿) symbol between words.

7.9 **B** Play the recording and give students time to mark the connected speech. Give feedback as a class, practicing natural pronunciation.

VOCABULARY

A In pairs, students discuss their ideas for a great vacation.

B Students complete the exercise alone. Give feedback as a class.

C Students complete the phrases with the verbs in the box.

D Direct students to the **Communication Hub** for further practice. Use the **Vocabulary Worksheet** on W38 for extra practice.

SPEAKING HUB

A Students work individually to write notes on a vacation where something unusual or funny happened.

B Elicit the four questions from the prompts and ask students to think of other questions they could ask.

C In groups, students talk about their partner's vacation.

TEACHING IDEA by David Seymour and Maria Popova

Vocabulary: Things to do

Use this activity to review the vocabulary section. Say this to your students:

In groups, brainstorm different kinds of activity-related vacations, e.g. *skiing*. (Write each vacation on the board as it is mentioned.) Take turns telling the class which kinds of vacations you have been on, and answer a few questions about each one.

Copy the vacations down in the order you would like to experience them, from most to least favorite. Compare your list with a partner. Work in pairs. Imagine you are going on vacation to India, where you will take part in a number of activities. (Elicit activities like these and write them on the board.)

mountain hiking, sightseeing, sunbathing, watching cricket, canoeing, nightlife, elephant riding in the jungle, guided tour of Bollywood, yoga

Write two lists: things you need to do before you go and things you need to take with you. Swap lists with another pair and see how many things they missed.

METHODOLOGY HUB by Jim Scrivener

Fluency, accuracy and communication

Imagine a switch inside your head – it swings between two settings: 'working mainly on accuracy' and 'working mainly on fluency'.

It's probably a huge simplification, but I suspect that something like this is at work in my head through most of my language teaching, changing its setting from activity to activity, stage to stage – and, in some teaching, changing minute by minute in response to things happening in class. And I think initially getting that switch installed and working may be a key skill for anyone learning to be a language teacher.

Certainly there are activities in which you are arguably working on both accuracy and fluency in relatively equal measure, but many everyday language teaching lesson stages are focused on one more than the other, and at any one moment, in any one activity, it is likely you will be aiming to focus on accuracy rather than fluency, or fluency rather than accuracy. The danger of correcting students in the middle of a mainly fluency task is that you interrupt their flow and take the focus off their message. Students usually find it hard to continue after a correction, while others in class may become more reluctant to speak for fear of similar interruptions.

GRAMMAR HUB

7.3 Simple past questions

A Use the prompts to write questions and short answers.

1 they / go / with their friends
Did they go with their friends? (?)
Yes, they did. (+)

2 you / visit / a lot of cities
Did you visit a lot of cities? (?)
No, I/we didn't. (-)

3 she / meet / many people
Did she meet many people? (?)
Yes, she did. (+)

4 your company / pay / for the flight
Did your company pay for the flight? (?)
Yes, it/they did. (+)

5 they / visit / the Eiffel Tower
Did they visit the Eiffel tower? (?)
No, they didn't. (-)

6 you / sleep / on the plane
Did you sleep on the plane? (?)
No, I/we didn't. (-)

B Complete the questions with *you* and a verb from the box.

eat get go ~~have~~ stay swim travel visit

1 *Did you have* a good vacation?
2 Where did you go on vacation this year?
3 How did you get there? By plane?
4 Did you visit any interesting museums?
5 Did you eat any local food?
6 Did you swim in the ocean?
7 How long did you stay for?
8 Did you travel by bus or train?

➤ Go back to page 66.

PRONUNCIATION
Connected speech

7.8 **A** Listen to the sentences. What do you notice about them?

1 Where did‿you go?
2 She went to‿a temple.
3 Did she stay‿in‿a hotel?

When spoken, the words *did you* are linked. There are no breaks between the words *did* and *you*.

7.9 **B** Listen and repeat the sentences. Mark the links between the words.

1 Did‿Emma see‿a panda?
2 Did she stay with‿a family?
3 She visited‿a lot‿of cities.
4 Did she have‿a good time?

VOCABULARY
Verb phrases

A SPEAK Work in pairs. What do you think makes a great vacation?

B READ Read the three travel stories. Answer the questions.

1 What did TravelBob do every day in Ibiza?
He swam in the ocean.
2 What happened to Kate956 one evening in New York?
She got lost.
3 Where did LisaChorley lose her camera?
She lost her camera in Bangkok.

Kate956
January 7, 1:36

Last year, my husband and I went to New York. We **visited museums** and we **went shopping**. But New York is really big, and one night we **got lost**. After an hour, we were tired, so we stopped at a nice, small restaurant. We **ate some delicious food**, and then got a taxi back to our hotel!

LisaChorley
January 7, 1:41

Three years ago, I went to Thailand. I traveled around for two months, and I **met some really nice people**. In Bangkok, I went sightseeing and **took a lot of pictures**. But I **lost my camera**! I was really sad, but two days later a man brought it back. He saw a picture of me and my hotel!

C READ Read the comments again. Use the words in the box to create verb phrases.

eat get go have lose
meet read swim take visit

1 swim in the ocean
2 go shopping
3 visit museums
4 take pictures
5 meet people
6 read a book
7 get lost
8 eat food
9 have a good time
10 lose your camera

D SPEAK Work in pairs. Go to the Communication Hub on page 155.

SPEAKING HUB

A PREPARE Think of a vacation you went on where something unusual or funny happened. Write notes about the vacation using the ideas below.

- accommodations
- people
- place
- the ending
- the problem or a funny situation
- transportation

B DISCUSS Work in pairs. Ask and answer questions about your vacations using the prompts.

1 Where / go?
2 How / travel / there?
3 Where / stay?
4 What / happen?

Where did you go?

I went to Moscow.

C DISCUSS Work in groups. Tell your group about your partner's vacation. Take a group vote on the most unusual or funny vacation.

TravelBob
January 7, 1:25

One spring, I went to Ibiza with my family. The hotel was really nice, and we **swam in the ocean** every day. But on the last day of our vacation, we lost our passports and we couldn't fly home! We stayed for ten more days. We didn't have any money, but we **read a lot of books**! We **had a great time**.

Talk about a vacation

Café Hub

7.4 New York

F – check in and out of a hotel   P – intonation in questions

COMPREHENSION

A ▶ 00:00–00:42 **Work in pairs. Watch the first part of the video. Answer the questions.**

1 Where did Sam and Zac meet? In New York

2 What did Zac hate? His job in the hotel

3 Why do you think he hated it? **Suggested answer:** Because he's not good at it and makes a lot of mistakes.

B ▶ 00:42–04:38 **Watch the second part of the video. Look at the hotel manager's checklist. Check (✓) the things Zac does. Put an ✗ on the things Zac doesn't do.**

NEW HOTEL RECEPTIONIST

1. Greet guests correctly. ✗
2. Check guests' identity. ✗
3. Give correct information: breakfast time/price. ✗
4. Offer to help with bags. ✗
5. Check guests' room number and print out the bill. ✗

USEFUL PHRASES

A ▶ **Complete the useful phrases with the words in the box. Then watch the video again and check your answers.**

can it look mean new nice things what

1 Hey guys. How are ___things___?

2 Hi! How's ___it___ going?

3 I ___mean___, good afternoon, sir!

4 I'm so sorry, sir. He's ___new___.

5 So, ___what___ happened next?

6 OK, ___look___ – it's fine!

7 You ___can___ call me Sam.

8 Have a ___nice___ day!

B How do you say these useful phrases in your language?

FUNCTIONAL LANGUAGE

Checking in and out of a hotel

SPEAK **Work in pairs. Practice the conversation. Change the words and phrases in bold. Use the words in the box to help you. Change numbers, times and prices, too.**

dinner double evening ID card ma'am would you like

Receptionist: Good **afternoon, sir**. How can I help you?
Guest: I have a reservation for a **single** room for **two** nights.
Receptionist: Could I have your **passport**, please?
Guest: No problem. Is **breakfast** included?
Receptionist: No, it isn't. Sorry. **Breakfast** is an extra **$14**.
Guest: What time is **breakfast**?
Receptionist: **Breakfast** is served from **7** till **11 am**.
Receptionist: **Do you need** help with your bags?
Guest: Great. Thanks.
Guest: Can I have my bill please?
Receptionist: Certainly, **Mr. King**. Which room was it?
Guest: Room **305**.

Suggested answer:
Receptionist: Good morning, ma'am. How can I help you?
Guest: I have a reservation for a double room for three nights.
Receptionist: Could I have your ID card, please?
Guest: No problem. Is dinner included?
Receptionist: No, it isn't. Sorry. Dinner is an extra $40.
Guest: What time is dinner?
Receptionist: Dinner is served from 6 pm till 9:30 pm.
Receptionist: Would you like help with your bags?
Guest: Great. Thanks.
Guest: Can I have my bill please?
Receptionist: Certainly, ma'am. Which room was it?
Guest: Room 201.

MILLY SAM NEENA ZAC GABY

PRONUNCIATION

Intonation in questions

7.10 **A** Listen and repeat the questions. Does the intonation go up or down at the end? Draw ↑ if the intonation goes up. Draw ↓ if the intonation goes down.

1 How can I help you? ↓
2 What's your name, please? ↓
3 Could I have your passport, please? ↑
4 Is breakfast included? ↑
5 What time is breakfast? ↓
6 Do you need help with your bags? ↑

7.10 **B** Listen again. Underline the words and syllables that are stressed in Exercise A.

C SPEAK Work in pairs. Practice asking the questions in Exercise A. Remember to use the correct stress and intonation.

SPEAKING

A PREPARE Work in pairs. Write a hotel check-in conversation. Use the information below. Use some of the phrases in Functional Language.

Guest

Ask about:

- Reservation for two adults and two children
- Wi-fi
- TV
- Cost of breakfast for you and children
- Restaurant opening times
- Check-out time

Receptionist

Give information about:

- Family room with one double and two single beds
- Free wi-fi 24/7
- All rooms have a TV
- Free breakfast for children
- Breakfast: $8.99 / 7 am to 11 am
- Dinner: $24.99 / 5 pm to 11 pm
- Check-out: noon

B PRESENT Practice your conversation. Perform it for the rest of the class.

Check in and out of a hotel

➤ Turn to page 166 to learn how to write a short article about a travel experience.

7.4 New York

LEAD-IN

Write *New York* on the board and ask the class what they know about the city (not the state). If anyone has visited the city, invite them to share their experiences with the class. Ask who would like to visit and why (or why not).

COMPREHENSION

A ▶ 00:00-00:42 Go through the questions with students. Then play the first part of the video for students to answer the questions. Check answers as a class.

B ▶ 00:42-04:38 Focus students on the checklist, checking understanding of the items. Then play the rest of the video. Students put a check mark or an X on the items on the list.

USEFUL PHRASES

A ▶ Students complete the useful phrases and compare their answers in pairs. Play the video again for students to check.

B If you have a monolingual class, allow time for students to discuss together how to say the phrases in their own language. If you have a multilingual class, give students time to record the phrases individually in their own languages.

FUNCTIONAL LANGUAGE

Students practice the conversation in pairs. Encourage students to look up when saying the conversation, rather than just reading from the page. Put students into different pairs. Students then replace the words in bold with those in the box and practice again. At the end, invite pairs to perform the conversation to the whole class. Make a note of any useful, topic specific emergent vocabulary to teach after each conversation has finished.

PRONUNCIATION

7.10 **A** Focus students on the questions. Then play the recording, pausing after each question. Students decide if the intonation goes up or down at the end of the question. Check answers as a class, and play the recording again if required. Explain/confirm that we usually use a falling intonation for *Wh-* questions and a rising intonation for yes/no questions.

7.10 **B** Write the first question from Exercise A on the board. Mark the intonation and then say the question or play the recording for it. Ask students which words and syllables are stressed and underline them. Play the rest of the recording for students to underline the stressed words and syllables.

C Students practice asking the questions, helping each other to pronounce them correctly.

SPEAKING

A In pairs, students write a conversation set at a hotel front desk. Go through the information they should include in the conversation and the two characters: the guest and the receptionist. Monitor, encouraging students to think about their stress and intonation when asking questions.

B Give students time to practice their conversations in pairs. They could record and review the conversations on their phones. Pairs then perform their conversations in front of the rest of the class.

Extra activity

Choose a pair to perform their role play again. Before they start, take one student aside and tell them to act in a certain way (e.g. you have a bad cold, you're very angry, you're a famous person, etc). Then, ask the pair to perform the conversation again and have the class guess what you told the first student. Repeat with other pairs, ideally reviewing vocabulary (e.g. personality adjectives) from previous units.

▶ VIDEO SCRIPT

S = Sam G = Gaby Z = Zac M = Manager

S: Hey guys. How are things?
G: Great! I just booked a trip to New York.
S: Amazing! I love New York! Did you know I met Zac in New York?
G: No, I didn't!
Z: It's true. I worked in a hotel downtown. I hated it.
S: Yeah, I remember. When I arrived in New York … I took a taxi from the airport and went to the Central Inn hotel.
Z: Hi! How's it going? I mean, good afternoon sir! Uh … How can I help you?
S: I have a reservation for a single room for two nights.
Z: Your name, please?
S: It's Sam King.
M: I'm so sorry, sir. He's new. Welcome to New York, Mr. King. Could I have your passport, please? Thank you.
S: No problem. Is breakfast included?
Z: Yes, it is.
M: No, it isn't. Zac, this reservation doesn't include breakfast. It's here on the screen.
Z: Oh, of course. Sorry, sir. Breakfast is an extra 12 dollars.
M: 14 dollars.
S: OK, that's fine. What time is breakfast?
Z: Um … 8 till 12.
M: No, it's not! Zac! Breakfast is served from 7 till 11 am. Your room is on the third floor. Room 305. Do you need help with your bags?
S: Great. Thanks.
Z: I think she hates me.
S: Yeah, I think she does.
Z: I'm not good at this job …
G: So, what happened next?
S: I did some sightseeing. Zac told me where to go, so I visited the Museum of Modern Art, went shopping, took photos from the top of the Empire State Building, ate some lovely food, took the subway, got lost. I had a great time!
Z: Hey, Sam.
M: It's Mr. King. Mr. King, Zac, is a hotel guest.
S: OK, look - it's fine! Can I have my bill please?
Z: Certainly, Mr. King. Which room was it?
S: Room 305. You can call me Sam.
Z: Thanks, Sam. When do you leave?
S: Today. I have a flight home tonight. I have a few hours free until then.
Z: Do you like pizza?
S: Pizza? Zac. I love Pizza.
M: Zac? Get back to work!
Z: I quit!
M: You can't quit now! You finish at 12 pm.
Z: Have a nice day!
M: You're fired!

7 Writing

Write a short article about a travel experience

W *so* and *because*

A Work in pairs. What makes a vacation good or bad?

B Read *Travel spotlight: Tulum*. Which of the things you discussed in Exercise A are mentioned?
beautiful beaches, delicious food, sunny weather

Travel spotlight: TULUM

Ex C Q1 Last month, I traveled to Tulum, in Mexico. It's
Ex C Q2 fairly easy to get there. I flew to Cancún, and then took a bus. I wanted to be near the ocean,
Ex C Q3 so I stayed in a small hotel on the beach. It was really beautiful. For three days, I read books and swam in the clear, blue ocean.

Tulum is a small town, but there are lots of things to do, so it isn't boring! During the day, you can visit historic places near the beach or go kite surfing. You can also visit the Sian Ka'an nature
Ex C Q4 park and see birds, animals and fish. I went on a day trip to Chichen Itza because I like history.

Ex C Q5 At night, you can eat dinner in one of the great restaurants in town, or you can go salsa dancing
Ex C Q6 in a club. The food at the hotel was really good – I ate fresh fish every day!

Tulum is a great place for a nice beach vacation with some interesting places to visit. A return
Ex C Q7 flight to Cancún costs around $500. The best time of year to go to Tulum is between December and April because it's sunny, but not too hot.

C Read again and answer the questions.

1 Where did the writer go? Tulum, Mexico
2 How did she travel there? She flew to Cancún and then took a bus
3 Where did she stay? In a small hotel
4 What did she do during the day? She went to Chichen Itza.
5 What can you do at night? Eat dinner or go salsa dancing
6 What was the food like? Really good
7 When is the best time to visit? Between December and April

D Complete the sentences with *so* or *because*. Use the information in the box to help you.

so and because

- We use *so* to talk about the result of something.
  I wanted to be near the ocean, ***so*** *I stayed in a small hotel on the beach.*
  But there are lots of things to do, ***so*** *it isn't boring!*
- We use *because* to explain the reason for something.
  I went on a day trip to Chichen Itza ***because*** *I like history.*
  The best time of year to go to Tulum is between December and April ***because*** *it's sunny, but not too hot.*

1 The writer flew to Cancún *because* it's near Tulum.
2 She stayed in the hotel because it was on the beach.
3 She is interested in history, so she went to Chichen Itza.
4 She ate fish every day because it was really fresh.
5 It isn't too hot between December and April, so it's the best time of year to go.

WRITING

A PREPARE You are going to write a travel blog about a place that you know. Write notes about the place. Use the questions in Exercise C to help you.

B PLAN Add more information to your notes. Use the travel blog in Exercise B to help you.

C WRITE Write your article. Use *so* and *because*.

166 WRITING

Refer students to this article as a model for the writing task.

Tell students that using words like this allows them to write longer sentences with more ideas.

If students don't have a travel experience to write about, they could invent one.

WRITING

In this writing lesson, students will learn how to write a short travel article, paying attention to how to use *because* and *so* to show reasons and results.

A Choose one of your stronger students and ask them to tell you about an amazing vacation they've had. Elicit what was good about it and write a bulleted list on the board under the heading *Good*. Now write the heading *Bad*. Tell students about a bad vacation that you went on, making a bullet list of issues on the board. Next, put students into pairs to discuss the question. Give feedback as a class, adding interesting/new ideas to your lists on the board.

B Give students up to three minutes to read the travel article and check if it mentions any of their ideas from Exercise A.

C Students read the article again and answer the questions. Students compare answers in pairs before checking as a class.

D Go through the *so* and *because* box with students. Explain that *so* shows what happens next. *Because* explains why something happens. Students then work alone to complete the sentences.

WRITING TASK

A Students think of a place they would like to write about. Ask students to use the questions in Exercise C to help them write notes about the place.

B Focus students on the travel blog and have them add information to their notes. If you have time, students could do some online research to check facts about the place.

C Students write their article, using their notes. Encourage them to use *so* and *because* to describe result and reason. Monitor and assist as required. Students can read each other's travel blogs, and decide where they would like to go.

Unit 7 Review

GRAMMAR

A Choose the correct words to complete the sentences.

1 Ten years ago, you *take could* / *could take* a ferry to the island from here.
2 You can't use the trolley in my town these days, but you *can* / *could* 50 years ago.
3 Before 2010, we *couldn't* / *not could* use the subway in my city.
4 When I had a scooter, I could *got* / *get* to school in 15 minutes.
5 *I could* / *Could I* ride a bicycle when I was six years old. How about you?
6 When we went to Venice, we *couldn't saw* / *couldn't see* any cars.
7 I couldn't *swim* / *swam* until I was ten years old.
8 When I was younger I *could* / *couldn't* run really fast, but I can't now!

B Complete the sentences with negative simple past form of the verbs in parentheses.

1 We *didn't travel* (*travel*) to Thailand.
2 They didn't fly (*fly*) to Osaka.
3 He didn't take (*take*) the bus to Prague.
4 The people weren't (*be*) friendly.
5 She didn't stay (*stay*) in a hotel.
6 I didn't have (*have*) a good time.
7 I didn't have (*have*) time to visit the Statue of Liberty.
8 She wasn't (*be*) on the same flight as me.

C Use the prompts to write simple past questions.

1 you / go on vacation / last year?
Did you go on vacation last year?
2 where / you / go?
Where did you go?
3 how / you / get there?
How did you get there?
4 where / you / stay?
Where did you stay?
5 you / go / with friends?
Did you go with friends?
6 you / do?
What did you do?

D Think about your last vacation. Write short answers to the questions in Exercise C.

E SPEAK Work in pairs. Ask and answer questions about your last vacation.

A: Where did you go?
B: I went to Sweden. Where did you go?

VOCABULARY

A Label the pictures (1–4) with the words in the box.

bus ferry scooter trolley

1 trolley

2 ferry

3 scooter

4 bus

B Choose the correct verbs to complete the text.

We [1]*left* / *missed* New York City early in the morning and [2]*arrived* / *left* in Bogotá five hours later. We [3]*took* / *left* the train to the center. We stayed in Bogotá for two weeks. On the way home, we [4]*missed* / *arrived* the train to the airport, so we [5]*left* / *took* a taxi instead. We then [6]*took* / *returned* a plane to Philadelphia.

C SPEAK Work in pairs. Tell your partner about the type of transportation you take every day. Then talk about the type of transportation you took on your last vacation.

D Complete the phrases with an appropriate verb.

1 g e t lost
2 t a k e pictures
3 m e e t people
4 s w i m in the ocean
5 h a v e a good time
6 v i s i t museums
7 l o s e your camera

FUNCTIONAL LANGUAGE

Complete the conversation with the words in the box.

346 bill (x2) minibar room stay taxi

Fumi: Hello. Can I have my [1] bill, please?
Receptionist: Good morning, sir. Which [2] room was it?
Fumi: Room [3] 346.
Receptionist: Did you have anything from the [4] minibar?
Fumi: No, I didn't have anything.
Receptionist: Here you are. Here's your [5] bill. Did you enjoy your [6] stay?
Fumi: Yes, very much, thank you.
Receptionist: That's good. Do you need a [7] taxi?

A selection of healthy fruits, vegetables and nuts.

Ask students to label the photo if you need time to set up the class.

A selection of healthy fruits, vegetables and nuts.

Virginia Woolf (1882–1941) was a British writer and an important thinker and author in the 20th century. Her first novel was published in 1915, and she went on to write several classic novels and collections of short stories.

The quote argues that in order to do basic tasks effectively, we need to eat well. Without food, we can't do anything properly.

OBJECTIVES

- talk about the food you eat
- talk about the food your family eats
- talk about ingredients and recipes
- order food in a restaurant
- write an online restaurant review

Work with a partner. Discuss the questions.

1 What's your favorite food?
2 Do you prefer eating at home or going to restaurants? Why?
3 Are you good at cooking?

FOOD AND DRINK 71

OBJECTIVES

Read the unit objectives to the class.

UNIT OPENER QUESTIONS

Ask students to look at the picture and describe what they see. Elicit the names of the food items and write them on the board. Ask students which of the fruits and vegetables they like eating and which they eat regularly.

Ask students to read the questions at the bottom of the page. Check that students understand the questions.

Put them into pairs to discuss the three questions. Monitor and help with grammar and vocabulary as required. Encourage students to listen to each other and ask follow-up questions to find out more. For whole-class feedback, ask two or three students to share their opinions with the rest of the class.

WORKSHEETS

Lesson 8.1 I'm hungry!

Food and drink (W39)

Countable and uncountable nouns (W40)

Lesson 8.2 What we eat

Containers (W41)

much, many, a lot of (W42)

Lesson 8.3 Yes, chef!

a/an, the, no article (W42)

Food preparation (W43)

8.1 I'm hungry!

Talk about the food you eat

V – food and drink G – countable and uncountable nouns; *some* and *any* P – plurals

VOCABULARY
Food and drink

A SPEAK Work in pairs. Discuss the questions.

1 What's your favorite food?

2 What food do you have in your fridge at home?

B Go to the **Vocabulary Hub** on **page 150**.

C SPEAK Work in groups. What kind of food is popular in your country?

GRAMMAR
Countable and uncountable nouns

A WORK IT OUT Read the conversation. Look at the nouns in bold. Which nouns are plural? eggs; mushrooms

Waitress: Hi! What can I get you?

Customer: Hey. I'd like two **eggs**, a **tomato** and some **mushrooms**, please.

Waitress: OK. Anything to drink?

Customer: Uh … yes. Some **coffee**, please.

B Complete the rules.

Countable and uncountable nouns

1 We *can* / *can't* count countable nouns (e.g. eggs, tomatoes).

2 We *can* / *can't* count uncountable nouns (e.g. coffee, pasta).

C Complete the table with the words in the box.

apples bread butter a carrot chicken ~~coffee~~ ~~eggs~~ mushrooms an onion an orange hamburgers ~~a tomato~~

Countable singular	Countable plural	Uncountable
a tomato	*eggs*	*coffee*
a carrot	apples	bread
an onion	hamburgers	butter
an orange	mushrooms	chicken

D Go to the **Grammar Hub** on **page 136**.

E SPEAK Work in pairs. Answer the questions.

1 How often do you drink tea or coffee?

2 How much fruit do you eat every day?

3 Are there any foods you didn't like when you were a child?

PRONUNCIATION
Plurals

8.1 **A** Listen and repeat. Do we always pronounce plural nouns the same way? No, we don't. There are three different ways to pronounce plural nouns in English: /s/, /z/ and /ɪz/.

cakes, bananas, oranges

8.2 **B** Listen and complete the table with the words in the box.

apples ~~bananas~~ beans ~~cakes~~ carrots chips eggs mushrooms ~~oranges~~ potatoes hamburgers sandwiches

/s/	/z/	/ɪz/
cakes	*bananas*	*oranges*
carrots	apples	sandwiches
chips	beans	
	eggs	
	hamburgers	
	mushrooms	
	potatoes	

8.2 **C** Listen again and repeat.

8.1 I'm hungry

LEAD-IN

Put students into groups. Ask them to think of a food or drink starting with each letter of the alphabet. When they are unable to think of anymore, allow them to think of the words in their own language and then check how to say these words in English. Award one point for the word thought of in English and half a point for the word in their own language. Write all useful/interesting language on the board, remembering to include the phonemes and practicing the correct pronunciation. Use images to explain the vocabulary if necessary.

VOCABULARY

A Put students into pairs to discuss the questions. Monitor, helping them with any new or challenging language. Give feedback as a class adding any useful/interesting vocabulary to the board. Again, remember to add the phonemes and practice the correct pronunciation. Use images to explain the vocabulary if necessary.

B Direct students to the **Vocabulary Hub**. Give them time to complete the exercise alone before checking answers in pairs. If you have time, you could ask students to test each other in pairs. One student takes turns saying a word, and the other student says the word group it's from (*dairy*, *meat* and *fish*, etc).

C Put students into groups to discuss the question. If possible, put students from different countries in each group. Use the **Vocabulary Worksheet** on W39 for extra practice.

GRAMMAR

A Before starting, clarify what a noun is. Write the following sentence on the board. *I love strawberries! They're delicious.* Elicit what part of speech the following words are: *love* (verb), *strawberries* (noun) and *delicious* (adj.). Elicit other examples in each category, encouraging students to use words they suggest in a sentence. Ask if *strawberries* is singular or plural (plural) and how you can tell (it ends in *ies;* the next sentence starts with *They're*). Next, give students time to read through the conversation and identify the plural nouns. Check answers as a class.

B Students complete the rules and compare answers in pairs, before checking as a class.

C Focus students on the examples in the table. Give them time to add the words to the correct column. Check answers by building up the table on the board.

D Direct students to the **Grammar Hub** (see below and TB73). Read the examples and go through the rules with the class.

E Model the answers by talking about yourself. Ask students to report back what you said. Reformulate as required. Students then ask and answer the questions in pairs. Monitor and encourage students to ask follow-up questions to find out more. For whole-class feedback, ask pairs to report back on how similar or different they are. Use the **Grammar Worksheet** on W40 for extra practice.

GRAMMAR HUB

8.1 Countable and uncountable nouns; *some* and *any*

Singular countable nouns	Plural countable nouns	Uncountable nouns
an apple	apples	bread
a banana	bananas	butter
a carrot	carrots	cheese
an egg	eggs	chicken
a mushroom	mushrooms	fish
an orange	oranges	lettuce
a potato	potatoes	milk
a tomato	tomatoes	rice
		water

- Countable nouns are nouns you can count.
- Most nouns are countable. They can be singular or plural.

  a banana *six bananas*
- Uncountable nouns don't have a plural form and we can't count uncountable nouns.

  beef NOT ~~beefs~~ OR ~~one beef, two beefs~~

	Singular countable nouns	Plural countable nouns	Uncountable nouns
Positive	*a/an*	*some*	*some*
	I have **a banana** in my bag. I had **an apple** for breakfast.	There are **some apples** in the fridge. I have **some tomatoes** for the salad.	I can buy **some milk** on the way home.
Negative	*a/an*	*any*	*any*
	I don't have **a banana**. No, I don't want **an orange**, thank you.	There aren't **any burgers** left. I'm afraid we don't have **any mushrooms**.	Sorry, I don't have **any tea**.
Question	*a/an*	*any*	*any*
	Do you want **a banana**? Is there **an onion** in this recipe?	Do we have **any mushrooms**? Are there **any sausages** left?	Do you have **any cake**? Is there **any yogurt** in the fridge?

Be careful!

- With questions, we often use *some* when we make an offer.

  Do you want some bread?
- We use *some* not *any* when we make a request.

  Can I have some rice, please? NOT ~~Can I have any rice, please?~~

8.1 I'm hungry

PRONUNCIATION

8.1 **A** Play the recording for students to listen and repeat the words. Model and practice correct pronunciation of the three different endings.

8.2 **B** Play the recording. Students complete the table then check their answers with a partner. Give feedback as a class.

8.2 **C** Play the recording again and practice correct pronunciation of each word. Highlight the extra syllable in words ending in /ɪz/.

LISTENING

8.3 **A** Play the recording, then give feedback as a class.

8.3 **B** Play the recording again. Give students time to check answers in pairs before giving feedback as a class.

C Students discuss the questions in pairs. Monitor and help with any new or challenging vocabulary.

GRAMMAR

8.4 **A** Students listen to part of the conversation again and add *some* or *any* to the sentences and questions. Check answers as a class.

B Give students time to complete the table before giving feedback as a class. Read through the information box together and refer students to the section on *some* and *any* in the **Grammar Hub** if necessary.

C Put students into pairs. Direct students to the **Communication Hub**. Give students time to identify the items in their own fridges, before completing the activity. Monitor and assist as necessary.

SPEAKING

A Go through the questions with students. Point out that Question 3 is a simple past question. Students then work alone to write notes on their answers to each question. Monitor and encourage them to use target language from the unit.

B In pairs, students ask and answer the questions. Monitor and encourage them to ask follow-up questions to find out more. Ask students to report back on the two most interesting things they found out about their partner.

AUDIO SCRIPT

8.3

Listening, Exercise A
M = Marta S = Stefan

M: Stefan, what are you doing?
Ex A **S:** I'm looking for something to eat for dinner tonight, but we don't have anything I can eat.
M: What do you mean? There's lots of food in there. Why don't we have pizza?
S: Oh, no. No, no. I can't have pizza.
M: Why not? You love pizza.
Ex B Q1 **S:** I do, I do … but I'm on a diet and pizza is one of the things I can't eat.
M: Is this the diet in your magazine? I told you – you *don't* need to lose weight.
S: I know, but I want to. Anyway, it's a very healthy diet.
M: OK, so what *can* you eat then?
S: Oh, lots of things. Beef, chicken, fish …
M: Vegetables?
S: Of course!
M: So why not pizza?
S: Oh, well I can't eat bread. So, no pizza. Now, what's in the fridge? Is there any chicken?
M: Uh … So, about the chicken …
S: Where is it? I'm sure we had some chicken …
Ex B Q2 **M:** There isn't any chicken. I … uh … ate it yesterday.
S: Oh, OK. Right. Well, I can eat vegetables. Now, what do we have … Oh, yes. We have some mushrooms and some broccoli. Oh, and we have a carrot too … That's good.
Ex B Q3 **M:** Mushrooms, broccoli and a carrot? We can't eat mushrooms, broccoli and a carrot for dinner! What else is there?
S: Uh … we might have some fruit … There's an orange! It's a little old, but it's OK. Hmm … we don't have any apples or bananas … we need to get some fruit next week …
Ex B Q4 **M:** We can't just eat fruit for dinner! I'm not sure about this diet. Why do we need to change? I think we have a healthy diet. We eat a lot of fresh food.
S: Hmm … Maybe …
Ex B Q5 **M:** … and we never eat unhealthy food like cake or chips.
S: Hmm. Yes, you're right. This diet is a terrible idea.
M: Great. So, let's make dinner. Pizza?

GRAMMAR HUB

8.1 Countable and uncountable nouns; *some* and *any*

A Choose the correct options to complete the sentences.

1 I'm a vegetarian so I don't eat *__meat__ / meats*.
2 Would you like some *chip / __chips__*?
3 She never drinks *__coffee__ / coffees* after 9 pm.
4 What's your favorite *__pizza__ / pizzas*?
5 Can you buy some *__bread__ / breads* on your way home?
6 Is there *__an onion__ / onions* in this recipe?

B Complete the sentences with *some, any, a* or *an*.

1 Did you buy ___any___ carrots at the grocery store?
2 Are there ___any___ good restaurants near here?
3 Would you like ___some___ more tea?
4 There's ___some___ pasta in the cupboard.
5 Do you want ___an___ orange?
6 There's ___a___ bottle of water in the fridge.

➤ Go back to page 72.

LISTENING

8.3 **A LISTEN FOR GIST** Listen to Marta and Stefan. What is their conversation about? What to have for dinner

8.3 **B LISTEN FOR DETAIL** Listen again and circle M (Marta), S (Stefan) or B (both).

Who …

1 can't eat pizza because they're on a diet? M / (S) / B
2 ate the chicken yesterday? (M) / S / B
3 doesn't want to eat vegetables for dinner? (M) / S / B
4 thinks they have a healthy diet? (M) / S / B
5 doesn't eat unhealthy food? M / S / (B)

C SPEAK Work in pairs. Answer the questions.

1 Do you want to try Stefan's diet? Why/Why not?
2 Do you think you have a healthy diet? Why/Why not?

A: I don't think I have a healthy diet. I eat a lot of fast food!
B: Really? I never eat fast food. I think I have a very healthy diet.

GRAMMAR

some and *any*

8.4 **A WORK IT OUT** Listen to part of the conversation between Marta and Stefan again. Then complete the sentences with *some* or *any*.

1 Is there __any__ chicken?
2 There isn't __any__ chicken. I ate it yesterday.
3 We have __some__ mushrooms and __some__ broccoli.
4 We don't have __any__ apples or bananas.

B Look at the sentences in Exercise A. Complete the table with *some* and *any*.

some and *any*	
	countable and uncountable nouns
Positive +	1 __some__
Negative -	2 __any__
Questions ?	3 __any__

Questions with *some*

When we make an offer or a request, we use *some* and not *any*.

*Do you want **some** bread?*
*Would you like **some** water?*

C SPEAK Work in pairs. Student A – go to the **Communication Hub** on **page 156**. Student B – go to the **Communication Hub** on **page 159**.

SPEAKING

A PREPARE Think about the food you eat. Read the questions and write notes.

1 What do you normally eat for breakfast, lunch and dinner?
2 Which foods do you eat that are really unhealthy?
3 What did you eat for dinner last night?
4 Which do you prefer – cooking dinner or eating at restaurants? Why?

B SPEAK Work in pairs. Answer the questions in Exercise A. Try to ask for more information if possible.

A: I ate pepperoni pizza for dinner last night.
B: Really? Did you cook it at home or go to a restaurant?
A: I went to a restaurant with my friend.
B: Which restaurant did you go to?

Talk about the food you eat

8.2 What we eat

● Talk about the food your family eats

V containers P short and long vowel sounds G *much, many, a lot of*

GRAMMAR Ex A

Let's eat
Around the world

How many people are there in your family? How much food do you eat in a typical week? Do you eat more packaged food or fresh food? What's your favorite food? And how much do you spend on food each week? Here, we take a look at food habits in different countries. GRAMMAR Ex A

Ecuador

Ex D Q5 GRAMMAR Ex A

In Ecuador, most families don't eat any packaged food at all. People usually buy fresh food in local markets and they eat a lot of fruits and vegetables, as well as rice and potatoes. People usually buy food every day to cook at home. Lunch is an important meal and most children go home for lunch in the afternoon. Families usually eat together. Ex D 1 & 2

Average cost of food per week: $30
Popular food: rice, potatoes, chicken

The US

Ex D Q5 GRAMMAR Ex A

Most people in the US eat a lot of packaged food. They don't eat a lot of fresh fruit and they don't eat many vegetables. Meat is very popular here, as well as dairy products, like milk and cheese. Most Americans go to a big grocery store once a week to buy food. There aren't many markets, but some towns have a farmer's market once a week. A lot of families regularly eat at restaurants or eat fast food in front of the TV or in the car. Ex D Q4 GRAMMAR Ex A

Average cost of food per week: $400
Popular food: corn, chicken, hamburgers

Italy

Italy is famous for its food, and for most Italians, food is a very important part of their day! Markets are very popular, but most people buy their food at a grocery store. Most people buy fresh bread every day, and they use milk mainly with coffee. Italians don't eat much packaged food, but people often buy cans of tomatoes and beans. The main meal of the day is usually lunch. Ex D Q3 Ex D Q5

GRAMMAR Ex A

Average cost of food per week: $200
Popular food: pasta, rice, fish, bread

Source
https://www.dosomething.org/us/facts/11-facts-about-american-eating-habits

READING

A PREPARE Answer the questions. Use the places in the box to help you. Write notes.

in a market | in a grocery store | in local stores | online

1 Where do you buy fresh food? Why?
2 Where do you buy packaged food? Why?

B SPEAK Work in pairs. Look at the photos in *Let's eat - Around the world* and answer the questions.

1 What type of food can you see?
2 What kind of people can you see in the pictures?

C READ FOR GIST Read *Let's eat - Around the world* and check your answers to Exercise B.

D READ FOR DETAIL Read again and answer the questions.

1 Which meal is important in Ecuador? Lunch
2 Where do children in Ecuador have their lunch? At home
3 How often do most Italians buy bread? Every day
4 In which country do people drink a lot of milk? the US
5 In which two countries do people eat packaged food? the US, Italy

E SPEAK Work in pairs. Answer the questions.

1 Why are the diets in Ecuador, Italy and the US so different?
2 Which diets are healthy? Why?
3 Which diet in the article is like yours? Which of the food in the pictures do you eat every week?

LEAD-IN

Show students pictures of famous food/dishes from your country. Elicit/Tell students what each is called, what it's made of and whether or not you like it. Put students into groups. If you're in a bilingual class, ask students to discuss famous food/dishes in their country. Monitor and encourage them to say whether they'd like to try any of the new dishes. If you're in a monolingual class, ask students to make a list of famous food/dishes from around the world. Monitor and ask students which dishes they tried and whether they liked them or not.

READING

A Do this activity with the whole class. Ask students the questions, using follow-up questions to extend their responses (e.g. *Why? Which one?*). If necessary, clarify the difference between fresh food (food that has recently been picked or caught) and packaged food (food sold in a package).

B Students work in pairs to answer the questions. Don't confirm answers at this point.

C Give students up to two minutes to find the answers in the text. Check answers as a class.

1 fruits and vegetables, junk food (pizza), spaghetti; 2 a customer and sales clerks in a market, friends/family, family.

D Give students a longer time limit of up to five minutes to read through the text and answer the questions. Allow students to compare answers. Check answers as a class.

E In pairs, students discuss the questions. Monitor and encourage students to ask follow-up questions to find out more. If you have time, you could put pairs together to summarize the main points of their discussion.

1 In Ecuador and Italy, people rarely eat packaged food. Instead, they buy fresh ingredients to cook with at home.; 2 + 3 Students' own answers.

METHODOLOGY HUB by Jim Scrivener

Extensive reading

There is a great deal of evidence that **extensive reading** (i.e. reading longer texts, such as a novel, over time) has a powerful impact on language learning. The more someone reads, the more they pick up items of vocabulary and grammar from the texts, usually without realizing it, and this widening language knowledge seems to increase their overall linguistic confidence, which then influences and improves their skills in other language areas, too (though this is probably only true in cases where the material they read is self chosen and is genuinely relevant and interesting to them).

So, there are strong arguments for actively encouraging students to read a lot in the target language, both in and outside the classroom. We can help by:

- providing a library of books, magazines, newspapers, leaflets, etc;
- training learners how to select suitable reading material and in ways to read it;
- creating a 'book club' environment that encourages learners to choose what books to purchase, talk about favorite books, share them with each other, write brief recommendations, etc;
- allowing sections of classroom time purely for students to read; some teachers who have five or six lessons a week set aside one of these lessons as quiet reading time.

TEACHING IDEA by David Seymour and Maria Popova

Vocabulary: Odd one out

Use this activity to review the vocabulary section. Say this to your students:

Work in small groups. I'm going to dictate ten sets of four words, e.g. *cabbage, orange, potato, onion*. After each set, choose the odd one out and circle it. (Give the students a short time to choose between each set. More than one answer is possible.) Take turns explaining your decisions, e.g. *A cabbage, because it's the only one that's green. / An orange, because it makes terrible soup.*

1. lemon, grapefruit, grape, lime
2. fridge, oven, microwave, toaster
3. Indian, Chinese, French, Italian
4. bacon, eggs, tomatoes, toast
5. bread, cake, pie, pudding
6. scramble, boil, fry, roast
7. box, bottle, can, jar
8. cows, chicken, sheep, fish
9. rice, wheat, potatoes, pasta
10. slice, chop, mince, mash

In your groups, write five more sets and read them aloud. See if the rest of the class can decide which is the odd one out.

TEACHING IDEA by David Seymour and Maria Popova

Grammar: Countable and uncountable

Use this activity to review the grammar section. Say this to your students:

Work in small groups. Are these words countable or uncountable?
news, meat, money, eggs, stairs, person, butter, pasta, information

Listen to these words and put them under three headings: countable, uncountable or both.
book, job, pepper, bread, energy, work, orange, sandwich, cake, furniture, snow, fish, literature, window, bottle, country, sleep, time, juice, mouse, glass, word, paper, table, question, salt, hair

Write two sentences using each of the words in the third column, once as a countable noun and once as an uncountable noun, e.g. *I like red peppers. I always add some pepper to my food.*

8.2 What we eat

VOCABULARY

A Write the following sentence on the board: *Can you buy two pastas on your way home?* Ask students whether this sentence is correct (*it isn't*) and why not (*pasta is uncountable*). Draw a large red X next to the sentence. Elicit ideas about how to correct the sentence, before writing the following correction underneath: *Can you buy two boxes of pasta on your way home?* Draw a large green check mark next to the sentence. Draw a box around *boxes* and highlight that this is a type of *container*. Highlight that we usually use containers to make uncountable nouns countable. Give students time to complete the exercise alone, before giving feedback as a class.

B Direct students to the **Vocabulary Hub**. Give students time to complete the exercise alone before checking answers in pairs.

C In pairs, students brainstorm a list of food items and the containers each one comes in. Build up the list on the board. Use the **Vocabulary Worksheet** on W41 for extra practice.

PRONUNCIATION

8.5 **A** Write *fish* and *meat* on the board, with the vowels underlined. Ask students if the *i* in *fish* is pronounced in the same way as the *ea* in *meat*. Play the recording for students to check. Model the two words, showing students how the mouth changes shape when saying the two vowel sounds. Elicit that *fish* has a short vowel sound /ɪ/; *meat* has a long vowel sound /iː/.

8.6 **B** Play the recording, for students to repeat the words. Give feedback as a class, practicing correct pronunciation as necessary.

C Put students into pairs to discuss the questions.

GRAMMAR

A Go through the task with students. Give them time to identify the phrases in *Let's eat - Around the world*.

B Students complete the table with *much, many* and *a lot of*. Check answers as a class.

C Direct students to the **Grammar Hub** (see below).

D Go through the example with students. Elicit when we need to use *How many* (with countable nouns) and *How much* (with uncountable nouns). Point out that *bread* in Question 1 is an uncountable noun, so we need to use *How much*.

E In pairs, students ask and answer the questions. Use the **Grammar Worksheet** on W42 for extra practice.

SPEAKING

A Students work through the prompts, writing questions to ask their partner in the next stage. Monitor and check questions for accuracy as they write.

B In pairs, students use their questions to find out about the food they eat. As their partner answers, they listen and write notes.

C Ask students to interview you with some of their questions and make a note of your answers. Then using these notes, work together as a whole class to build up a paragraph about you on the board. Leave this on the board to support students in the next stage. Monitor and assist as required.

D Allow students time to prepare what they're going to say.

GRAMMAR HUB

8.2 *much, many, a lot of*

	Countable nouns	Uncountable nouns
Positive	*a lot of*	*a lot of*
	There are **a lot of carrots** in this recipe!	She drinks **a lot of coffee**.
Negative	*not many*	*not much*
	We don't have **many tomatoes**.	There isn't **much milk** left.
Question	*How many?*	*How much?*
	How many potatoes do we need?	**How much pasta** do you want?

- We use *a lot of* with countable and uncountable nouns.
- We use *many* with countable nouns.
- We use *much* with uncountable nouns.

Be careful!

- We use **a lot of** for a large amount.
  There are a lot of eggs in this recipe.
- We use **some** for a medium amount.
  There is some milk in this recipe.
- We use **not many/much** for a small amount.
  There isn't much sugar in this recipe.

8.2 *much, many, a lot of*

A Complete the paragraph with *a lot of, much* or *many*.

Although we're not vegetarians, we eat [1] ___a lot of___ vegetables. I like tomatoes, but there aren't [2] ___many___ in our local market at the moment because it's winter. At breakfast we usually have cereal and [3] ___a lot of___ fruit. Fresh fruit is really good for you. We don't eat [4] ___much___ meat, but we sometimes have chicken on Sundays. My son loves potatoes so we always have [5] ___a lot of___ potatoes with our Sunday dinner. We all like a delicious dessert, but we don't eat [6] ___much___ chocolate.

B Complete the sentences with *much* or *many*.

1 How ___*much*___ money do you have?
2 How ___many___ people are coming to dinner?
3 How ___much___ water do you drink every day?
4 How ___much___ do you spend on food every month?
5 How ___much___ sugar do you want in your coffee?
6 How ___many___ bottles of water do we need?
7 How ___many___ packages of cookies do you have?

➤ Go back to page 75.

VOCABULARY

Containers

A Label containers (1–3) with the items in the box.

a bag of rice   a bottle of fruit juice   a can of tomatoes

B Go to the **Vocabulary Hub** on **page 150**.

C SPEAK Work in pairs. What other types of food and drinks come in containers?

A: A carton of juice.
B: A can of soda.

PRONUNCIATION

Short and long vowel sounds

8.5 **A** Underline the vowels (*a*, *e*, *i*, *o*, *u*) in the words below. Then listen to the words. How is the vowel sound different? *fish* has a short vowel sound /ɪ/; *meat* has a long vowel sound /iː/

1 fish   2 meat

8.6 **B** Listen and repeat the words. Are the vowel sounds long or short?

1 beef   long / short
2 biscuit   long / short
3 milk   long / short
4 eat   long / short
5 chips   long / short

C Work in pairs. Discuss the questions.

1 How often do you eat chips?
2 Do you eat a lot of fish?

GRAMMAR

much, many, a lot of

A Look at *Let's eat - Around the world* again. Find and underline the phrases with *much*, *many* and *a lot of*.

B WORK IT OUT Look at the phrases you underlined in Exercise A. Complete the table with *much*, *many* and *a lot of*.

much, many and *a lot of*		
	Countable nouns	Uncountable nouns
Positive +	She eats [1] *a lot of* bananas.	He eats [2] a lot of pasta.
Negative -	She doesn't eat [3] many apples.	He doesn't drink [4] much coffee.
Questions ?	How [5] many cookies are there?	How [6] much rice is there?

C Go to the **Grammar Hub** on **page 136**.

D PRACTICE Use the prompts to write questions with *How much* and *How many*.

1 bread / you / eat? *How much bread do you eat?*
2 tea / you / drink? How much tea do you drink?
3 chips / you / eat? How many chips do you eat?
4 meat / you / eat? How much meat do you eat?
5 rice / you / eat? How much rice do you eat?

E SPEAK Work in pairs. Answer the questions in Exercise D.

I don't eat much bread, but I eat a lot of pasta.

SPEAKING

A PREPARE Write questions to ask your partner about these things:

- his/her family (people, ages)
  How many people are there in your family?
- cost of food per week
  How much do you spend on food each week?
- food shopping (where? how often? what?)
- fresh food (fruits and vegetables, dairy, meat and fish)
- packaged food

B SPEAK Work in pairs. Ask your partner about the food they eat each week. Write notes.

C ORGANIZE Write a paragraph about your partner.

D PRESENT Tell the rest of the class about your partner. Do people eat similar or different food?

Talk about the food your family eats

G a/an, the, no article V food preparation P consonant clusters S decoding

READING

A Work in pairs. Are the following sentences true for you?

1 I cook dinner every night.
2 I love making unusual dishes.
3 I buy a lot of food online.

B READ FOR GIST Read *Thanks for trying Homecook*. Which sentence best describes it?

1 It's a survey about people's cooking habits.
2 It's an advertisement about a food business. (circled)
3 It's a description of a cooking school.

C READ FOR DETAIL Read the advertisement again. Are these sentences true (T), false (F) or not given (NG)? Correct the false sentences.

1 *Homecook* delivers ready cooked meals to your home. T / (F) / NG — *Homecook* delivers the ingredients, you cook the meals.
2 Customers can order a box for between two and four people. (T) / F / NG
3 Both Carlo and Frankie, who started the business, are Australian. T / (F) / NG — Carlo is Italian.
4 The business gets bigger every year. and now has over 100 staff. T / F / (NG)
5 Customers can order a maximum of 12 meals a week. T / F / (NG)
6 According to one customer, they now spend less on food with *Homecook*. (T) / F / NG

D Work in pairs. Look at the words in bold in the *Homecook* advertisement. What part of speech are they – nouns, adjectives or verbs?
1 adjective 2 noun 3 noun 4 verb 5 noun

E Complete the definitions with the words in Exercise D. Use the information in the box to help you.

Decoding

Noun, adjective, verb and adverb are all parts of speech. Thinking about parts of speech helps you work out the meaning of words.

1 dessert sweet food after main meal
2 recipe cooking instructions
3 ingredient one of the foods you use to make a particular meal
4 deliver to take things like letters and goods to a place
5 delicious extremely tasty or enjoyable

F SPEAK Work in pairs. Answer the questions.

1 Where do you buy fresh ingredients from?
2 Would you use *Homecook* to get fresh ingredients? Why/Why not?

Thanks for trying Homecook

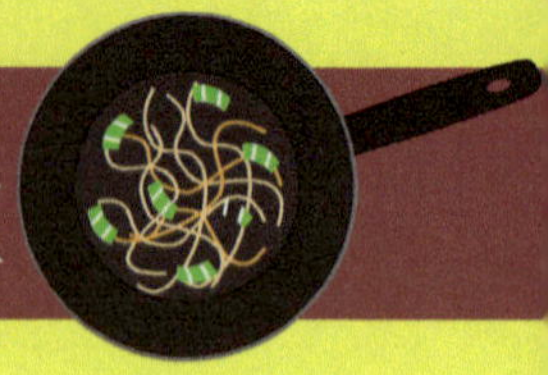

Our promise
With *Homecook*, you can cook quick, **delicious** meals at home with tasty ingredients. Ex C Q1

Our offer
We offer boxes of fresh **ingredients** for a main course for two, three or four people. You can also order appetizers and **desserts**. Each box comes with a recipe. Follow the recipe to create a delicious meal. Ex C Q2

Our story
Friends Carlo Vallone and Frankie Benn started *Homecook* in 2014 in Frankie's home city of Melbourne, Australia. Carlo, from Naples, is a chef and Frankie's speciality is business. Ex C Q3

We started *Homecook* because we wanted to offer fresh ingredients that are ready to cook. And we did it. Last year we **delivered** over a million boxes!

How does *Homecook* work?
WE deliver thousands of boxes to homes around the country every week.
YOU choose from 12 delicious, healthy recipes each week.
WE deliver fresh ingredients and **recipe** cards for each meal you choose.
YOU cook, serve and eat!

Ex C Q6 "The ingredients are really good quality. We save money on our food shopping now. We're really excited when the box arrives each week."
Leanne, Geelong

GRAMMAR

a/an, *the*, no article

A WORK IT OUT Read the sentences from the *Homecook* advertisement. Match sentences (1–3) to rules (a–c).

1 Friends Carlo Vallone and Frankie Benn started *Homecook* in 2014 in Frankie's home city of Melbourne, Australia.
2 Each box comes with a recipe. Follow the recipe to create a delicious meal.
3 We deliver thousands of boxes to homes around the country every week.

***a/an*, *the*, no article**

a 2 We use *a/an* the first time we talk about something. Then we use *the* to talk about it again.
b 1 We usually use no article in front of names, places, companies and cities.
c 3 We use *the* when there is only one or it is clear what is being talked about.

B Go to the **Grammar Hub** on **page 136**.

8.3 Yes, chef!

LEAD-IN

Write three meals you have had recently on the board, including one from a takeout restaurant, one someone else made for you and one you cooked yourself. Ask students to guess which is which. Encourage questions and discussion. Students then do the same in small groups.

READING

A Students discuss the sentences in pairs, saying which ones are true.

B Go through the three descriptions with students, checking understanding. Then give students one minute to look through the advertisement and decide on the best description.

C Give students a longer time limit of up to five minutes. Students read the advertisement in detail and decide if the sentences are *true*, *false* or *not given*. Ask them to underline the parts of the text which show that the sentences are true or false and to correct the false sentences.

D Write the first sentence from the text on the board (ideally with *delicious* in a different color). Elicit that *delicious* describes *meals*, which is a noun, so *delicious* is an adjective. Ask students to identify the verbs in the sentence (*can* and *cook*), before putting them in pairs to complete the exercise. Give feedback as a class.

E Allow students time to go through the *Decoding* box. Point out that knowing what part of speech a word is can help guess its meaning. Students work alone to match the words with their definitions. Students compare answers in pairs before checking as a class.

F Students discuss the questions in pairs. Open up the discussion to the whole class.

GRAMMAR

A Students match the examples to the rules in the box. Allow students time to compare and discuss their answers in pairs. Check answers as a class.

B Direct students to the **Grammar Hub** (see below). Read the examples and go through the rules with the class. Use the **Grammar Worksheet** on W42 for extra practice.

GRAMMAR HUB

a/an	We use *a/an* the first time we talk about a singular noun.	I have **a recipe** for lasagna. There's **an onion** in the cupboard over there.
the	We use *the* with singular nouns when it is clear what we are talking about or when there is only one.	Fry **the onion** for five minutes. Where's **the waitress**?
	We use *the* with plural nouns when it is clear what we are talking about.	**The ingredients** for this recipe are unusual.
no article	We use no article with the names of people, companies, cities and countries (except *the UK*, *the US*, *the Netherlands*).	This is **Erica**. She's a chef from **Sydney, Australia**.
	We use no article when we talk about things in general.	Do you like **pizza**? **Chips** are not very healthy.

8.3 *a/an*, *the*, no article

A Choose the correct options to complete the paragraph.

Levain Bakery is [1]*the / a / an* company that makes [2]*the / – / an* chocolate cookies. [3]*The / A / –* company is in [4]*the / a / –* New York, but it sells cookies all across [5]*the / a / an* US.

B Complete the paragraphs with *the*, *a*, *an* or –.

[1] __–__ Jamie Oliver is [2] __an__ English chef who is famous in [3] __the__ UK and across [4] __the__ world. He has a lot of restaurants and [5] __–__ popular TV shows. [6] __–__ People love cooking and eating his Italian recipes.

[7] __–__ Wellington Froots is [8] __a__ company that grows and delivers fresh [9] __–__ fruits and vegetables. Friends Isabella Sheridan and Akiko Okamura started their business in Isabella's home city of [10] __–__ Wellington, in [11] __–__ New Zealand. [12] __The__ company delivers [13] __a__ new box of locally grown, fresh ingredients to its customers every week.

C Correct the mistakes in each sentence.

1. My dad has ~~an~~ a great recipe for carrot cake!
2. Let's go to ~~a~~ the new French restaurant on Broad Street.
3. Ramen is a popular noodle dish from ~~the~~ Sapporo, Japan.
4. Could you get me ~~a~~ the grater? It's in that cupboard over there.
5. ~~The junk~~ Junk food is bad for your health.
6. Could you buy ~~the~~ an onion on your way home? I need one for this recipe.

➤ Go back to page 76.

8.3 Yes, chef!

VOCABULARY

8.7 **A** Write *recipe* on the board. Point out the pronunciation /ˈresəpi/. Then write *ingredients* on the board and point out its pronunciation /ɪnˈgriːdiənts/. Focus students on the picture of the hash browns. Find out if students know what this is and if they have tried it. Explain that they will listen to a recipe for making hash browns, using simple ingredients.

Students read through the different parts of the recipe. At this stage, they could predict the order. Play the audio. Students number the instructions in the correct order.

> *C: OK, guys, here's my hash browns recipe. You need four large potatoes, one white onion, one egg, salt and pepper and vegetable oil. First, grate the potatoes and squeeze out the water into the sink. Then, peel and chop an onion. After that, crack an egg into a bowl and beat it. Add the potato, onion, salt and pepper to the egg and mix them together. Then, put one tablespoon of vegetable oil in a frying pan and, when it's hot, put spoonfuls of the mixture into the pan and make them flat. Fry them for two to three minutes on each side, or until they're crisp. And finally, serve! I hope you enjoy it!*

B In pairs, students match the instructions with the images. Check answers as a class.

C Allow time for students to prepare to talk about their favorite dish. They can use dictionaries to check key words if required. Then put students into pairs or small groups to share their favorite dishes and ideas on how to cook them. Use the **Vocabulary Worksheet** on W43 for extra practice.

PRONUNCIATION

A Write *salt and pepper* on the board. Ask students to identify the consonants. Highlight that a consonant cluster is when there is more than one consonant sound together. So, the *pp* in *pepper* is not a consonant cluster but the *lt* in *salt* is. Students identify the consonant clusters in the words. Check answers as a class.

8.8 **B** Play the recording. Students repeat the words. Back-chaining while practicing can help students with the pronunciation of consonant clusters (e.g. *-ack, -nack, snack*).

SPEAKING HUB

A In pairs, students make a list of meals they could cook.

B Students select one of the meals and work together to write a simple recipe. Allow students time to check any key words in a dictionary.

C Students present the recipes to the class. Encourage the audience to ask follow-up questions to find out more.

D In pairs, students discuss the recipes they heard in the class presentations. Ask them to decide which ones they would and wouldn't like to try and give reasons. If students don't cook, they can discuss which meals they would like to try. For class feedback, find out which were the most popular recipes.

Extra activity
Set this task for homework. Ask students to prepare presentation slides with images or make a video showing them cooking the meal. They can use this in the presentation stage.

METHODOLOGY HUB by Jim Scrivener

Using English in class

Some teachers have found that competition and bribery are techniques that get results (e.g. *'Every time you speak Spanish, I'll give a red mark to your team. The team with the fewest red marks at the end gets a bar of chocolate.'*). I have some problems with this, because it seems to be building a motivation fairly separate from the genuine interest in the subject matter that I am hoping to arouse; it seems to be a case of 'Do this to please the teacher'.

I am sure that inducements, threats, prizes, etc can all have limited success in creating an 'English-only' classroom, but I believe that a more complete solution involves looking at the whole atmosphere of the class.

As an ideal, I would like a classroom where learners were free to use their own tongue whenever they wanted but in fact mostly chose to use English. How would this be possible? Maybe by creating a climate where it was OK to use English, where using English was normal and natural and not special or frightening. There is no easy way to get to this, but here are some ideas that might help:

- Use a lot of listening material to surround them with the sound of English.
- Put English language posters on the walls.
- Have short, clearly demarcated sections of the lesson when English is the first language; at other times, other languages are possible.
- Negotiate the ground rules with the students or – better yet – let them set rules completely by themselves.
- Discuss (as opposed to 'Tell') the point of the activity, lesson, course. Agree how it will be done, why using English is important.
- Respond positively to every effort at using English.
- Don't reprimand learners for not using English, but keep operating in English yourself.
- Only 'hear' English.
- Spend a lot of time on fluency work without correction.
- Establish that you are delighted for them to speak anything at all; communication is your priority, rather than accuracy.
- Create a lot of pair and small group activities that require them to do something with English to avoid possibly feeling humiliated for getting it wrong in a bigger group.
- When it becomes a big problem, stop the activity and negotiate again; *'I notice that many of you are using (Portuguese). Is this OK?'*
- Be prepared for English use to grow gradually, rather than be established for a whole lesson at the start of the course.

VOCABULARY
Food preparation

8.7 **A** Listen to Carlo's recipe for hash browns and number the instructions 1–7.

Hash browns

Ingredients:
4 large potatoes
1 white onion
1 egg
salt and pepper
vegetable oil

Instructions:

1 **Grate** the potatoes and squeeze out the water.

2 **Peel** and **chop** an onion.

6 **Fry** for 2–3 minutes on each side, or until crispy.

5 **Put** one tablespoon of vegetable oil in a frying pan. When it's hot, put spoonfuls of the mixture into the pan. Make them flat.

3 **Crack** an egg into a bowl and **beat** it.

7 **Serve!**

4 **Add** the potato, onion, salt and pepper to the egg and **mix** them together.

B Match the instructions (1–7) in Exercise A with the pictures (a–g).

a 4

b 1

c 7

d 3

e 6

f 2

g 5

C **SPEAK** Work in pairs. What are your favorite dishes? Do you know how to cook them? Tell your partner.

A: I love pasta. I make it all the time.

B: Me too. I make a sauce with fresh tomatoes. You chop the tomatoes and fry them in olive oil with some garlic.

PRONUNCIATION
Consonant clusters

A Consonant clusters are groups of two or more consonant sounds. Underline the consonant clusters in these words.

1 bowl
2 chips
3 fridge
4 mushroom
5 shrimp
6 snack

8.8 **B** Listen and repeat the words in Exercise A.

SPEAKING HUB

A **PLAN** Work in pairs. Make a list of five meals that you can cook.

B **PREPARE** Choose one of the meals from Exercise A. List the ingredients and write a simple recipe for it.

C **PRESENT** Read your recipe to the class.

D **DISCUSS** Work in pairs. Which meals would you like to make? Which wouldn't you like to make? Why?

Talk about ingredients and recipes

Café Hub

8.4 More cheese

F– order food in a restaurant P– stress and intonation

COMPREHENSION

A ▶ Watch the video. Complete the sentences with *Sam* or *Zac*.

1 ___Sam___ wanted to cook dinner.
2 ___Zac___ suggests they go out.
3 ___Sam___ orders chicken and rice.
4 ___Zac___ orders pasta and a large bottle of water.
5 ___Zac___ has a dessert.
6 ___Sam___ thinks ___Zac___ is strange.

B Test your memory! Check (✓) the ten items of food you can see in the video.

✓ 	☐ 	✓ 
✓ 	☐ 	☐ 
✓ 	✓ 	✓ 
✓ 	✓ 	☐ 
✓ 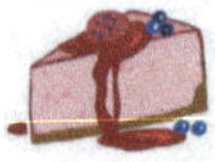	☐ 	✓ 

C ▶ **SPEAK** Work in pairs. Compare your answers to Exercise B. Then watch the video again and check your answers.

A: Was there any bread?
B: Yes, I think so. Were there any bananas?

FUNCTIONAL LANGUAGE

Ordering food in a restaurant

A Complete the conversations. Write *have*, *like* or the correct form of *be*.

Zac: Hi. A table for two please.
Waiter: Do you 1 ___have___ a reservation?
Sam: I 2 ___'m___ afraid not. Could we 3 ___have___ a table over there, please?
Waiter: That 4 ___'s___ fine, please come this way.

Waiter: 5 ___Are___ you ready to order?
Sam: Yes, I think we 6 ___are___. I'll 7 ___have___ the chicken and rice, please. And a side salad.
Waiter: OK, one chicken, one side salad.
Zac: I'll 8 ___have___ the steak and fries, please.
Waiter: OK, one steak.
Zac: No wait. Sorry. I'll 9 ___have___ the pasta.
Waiter: Sure, one pasta. Would you 10 ___like___ something to drink?
Sam: Water, please.
Zac: Can we 11 ___have___ a large bottle of water?
Waiter: No problem.
Sam: Thanks.

Waiter: Would you 12 ___like___ to see the dessert menu?
Sam: I 13 ___'m___ OK, thanks.

Sam: Can we 14 ___have___ the bill, please?
Waiter: Of course.

B ▶ Watch the video again and check your answers.

C **SPEAK** Work in pairs. Practice the conversation.

MILLY

SAM

NEENA

ZAC

GABY

PRONUNCIATION

Stress and intonation

A 01:38–02:10 Watch the scene in the restaurant again. Notice the word stress and intonation.

Waiter:	Are you ready to order?
Sam:	Yes, I think we are. I'd like the chicken and rice, please. And a side salad.
Waiter:	OK, one chicken, one side salad.
Zac:	I'll have the steak and fries, please.
Waiter:	OK, one steak.
Zac:	No wait. Sorry. I'll have the pasta.

B 01:38–02:10 Watch again and repeat the conversation. Copy the stress and intonation.

C SPEAK Work in pairs. Practice the conversation in Exercise A. Remember to use the correct stress and intonation.

MENU

MAIN COURSES

Chicken and rice

Steak with mushrooms and fries

Pasta with olives and tomatoes

SIDES

Fries

Rice

Salad

DESSERTS

Fruit salad

Cheesecake

Ice cream

SPEAKING

A PLAN Look at the menu. Underline the food you'd like to eat.

B SPEAK Work in pairs. Write and practice a conversation in a restaurant. Do these things:

- Order food from the menu.
- Change your order.
- Do or say something strange.

C PRESENT Perform your conversation for the class.

D Take a class vote for the best conversation and food selection.

Order food in a restaurant

➤ Turn to page 167 to learn how to write an online restaurant review.

8.4 More cheese

LEAD-IN

Focus students on the photo and ask what they can see and what they think is happening. Then ask pairs to share an experience of either a very good or a very bad experience at a restaurant or a café. Get feedback from the whole class.

COMPREHENSION

A ▶ Play the video. Students complete the sentences. Allow them time to compare answers with a partner before checking as a class.

B Individually, students apply a check mark to the eight items they saw in the video. Do not play the video again at this point.

C ▶ In pairs, students discuss their answers. Then check as a class by playing the video again.

FUNCTIONAL LANGUAGE

A Students work alone to complete the four conversations. Then allow students time to compare their answers in pairs.

B ▶ Play the video again for students to check their answers.

C In pairs, students practice the conversations. Encourage them to look up and say the conversations, rather than reading off the page.

PRONUNCIATION

A ▶ 01:38-02:10 Before playing the video, go through the conversation with students. Point out the underlined words and syllables. These show the stressed sounds. Students watch the scene from the video again, listening for the stressed sounds and the way the voices move up and down.

B ▶ 01:38-02:10 Students watch again and repeat the conversation, focusing on the stress and intonation.

C In pairs, students practice saying the conversation. Ask them to do this at least twice, swapping roles, until they sound natural.

SPEAKING

A Focus students on the menu. Check any unknown vocabulary and practice the pronunciation of *dessert* /dɪ'zɜrt/, which has the stress on the second syllable.

B Put students into pairs to write a conversation. Point out that there should be two characters: a customer and a waiter. Go through the three stages of the conversation, and make sure students include these. Monitor and assist.

C Students perform their conversations for the whole class.

D Take a vote on the most interesting or funniest conversation. Also, find out what the most popular food selections are.

METHODOLOGY HUB by Jim Scrivener

Running a role play: some guidelines

- Make sure the students understand the idea of role play. Do they know what's going to happen? Do they know what is required of them? Are they comfortable doing that or not?
- Make sure the context or situation is clear.
- Do they understand the information on their own card? Allow reading / dictionary / thinking time (during which you go around and help if necessary).
- Give them time to prepare their ideas before they start - maybe encourage note-writing - but when the activity starts, encourage them to improvise rather than rely on prepared speeches and notes. The preparation work they have done will inform their role play, but could simply get in the way if they over-rely on it. It may help to take away the cards when the role play starts.
- At the end of the role play, make sure that you give some feedback on how well (or not) the students completed the activity. Remember to comment on the language used as well as the appropriacy of what was said. Students will need to feel that they have achieved something.

▶ VIDEO SCRIPT

S = Sam Z = Zac W = Waiter

S: Hi.
Z: Hi.
S: OK! I'm ready to cook! Let's go to the flat. Did you do the shopping? I sent you a list. Bread, eggs, vegetables, pasta and … cheese.
Z: Uhhhhhhhhhhhhh … Uhhhhhhhhhhhhh … Let's go out for dinner?
S: OK.
W: Good evening, gentlemen.
Z: Hi. A table for two please.
W: Do you have a reservation?
S: I'm afraid not. Could we have a table over there, please?
W: That's fine, please come this way. Are you ready to order?
S: Yes, I think we are. I'd like the chicken and rice, please. And a side salad.
W: OK, one chicken, one side salad.
Z: I'll have the steak and fries, please.
W: OK, one steak.
Z: No wait. Sorry. I'll have the pasta.
W: Sure, one pasta. Would you like something to drink?
S: Water, please.
Z: Can we have a large bottle of water?
W: No problem.
S: Thanks.
Z: More, please. More, please. More, please. More, please. More, please. More, please. That's enough. Thank you.
W: OK. Can I get you anything else?
S: We're fine, thanks.
Z: What? What?
S: The cheese? That's a lot of cheese.
Z: Oh right, yeah. I love cheese.
S: So do I, Zac, but that's just strange. And the ketchup?
Z: Yeah! But it tastes SO good.
S: How was your cheese?
Z: Delicious!
W: Would you like to see the dessert menu?
S: I'm OK, thanks.
Z: Do you have any cheesecake?
S: Seriously Zac? More cheese?
Z: I love cheesecake.
W: OK. One cheesecake then.
Z: Thanks.
S: Can we have the bill, please?
W: Of course.
S: No.

8 Writing

Write an online restaurant review

W – pronoun referencing

A SPEAK Work in pairs. Answer the questions.

1 Do you like eating out?
2 How often do you eat out?
3 What's your favorite type of restaurant?
4 Do you ever write online reviews about restaurants you visit?

B Read the two restaurant reviews. Who didn't have a good time? Nor didn't have a good time.

Posted on 1/3/19 at 10:32am

Primavera ★

We chose Primavera because **it** had amazing reviews and we love Italian food. When we arrived, the music was really loud. I called the waitress and asked **her** to turn **it** down. **She** just walked away! It wasn't much better when we ordered our food. When the appetizers arrived, my fish wasn't cooked so I sent **it** back. My boyfriend said there was too much garlic on **his** shrimp – he didn't even finish **them**! For the main course, we had a salad and a steak. **They** were OK but nothing special. We didn't have a dessert. Overall, **it** cost too much and the food wasn't good. We didn't enjoy our meal and we won't go again.

Nor, Singapore

Share Like Comment

Ex C Q1, Ex C Q4, Ex C Q5

Posted on 3/17/19 at 3:25pm

Allium ★★★★

I wanted somewhere special for my wife's 30th birthday, so I chose the French restaurant, Allium. **It's** very popular and so it wasn't easy to get a table. The piano player was really good and the service was great. There were fresh flowers on every table. **They** smelled wonderful. We ordered the soup and the mushrooms as appetizers. Then for the main course, I had the chicken and my wife had beef. We both had the lemon parfait for dessert. It was a fairly expensive meal, but the food was great so **it** was good value. Our waiter, Pascal, was really good, too, so we left **him** a big tip! We loved Allium. I really recommend **it** for a special occasion.

Dieter, Germany

Share Like Comment

Ex C Q3, Ex C Q2

Refer students to these reviews as models for the writing task.

C Read the reviews again and answer the questions. Choose Nor (N) or Dieter (D).

1 Who wasn't happy with the staff? (N) / D
2 Who thinks the food was good? N / (D)
3 Who liked the music? N / (D)
4 Who thinks their meal was too expensive? (N) / D
5 Who doesn't recommend it? (N) / D

D Complete the sentences with a pronoun. Use the information in the box to help you.

Pronoun referencing

The first time we talk about something, we use a noun. After that, we use pronouns to avoid repeating the noun and to make our writing flow.

*When we arrived, **the music** was really loud. I called **the waitress** and asked **her** to turn **it** down.*

Tell students that using pronouns like this helps them write longer paragraphs.

1 We enjoyed our meal. It was delicious.
2 The waitress and the manager were unfriendly. They didn't help us at all.
3 The waiter only came to our table after I called him three times.
4 The appetizers were amazing. I can't recommend them highly enough.
5 My wife loved the restaurant. She wants to go back soon.
6 We liked our waitress and left her a good tip.

WRITING

A PREPARE Think about a good or bad experience you had at a restaurant. Write notes. Think about:

- who you were with
- the name of the restaurant
- what it looked like
- the type, choice and quality of the food
- the staff
- the cost

If students don't have a real experience to write about, they could invent one.

B WRITE Write a review of your restaurant. Use your notes from Exercise A to help you. Remember to use pronouns and to write about what you liked and didn't like.

C REVIEW Work in pairs. Read each other's reviews. Do you want to go to the restaurant your partner went to?

WRITING 167

WRITING

In this writing lesson, students will learn how to write an online restaurant review, paying attention to how to use referencing words to make a text more cohesive.

A Students discuss the questions in pairs. Share answers as a class and contribute your own ideas. Ask follow-up questions to encourage students to extend their answers.

B Students read the two restaurant reviews. For whole-class feedback, elicit that the last few lines of a review usually summarize the writer's main opinion.

C Students read the reviews again and decide which person each question relates to. Allow students time to compare answers, before checking answers as a class.

D Read through the *Pronoun referencing* box with students. Point out that we use pronouns like this after a person or thing has been mentioned for the first time. If we use a pronoun before we make it clear what we are talking about, our writing can become very unclear (e.g. *When we arrived, it was really loud.*). Students work alone to complete the sentences. Check answers as a class.

WRITING TASK

A Describe a good or bad experience you had at a restaurant. Build up notes about the experience on the board as you speak. Students write notes about an experience of their own. Once their notes are complete, students describe the experience to their partner, adding to their own notes as they think of more information or as their partner asks questions.

B Students write a review of the restaurant using their notes to help. Remind students to use pronouns and to include what they liked and what they didn't like. They should also summarize their own opinion at the end of the review. If they like, students can add a star rating to the review. Monitor and assist as required.

C Students read each other's reviews and decide if they want to go to the restaurant. If you have time, you could ask students to read all the reviews and take a vote to find the most and least popular restaurant.

Unit 8 Review

VOCABULARY

A Match the food items in the picture (a–m) with the words in the box.

a banana h a loaf of bread k a slice of cake m
carrots e cheese g chicken a an apple i
a mug of coffee l eggs b milk c
mushrooms f an orange j yogurt d

B Choose the correct words to complete the phrases.

1 a *can* / *bottle* of beans
2 a *carton* / *bag* of fruit juice
3 a *bag* / *container* of yogurt
4 a *can* / *box* of tomatoes
5 a *bag* / *carton* of rice
6 a *jar* / *can* of mayonnaise
7 a *carton* / *bag* of chips
8 a *can* / *bottle* of lemonade.

C Complete the recipe with the verbs in the box.

add beat ~~chop~~ crack fry mix peel put

Spanish omelette

1 Peel and ___chop___ an onion.
2 ___Peel___ the potatoes and cut them into small pieces.
3 ___Put___ one tablespoon of oil in a frying pan.
4 ___Fry___ the onion and potatoes together for 20 minutes.
5 ___Crack___ eight eggs into a bowl and ___beat___ them.
6 ___Add___ salt and pepper to the eggs and ___mix___ them together. Then add the mixture to the onions and potatoes.
7 Cook for 10 minutes, or until brown.

GRAMMAR

A Find and correct six mistakes in the conversation.

Eloise: What do you want to cook for the party?
Gemma: Hmm. How about ~~fishes~~ and ~~beefs~~? fish; beef
Eloise: Good idea! We can make some ~~rices~~ too. rice
Gemma: But Lola doesn't eat ~~meats~~. She's vegetarian. meat
Eloise: We can make ~~pastas~~ with ~~vegetable~~ for Lola. pasta; vegetables

B Complete the sentences with *a/an*, *some* and *any*.

1 I have ___an___ apple and ___a___ sandwich for my lunch.
2 Do we have ___any___ mushrooms?
3 I want to make ___a___ pizza, but I don't have ___any___ cheese.
4 Is there ___any___ milk in the fridge?
5 Can you buy ___some___ potatoes at the store, please?

C Choose the correct words to complete the sentences.

1 Do you eat *a lot of* / *many* meat?
2 How *much* / *many* potatoes do you eat every week?
3 How *much* / *many* bread do we need?
4 We have *a lot of* / *many* eggs. Let's make a cake!
5 There isn't *much* / *many* fruit. Can you buy some?

D Find and correct the mistakes in four of these sentences.

1 Is there ~~recipe~~ for this meal? a recipe
2 My hometown is ~~the~~ New York City.
3 We need two lemons and ~~orange~~. an orange
4 They always put the ingredients at the top of the recipe.
5 My friend is very good at cooking delicious ~~the~~ meals.

FUNCTIONAL LANGUAGE

A Look at the conversation. Put the sentences in the correct order (1–7).

6 Waiter: Anything to drink?
2 Customer A: Yes, I'll have the chicken.
7 Customer A: Just water please.
3 Customer B: And I'll have the fish. No, wait. I'll have the steak.
1 Waiter: Are you ready to order now?
5 Customer A: Yes, we'd both like potatoes and vegetables please.
4 Waiter: Would you like anything with your chicken and steak?

B SPEAK Work in pairs. Student A is the waiter. Student B is the customer. Practice ordering food in a restaurant. Use the ideas in Exercise A to help you.

A: Are you ready to order now?
B: Yes, I'll have the fish, please.

Ask students to label the photo if you need time to set up the class.

Shoppers on Black Friday in Maine, US.

The quote suggests that if something feels right or we enjoy it, we should take advantage and do it as much as possible.

OBJECTIVES

- talk about clothes and what people are doing
- talk about what people do at different times
- talk about shopping habits and tastes
- shop for clothes
- write a social media post

Work with a partner. Discuss the questions.

1 How often do you go shopping?
2 Look at the picture. Who do you think they're shopping for? Why?
3 Do you like shopping online? Why/Why not?

SHOPPING 81

OBJECTIVES

Read the unit objectives to the class.

UNIT OPENER QUESTIONS

Ask students to look at the picture on the page and describe what they see. Ask students where they think the shoppers were and what they bought. Point out that Black Friday is an event which happens in many countries in November. Prices are lower than usual, and many people buy things in stores or online. Ask students if they know about Black Friday or have anything similar in their countries.

Ask students to read the questions at the bottom of the page. Check that students understand the questions.

Put them into pairs to discuss the three questions. Monitor and help with grammar and vocabulary as required. Encourage students to listen to each other and ask follow-up questions to find out more. For whole-class feedback, ask two or three students to share their opinions with the rest of the class.

WORKSHEETS

Lesson 9.1 People watching

Clothes (W44)

Present progressive (W45)

Lesson 9.2 Job swap

Present time expressions (W46)

Simple present vs present progressive (W47)

Lesson 9.3 Shop till you drop

Object pronouns (W48)

Stores and services (W49)

9.1 People watching

Talk about clothes and what people are doing

V clothes P /ɜːr/ G present progressive

VOCABULARY
Clothes

A Work in pairs. What clothes can you see in pictures (1–4)? Use the words in the box to help you.

cap coat jeans hat scarf shorts socks skirt sunglasses sneakers pants

B Go to the **Vocabulary Hub** on **page 151**.

C **SPEAK** Work in pairs. Look at the pictures in Exercise A.

1 Which clothes do you like? Why?
2 Which don't you like? Why?

PRONUNCIATION
/ɜːr/

9.1 **A** Listen and repeat. Notice that the underlined syllables are all pronounced as /ɜːr/.

early first learn prefer shirt

9.2 **B** Check (✓) the words that have the /ɜːr/ sound. Then listen, check and repeat.

- [ ] ear
- [x] her
- [x] skirt
- [ ] there
- [x] thirty
- [x] Thursday
- [ ] we're
- [x] work

C **SPEAK** Work in pairs. Say this tongue twister.

I prefer to wear a shirt to work on Thursdays.

LISTENING

A What do you like to do when you are alone in a café? Which sentence describes you?

- I sit quietly and read.
- I usually use my phone.
- I watch the people around me.
- I call my friends.

9.3 **B** **LISTEN FOR KEY WORDS** Listen to Johan's conversation. Which of the activities in Exercise A does he do?

watches people around him, calls his friend

9.3 **C** **LISTEN FOR DETAIL** Listen again. Match the people (1–5) with their clothes (a–e).

1 customer	a pink dress
2 angry woman	b tie
3 tall man	c pajamas
4 short woman	d sneakers
5 young girl	e hat

D **SPEAK** Work in pairs. Answer the questions.

1 Do people in your town or city wear interesting clothes?
2 Do you know any celebrities who wear unusual clothes?
3 Why do you think people wear unusual clothes?

A: There is a charity run in my town every year. Lots of people wear funny clothes.
B: I think Lady Gaga wears unusual clothes.

9.1 People watching

LEAD-IN

Walk confidently into class, adjusting your clothing (e.g. checking buttons, brushing imaginary dirt off your shoulder, etc). Ask students if they like your clothes. Highlight each piece of clothing, eliciting the word for it and asking students to give their opinions. Put students into pairs; ask them to make a list of clothing you should never wear and clothes they think you should buy.

VOCABULARY

A In pairs, students match the items of clothing to the pictures. Check answers as a class.

B Direct students to the **Vocabulary Hub**. Give them time to complete the exercise alone before checking answers in pairs.

C Students discuss the clothes in Exercise A, saying which they like. Use the **Vocabulary Worksheet** on W44 for extra practice.

PRONUNCIATION

9.1 **A** Play the recording. Elicit the sound and emphasize that the mouth needs to be relaxed.

NOTE: The international phonetic alphabet has been used in this course. However, /ɜː/ is represented as /ɝ/ in the American English phonetic alphabet.

9.2 **B** In pairs, students say the words and identify which have the target sound.

C Students practice the tongue twister in pairs. Encourage students to try saying it very slowly at first, then saying it faster and faster.

LISTENING

A Describe the setting for the students; they are alone in a café, with no plans to meet anyone. Ask students what they would do. Then ask students to identify which sentence describes them best. Add your own opinion.

9.3 **B** Go through the task for students. Students then listen and decide which activity from Exercise A Johan does.

9.3 **C** Allow students time to read the task. Then play the recording again. After listening, students compare answers with a partner.

D Provide your own answers using the target language.

TEACHING IDEA by David Seymour and Maria Popova

Vocabulary: My clothes

Use this activity to review the vocabulary section. Say this to your students:

Find someone in class who is wearing …

something green, designer clothes, jeans, nylon, sandals, no socks, silk, a belt, something striped

I will tell each of you the name of someone else in class. On your own, write a description of what this person is wearing. (Collect the descriptions and read them aloud to see how quickly the class can identify each person.)

Point to these things, either on yourself or on another student.

zipper, pocket, button, collar, laces, sleeve, hem, heel, lapel

Find out who has:

the most zippers, the deepest pockets, the brightest socks, the longest laces, the highest heels, the biggest collar, the most interesting buttons

Everybody stand up. Sit down if you are wearing the things I say. The last person standing is the winner. (Read the list aloud one at a time. Vary or add to the list according to what your students are wearing.)

green socks, a jacket with zippers, a belt, sneakers, jeans, a blue shirt, a sweatshirt with a logo, high heels, a short-sleeved top, something with more than six buttons, a baseball cap

TEACHING IDEA by David Seymour and Maria Popova

Grammar: Clothes

Use this activity to test understanding of the present progressive. Say this to your students:

Ask a student what he/she wears or is wearing and then to repeat the question to another student, e.g.

Teacher: Manuel, are you wearing jeans?
Manuel: No, I'm not. Are you wearing jeans, Ilona?
Ilona: Yes, I am.
Teacher: Brigit, do you wear a scarf?
Brigit: Yes, I do, during the winter. Do you wear a scarf, Peter?

AUDIO SCRIPT

9.3

Listening, Exercise B
S = Sophie J = Johan

S: Hey, Johan.
J: Hey!
S: How are things? What are you doing?
J: I'm well, thanks. I'm having a coffee at the café in the park.
S: Oh, I miss the café in the park. Is Tom there?
J: No, just me. Excuse me – espresso, please? Oh, sorry! How embarrassing! I just ordered a coffee from a customer. I thought he was a waiter – he's wearing a white shirt and a tie and carrying some cups. (Ex C Q1)
S: Oops! Is the park busy?
J: Yes, it's very busy. Ooh! There's a woman near me. I *think* she's a runner – she's wearing a T-shirt and sneakers. She's very angry. She's trying to get a bottle of water, but no one is serving her. (Ex C Q2)
S: Mm.
J: Oh, Sophie, you should see this – there's a tall man and a short woman coming this way. They're wearing *really* strange clothes. She's in pajamas! (Ex C Q4)
S: What? They're in pajamas?
J: No, the *man* isn't wearing pajamas. He's dressed like a pirate! Haha! He's in a black jacket, a bandana and a hat with three corners. (Ex C Q3)
S: Haha! That's odd. I wonder why they're dressed like that …
J: Hang on, I'll ask … Excuse me, why are you wearing those clothes? Oh, I see. Thanks. Apparently, they're doing a charity run.
S: Oh, I see!
J: Aww! How cute …
S: What's happening now?
Ex C Q5 **J:** There's a little girl in a pretty pink party dress with a pink ribbon in her hair. She's holding her mother's hand. I think it's her first party. She looks very sweet!
S: Awww …
J: Anyway, tell me about you. What are you doing?
S: Well, it was really cold this morning, so …

9.1 People watching

GRAMMAR

A Display the sentences on the board and ask students to identify the verbs. Underline them, including the form of *be* (e.g. *What are you doing?*).

B Students work alone to complete the rules. Check answers as a class. Read through the *Present progressive spelling* box with students, and give more examples as required, to check understanding.

C Direct students to the **Grammar Hub** (see below). Read the examples and go through the rules with the class.

D Students work alone to write present progressive questions using the prompts. Monitor and assist as required.

E In pairs, students ask and answer the questions. Monitor and focus on accuracy of the target language. Use the **Grammar Worksheet** on W45 for extra practice.

SPEAKING

A–D Students review the photos and, working individually, choose someone to describe. Students complete the remaining exercises and discuss the questions in pairs.

GRAMMAR HUB

9.1 Present progressive

	Positive	Negative
I	**I'm talking** to my friend.	**I'm not feeling** very well.
he/she/it	**She's wearing** shorts and a t-shirt.	**She isn't working** today.
you/we/they	**They're playing** cards.	**They aren't wearing** uniforms.

	Question	Short answers	
I	**Am I saying** it correctly?	Yes, **you are**.	No, **you aren't**.
he/she/it	**Is she wearing** a backpack?	Yes, **she is**.	No, **she isn't**.
you/we/they	**Are you doing** it together?	Yes, **we are**.	No, **we aren't**.

Spelling rules	base form	*-ing*
Add **-ing**.	look	look**ing**
Drop the **-e** with verbs ending **-e**.	giv**e**	giv**ing**
Double the final consonant with verbs ending consonant, vowel, consonant + **-ing**.	sto**p**	sto**pping**

- We use the present progressive to talk about things happening now.
- In the negative, with *you*, *he*, etc we can also say: *You're not + -ing, He's not + -ing, She's not + -ing, It's not + -ing, We're not + -ing, They're not + -ing.*

  It ***isn't*** *raining. OR* ***It's not*** *raining.*
- In negative short answers, with *you*, *he*, etc we can also say: *No, you're not., No, he's not., No, she's not., No, it's not., No, we're not., No, they're not.*

  Are they driving to work at the moment? No, ***they aren't****. OR No,* ***they're not****.*

9.1 Present progressive

A Complete the conversations with the present progressive form of the verbs in parentheses. Use contractions where possible.

1 A: Where are you?
B: We 're getting (get) off the bus right now.

2 A: Is he coming (come) now?
B: Yes, very soon.

3 A: Where's Ahmed?
B: He 's having (have) lunch.

4 A: Are you at work?
B: No, I 'm sitting (sit) in the park.

5 A: What are you reading (read) at the moment?
B: *The Secret History* by Donna Tartt. It's amazing!

6 A: What are you up to?
B: I 'm watching (watch) the rugby

B Use the prompts to complete the text messages. Use contractions where possible.

What *are you doing* (you / do) now?

1 I'm watching (I / watch) TV. What about you?

2 I'm walking (I / walk) the dog. 3 She's wearing (she / wear) her new collar. Is Elle with you?

No, she isn't here. She's with Wes. 4 They're going (they / go) to the gym now.

5 Are you going (you / go) too?

No, I'm too tired.

➤ Go back to page 83.

GRAMMAR

Present progressive

A WORK IT OUT Look at the sentences from the conversation between Johan and Sophie. Underline the verbs.

1 What are you doing?
2 I'm having a coffee.
3 They're wearing really strange clothes.
4 No, the man isn't wearing pajamas.

B Choose the correct words to complete the rules.

Present progressive

1 We use the present progressive to describe *what is happening now / routines*.
2 We make the present progressive with *be + verb + base form / -ing*.
3 In present progressive questions, *be* comes *before / after* the subject.

Present progressive spelling

- We add *-ing* to most verbs in the present progressive.
  read – reading
  think – thinking
- With verbs ending in *-e*, we drop the *-e*, and add *-ing*.
  give – giving
- When the last three letters of a verb are consonant, vowel, consonant, we usually double the final consonant and add *-ing*.
  run – running
  stop – stopping
  Traveling is the exception to this rule in American English.

C Go to the **Grammar Hub** on **page 138**.

D PRACTICE Use the prompts to write present progressive questions.

1 what / you / wear?
What are you wearing?
2 you / wear / warm clothes?
Are you wearing warm clothes?
3 what book / you / read / at the moment?
What book are you reading at the moment?
4 you / eat / something?
Are you eating something?
5 what / you / think / right now?
What are you thinking (about) right now?

E SPEAK Work in pairs. Take turns asking and answering the questions in Exercise D.

A: What are you wearing?
B: I'm wearing blue jeans, black sneakers and a white T-shirt. What are you wearing?

a

b

SPEAKING

A PREPARE Look at the pictures (a and b). Choose a person to describe. Think about:

- what they are wearing
- what they are doing
- where they are

B ORGANIZE Write notes about what you want to say.

This man is wearing sunglasses and a white shirt. He's taking a selfie with his friend.

C SPEAK Work in pairs. Describe the person to your partner. Can they guess who you are talking about?

D DISCUSS Work in groups. Discuss the questions.

1 What do you think of the clothes people are wearing in the pictures above?
2 Would you wear the same clothes? Why/Why not?
3 What kind of clothes are fashionable in your country at the moment?

Talk about clothes and what people are doing

9.2 Job swap

Talk about what people do at different times

V present time expressions G simple present vs present progressive P /ŋ/

LISTENING

A SPEAK Work in pairs. Look at pictures (1–3). Would you like to do these jobs? Why/Why not?

9.4 **B LISTEN FOR GIST** Listen to the announcement. What is it about? Choose the correct answer.

- **a** a competition (circled)
- **b** a job offer
- **c** a sale

9.4 **C LISTEN FOR KEY WORDS** Listen again and complete the sentences.

1. The prize money is $ 1,000 .
2. To win the money, shoppers must do a different job for one day.
3. The Clothing Department is on Level 2 .
4. The Clothing Department is next to the café .
5. Registration closes at 4 pm.

D SPEAK Work in pairs. Answer the questions.

1. What do you do? Are you a student? Do you have a job?
2. Do you like what you do? Why/Why not?
3. Do you want to change what you do?

READING

A Match jobs (1–6) with what the person does (a–f).

1 doctor	a teach children
2 mechanic	b plan events, book models
3 teacher	c fix engines
4 personal shopper	d help sick people
5 fashion show director	e take pictures
6 photographer	f give advice, choose clothes for shoppers

(Answers: 1–d, 2–c, 3–a, 4–f, 5–b, 6–e)

B READ FOR GIST Read the social media posts. Are Bryony, Lee and Adal enjoying their job swap?
Adal is really enjoying the job swap; Bryony is enjoying it (but less than Adal); Lee isn't enjoying it.

C READ FOR SPECIFIC INFORMATION Read the posts again and answer the questions. Choose Bryony (B), Lee (L) or Adal (A).

1. Who loves his job swap? B / L / (A)
2. Who doesn't have a specialist to help her? (B) / L / A
3. Who wants to go back to his usual job? B / (L) / A
4. Who usually repairs things? B / (L) / A
5. Who usually helps sick people? (B) / L / A
6. Who is thinking about changing his job? B / L / (A)

D SPEAK Work in pairs. Answer the questions.

1. Do you think a job swap is a fun idea? Why/Why not?
2. Which job in *Job swap* would you like to try? Why?

VOCABULARY

Present time expressions

A Read *Job swap* again. Find and underline the present time expressions. The first two have been done for you.
right now; at the moment; Currently,

B Choose the correct time expression to complete the sentences.

1. I spend a lot of time at the gym *now* / *these days*. I'm trying to get in shape for the London Marathon next year.
2. I'm *currently* / *today* working at St. Crispin's Hospital in London. It's just for a few weeks.
3. I'm afraid Mr. Stevens isn't here *at the moment* / *these days*. Can I take a message?

C SPEAK Work in pairs. Answer the questions.

1. What is your teacher wearing today?
2. What are you currently studying?
3. What are you doing more often these days?
4. What is your favorite TV show at the moment?

A: *My favorite TV show at the moment is Game of Thrones. It's amazing!*
B: *Oh, really? That's my favorite show, too!*

9.2 Job swap

LEAD-IN

Tell students about your work day routine (e.g. what time you get up, when you start work, etc). Explain some of the good aspects of your job as well as things you don't like. Next, ask one of your stronger students about their job/studies. Elicit their daily routine and the pros and cons of what they do. Ask them if they'd like to swap roles with you for the day, and encourage them to explain their reasoning. Now put students in pairs and ask them to explain what they do and to decide whether they'd like to swap roles for a day and why. Give feedback as a class, adding any useful emergent language to the board.

LISTENING

A Focus students on the pictures. Identify what the jobs are, and ask them which they would like to do (*1 the person is washing a car; 2 this person could be a stuntman or stuntwoman; 3 this person is a designer or architect*). Open up the discussion to the whole class and use follow-up questions to encourage the students to extend their answers.

9.4 **B** Go through the task with the students. Then play the recording. Ask students to explain their choice.

A: *Hello shoppers and welcome to Greenfield Department Store. Would you like to win 1,000 dollars? Then enter our job swap competition! Swap your job for one day and you could win the money. To enter our job swap competition, go to the clothing department on level two, which is by the café. Make sure you enjoy some coffee and a sandwich while you're there! Registration opens this morning at ten o'clock and stays open until four o'clock this afternoon, so make sure you register your name and contact information today.*

9.4 **C** Allow students time to read through the sentences before listening again. Students compare answers in pairs and listen again as required. Check answers as a class.

D Students ask and answer the questions in pairs. Open up the discussion for the whole class, and give your opinion, too.

READING

A Students match the jobs with the actions. Allow students time to compare answers in pairs and then check as a class. If necessary, help with the pronunciation of *mechanic* **/mə'kænɪk/**.

B Focus students on the *Job swap* text. If you didn't use the Lead-in above, remind students that a *swap* is when two people give each other something for a short time. Elicit what a *job swap* might be (it's when two people do the job that the other person was doing).

Give students up to two minutes to find out if the people are enjoying their job swaps. Check answers as a class.

C Set a longer time limit. Students read the text again and decide who each question relates to. Allow students time to compare answers in pairs and review the text as required. Give feedback as a class, encouraging students to explain what part of the text gave them the answers.

D Students discuss the questions in pairs. Then put two pairs together for students to report the main point of their discussion with their partner and to extend the discussion further. For whole-class feedback, ask a few groups to summarise the main points of their discussion.

VOCABULARY

A Focus students on the underlined time expressions in the text. Then ask students to find and underline the rest. Check answers as a class.

B Individually, students complete the sentences with the correct time expression. Check answers as a class.

C In pairs, students discuss the questions. Monitor and encourage students to ask follow-up questions to find out more about each other. Make a note of effective use of the present time expressions (as well as the present progressive) and highlight these in whole-class feedback. Use the **Vocabulary Worksheet** on W46 for extra practice.

METHODOLOGY HUB by Jim Scrivener

Flashcards

Flashcards is ELT jargon for pictures (or diagrams, words, etc) that you can hold up when standing in front of the whole class. They are also useful for handing out as part of various activities.

The easiest way to find good pictures is to do an Internet image search – though, you also need access to a color printer or IWB to show them. Many schools have their own library of published flashcards.

If you find a good picture, rather than using it once, keep it and slowly build up your stock of resources. To start collecting, you need to approach the world with a 'flashcard' frame of mind! Whenever you look at a magazine, advertising flyer, etc, keep your eyes open for suitable pictures. When the publication is ready to head for the trash can, cut out the pictures you need. Generally, choose larger pictures that will be clearly visible even from the back of the classroom. You will find some subjects are very easy to find (cars, food products, perfumes, etc) whereas others (people doing specific everyday tasks, faces expressing different moods, etc) are harder. After a while, you'll need to start looking for specific things that fill in the blanks in your set.

When you have a number of pictures, you'll have to find some way to organize them, maybe in folders sorted by topic. It may also be worth taking the extra time to make cards longer lasting, by gluing them down on cardboard, keeping them in plastic pockets or even by laminating them. What can you do with them? Here are a few typical uses:

- to quickly show the meaning of a lexical item, e.g. *to iron*;
- to illustrate presentations of language, for example, by giving a visual image to an imaginary character, e.g. *This is Marilyn. Every day she gets up at six o'clock …*, etc;
- to tell a story, providing occasional images to give students something tangible to look at and help their understanding, e.g. *… and then a large green truck turned around the corner and drove toward them*;
- as prompts to remind them of a specific grammar point or typical error, e.g. a flashcard with the word *past* on it to quickly remind students to make verbs in the past form;
- as seeds for student-based storytelling activities, e.g. handing out a small selection of pictures to groups of students and asking them to invent a story that incorporates all those images;
- as prompts for guessing games, definition games, description games, etc. For example, one person on a team has a picture of a person, which they describe. Then the other students are shown a pile of seven pictures (including the original one) and have to work out which picture was described.

9.2 Job swap

GRAMMAR

A Give students time to complete the rules alone, before checking their answers with a partner. Give feedback as a class, providing new examples to help clarify the rules if necessary. Then read through the *Time expressions* box as a class. Point out that we usually use expressions like *at the moment* or *right now* with the present progressive, to make it clear that we are talking about something that doesn't always happen and will end soon.

B Direct students to the **Grammar Hub** (see below). Read the examples and go through the rules with the class.

C Put students into pairs or small groups to discuss the questions. Monitor, focussing on use of the two tenses. Give feedback as a class, encouraging students to ask follow-up questions to stimulate discussion (e.g. *Do you think you should speak to your parents more? What's the TV show about?* etc). Use the **Grammar Worksheet** on W47 for extra practice.

> **Extra activity**
> Ask students to write six new questions: three in the simple present and three in the present progressive. Monitor, ensuring the questions are as interesting as possible. Then, ask students to stand up and walk around the class asking their questions. Monitor and answer anything you're asked!

PRONUNCIATION

9.5 **A** Play the recording so students can listen and repeat the pairs. Focus on the final sound in each word. Highlight that the first word in each pair has a /n/ sound and the second has a /ŋ/, writing these phonemes on the board. Practice the two sounds multiple times.

9.6 **B** Explain that the /ŋ/ isn't always at the end of a word, using *angry* as an example. Next, play the recording for students to repeat the words.

SPEAKING

Direct students to the **Communication Hub** for further practice.

A Elicit the question for the first prompt (*What do you do?*). Point out that students need to decide if each question is asking about general habits and routines or about what the other student is doing right now. Give students time to write the questions, and then check they have written them correctly.

B Put students into pairs to ask and answer the questions. They should write notes on what their partner says.

C Put students into small groups with different people. Ask them to use their notes to suggest interesting job swaps for the people in the class.

GRAMMAR HUB

9.2 Simple present vs present progressive

- We use the simple present to talk about habits and routines.
  He wears a suit to work every day.
- We also use the simple present to talk about things that are true in general.
  They usually dress up for a party.
- We use the present progressive to talk about things happening now.
  Take a coat – it's raining outside.
- We also use the present progressive to talk about things happening around now.
  I'm working in Berlin for a month. I usually work in New York.

> **Be careful!**
> - We often use the simple present with the time expressions *all day*, *every week*, *once a year*, and adverbs like *always*, *often*, *usually* and *never*.
> - We often use the present progressive with the time expressions *(right) now* and *at the moment*.

9.2 Simple present vs present progressive

A Choose the correct option.

1. The department store ***opens*** / *is opening* at nine o'clock every day.
2. I ***don't usually give*** / *am not usually giving* fashion advice.
3. He *wears* / ***'s wearing*** a Hugo Boss suit and Prada shoes.
4. It looks like she *enjoys* / ***'s enjoying*** the fashion show.
5. In the US, students usually ***don't wear*** / *aren't wearing* a uniform to school.
6. Today, I *work* / ***'m working*** on a report for Gemma.
7. It usually ***snows*** / *is snowing* at this time of year.
8. I can't meet tomorrow. I ***work*** / *'m working* from home on Tuesdays.

B Complete the conversations with the simple present or present progressive forms of the verbs in parentheses.

1. A: Can __I speak__ (I / speak) to Rosanna Francis?
   B: Sorry, __she isn't / is not__ (she / not / be) here. Can I take a message?
2. A: Hey! Where __are you?__ (you /be)?
   B: __I'm / I am leaving__ (I / leave) now.
3. A: __Are you watching__ (you / watch) the news?
   B: No. Why? What __is happening?__ (be / happen)?
4. A: Where __are you from__ (be / you / from)?
   B: I __'m / am from__ (be / from) a small town in Northern Spain.
5. A: What __are you cooking__ (you / cook)?
   B: I __am making__ (be / make) spaghetti.

➤ Go back to page 85.

Job swap

Greenfield Department Store
October 23, 8:57 am

It's job swap day! We've asked the winners of our job swap competition (Bryony, Lee and Adal) to post updates here every hour to tell us how their new job is going.

Bryony Williams
October 23, 10:05 am

I'm enjoying my job swap, but it's completely different from what I usually do. I work as a doctor, but today I'm organizing a fashion show. It's hard work and there's a lot to do, but I'm having an interesting time. I love fashion and clothes, so I expected this to be easy, but it isn't. Today, I'm booking models and planning the event. The other job swappers have experts to help them, but I don't, so I'm feeling under pressure now!

Share Like Comment

Lee Cartwright
October 23, 10:17 am

Yesterday, I was a mechanic, but today I'm working as a personal shopper! I usually test cars and fix them, but today I'm giving people advice on buying clothes. I love my job at the garage, but I'm not enjoying this job at the moment. I can only write this now because my expert, Katrina, is talking on the phone. When she finishes, it's back to work for me. I don't want to do this anymore. I'm not having fun. I want to go back to my workshop.

Share Like Comment

Adal Khan
October 23, 10:21 am

I usually teach eight-year-old children, but right now I'm taking pictures of models. Currently, I'm working as a fashion photographer! I took over 200 pictures this morning and it isn't even lunchtime yet. I'm learning so many things and I'm having the best time. As a teacher, I usually tell people what to do at school, but today Santos, my expert, is teaching me. Who knows, maybe I'm starting a new career … 😃

Share Like Comment

Glossary

career (n) a job that you want to do for a long period of your life
expert (n) someone with a particular skill or who knows a lot about a particular subject
swap (v) to give something to someone in exchange for something else

GRAMMAR

Simple present vs present progressive

A WORK IT OUT Read the examples in the box. Then choose the correct words to complete the rules.

Simple present and present progressive

1 We use the present progressive to talk about events that *happen every day / are happening now*.
… but today I'm organizing a fashion show.
… so I'm feeling under pressure now.

2 We use the simple present to talk about *events that happen every day / events happening now*.
I work as a doctor …
I love fashion and clothes …

Time expressions

Time expressions like *all day*, *every week* and *once a year* are used with the simple present.
I visit my grandmother once a week.
Adverbs of frequency (*always*, *usually*) are also used.
I usually test cars and fix them.
Time expressions like *today*, *now* and *at the moment* are used with the present progressive.
Today, I'm booking models.

B Go to the **Grammar Hub** on **page 138**.

C SPEAK Work in groups. Discuss the questions.

1 What's something that you only do once a year?
2 How often do you speak to your parents?
3 What are you watching on TV at the moment?
4 What time do you usually finish work or college classes?
5 What's something that you never do?

PRONUNCIATION

/ŋ/

9.5 **A** Listen and repeat the pairs of words. Can you hear the difference between the final sounds?

1 ban / bang
2 thin / thing
3 win / wing

9.6 **B** Listen and repeat. All of the words have the /ŋ/ sound.

angry bank banking enjoying
finger having helping long shopping
taking talking thinking

SPEAKING

Work in pairs. Go the **Communication Hub** on **page 157**.

Talk about what people do at different times

9.3 Shop till you drop

Talk about shopping habits and tastes

G object pronouns **V** stores and services **P** /tʃ/ and /ʃ/ **S** reading for genre

READING

A Work in pairs. Answer the questions. Use the words in the box to help you.

designer brands discount stores expensive things full price things good quality products local stores

1 What kind of things do you usually buy online?
2 What do you like spending money on? Why?
3 What don't you like spending money on? Why?

B Read *How to market your business* quickly. Where is it from? Who is the author writing to? Use the information in the box to help you.

Reading for genre

When you read something, it is important to know why the author wrote it. Think about:

- *Where is the text from (e.g. a website, magazine)?*
- *Who is the text for (e.g. students, doctors)?*

C READ FOR DETAIL Read the article again. Are the sentences true (T) or false (F)? Correct the false sentences.

1 Mike's store sells designer clothes. T / (F) Mike's store sells fruits and vegetables, cheese, bread and cakes.
2 Mike isn't getting enough customers. (T) / F
3 Discount shoppers spend a lot of time in stores because they love shopping. T / (F) Discount shoppers want good prices.
4 Luxury shoppers don't worry about the price of things. (T) / F
5 Quality shoppers go to local stores because they are cheap. T / (F) Quality shoppers want to support local businesses.

D SPEAK Work in pairs. Answer the questions.

1 What kind of shopper would be interested in Mike's business? Why?
2 What kind of shopper are you?

A: *Mike could raise his prices. Then luxury shoppers might be interested in his business.*
B: *That's true. Quality shoppers might also be interested because they like to support local businesses.*

How to market your business

Mike owns a small store. He spends all of his time working in it. It sells fruits and vegetables, cheese from a local farm, fresh homemade bread and delicious cakes. The store is on a busy road, full of cafés and restaurants. The local people have a lot of money and they know how to spend it. But Mike's business is slow. He's worried. He's trying different things to sell more food, but nothing is working. So what's he doing wrong? Maybe he isn't selling to the right people. It's the first rule of business: find out who your customers are, and listen to them. So, is business in your store slow? Read on to find out how to attract three kinds of shoppers. Ex C Q1 Ex C Q2

Drop your prices

Discount shoppers like saving money! They like spending time in stores because they want to find everything at a good price. These shoppers like big grocery store markets and cheap local stores. Department stores are usually too expensive for them. They aren't interested in designer brands. They often shop online and travel to find the best price. They don't like paying full price for anything, and often buy clothes or big items when there's a sale. Ex C Q3

Offer something special

Luxury shoppers love shopping, fashion and expensive products. Shopping is a serious hobby for them. They don't mind paying a lot for their favorite designer brands! Luxury shoppers hate cheap stores and prefer elegant department stores in the city center, where they can have a cup of coffee and meet their friends for lunch. Luxury shoppers buy what they want, when they want. Ex C Q4

Which kind of shopper do you think would be interested in your business?

Offer quality

Quality shoppers look for products that they can use for many years and they are happy to pay a little more for something special. They look for good quality things in shopping malls. They also like local stores because they want to support businesses in their area. They often shop at markets, or at traditional local bakeries and butchers'. They also like to touch the things they are buying and they often spend a long time looking at them. Ex C Q5

Glossary

brand (n) a product, or products, that has its own name and is made by a particular company
designer (adj) designer clothes are made by a famous designer and are usually expensive
local (adj) in or close to the area that you live in, or to the area that you are talking about
luxury (n) something expensive that you enjoy, but do not really need
quality (n) how good or bad something is
sale (n) an event or period of time when a store reduces some of its prices

9.3 Shop till you drop

LEAD-IN

Write the names of five stores you think students will know on the board. Put students into pairs. Ask them to rank the stores from their favorite to their least favorite. Monitor and encourage discussion. Give feedback as a class, encouraging students to explain why they like or don't like the stores on the list. Explore any major differences in opinion. Encourage students to give examples of stores they prefer and why.

READING

A Read through the phrases in the box as a class, making sure that students understand them. Point out the *Glossary* at the bottom of the article on page 86, where students can find definitions of some of these words. You could also pre-teach the following items: *luxury* and *sale*.

Students answer the questions in pairs, using the words in the box to help. Ask pairs to share main points with the whole class.

To practice these words further, you could ask students to discuss these questions in pairs: *Is there a brand of clothes you like to buy? Is the quality of clothes important to you? Do you like designer or luxury brands? Do you usually buy clothes when there is a sale?*

B Read through the *Reading for genre* box with students. Point out that a good writer always writes for a particular audience in mind. Then ask students the questions in Exercise B. Ask students to explain their choice of answer.

The article might be from a business magazine or from a website. The article is for business owners. It isn't for shoppers. These extracts from the article tell us who the article is for: How to market your business; It's the first rule of business: find out who your customers are, and listen to them. Which kind of shopper do you think would be interested in your business?

C Go through the task with students. Set a time limit of five minutes. Students read the text in detail and decide if the sentences are true or false. They should identify the part of the text which gives them the answer, and they should also correct the false answers. Allow students time to compare and answer in pairs before checking as a class.

D Students discuss the questions in pairs. Then open up the discussion to the whole class, and include your own opinions, too.

METHODOLOGY HUB by Jim Scrivener

Dealing with lexis during reading or listening work

While students are mainly working on reading or listening skills, you are less likely to spend time on lexis, as this might clash with the reading, listening or other aims.

Once the learners have become comfortable with the text, you can focus attention on lexical items in the text and how they are used. Here are some things that you could ask:

- Can you guess the meaning of this word from the meaning of the text around it?
- Find some words in the text that mean …
- Find some words in the text connected with the subject of …
- In line X, what does … mean?
- Find words and sort them into three separate groups under these headings: …
- Why does the writer use the word … here?
- Find words in the text that match this list of synonyms.
- What words come before / after the word … . What other words collocate with this word?
- Can you remember any other phrases you know with this word in them?
- Can you find any multiword items (i.e. groups of words that go together / chunks)?
- What's the opposite of this word?
- How many different words does the writer use to describe the …?

TEACHING IDEA by David Seymour and Maria Popova

Grammar: Personal pronouns

Use this activity to prepare for the grammar focus on page 87.

Personal pronouns (Write this table on the board, eliciting the pronouns as you do so.)

I	love	me
you	like	you
he	hate	him
she	want	her
it	don't like	it
we		us
they		them

Take turns saying a sentence and then a question using the words in the table, e.g.

A: She likes him.

B: Why does she like him?

A: Because …

In small groups, take turns saying as many sentences as you can using these words, as quickly as possible, e.g. *He wants us to listen.*

I	want(s)	me	to	speak
you	would like	you		go
he	need(s)	him		write
she	asked	her		listen
it	told	it		look
we	don't want	us		
they		them		

Add another preposition, where possible, and another pronoun, e.g. *He wants us to listen to him.*

9.3 Shop till you drop

GRAMMAR

A Write the first sentence on the board. Analyze it with students and underline the preposition and circle the object pronoun. Students then do the same with the remaining sentences. Check answers as a class, using the board for support.

B Students work alone to complete the rules. Check answers as a class.

C Direct students to the **Grammar Hub** (see below). Read the examples and go through the rules with the class.

D Model the answers for students by talking about yourself. Then elicit the object pronouns you used and what they referred to. Then put students into pairs, to ask and answer the questions. Monitor and focus on accuracy of the target language. Use the **Grammar Worksheet** on W48 for extra practice.

VOCABULARY

A Focus students on the text. Ask them to underline eight words for stores or services. Check as a class.

apples: grocery store, market
a cake: café; grocery store, market, bakery
cheese: a restaurant, grocery store, market
a cup of coffee: café, restaurant
meat: grocery store, market, butcher's
a pair of shoes: market, department store, shopping mall
a pizza: café, restaurant, grocery store, shopping mall, bakery
a TV: department store, shopping mall

B In pairs, students say where they could buy each of the items in the box.

C Direct students to the **Vocabulary Hub**. Give students time to complete the exercise alone before checking answers in pairs.

D Model the answers by talking about your own views, explaining and extending your answers using target language from the unit. Students then discuss the questions in pairs. Use the **Vocabulary Worksheet** on W49 for extra practice.

PRONUNCIATION

9.7 **A** Play the recording for students to repeat the words. Highlight the difference in the sounds, particularly that the /ʃ/ sound can be continued, whereas /ʧ/ cannot.

9.8 **B** In pairs, students complete the table with the words from the box. Encourage students to say the words out loud to identify the sounds.

SPEAKING HUB

A In groups, students read through the instructions. They think of ideas for questions based on the three bullet points.

B Students work together to write questions. Monitor and assist with accuracy as required.

C Students mingle with students from a different group. They ask and answer questions, making a note of the answers.

D Put students into their original groups to share their findings.

GRAMMAR HUB

9.3 Object pronouns

Subject pronoun	Object pronoun
I	me
he	him
she	her
it	it
we	us
you	you
they	them

- We use object pronouns after a verb or after a preposition.
  After a verb: *Can you show me a different dress, please?*
- After a preposition: *It's Dinu's birthday. I'm buying a present for her.*

9.3 Object pronouns

A Complete the sentences with the object pronouns in the box.

me you him her it them

1 My sister loves clothes. I always go shopping with ___her___.
2 I love blue. It's the best color for ___me___.
3 Alison loves shoes. She spends a lot of money on ___them___.
4 Tom's very friendly. His customers like ___him___.
5 Jin want's a new cell phone. She's saving up for ___it___.
6 I bought ___you___ a cup of coffee, Doug. Be careful – it's hot!

B Complete the sentences with subject or object pronouns.

1 I need some new clothes, but ___I___ don't want to spend a lot of money on ___them___.
2 My sister gives great fashion advice. ___I___ always enjoy clothes shopping with ___her___.
3 Daniel doesn't have a lot of money, so ___I___ don't think ___he___ can afford those shoes.
4 I follow Mark Greenwood on Instagram. ___He___'s a fashion blogger.
5 Jo has three sisters. ___They___ always borrowed each other's clothes when ___they___ were younger!

➤ Go back to page 87.

GRAMMAR
Object pronouns

A Look at the sentences from *How to market your business*. Underline the prepositions and circle the object pronouns.

1 He spends all of his time working in it.
2 Department stores are usually too expensive for them.
3 Shopping is a serious hobby for them.
4 They like to touch the things they are buying and they often spend a long time looking at them.

B **WORK IT OUT** Choose the correct words to complete the rules.

Object pronouns

1 Object pronouns usually go at the ***beginning / end*** of sentences.
2 Prepositions usually go ***before / after*** object pronouns.

C Go to the **Grammar Hub** on **page 138**.

D **SPEAK** Work in pairs. Answer the questions. Use object pronouns.

1 Do you have any brothers or sisters? How often do you see them?
2 What's your favorite movie? When did you last watch it?
3 Who do you like to go shopping with? Why?

I have one brother named Tom. I see him about once a month.

VOCABULARY
Stores and services

A Read *How to market your business* again. Find and underline eight words for stores or services.

B **SPEAK** Work in pairs. Where could you buy the things in the box? Use the words you found in Exercise A to help you.

apples a cake cheese a cup of coffee meat a pair of shoes a pizza a TV

C Go to the **Vocabulary Hub** on **page 151**.

D **SPEAK** Work in pairs. Answer the questions.

1 Do you prefer buying things online or in a store? Why?
2 Do you usually buy fruits and vegetables from a market or a grocery store? Why?
3 Is there a shopping mall near where you live? How often do you go there?

A: I prefer buying things online because it's quick and easy.
B: Really? I prefer buying things in stores because you can see things before you buy them.

PRONUNCIATION
/tʃ/ and /ʃ/

A 9.7 Listen and repeat. Can you hear the difference between /tʃ/ and /ʃ/?

/tʃ/ choose, rich, chocolate
/ʃ/ shoes, shower, finish

B 9.8 Complete the table with the words in the box. Then listen, check and repeat.

~~butcher's~~ ~~cash~~ change cheap choose fashion fresh lunch shoes touch

/tʃ/		/ʃ/	
butcher's	choose	*cash*	shoes
change	lunch	fashion	
cheap	touch	fresh	

SPEAKING HUB

A **PREPARE** Work in groups. You are going to interview your classmates about their shopping habits. Think about:

- type of stores
- cost
- location

B **PLAN** Write questions for a shopping survey.

How often do you go shopping?
What kind of things do you usually buy online?
What do you like shopping for?

C **DISCUSS** Interview students in other groups. Write down their answers.

D **PRESENT** Get back into groups and compare your findings. Then present the information to the class.

Lots of people shop in grocery stores because it's easy and cheap.

Talk about shopping habits and tastes

9.4 Meeting Milly

F– shop for clothes P– connected speech

COMPREHENSION

A SPEAK Work in pairs. Look at the picture of Milly's clothing store. Answer the questions.

1 How often do you go shopping for clothes?
2 Do you like clothing stores like Milly's?
3 What are your favorite kinds of clothing stores?

B Watch the video. Complete the sentences. Write *Milly*, *Neena* or *Zac*.

1 *Neena* and *Zac* are housemates.
2 Milly and Neena are old friends.
3 Milly and Zac meet for the first time.
4 Milly and Zac are American.
5 Milly and Zac are from Seattle.
6 Milly and Zac don't try on any clothes.
7 Neena and Zac leave the store together.

C SPEAK Work in pairs. Why can't Zac speak? How does he feel about Milly? Zac is very shy. He likes Milly a lot.

FUNCTIONAL LANGUAGE

Shopping for clothes

A Complete the conversations (A–F). Then watch the video again and check your answers.

A

Sales clerk: [1] Can I help [2] you?
Customer: No, I'm just looking, thank you.

B

Customer: Can [3] I try it [4] on?
Sales clerk: Sure.

C

Customer: Where [5] are the changing [6] rooms?
Sales clerk: They're over there next to the scarves and shirts.

D

Customer: [7] What do [8] you think, guys?
Sales clerk: It looks great!

E

Customer: Have [9] you got [10] a medium?
Sales Clerk: Yeah, I think so.

F

Customer: I [11] 'll take [12] the jacket, the skirt and the shirt, please. [13] How much [14] is that?
Sales clerk: That's £85, please. Thank you.

B Work in pairs. Practice the conversations in Exercise A.

MILLY SAM NEENA ZAC GABY

PRONUNCIATION
Connected speech

9.9 **A** Listen and repeat the questions. Is there a pause between the words connected with a ‿?

1 Can‿I try‿it‿on? No, there isn't.
2 How much‿is‿it?

9.10 **B** Draw a ‿ to show the connected words. Then listen and check.

1 Can‿I‿try them‿on?
2 How much‿are‿they?
3 It's‿over there.
4 Your store‿is‿awesome!
5 Do‿you‿have‿an‿extra large?

9.10 **C** Listen again and repeat. Remember to use connected speech.

SPEAKING

A PREPARE Work in pairs. Look at the pictures. What do you like / not like about the clothes?

A: I really like the …
B: Do you? I think the …

B PLAN Work in pairs. Imagine you are in Milly's store. Student A – you are a sales clerk. Student B – you are a customer that needs help. Write a conversation.

- Offer to help the customer.
- Choose an item of clothing and ask to try it on.
- Tell the customer where the changing room is.
- Try it on and then ask for a different size.
- Give the customer a different size.
- Say you want to buy it and ask for a price.
- Tell the customer the price and ask how they want to pay.
- Buy the item and thank the sales clerk.

C PRESENT Perform your role play for the class.

Shop for clothes

➤ Turn to page 168 to learn how to write a social media post.

9.4 Meeting Milly

LEAD-IN

Write some items of clothing on the board (recycling language from earlier on in the unit). Ask students individually to make a note of the best place, in their opinion, to buy each item. Put students into groups to discuss and justify their answers, seeing if they can change anyone's mind.

COMPREHENSION

A In pairs, students look at the picture and discuss the questions. Give your own answers to start the feedback and then invite students to join in. Encourage students to extend their responses by asking follow-up questions.

B ▶ Allow students time to review the sentences. Play the video. Students complete the sentences with the three names. Students compare answers and then check as a class.

C Students discuss the questions in pairs. Share ideas as a class.

FUNCTIONAL LANGUAGE

A ▶ In pairs, students predict how to complete the conversations. Play the video again to check.

B Put students into pairs to practice the conversations twice. Ask them to take turns being the customer.

PRONUNCIATION

9.9 **A** Write *connected speech* on the board, and elicit what it might mean. Point out that in English, we often pronounce words together as one sound, linking them. Remind students that if a word ends with a consonant sound and the next word begins with a vowel sound, then these words are often connected when we speak.

Focus students on the two questions and the linking lines. Play the recording for students to hear them. Make sure they notice how the consonant and vowel sounds are connected. Play the recording again for students to check if there is a pause where the linking lines are marked.

9.10 **B** Write the first example on the board. As a class, identify the linking words. Students then work in pairs to identify the linking sounds in the other examples. Play the recording for students to check their answers.

9.10 **C** Play the recording again. Students listen again and repeat, focusing on producing the linking sounds.

SPEAKING

A Focus students on the pictures. In pairs, students discuss the clothes, talking about what they like and don't like about them. Encourage students to think about different aspects of the clothes (e.g. the style, color and price).

B In pairs, students write a conversation following all the stages given. Encourage them to use the *Functional Language* they have studied. Monitor and help as students prepare. Allow students time to practice their conversations. If you have time, ask students to record themselves. They can play back their conversations and notice whether they are using connected speech or whether they are pronouncing each word separately.

C Students take turns performing their role plays to the whole class. For whole-class feedback, praise any example you heard of good connected speech.

Extra activity

Put students into groups to discuss the following questions.

1 Do you like clothes shopping? Why/Why not?

2 How much money do you spend on clothes every month?

3 Do you prefer buying clothes online or in a store? Why?

Monitor, helping with new vocabulary as necessary. Try to encourage students to ask follow-up questions to get more information (e.g. *What kind of things do you like shopping for?*). If you have time, give feedback and open the questions up for class-wide discussion.

▶ VIDEO SCRIPT

Z = Zac M = Milly C = Customer N = Neena

Z: Sure. Let's go.
M: Hi! Can I help you?
C: No, I'm just looking, thank you.
M: OK. No problem.
Z: Cool!
N: Milly?
M: Neena! How are you?
N: I'm good. How are you?
M: Really well. Welcome, welcome! So, what do you think of the store?
N: It's great! I love it! Oh, this is … Zac?
Z: Yeah?
N: This is Milly … … And this is Zac.
M: Hey, Zac.
N: Zac's my new housemate. He's American too.
M: Cool. Where are you from?
Z: Sea … Seattle.
M: No way! Me too!
Z: That's cool! Your store is awesome.
M: Thanks.
N: Yeah … Umm … Oh, I like this! I'm looking for a new jacket. Can I try it on?
M: Sure.
N: Where are the changing rooms?
M: They're over there next to the scarves and shirts.
Z: So uh … When … When did you open?
N: What do you think, guys?
Z: It looks great!
M: Yeah! But it's a bit small, maybe.
N: I think you're right, Milly. Have you got a medium?
M: Yeah, I think so.
Z/M: Yes!
M: Yes.
Z: Ummm. No.
Z/M: Perfect!
N: Great. I'll take the jacket, the skirt and the shirt, please. How much is that?
M: That's £85, please. Thank you.
N: So nice to see you, Milly. I love the shop.
M: Thank you, Neena. See you soon. And bye Zac.
Z: Bye Milly.

9 Writing

Write a social media post

W– checking your work

A Work in pairs. Answer the questions.

1 What social media sites do you use?
2 Do you follow anyone on social media? Who?
3 Do you ever post pictures of yourself or friends/family on social media?
4 What kinds of pictures do people usually post on social media?

B Look at the pictures and read the social media posts. Match posts (a–d) with pictures (1–5). There is one picture you do not need. 1 d; 2 b; 3 c; 5 a

C Read the posts again and answer the questions.

1 Why is the woman trying on sunglasses?
2 What are Daria and her friend looking for?
3 What are the people doing at the beach?
4 Why is the man having breakfast in a café?

D Find and correct two mistakes in each sentence. Use the information in the box to help you.

Checking your work

Always check your work for mistakes after you write something. Make sure you:

- use the correct punctuation (capital letters, apostrophes, periods).
- avoid common spelling mistakes, for example ~~fourty~~ *forty*.
- use the correct grammar, for example, *I'm watching* ~~watch~~ *a movie at the moment.*

1 ~~Were~~ at the market and I ~~eat~~ an ice cream cone. We're; 'm eating
2 ~~Like you thees~~ shoes? Do you like these
3 What ~~you do~~ at the moment? are you doing
4 ~~I having~~ a party ~~beacause~~ it's my birthday. I'm having; because

E Read post c again and correct:

- three punctuation mistakes
- three grammar mistakes
- three spelling mistakes

a I'm having breakfast at my favorite café today. And I'm with my favorite person – my wife, Lucy! The eggs here at Kevin's are delicious. It's the perfect start to my birthday! #goodtimes

b We're at the market. I'm looking for some new sunglasses because it's really sunny here. What does everyone think of these? They're really funny! Everyone is looking at us! #Spain

c Im spending the day with my best ~~freind~~ ~~daria~~ – friend; D we're shoping, obviously! I ~~buyed~~ a new top in bought a great little store. Now were looking for a place to have lunsh. Does anyone know a restaurant in Mango Grove that ~~have~~ good food. #bestfriends has; ?

d It's Saturday! Can you see where we are? That's right – at the beach! It's a beautiful day. The kids are eating ice cream cones. Rita's sleeping and I'm just relaxing!

Share Like Comment

Refer students to these posts as models for the writing task.

Answers

1 Because it's really sunny where she is.; 2 A place to have lunch.; 3 The kids are eating ice cream cones, Rita's sleeping and the writer is relaxing.; 4 Because it's his birthday.

Tell students that being able to check your own work is an important skill.

WRITING

A PREPARE Find a picture of yourself. (If you don't have one, imagine a picture that you want to describe.) Write notes about:

- where you are
- who you are with
- what you are doing

B WRITE Write a social media post about your picture. Use the posts in Exercise B to help you.

C REVIEW Check your work for mistakes. Use the strategies in the box to help you. Then swap with a partner and check their work.

Students can also check each other's work.

168 WRITING

WRITING

In this writing lesson, students will learn how to write a social media post, paying attention to what to focus on when checking their own work.

A Students discuss the questions in pairs. For whole-class feedback, students share the most interesting points of their discussion. Add your own views and opinions.

B Students work alone to match the social media posts to the pictures. Highlight that there is one picture they do not need. Check answers as a class and ask students to explain how they decided.

C Students read the posts again in more detail and answer the questions. Allow time for pairs to compare and discuss answers before checking as a class.

D Read through the *Checking your work* box with students. Then, with books closed, elicit the three main things students should look for when checking their work, as listed in the box. Students then review the four sentences and find and correct two mistakes in each.

E Students read post c again and find three of each type of mistake. If possible, display the post on the board and ask students to correct it for the whole class to see.

WRITING TASK

A If possible, display a photo of yourself to the class and write notes on the board about where you are, who you are with and what you are doing. Encourage students to ask you questions about it. Students then, if possible, find a photo of themselves on their phones and write notes about it.

B Demonstrate writing a social media post from the notes you put on the board. Students then use their notes to write their own social media post. Encourage them to write in an informal, friendly style.

C Elicit the three strategies from the *Checking your work* box, and students use these to check their own work.

Unit 9 Review

VOCABULARY

A Choose the correct words to complete the descriptions.

He's wearing a [1]*suit* / *coat* and has brown [2]*shoes* / *boots*. His [3]*shirt* / *skirt* is white and his [4]*scarf* / *tie* is red.

She's wearing a blue [5]*dress* / *shirt*, with white [6]*sneakers* / *boots* and a pink [7]*sweater* / *coat*. She also has a yellow [8]*hat* / *bag*.

B Complete the sentences with the time expressions in the box.

at the moment	currently	today	this week	this year

1 Mom doesn't want to celebrate her birthday ___this year___.

2 I have a doctor's appointment ___today___ at 3 pm.

3 I'm ___currently___ studying history at Cambridge.

4 I live with my parents ___at the moment___, but I want to move out soon.

5 I have so much work to do ___this week___! Five days isn't enough time.

C Complete the definitions with the words in the box.

bakery	bank	bookstore	butcher's	dentist's	hairdresser's	newsstand	pharmacy

1 ___bookstore___ a store that sells books

2 ___butcher's___ a store that sells meat

3 ___bank___ a place where you can borrow or save money

4 ___dentist's___ a place where you can have your teeth examined

5 ___bakery___ a store that sells cakes, bread, pastry

6 ___pharmacy___ a place where you get medicine

7 ___hairdresser's___ a place where you can get your hair cut

8 ___newsstand___ a place that sells magazines, newspapers, chocolate

D SPEAK Work in pairs. Answer the questions.

1 What kind of clothes do you wear at work/college?

2 What kind of clothes do you wear at home?

3 What are you wearing today?

GRAMMAR

A Choose the correct words to complete the sentences.

1 I usually *am working* / *work* on Saturdays, but I *'m taking* / *take* this Saturday off.

2 She *'s crying* / *cries* because romantic movies always *are making* / *make* her sad.

3 I usually *am going* / *go* camping, but this year I *'m staying* / *stay* in a hotel.

4 He *'s wearing* / *wears* white today, but he usually *is preferring* / *prefers* black.

5 I usually *am working* / *work* from home on Thursdays, but I *'m coming* / *come* in this week for a meeting.

6 She *'s meeting* / *meets* her friends tonight. I think they *'re going* / *go* to the movie theater.

B Complete the story with the correct form of the verbs.

My name is Marc Sands and I [1]___work___ (*work*) in a clothing store. A lot of tourists [2]___come___ (*come*) to our store every day. At the moment, we [3]___are having___ (*have*) a sale. It's only 9:30 am and people [4]___are coming___ (*come*) through the door already. The store [5]___is getting___ (*get*) busy.

C SPEAK Work in pairs and discuss things you do every day, and say what you are doing now.

D Complete the sentences with the correct object pronoun.

1 My brother knows a lot about luxury brands. He spends a lot of money on ___them___.

2 Alicia is an expert on saving money. I need to listen to ___her___.

3 We need more staff. How can we get more people to work for ___us___?

4 Tariq owns a busy café in the center of town. It is the most important thing to ___him___.

5 My daughter has a new party dress. She wants to wear ___it___ every day.

6 It's Mom's birthday on Saturday. Don't forget to call ___her___!

FUNCTIONAL LANGUAGE

Match the beginnings of sentences (1–5) with the ends of sentences (a–e).

1 Can I	a are over there.
2 I'm looking for	b pants are over here.
3 Yes, our	c help you?
4 Can I try	d them on?
5 Yes, the changing rooms	e a pair of pants.

A young traveler at Iskanderkul Lake, Tajikistan

The great outdoors (n) the countryside, especially when used for activities such as walking or camping Synonyms: countryside (n), nature (n)

Ask students to label the photo if you need time to set up the class.

A young traveler at Iskanderkul Lake, Tajikistan.

The quote suggests that answers to life's questions are to be found all around us in nature.

Albert Einstein (1879–1955) was a German-born mathematician and physicist. He won the Nobel Prize for physics in 1921. His theory of relativity is one of the major ideas in modern physics, and his work changed scientific knowledge fundamentally.

OBJECTIVES

- talk about and compare outdoor places
- talk about places around the world
- talk about living outdoors
- make and respond to invitations
- write a product review

Work with a partner. Discuss the questions.

1. Do you prefer cities or the countryside?
2. Look at the picture. Would you like to go there?
3. Which parts of your country are beautiful?

THE GREAT OUTDOORS 91

OBJECTIVES

Read the unit objectives to the class.

UNIT OPENER QUESTIONS

Ask students to look at the picture on the page and describe what they see. Ask students if they know anywhere like the place in the picture. Write the word *remote* on the board, and explain what it means (far away from towns, cities or other people). Ask students to share any experiences they have of spending time in remote places.

Ask students to read the questions at the bottom of the page. Check that students understand the questions.

Put them into pairs to discuss the three questions. Monitor and help with grammar and vocabulary as required. Encourage students to listen to each other and ask follow-up questions to find out more. For whole-class feedback, ask two or three students to share their opinions with the rest of the class.

WORKSHEETS

Lesson 10.1 The right location

Landscape features (W50)

Comparatives (W51)

Lesson 10.2 Where on Earth?

Seasons and weather (W52)

Superlatives (W53)

Lesson 10.3 Survival

Phrasal verbs (W54)

Verb + infinitive (W55)

10.1 The right location

Talk about and compare outdoor places

V – landscape features   G – comparatives   P – weak forms: /ə/ in *than*

FAMOUS MOVIE LOCATIONS

A lot of directors use studios or computers to make their movies. But some still like to use real places. Here are some famous movie locations that you can actually visit.

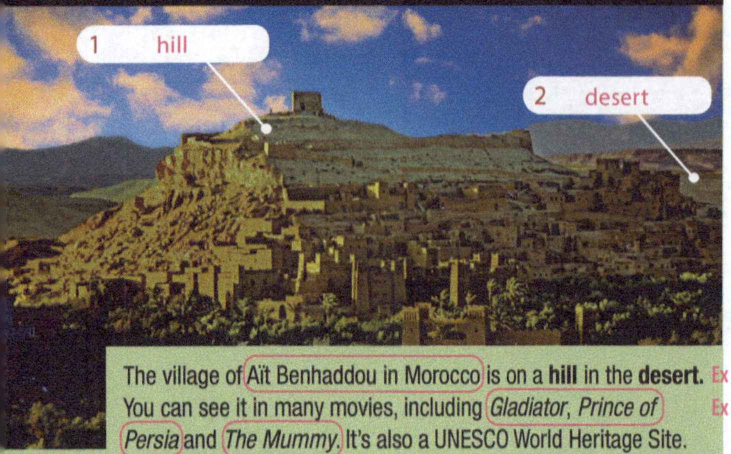

The village of Aït Benhaddou in Morocco is on a **hill** in the **desert**. You can see it in many movies, including *Gladiator*, *Prince of Persia* and *The Mummy*. It's also a UNESCO World Heritage Site.

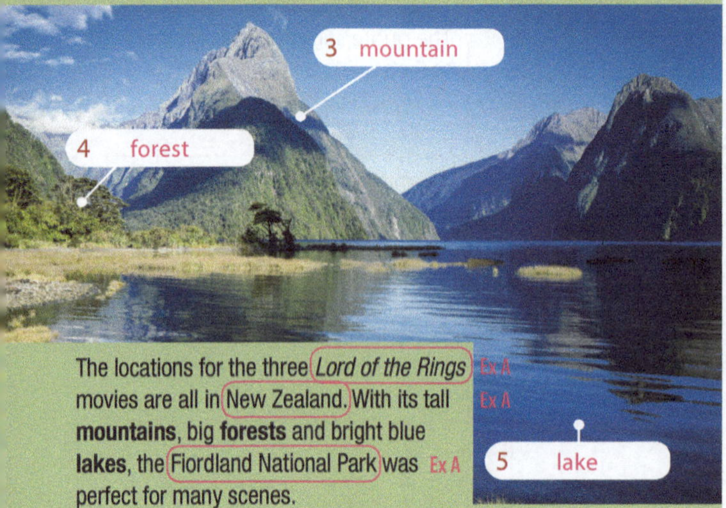

The locations for the three *Lord of the Rings* movies are all in New Zealand. With its tall **mountains**, big **forests** and bright blue **lakes**, the Fiordland National Park was perfect for many scenes.

The **beach** of Maya Bay was the location of Danny Boyle's movie *The Beach*, with Leonardo DiCaprio. It's on the **island** of Koh Phi Phi Leh near Phuket. There are 32 islands here, surrounded by the beautiful blue **sea**.

Do you know this place? They made *Avatar* in this **jungle**, on the Hamakua Coast of Hawaii. This part of the island has around 200 cm of rain every year, and it's full of tall, green trees and beautiful **rivers**.

VOCABULARY
Landscape features

A Work in pairs. Look at the pictures in *Famous movie locations*. Where are they? What movies did they make there?

B Read the article quickly and check your answers to Exercise A.

C Read the article again. Label the pictures with the words in **bold**.

D SPEAK Work in pairs. Can you see any of these landscape features in your country? Tell your partner.

I'm from Spain. There are lots of beautiful beaches near Barcelona.

LISTENING
The movie location

A LISTEN FOR GIST Listen to Clarice talking about the locations for her movie. What is a location scout? (10.1)

A location scout finds the best places to make a movie.

B LISTEN FOR SPECIFIC INFORMATION Listen again. Where did they film these scenes? Why? Write notes. (10.1)

1 the beach scenes
2 the desert scenes
3 the jungle scenes

C SPEAK Work in pairs and discuss the questions.

1 What are some of the good things about filming in a studio?
2 What are some of the problems of filming in a real location (e.g. a city)?

A: I think it's easier to film in a studio.
B: I agree. You don't need to worry about the weather.

D SPEAK Work in pairs and discuss good movie locations in your country. Explain your ideas.

Wadi Rum in Jordan is a great location for making movies. It's a desert. They made **Transformers: Revenge of the Fallen** *there.*

10.1 The right location

LEAD-IN

Write the word *location* on the board, and elicit what it means (the place where something is, or where something happens).

Show some images of outdoor locations you have been to, and ask students to describe them and guess where they are. Students could prepare to do the same with images from their phones. Then, they work in pairs and ask and answer questions about the images.

VOCABULARY

A If possible, display the images on the board. Students look at the photos and guess where the locations are. Ask students to justify their guesses. Then ask which famous movies they think were made there and why.

B Students read *Famous movie locations* and check their answers.

C Point out that the photos show different *landscapes* (an area of land that is beautiful to look at). Students label the pictures with the words in bold. Check answers as a class.

D If you are from a different country than your students, talk about where you are from and the landscape features you can find in your country. Students then do the same in pairs. To extend, if students are from different countries, or different areas of the same country, students could find photos of the landscapes to show examples of the places. Use the **Vocabulary Worksheet** on W50 for extra practice.

LISTENING

10.1 **A** Go through the task with students. Play the recording. Students discuss their ideas in pairs. Share ideas as a class.

10.1 **B** Play the recording again and allow students to take notes on the three types of scenes. Play it again if required. After listening, students compare notes in pairs.

1 In Mexico because the beaches in California are too busy and it was cheaper to film in Mexico; 2 In Morocco because the desert has some interesting buildings and the sand is red; 3 In a studio in Los Angeles because it's difficult to film in a real jungle.

C Students discuss the questions in pairs. Encourage the use of follow-up questions to help them to extend their responses. Share ideas as a class.

D If you are from a different country than your students, start the exercise by describing places in your country which would make good movie locations.

Extra activity

Ask students to research the movie locations used in their favorite movie. Encourage them to find out as much information as they can about where the locations are and why they were chosen. Then, have them report back to the class, ideally displaying locations on the board and asking the class to guess what was filmed there and why.

AUDIO SCRIPT

10.1

Listening, Exercise A
P = Presenter C = Clarice Mk = Mark
J = Janek Ma = Maria

P: With us today is Clarice Steinburg, a location scout. Clarice worked on this year's top movie, *The Adventurer*, which won eight Oscars! Clarice, welcome. Tell us about your job. What does a location scout do?

Ex A **C:** Well, I find the best places to make a movie. I don't mean a studio; I mean actual locations, like a building, a city or a landscape.

P: I see, I see ... Well, Clarice, we have a lot of questions for you tonight from people here in the audience. First up is Mark from London. What's your question, Mark?

Mk: Yes. Hi, Clarice. *The Adventurer* is a great movie, and the locations are amazing.

C: Thank you.

Mk: A lot of the story takes place on a beach in California. Which beach is it?

Ex B Q1 **C:** Well, we didn't actually film in California. We filmed the beach scenes in Mexico.

P: Mexico? Why was that?

C: It's very difficult to film in California because it's really crowded and there are people everywhere. Often, the beaches are busier than the city! It's difficult to close a busy beach for days to make a movie.

P: So, it was better to film in Mexico?

C: That's right. The beaches in Mexico are quieter than in California.

P: Was it expensive?

C: No. Actually, it was more expensive to film in the US than in Mexico. Even with the cost of flights and hotels, Mexico was cheaper than the US.

P: OK. We're ready for another question. Janek?

J: Thank you. The part in the desert is amazing. Is that Mexico, too?

Ex B Q2 **C:** No, we shot that bit in Morocco.

P: Wow. Why Morocco? That's so far from California!

C: Yes, Morocco is much farther than Mexico! But there are some old buildings in the part of the desert where we filmed, and the sand is very red, so it's more interesting.

P: Next question. Maria?

Ma: Hi, Clarice.

C: Hi!

Ma: I loved *The Adventurer*. The scenes in the jungle are really beautiful. Where did you film them? I want to go there!

Ex B Q3 **C:** I'm sorry. We filmed those right here in Los Angeles!

P: No! There aren't any jungles in L.A.!

C: I know! We created that location on a computer! It was all in a studio in downtown Los Angeles. It's very difficult to film in a real jungle.

10.1 The right location

GRAMMAR

A Display or write the two sentences on the board. Underline *cheaper than* and *more expensive than*. Ask: *Were Mexico and the US the same?* (*no*). Ask: *Which place cost more money to film in?* (*the US*). Students then work in pairs to complete the table of examples and rules. Check answers as a class by building up the table on the board. Highlight the irregular adjectives at the bottom of the table.

B Read through the *Comparative spellings* box as a class. Point out that these spelling rules only apply to one-syllable adjectives. Adjectives with two or more syllables don't change their spellings. Write the word *busy* on the board. Elicit the comparative form (*busier than*). Point out that two-syllable adjectives ending in *-y* change their spelling by adding *-ier*.

C Direct students to the **Grammar Hub** (see below). Read the examples and go through the rules with the class.

D Read through the example with students and elicit why the comparative form of *beautiful* is *more beautiful* (*beautiful* has more than one syllable). Students then complete the exercise individually.

E In pairs, students say whether they agree or disagree with the sentences in Exercise D. Use the **Grammar Worksheet** on W51 for extra practice.

PRONUNCIATION

10.2

A Go through the task with students and ask them how they pronounce *than*. Play the recording for students to decide which pronunciation of *than* they hear.

B In pairs, students are to practice saying the sentences. Remind students about word stress. They will find that stressing the sentences correctly will help them with the weak pronunciation of *than*.

SPEAKING

A In pairs, students choose two countries, two landscape features or two movies to compare. To support students, provide your own example.

B Students write comparative sentences. Monitor and assist as required, focusing on the accuracy of the target language. Pay attention to students' spelling of comparative adjectives.

C Put students into new pairs to discuss their ideas. Monitor, encouraging students to explain their reasoning. You could also take this opportunity to teach phrases to help them agree or disagree politely (e.g. *I'm sorry, I don't agree.*; *Yes, absolutely!* etc).

GRAMMAR HUB

10.1 Comparatives

		Adjective	Comparative
One syllable	Add **-er**.	high	higher
More than one syllable	Add **more** + adjective.	beautiful	more beautiful
Irregular	Use irregular comparative.	good	better
		bad	worse
		far	farther

Spelling rules		
Add **-er**.	cheap	cheap**er**
Add **-r** with adjectives that end in **-e**.	larg**e**	large**r**
Double the consonant and add **-er** with adjectives that end vowel + consonant.	h**ot**	ho**tter**

- We use comparatives to say how two or more things are different.

  *Mount Everest is **higher** than Ben Nevis.*
  *Thailand is **more beautiful** than Alaska.*

- Some two-syllable adjectives can form one-word comparatives.

  dirty → dirtier *quiet → quieter*
  narrow → narrower

- Comparatives are often followed by *than* but not always.

  *Avatar was better **than** The Beach. OR The Beach was good but Avatar was better.*

10.1 Comparatives

A Write the comparative form of each adjective.

1 old *older*
2 big bigger
3 dirty dirtier
4 expensive more expensive
5 bad worse

B Match to make sentences.

1 Moscow is colder than
2 December is hotter
3 The city is more
4 Riding a motorcycle is more
5 Is Romania more
6 The Burj Khalifa is taller

a crowded than the countryside.
b New York.
c beautiful than Ireland?
d than the Eiffel Tower.
e dangerous than driving a car.
f than July.

C Correct the mistakes in each sentence.

1 The mountains are ~~more cold~~ *colder* than the desert.
2 Mount Everest is ~~biger~~ than Mount Kilimanjaro. bigger
3 K2 is ~~the~~ more dangerous than Mount Everest.
4 The Nile is ~~more long~~ than the Amazon. longer
5 It's ~~difficulter~~ to film in the jungle than in a city. more difficult
6 The UK is bigger ~~as~~ Ireland. than
7 Ireland is ~~famouser~~ for mountains than beaches. more famous

➤ Go back to page 93.

GRAMMAR
Comparatives

A WORK IT OUT Look at these sentences from the TV interview with Clarice. Complete the table.

Mexico was **cheaper than** the US.

It was **more expensive** to film in the US **than** in Mexico.

Comparatives			
	Adjective	Comparative	Rule
One-syllable adjectives	cheap	[1] cheaper	We add [3] -er + *than*
Adjectives with two or more syllables	expensive	[2] more expensive	We add [4] more + adjective + *than*
Irregular adjectives	good	better	
	bad	worse	

B PRACTICE Complete the sentences with the comparative form of the adjectives in parentheses. Use the information in the box to help you.

Comparative spellings

For adjectives that end in *-e*, we add *-r*.

large → larger; close → closer

For adjectives that end with a consonant, we double the consonant and add *-er*.

hot → hotter; big → bigger

1 The mountains are colder (*cold*) than the desert.
2 Mexico is closer (*close*) to California than Morocco.
3 Hollywood is more famous (*famous*) for movies than nature.
4 Mexico is four times bigger (*big*) than Morocco.
5 Californian beaches are more crowded (*crowded*) than Mexican beaches.

C Go to the **Grammar Hub** on **page 140**.

D PRACTICE Use the prompts to write comparative sentences.

1 beautiful – New Zealand / Australia
New Zealand is more beautiful than Australia.
2 hot – Buenos Aires / Rio de Janeiro
Rio de Janeiro is hotter than Buenos Aires.
3 long – the Amazon / the Nile
The Amazon is longer than the Nile.
4 dangerous – the Sahara / Everest
The Sahara is more dangerous than Everest.
5 cold – New York City / Moscow
Moscow is colder than New York City.

E SPEAK Work in pairs. Look at the sentences in Exercise D. Say whether you agree or disagree.

A: New Zealand is more beautiful than Australia. What do you think?
B: I disagree. Australia has amazing beaches!

PRONUNCIATION
Weak forms: /ə/ in *than*

10.2 **A** Listen to five comparative sentences. Is *than* pronounced /ðæn/or /ðən/? It's pronounced / ðən /.

B SPEAK Work in pairs. Practice saying the sentences in Grammar Exercise B. Listen and check your partner's pronunciation. Be careful to pronounce *than* correctly.

SPEAKING

A PLAN Work in pairs. Choose two countries, two landscape features or two movies to compare. Then think of adjectives to describe them.

Canada: modern, cold, big …

Thailand: beautiful, wet, traditional, interesting …

B PREPARE Write sentences comparing the two things you chose in Exercise A.

Canada is colder than Thailand.

C SPEAK Work in another pair. Student A – tell your partner your ideas. Student B – say whether you agree or disagree. Take turns.

A: Canada is more modern than Thailand.
B: Hmm. I'm not sure. Bangkok is a very modern city.

Talk about and compare outdoor places

10.2 Where on Earth?

Talk about places around the world

V seasons and weather P /oʊ/ and /aʊ/ G superlatives

EXtreme places

This week, we look at some of the most difficult places to live on Earth. What's life like there? How do people survive in these places?

Yakutsk

It's winter in Yakutsk, Siberia. It's -42°C. It's snowing and it's foggy. Welcome to the coldest city on Earth. The lowest temperature in Yakutsk was -64°C. But about 270,000 people still live normal lives in this busy, modern city. They travel to work, go to school and meet friends. It's just like in any other city, Ex C Q1 except it's impossible to stay outside for too long. 'Yes, it's very cold, but I like it here,' says Nina. She's wearing a big fur hat, boots and a long coat, but she's smiling. 'Humans can survive anywhere,' she says. Ex C Q2

Tristan da Cunha

A population of about 265 people live in the middle of the Atlantic Ocean. They are British, but they are 9,000 km from London. Their home is Tristan da Cunha. It's the world's most remote inhabited island. The weather is a little windy, but this isn't the problem. There isn't an airport, and the nearest mainland is South Africa, 2,430 km away. To get to the island, there's a boat from Cape Town. The journey Ex C Q5 takes six days.

So, how do people survive on this island? Well, there's electricity and the internet. There's a grocery store, too, but food is expensive, Ex C Q6 so most people on the island grow potatoes. Why do people stay when life isn't easy? Erik, a worker at the fish factory, says, 'It's so quiet and beautiful. We don't have the problems of the modern world here'.

*data true as of 2017

Kuwait City

It's a Saturday in Kuwait City – the hottest city in the world. About 2.4 million people live here, but you don't see anyone walking around. Why? Because it's 50°C and nobody wants to be outside. Ex C Q3

The weather here is extreme. In the summer, it's hotter than the Sahara Desert. But this isn't the driest place on Earth – that's the Atacama Desert in Chile. In fact, there are a lot of thunderstorms in the fall.

What do people do here, then? During the hottest months, they live inside. Ex C Q4 Most people drive from their air-conditioned homes in their air-conditioned cars to air-conditioned offices and shopping malls. And there is another important thing. 'Water, water, water,' says Sharifa, an architect. 'We have to drink a lot!'

Glossary

extreme (adj) very great in degree
fur (n) the soft hair that covers the body of some animals
inhabited (adj) a place that is inhabited is a place that has people living in it
remote (adj) far away from other cities, towns or people
survive (v) to continue to exist, especially in a difficult or dangerous situation

READING

A Work in pairs. Look at the pictures in *Extreme places* and read the introduction. What problems do you think the people living in these places have? Write notes. **Suggested answers:** you have to wear warm / cool clothes; you can't go outside / you have to stay inside; there isn't a lot of food; it's far from other places; it's lonely; there's nothing to do.

B READ FOR GIST Read *Extreme places*. Are there any ideas you didn't think of in Exercise A?

C READ FOR DETAIL Read again. Choose the correct answer a, b or c to complete the sentences.

1 Yakustsk is …
- a a quiet town.
- b a small village.
- (c) a busy city.

2 People in Yakutsk …
- a never go outside in winter.
- (b) go outside in the winter in warm clothes.
- c only go outside in the summer.

3 In Kuwait City, the streets are empty because …
- (a) it's too hot to go outside.
- b not many people live there.
- c people are at work.

4 There are a lot of cars in Kuwait City because …
- a it's a very big city.
- b it's very rainy.
- (c) people drive everywhere.

5 To get to the island, people on Tristan da Cunha have to …
- a fly from Cape Town.
- (b) take a boat.
- c fly from London.

6 People on Tristan da Cunha grow potatoes because …
- (a) food is expensive in the grocery store.
- b they can't grow other vegetables.
- c there isn't a store.

D SPEAK Work in pairs. Are there any extreme places in your country? Tell your partner about them.

10.2 Where on Earth?

LEAD-IN

Write *Where on Earth?* on the board. Point out that this is an expression we can use in English when we want to emphasize that we don't know where something is (e.g. *Where on Earth are my glasses?*).

With books closed, write the typical summer and winter temperatures of your hometown on the board. Ask students to compare their hometowns to yours, using the target language of the previous lesson (e.g. *My country is hotter than yours in the summer*). At this point, you could test the level of knowledge of this lesson's target language by asking *Who lives in the hottest/ coldest country?* However, do not focus on accuracy at this point.

READING

A Pre-teach the word *extreme* (very great in degree) and the pronunciation /ɪk'striːm/. Write *extreme places* on the board, and ask students what this might refer to (e.g. *very cold, very high* or *very remote places*).

Focus students on the pictures. Ask them to read the introduction to *Extreme places*. They then discuss the question in pairs and write notes on the problems of living in extreme locations.

B Set a short time limit of up to three minutes. Students read the text and find out what problems are mentioned. Check answers as a class.

C Set a longer time limit of up to six minutes. Students read the text again and then answer the questions. Make sure they use the *Glossary* to check any unfamiliar words. Allow students time to compare answers in pairs. Give feedback as a class, encouraging students to explain where in the text they found the answers.

D Students discuss the question in pairs. Monitor, helping with any new or challenging vocabulary. Then open up the discussion to the whole class, with students sharing their knowledge of extreme places around the world. Join in with your own experiences.

TEACHING IDEA by David Seymour and Maria Popova

Grammar: Countries

Use this activity to review the grammar section on comparatives. Say this to your students:

In groups of three or four, discuss these questions about the UK/US.

Is the UK/US hotter or colder than your country? How much?

Is it wetter/grayer, etc?

Is it cheaper / more expensive?

What are the differences between your country and the UK/US?

Which things are better in your country than in the UK/US?

In pairs, compare two countries you know well using these ideas.

big, small, developed, mixed, green, corrupt, hot, cold,

mountainous, expensive, tolerant, soccer crazy, safe, rich

(Variation: Give a country to each pair of students. Ask them to write a list of comparisons between that country and the country they are in now. They read out their comparisons and the others try to guess the country.)

TEACHING IDEA by David Seymour and Maria Popova

Grammar: Advertising agency

Use this activity to review the grammar section on comparatives and to prepare for the grammar section on superlatives. Say this to your students:

Tell me things which are regularly advertised on TV. (Write the elicited list on the board.)

In small groups, choose one of these things and think of a new brand. Write a radio ad explaining why it's better than its competitors, e.g. *For the whitest teeth buy Afterglo. It whitens your teeth and leaves your breath fresher than mountain air. It's more effective than all its leading competitors. Choose Afterglo, for the brightest, most confident smile.*

Read your ad aloud to the class. When you're listening to the other groups' ad, make some notes for a complaint to the Advertising Standards Agency, e.g. *The ad says it's more effective than other toothpastes, but it contains much more sugar than other brands to make it taste better.*

METHODOLOGY HUB by Jim Scrivener

Monitoring

Monitor discreetly

Discreet monitoring is when you maintain a presence in the room, but do not overtly offer help, interfere, correct, etc. Your aim is that the students know you are there, but your watching and listening does not in any way disturb them. They will not feel tempted to call on you unless there is a significant problem – and when they do ask for help, do this swiftly and effectively, then return to the discreet monitoring role. You are sending a message that you are interested, but that the main task is for them to do using their own resources as much as possible.

Vanish

There are cases when any teacher presence can actually interfere with and diminish the usefulness of work being done. Sometimes the best option for you is to vanish, i.e. get out of immediate eyeshot. You could go into a corner of the room and sit quietly.

It is a good idea to have something concrete to do (e. g. read something) in order to prevent yourself from constantly worrying about how students are doing and getting drawn back into it. You need to keep a small percentage of attention on the room, in order to know when the activity is reaching an end or a crisis point, but otherwise restrain yourself from doing too much. Relax and stop being a teacher for a while.

Participate

You may sit down and join a group (temporarily or for the whole task) and take part as if you were one of the group, offering ideas, helping with questions, joining in discussions. You could quietly move on to another group. By the end of the task, you might have worked with a number of groups. Of course, while you are monitoring or working with one group, you will need to remain alert to what others are doing and if there are any problems.

10.2 Where on Earth?

VOCABULARY

A Focus students on the picture. They discuss the questions in pairs. Share ideas and views as a class. Point out that the picture shows a person with a bicycle in Vietnam.

B Direct students to the **Vocabulary Hub**. Give them time to complete Exercises A and B alone before checking answers in pairs.

C Students discuss the questions in pairs. Monitor and assist as necessary. Use the **Vocabulary Worksheet** on W52 for extra practice.

PRONUNCIATION

A Play the recording. Elicit the difference between the vowel sounds, modeling the sounds for the students and how your mouth moves differently for each sound. Play the recording again for students to listen and repeat.

10.4 **B** In pairs, students complete the table. Encourage students to try saying the words as they do so. Play the recording for students to check their answers. Play it again for students to repeat each word.

GRAMMAR

A Students complete the sentences using words from the text. Give feedback as a class.

B Students complete the table alone before checking their answers with a partner. Give feedback as a class.

C Direct students to the **Grammar Hub** (see below). Read the examples and go through the rules with the class.

D Focus on the example with students and elicit which part of the prompt changed (*the adjective*). Then elicit which word was added (*the*). Students work alone to complete the questions. Monitor and assist as required.

E Put students into pairs to ask and answer the questions. Monitor, focussing on the accuracy of their grammar, rather than general fluency. Use the **Grammar Worksheet** on W53 for extra practice.

SPEAKING

Put students into A/B pairs. Direct them to the **Communication Hub**.

GRAMMAR HUB

10.2 Superlatives

		Adjective	Superlative
One syllable	Add **the** + **-est**.	cold	the coldest
More than one syllable	Add **the most** + adjective.	remote	the most remote
Irregular	Use **the** + irregular superlative.	good	the best
		bad	the worst
		far	the farthest

Spelling rules		
Add **-est**.	cheap	cheap**est**
Add **-st** with adjectives that end in **-e**.	larg**e**	larg**est**
Double the consonant and add **-est** with adjectives that end vowel + consonant.	h**ot**	ho**ttest**

- We use superlatives to say that something is top or bottom of a group.

  *The Atacama is **the coldest** dry desert in the world.*

  *What's **the most** remote place in your country?*
- Some two-syllable adjectives can form superlatives without *most*.

  dirty → the dirtiest *quiet → the quietest*

  narrow → the narrowest
- We often put *the* before superlatives but not always.

  Megan is my best friend. NOT *~~Megan is my the best friend.~~*

  *Megan is **the best** friend I've ever had.*

10.2 Superlatives

A Write the superlative form of each adjective.

1. tall *the tallest*
2. hot the hottest
3. sunny the sunniest
4. beautiful the most beautiful
5. good the best

B Choose the correct options to complete the sentences.

1. Aconcagua is the *most tall* / *tallest* mountain in South America.
2. The Pacific is the *most big* / *biggest* ocean in the world.
3. I think the Newfoundland is the *most beautiful* / *beautifullest* dog in the world!
4. Mawsynram is the *most wet* / *wettest* place on Earth.
5. Hanoi is the *most ancient* / *ancientest* city in Vietnam.
6. Parinacota is the *most high* / *highest* city in Chile.

C Complete the sentences with the correct superlative form of the adjective in parentheses. Add *the*.

1. Yakutsk is the coldest (cold) city in the world.
2. Is Monaco the most expensive (expensive) country to live in?
3. Death Valley is the hottest (hot) place on Earth.
4. Tristan Da Cunha is the most remote (remote) island on the planet.
5. The Tata Nano is the cheapest (cheap) car in the world.
6. Valletta is the sunniest (sunny) place in Europe.

➤ Go back to page 95.

VOCABULARY
Seasons and weather

A Look at the picture and answer the questions.

1 Which country do you think this is? Why? The picture is of a person with a bicycle in Vietnam.
2 Is the weather good or bad?
3 Is the weather like this in your country?

B Go to the **Vocabulary Hub** on **page 152**.

C **SPEAK** Work in pairs. Answer the questions.

1 What's the weather like today?
2 What's the weather like in your country in each season?
3 What's your favorite season? Why?

PRONUNCIATION
/oʊ/ and /aʊ/

10.3 **A** Listen and repeat. Can you hear the difference between the sounds /oʊ/ and /aʊ/?

/oʊ/ snowing, go, throw

/aʊ/ cloudy, sound, brown

10.4 **B** Complete the table with the words in the box. Then listen and repeat.

~~around~~ cloudy ~~coat~~ grow home lowest now outside sound snowing town

/oʊ/		/aʊ/	
coat	lowest	around	outside
grow	snowing	cloudy	sound
home		now	town

GRAMMAR
Superlatives

A **WORK IT OUT** Look at *Extreme places*. Complete the sentences with words from the text.

1 Welcome to the coldest city on Earth.
2 It's a Saturday in Kuwait City – the hottest city in the world.
3 But this isn't the driest place on Earth – that's the Atacama Desert in Chile.
4 It's the world's most remote inhabited island.
5 There isn't an airport, and the nearest mainland is South Africa, 2,430 km away.

B Complete the table. Use the examples in Exercise A to help you.

Superlatives			
	Adjective	Superlative	Rule
One-syllable adjectives	cold	1 the coldest	We use *the* + adjective + 3 -est
Adjectives with two or more syllables	remote	2 the most remote	We use *the* + 4 most + adjective
Irregular adjectives	good bad	the best the worst	

C Go to the **Grammar Hub** on **page 140**.

D **PRACTICE** Use the prompts to write superlative questions.

1 What's / high / mountain / in the world?
What's the highest mountain in the world?
2 What's / big / ocean / in the world?
What's the biggest ocean in the world?
3 What's / beautiful / place / in the world?
What's the most beautiful place in the world?
4 What's / good / movie / ever made?
What's the best movie ever made?
5 Which / good / season to visit your country?
Which is the best season to visit your country?
6 What's / bad / thing about your city?
What's the worst thing about your city?

E **SPEAK** Work in pairs. Ask and answer the questions in Exercise D.

SPEAKING

Student A – go to the **Communication Hub** on **page 157**.
Student B – go to the **Communication Hub** on **page 159**.

Talk about places around the world

V – phrasal verbs   G – verb + infinitive   P – weak forms: /tuː/ and /tə/   S – identifying fact and opinion

READING

A Work in pairs. Tell your partner about the last time you got lost. What did you do?

A: I got lost on vacation in New York last year. I asked a policeman to help me!
B: Haha! I got lost in the mountains in France once. I called my friend for help.

B READING FOR GIST Read the article. Who is the article written for?

1 Someone who wants to go on vacation.
2 Someone who wants to go walking in a remote place. (circled)
3 Someone who wants to buy camping equipment.

C READ FOR DETAIL Read the article again. Match the beginnings of sentences (1–5) with the ends of sentences (a–e).

1 People die every year — c
2 The cold is more dangerous — b
3 You can't survive for a week — d
4 The safest way to drink water — a
5 Try to find — e

a is to boil it first.
b than almost anything else.
c because they don't prepare well.
d without water.
e plants to eat.

D Read these sentences from the article. Are they facts (F) or opinions (O)?

Identifying fact and opinion

Texts usually contain a mix of fact and opinion.

A fact is something that is true. Facts can include statements or statistics.

Most of them are between the ages of 20 and 29.

An opinion is what the speaker personally thinks about something.

Some people think it's important to take everything you need with you, like a tent, but I don't agree.

Opinions often include phrases such as: *I think …, I prefer …, I believe …, I feel …, In my opinion …, I agree, I don't agree / I disagree.*

1 I prefer to travel with only a few things and use what nature gives me. (I prefer) F / O (O circled)
2 I believe that the best thing to do is to make a dry place where you can sleep. (I believe) F / O (O circled)
3 The night is much colder than the day. F / O (F circled)
4 It's always safer to boil water before you drink it. F / O (F circled)
5 I feel that the best thing you can do is learn to read the night sky before you leave. F / O (O circled)
(I feel that the best thing)

E SPEAK Work in pairs. Put Chuck's advice in order from the most important (1) to the least important (5). Explain your ideas.

I think finding somewhere to sleep is the most important advice because …

FIVE WAYS to survive in the wild

By top survival expert **Chuck Adams**

Ex C Q1 Every summer, hikers die because they don't prepare for their adventure. Most of them are between the ages of 20 and 29. So what happens if you get lost? Don't give up! I believe you can survive anywhere! Here are five tips before you set off on your next trip. Ex B

1 Build somewhere to sleep

Some people think it's important to take everything you need with you, like a tent, but I don't agree. I prefer to travel with only a few things and use what nature gives me. I believe that the best thing to do is to make a dry place where you can sleep. Put some pieces of wood against a tree and make a bed of grass on the ground. Ex C Q2 Also, one of the most dangerous things is the cold. The night is much colder than the day, so put on all of your clothes when you go to bed.

2 Make a fire

You only need two pieces of dry wood to start a fire! Check my Survival in the wild video on how to do this. Remember to add some big pieces of wood to keep you warmer for longer during the night.

3 Find water

Ex C Q3 Water is more important than food – you can only live for three days without water. It's better to drink water in rivers than water in lakes. Ex C Q4 It's always safer to boil water before you drink it.

4 Find food

Ex C Q5 We get most of our food from nature. Learn how to look for plants or flowers that you can eat. You can also catch and eat small animals. Watch my Survival in the wild video to learn how.

5 Read the sky

Use the North Star and the shape of the moon to help find out where you are. I feel that the best thing you can do is to learn to read the night sky before you leave.

Glossary

hiker (n) someone who walks long distances in the countryside for pleasure
nature (n) the physical world, including land, sea and all living things
survive (v) to continue to exist, especially in a difficult situation
the wild (n) an environment that is natural

10.3 Survival

LEAD-IN

Write the word *survival* on the board. Elicit or explain that it means the fact or state of continuing to live or exist, especially in difficult conditions. Show a movie poster of a famous movie in which someone managed to survive in difficult conditions (e.g. *Cast Away* or *The Martian*). Ask students if they know the movie. If they do, ask them to explain the story. If they don't, tell them the story and ask them if they would like to see it.

READING

A Set up the exercise by describing a time you got lost. Tell students what you did. Encourage students to ask you questions to find out more. Students then work in pairs or small groups to share their stories. For whole-class feedback, ask students to share the most interesting stories.

B Go through the task with students. Set a short time limit of one minute, reminding students they are reading only to find out the answer to one question. Check answer as a class.

C Set a longer time limit of up to four minutes. Students read the article again to match the beginnings and ends of the sentences. Allow students time to compare answers with a partner before checking answers as a class.

D Read through the *Identifying fact and opinion* box with students. Remind students that in the previous lesson, they asked each other *What's the most beautiful place in the world?* Elicit whether the answer to this question would be a fact or an opinion (*an opinion*).

Give students up to two minutes to read Sentences 1–5 and decide if each one is fact or an opinion. Students compare answers with a partner before checking as a class.

E In pairs, students rank the five pieces of advice from the article from most to least important. If you have time, you could put students into groups. They should compare their rankings and try to agree on the top three pieces of advice. For whole-class feedback, groups explain their ideas to the class. Encourage them to give reasons.

GRAMMAR HUB

10.3 Verb + *to* + infinitive

	verb + infinitive
decide	We **decided to go** hiking in the mountains.
forget	Don't **forget to take** your cell phone.
help	The map **helped** us **to find** the way.
learn	They're **learning to use** a compass.
need	You **need to build** a place to sleep.
plan	I'm **planning to hike** through the jungle next summer.
prefer	She **prefers to travel** by car.
remember	**Remember to set off** early.
try	She's **trying to start** a fire.
want	I **want to know** more about survival.

- Many verbs are followed by the infinitive.

Be careful!

I plan to go to Rome next summer.
NOT ~~*I plan going to Rome next summer.*~~
NOT ~~*I plan go to Rome next summer.*~~

10.3 Verb + infinitive

A Complete the sentences with *to* and the verbs in the box.

bring (x2) carry go make read travel

1 I forgot ___*to bring*___ my raincoat with me.
2 I'm trying ___to read___ the map, but it's really dark.
3 They should get some wood. They need ___to make___ a fire to keep warm.
4 Did you remember ___to bring___ a bottle of water with you?
5 She's planning ___to go___ to Greece for a vacation next year.
6 We helped ___to carry___ the boxes into the house.
7 I don't like flying – I prefer ___to travel___ by train.

B Reorder the words to make sentences. Add *to* in the right place.

1 you / need / boil the water / don't
You don't need to boil the water.
2 for / they / decided / go / a / walk
They decided to go for a walk.
3 planning / we're / the / world / travel
We're planning to travel the world.
4 before dark / get / hope / there / we
We hope to get there before dark.
5 needs / some camping equipment / she / buy
She needs to buy some camping equipment.
6 in the jungle / must learn / they / survive
They must learn to survive in the jungle.
7 do / a survival course / I / don't want
I don't want to do a survival course.

➤ Go back to page 97.

10.3 Survival

VOCABULARY

A Read through the *Phrasal verbs* box with students. Then ask students to underline five phrasal verbs in *Five ways to survive in the wild*. Check answers as a class and write the phrasal verbs on the board.

Put students into pairs to try and work out what each phrasal verb means. They should use the context in *Five ways to survive in the wild* to help them. Do not confirm answers at this point.

B Students match the phrasal verbs from Exercise A to the definitions. Check answers as a class.

C Direct students to the **Vocabulary Hub**. Give them time to complete the exercise alone before checking answers in pairs.

D In pairs, students write their own sentences using the phrasal verbs. They should write one sentence for each phrasal verb. Stronger students could try to write a story using all five of them. Monitor and assist as required. Use the **Vocabulary Worksheet** on W54 for extra practice.

LISTENING

A In pairs, students discuss the pictures and whether Chuck Adams uses the items. Monitor and encourage discussion as to what people can use the items for. Check answers as a class.

10.5 **B** Go through the task. Play the recording for students to find out if Marcus James agrees. Check answer as a class.

10.5 **C** Allow students time to read through the sentences before playing the recording again. Students listen and decide if the sentences are true or false. Play the audio again if required. Put students into pairs to compare answers and correct the false sentences. Check answers as a class.

1 F (Marcus James says the easiest way to start a fire is to carry matches or a lighter.); 2 T; 3 F (You can live for up to three weeks without food.); 4 F (You don't need to build anything – just wear a raincoat.); 5 T.

D In pairs, students rank the nine items in order of importance. They then compare ideas with another pair. If you have time, you could encourage students to agree on the top five most important items. Share ideas as a class.

GRAMMAR

10.5 **A** Go through the task. Allow students time to read through the sentences and predict the missing words. Play the recording again. Check answers as a class.

B Students review the sentences in Exercise A and complete the rule. Check answer as a class.

C Direct students to the **Grammar Hub** (see TB96). Read the examples and go through the rules with the class. Use the **Grammar Worksheet** on W55 for extra practice.

PRONUNCIATION

10.6 **A** Go through the information with students. Then play the recording for students to hear the difference.

10.6 **B** Play the recording again to help students complete the rules. Give feedback as a class, practicing the correct pronunciation of each example. If you have time, put students into pairs to write five sentences using infinitives pronounced /tuː/ and five pronounced /tə/. Monitor and practice correct pronunciation.

SPEAKING HUB

Direct students to the **Communication Hub** for further practice.

Extra activity
This is a variation of the Speaking Hub task. Put students into groups and tell them that they have to survive on a desert island alone for 6 months. Next, write the names of (or display images of) six to ten things each group can take with them to the island. These should be a variety of useful items (e.g. a knife, a lighter, etc) and less practical items (e.g. a can of beans, a dog, etc). Tell groups that they must agree on three items to take. Monitor the discussions and assist as necessary. Give feedback, encouraging students to explain the reasons for their choices.

AUDIO SCRIPT

10.5

Listening, Exercise B
G = Greg M = Marcus

G: We're here with survival expert Marcus James to hear his advice on how to survive in the wild. Marcus, thank you for joining us.

M: You're welcome. Thanks for having me on the show.

G: So Marcus, if you're lost and you need to stay warm or cook some food, what's the best way to start a fire? Two pieces of dry wood?

Ex C Q1 **M:** Well, Greg, the easiest thing to do is to carry a box of matches or a lighter in your backpack and use that to light a fire.

G: Oh, yes … I suppose so. So how about some other tips? For example, what are the safest plants to eat? How can I catch animals?

Ex C Q2 **M:** Again, 95 percent of hikers have energy bars in their backpack! They don't need 'macho survival techniques'. Always plan to take a few important things with you, like a pocketknife, a lantern and a phone. Then, you don't have to catch animals! And, did you know, Greg, you can actually survive for up to three weeks without food? And that's a fact!

Ex C Q3

G: Really? So, what about Chuck Adams? Is his advice wrong?

M: It's not bad – I just don't think it's the most useful advice. For example, if you want to stay dry, take a raincoat. You don't need to build anything.

Ex C Q4

G: What's the most useful advice in your opinion?

M: The best advice I can give you is to be prepared. When you decide to go hiking, tell someone where you're going. On the hike, check your map and compass. Take lots of photos on your phone. They can help you find your way back later. And if you get lost, leave signs so people can find you. For example, leave pieces of clothing on a tree. And remember to keep warm. The truth is, most people don't die because they get lost – they die because they don't prepare.

Ex C Q5

VOCABULARY
Phrasal verbs

A Read the information in the box. Then read *Five ways to survive in the wild* and underline five phrasal verbs.

> **Phrasal verbs**
>
> Phrasal verbs have two parts, usually a verb and a preposition. The preposition often changes the meaning of the verb. For example, *give up* means 'stop doing something'.
>
> A: *I'm tired. This race is hard.*
>
> B: *Don't **give up**! We're almost there.*

B Complete the definitions with phrasal verbs from Exercise A.

1 put on to start wearing something
2 give up to stop doing something
3 find out to learn something
4 set off to leave
5 look for to try to find

C Go to the **Vocabulary Hub** on **page 152**.

D Work in pairs. Write sentences using the phrasal verbs in Exercise B.

LISTENING

A Work in pairs. Look at *Marcus James: Survival Kit*. Do you think Chuck Adams uses any of these items? Why/Why not?

MARCUS JAMES: SURVIVAL KIT

10.5 **B** **LISTEN FOR GIST** Listen to an interview with survival expert Marcus James. Does he agree with Chuck Adams?
No. Marcus James disagrees with lots of things Chuck Adams says.

10.5 **C** **LISTEN FOR DETAIL** Listen again. Are the sentences true (T) or false (F)? Correct the false sentences.

1 The easiest way to make fire is from dry wood. T / (F)
2 Almost all hikers travel with energy bars. (T) / F
3 You can live for ten days without food. T / (F)
4 You should build a shelter to stay dry. T / (F)
5 You should take a lot of photos. (T) / F

D **SPEAK** Work in pairs. Put the items in Exercise A in order of most important (1) to least important (9). Then compare your list with another pair.

GRAMMAR
Verb + infinitive

10.5 **A** Listen to the interview again and complete the sentences.

1 Always **plan** to take a few important things with you, like a pocketknife, a lantern and a phone.
2 For example, if you **want** to stay dry, take a raincoat.
3 You don't **need** to build anything.
4 When you **decide** to go hiking, tell someone where you're going.
5 And **remember** to keep warm.

B **WORK IT OUT** Look at the sentences in Exercise A and complete the rule.

> **Verb + infinitive**
>
> Lots of verbs in English are followed by *infinitive / -ing*.
>
> Examples include: *plan, want, need, decide, rememeber.*

C Go to the **Grammar Hub** on **page 140**.

PRONUNCIATION
Weak forms: /tuː/ and /tə/

10.6 **A** We pronounce *to* before an infinitive either /tuː/ or /tə/. Listen and repeat. Can you hear the difference?

/tuː/ to agree, to arrive, to open
/tə/ to believe, to prepare, to set off

10.6 **B** Listen again and complete the rules.

> **/tuː/ and /tə/**
>
> 1 we say **/tuː/** before infinitives starting with a *vowel / consonant* sound.
>
> 2 we say **/tə/** before infinitives starting with a *vowel / consonant* sound.

SPEAKING HUB

Work in pairs. Go to the **Communication Hub** on **page 157**.

Talk about living outdoors

Café Hub

10.4 Party invitation

F – make and respond to invitations   P – stress and intonation

Glossary

cinema **(n) (British)** = movie theater **(n) (American)**

COMPREHENSION

A SPEAK Work in pairs. Look at the picture. What are Zac, Neena and Gaby planning? What do they have to decide?

B ▶ **Watch the video. Choose the correct words to complete the sentences.**

1 It's Sam's birthday ***today*** / ***tomorrow***.
2 Neena has a birthday ***present*** / ***card*** for Sam.
3 Neena thinks the cinema is ***boring*** / ***expensive***.
4 Gaby thinks a party is ***cheaper*** / ***easier*** than a restaurant.
5 Zac checks the ***weather forecast*** / ***restaurant prices***.
6 They decide ***to have*** / ***not to have*** a picnic.
7 Zac suggests a surprise party ***in the flat*** / ***at Sam's café***.
8 Neena tells Milly to arrive at ***ten to*** / ***ten past*** six.
9 Sam's parents ***can*** / ***can't*** come to the party.

C SPEAK **Work in pairs. Answer the questions.**

1 What is the final plan for the party?
2 Why does Zac shout when Sam arrives at the flat?
3 Why do Sam, Gaby and Neena laugh at the end?

FUNCTIONAL LANGUAGE

Making and responding to invitations

A ▶ **Watch the video again. Check (✓) the invitations and replies you hear.**

Inviting people	Are you free on Friday? We're having a party. ☑
	Would you like to come to Sam's party tomorrow? ☑
	We're holding a party for Sam tomorrow evening. Can you come? ☐
Saying *yes*	That sounds great. ☑
	We'd love to come. ☑
	Sure! I'd love to. ☑
	That would be great. ☐
Saying *no*	Sorry, I'm busy. ☑
	I can't come. I'm working. ☑
	I'd love to, but I'm away. ☐

B SPEAK **Work in pairs. Student A – invite your partner using the questions in Exercise A. Student B – reply using the phrases in Exercise A . Then swap roles.**

MILLY SAM NEENA ZAC GABY

PRONUNCIATION

Stress and intonation

A Listen and repeat the replies. Copy the stress and intonation. 10.7

1 That sounds great.
2 We'd love to come.
3 Sure.
4 I'd love to.
5 Sorry, I'm busy.
6 I can't come. I'm working.

B Listen again. Underline the stressed word or syllable in the replies in Exercise A. 10.7

C SPEAK Work in pairs. Practice saying the replies in Exercise A. Remember to use the correct stress and intonation.

SPEAKING

A PREPARE Write notes about three activities to do with your partner.

- *See the new Avengers movie > Friday night.*
- *Go for a walk > Sunday afternoon.*
- *Play soccer > next Thursday.*

B SPEAK Take turns making invitations and saying *yes* or *no*. Use the phrases in the Functional language section and your notes to help you.

A: Would you like to see a movie with me this evening?
B: I'd love to, but I'm really tired.

C DISCUSS Work in pairs. Think about the last time you got an invitation. Did you go? If not, why not? Tell your partner about it.

A: I got an invitation to a work party last month.
B: Did you go?
A: No, I didn't. I was on vacation.

Make and respond to invitations

➤ Turn to page 169 to learn how to write a product review.

10.4 Party invitation

LEAD-IN

Tell students about the best birthday party you've ever had. Explain what you did, who was there and why it was so good. Then put students into pairs to discuss their own experiences. Monitor, helping with any new vocabulary or difficult grammar. Make a note of any useful emergent language, adding it to the board and, if possible, using it as the basis of further discussion.

COMPREHENSION

A Students discuss the questions in pairs. Encourage students to extend their answers by asking follow-up questions. Share answers as a class.

They are planning a party for Sam. They have to decide on a present, what to do and who to invite.

B ▶ Allow students time to read through the sentences before playing the video. Make sure students understand what a *surprise party* is (a party for someone who wasn't expecting it). Play the video so students can complete the sentences. Give students time to check their answers with a partner, before giving feedback as a class.

C Students discuss the questions in pairs. Open up the discussion to the whole class.

1 Zac invites Sam to dinner when Sam finishes work at 6 pm. Party guests arrive at 6:10 pm. Zac tells Sam he left his bag at the café. They go back to the café and everyone yells 'surprise!'; 2 Because he wants to warn Neena and Gaby to hide information about the party.; 3 Because they see that Zac is embarrassed about a picture he has drawn of Milly.

FUNCTIONAL LANGUAGE

A ▶ Allow students time to review the invitations and replies in the table. Students then watch the video again and apply a check mark to the ones they hear.

B Put students into pairs. They take turns inviting their partner to do something (e.g. come to a party), using the invitations and replies from Exercise A.

PRONUNCIATION

10.7 **A** Play the recording. Students listen and repeat the replies.

10.7 **B** Play the recording again. In pairs, students identify and underline the stressed syllables. Check answers, writing the answers on the board.

C In pairs, students practice the replies. Monitor, helping students to use the correct stress and intonation.

SPEAKING

A Students work alone to think of three activities they could do with a partner. They should write notes about the activities and when to do them. Monitor and assist as required.

B In pairs, students take turns making invitations and reply to their partners' invitations. Point out that they should use *Functional Language* they learned. They should also use the notes they wrote.

C Put students into new pairs or small groups to discuss the questions. Encourage them to use follow-up questions to find out more.

▶ VIDEO SCRIPT

Z = Zac G = Gaby N = Neena D = David
Mi = Milly Mu = Sam's Mum S = Sam

Z: Guys, guys, guys! BIG NEWS!
G: What?
Z: It's Sam's birthday!
N: Today?
Z: Tomorrow.
N: We need a present!
G: We need a party!
Z: We need a plan! OK – number 1 – present?
N: Check.
Z: Number 2 – what should we do?
G: Let's go out.
N: Good idea! Where?
G: How about the cinema?
N: No, that's boring. Let's go to a restaurant.
Z: What about a surprise party?
G: Yes! A party's cheaper than a restaurant.
Z: Our flat is too small. I have another idea … a picnic in the park.
G: It's raining, again.
Z: Ohhh … it's a thunderstorm. And tomorrow … a bigger thunderstorm!
G: It's not like this in Spain. Madrid has the best weather in the world. It's hotter than London and always sunny.
N: Well, this is summer in England.
G: No picnic then.
Z: Where is it? Aha! This is a key to Sam's Cafe.
N: And …?
Z: I invite Sam to a restaurant for a birthday meal. Sam finishes work at 6 pm and I meet him at the cafe. We leave and you arrive. I tell Sam I left my bag at the cafe and we come back. We walk into the cafe and everyone shouts 'surprise'. What do you think?
N: That's a great plan.
Z: OK! Number 3. Invitations!
G: Hi, David. Are you free on Friday? We're having a party.
D: Sorry, I'm busy. I can't come. I'm working.
G: No problem. Bye.
N: Hi Milly. Would you like to come to Sam's party tomorrow?
Mi: Sure! I'd love to.
N: Great! It's a surprise so come to the cafe at ten past six.
Mi: Cool. Um … What about Zac?
N: Yes. Zac's coming.
Mi: Awesome.
G: And ask his parents?
Z: OK.
Mu: Hello?
Z: Hi Sue? It's Zac. Are you and Gary free tomorrow evening? We're having a surprise party for Sam.
Mu: That sounds great. We'd love to come.
Z: OK, great. See you then. Oh, hi Sam! What a nice surprise!
N: Quick. Turn the page!
Z: Let's go into the living room!
S: Why are you shouting? Hey. What's that?
Z: Thanks, guys.

10 Writing

Write a product review

adverbs of manner

A Work in pairs. Look at the pictures. Answer the questions.

1 Do you own any of these items?
2 Where did you buy them?
3 Are they good quality?

1 a flashlight 2 a pocketknife 3 a backpack 4 a pair of walking boots 5 a tent 6 a first aid kit 7 a small camping stove

B Read three customer reviews. Which of the items in Exercise A are they for?

a flashlight ① **I bought this to use at night on a camping trip.** I already have one, but this one is smaller and stronger. But it's also expensive and the batteries die very quickly. The most important thing is that it has a strong light! And it works really well, so I recommend it for beginner campers or hikers.

Published 1 week ago by Bob Smith

a pocketknife ② **I got this to use when I go fishing.** It's great and it does a lot of different things. It cuts nicely. It also has scissors and a can opener. Use it carefully, though. It can be dangerous! I'd recommend this to everyone!

Published 5 days ago by Greg Barnett

a tent ③ **I got this for our family vacation.** We understood the instructions easily, but it's too small. It says it's for four people, but I don't think that's true. It's also made very badly. And they have the worst customer service, too! After just one week, it broke, and now I can't get my money back. Don't buy this!

Published 2 days ago by Elizabeth Brown

C Which is a five-star (★★★★★) review, which is a three-star (★★★) review and which is a one-star (★) review? Why?

D Read the reviews again. Write notes about each using the table below.

	Review 1	Review 2	Review 3
What is the product?	a flashlight	a pocketknife	a tent
What are its bad points?	expensive, batteries die very quickly	it can be dangerous	small, made badly
What are its good points?	small, strong, good light	does lots of different things, cuts nicely	-
Would the reviewer recommend it?	yes	yes	no

E Find two adverbs of manner in each online review. Which adverb is irregular? Use the information in the box to help you.

Adverbs of manner

Adverbs of manner tell us how something happens.
It cuts nicely.
We add *-ly* to an adjective to make a regular adverb.
quick – quickly
For adjectives ending in -y, we drop the *-y* and add *-ily*.
easy – easily
Some adverbs are irregular.
hard – hard
good – well
Adverbs come after the main verb.
We understood the instructions easily.
Use it carefully.
We use words like *fairly*, *very* and *really* to add more information.
It's made very badly.
It works really well.

F Complete the sentences by making adverbs from the adjectives in parentheses.

1 The flashlight broke ___easily___ (*easy*).
2 The boots arrived very ___quickly___ (*quick*).
3 Everything fits ___perfectly___ (*perfect*) into one bag.
4 The camping stove didn't work very ___well___ (*good*).
5 Please use the pocketknife ___carefully___ (*careful*) because it's very sharp.
6 The instructions say very ___clearly___ (*clear*) there aren't any scissors in the first-aid kit.

WRITING

A PREPARE Imagine you have bought one of the items in Exercise A. Write down some good and bad things about it.

B WRITE Write a review of your product. Use the questions in Exercise D to help you. Use some adverbs of manner. Write about 50 words.

C REVIEW Work in pairs. Read each other's reviews. Can you find any mistakes? How many adverbs of manner can you find?

WRITING 169

Answers
1 quickly, well (irregular); 2 nicely, carefully; 3 easily, badly.

Tell students that using adverbs like this helps them to give clearer explanations.

Refer students to these reviews as models for the writing task.

Answers
The first review is three-star. The reviewer was fairly happy but there were a couple of bad things. The second is five-star. The reviewer is very happy and only warns about it being dangerous as a bad thing. The last is one-star. The reviewer only gives one advantage and warns people not to buy it.

Encourage students to peer-correct each other's work.

WRITING

In this writing lesson, students will learn how to write a product review, paying attention to how to use adverbs to explain how something happens.

A In pairs, students answer the questions. Share answers as a class. Ask students how, in general, they decide which items to buy and whether they ever read product reviews online.

B Students read the customer reviews and match them to three items from Exercise A. Check answers as a class.

C Students match the star ratings to the reviews. When checking answers as a class, ask students to explain their answers.

D Students read the reviews again in more detail. They write notes on each one. Allow students time to compare notes in pairs and to add to their notes.

E Read through the *Adverbs of manner* box with the class. If possible, display the first review and work together as a class to identify two adverbs of manner. Students then work alone to identify the adverbs of manner in the other two reviews. Check answers as a class.

F Students work alone to complete the sentences by changing the adjective in parentheses into an adverb. Check answers as a class.

WRITING TASK

A Tell students to imagine they bought an item from Exercise A. Ask them to write notes on the good and bad things to say about the item.

B Students write a review of the product. Remind them to use the questions from Exercise D and to use adverbs of manner. Monitor and assist as required.

C Students read each other's reviews to identify any mistakes and help correct them. For whole-class feedback, ask who would buy the product their partner reviewed and why (or why not).

Unit 10 Review

GRAMMAR

A Look at the advertisements for two apartments. Use the prompts to write comparative sentences.

$150 a night | Beautiful apartment, five minutes from the city center
Apartment / three bedrooms
★★★★ 3,256 reviews

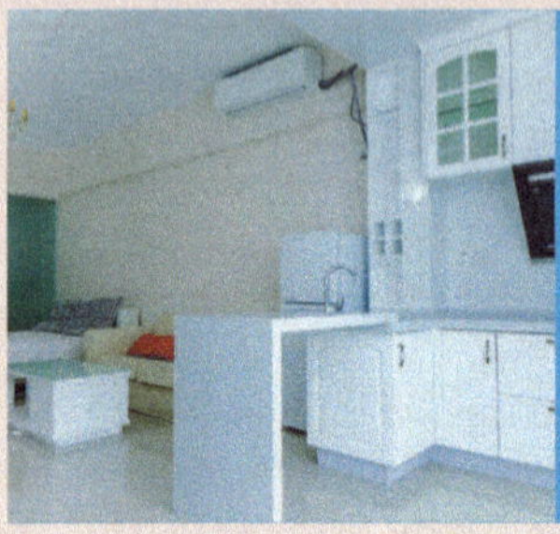

$60 a night | Excellent apartment, 20 minutes from the city center
Apartment / one bedroom
★★★★ 2,988 reviews

1 Apartment B / small / Apartment A
Apartment B is smaller than Apartment A.

2 Apartment A / expensive / Apartment B
Apartment A is more expensive than Apartment B.

3 Apartment A / good / Apartment B
Apartment A is better than Apartment B.

4 Apartment A / big / Apartment B
Apartment A is bigger than Apartment B.

5 Apartment A / close / to the city center / Apartment B
Apartment A is closer to the city center than Apartment B.

B Complete the sentences with the superlative form of the adjective in parentheses.

1 Death Valley is *the hottest* (*hot*) place in the US.
2 Lake Superior is the biggest (*big*) lake in Canada.
3 Manchester is the rainiest (*rainy*) city in the UK.
4 Quito in Ecuador is the most ancient (*ancient*) city in South America.
5 Mount Kilimanjaro is the highest (*high*) mountain in Africa.
6 Tristan de Cunha is the most remote (*remote*) island in the world.
7 Sushi is the best (*good*) food in the world!
8 Laos is the most beautiful (*beautiful*) country I visited in South East Asia.

C Choose the correct form of the verbs to complete the sentences.

1 I'm planning ***to go*** / ***going*** hiking this weekend.
2 I really enjoy ***to watch*** / ***watching*** horror movies.
3 Remember ***to take*** / ***taking*** a coat – it's cold outside!
4 It was raining, so I decided ***to take*** / ***taking*** the bus.
5 I keep ***to wake up*** / ***waking up*** at 6:30 am.
6 I really need ***to get*** / ***getting*** a haircut!

VOCABULARY

A Complete the descriptions with the words in the box.

beach desert forest hill island lake mountains river ocean

The [1] *desert* here is beautiful. The [2] mountains are very tall and there's snow on them. We can't swim in the [3] river because it's too cold.

We're camping here in the [4] forest. There are so many trees! We swam in the [5] lake this morning; then climbed the [6] hill next to the campsite.

This small [7] island is beautiful. We swam in the [8] ocean yesterday, then sat on the [9] beach.

B Look at the pictures. Complete the phrases.

1 It's *cloudy*.
2 It's hot.
3 It's snowing.
4 It's cold.
5 It's windy.
6 It's raining.

C Complete the sentences with the phrasal verbs in the box.

found out give up look for put on set off

1 We set off at five o'clock.
2 Don't give up! You're almost there.
3 Can you help me look for my keys?
4 I just found out that I failed my exam.
5 You should put on a scarf. It's cold outside!

FUNCTIONAL LANGUAGE

Complete the conversation with the words in the box.

busy can't free sounds would

A: Are you [1] free tonight?
B: Why?
A: [2] Would you like to go to the movies?
B: Sorry, I [3] can't. I'm [4] busy. Maybe another time.
A: How about tomorrow night?
B: That [5] sounds good. What's playing?

Ask students to label the photo if you need time to set up the class.

A woman doing yoga on an empty beach.

The quote tells us to value our health. We should not spend time worrying about things such as cars, clothes, jewelry or houses. All of these are meaningless if we do not have good health.

Lao Tzu was a Chinese philosopher and writer. He is thought to have lived in the 4th or 5th century BC.

OBJECTIVES

Read the unit objectives to the class.

UNIT OPENER QUESTIONS

Ask students to look at the picture on the page and describe what the person is doing (*yoga*) and what time of day it is (*sunset* or *sunrise*). Ask students if they think this is a healthy activity. Share answers as a class.

Ask students to read the questions at the bottom of the page. Check that students understand the questions.

Put them into pairs to discuss the three questions. Monitor and help with grammar and vocabulary as required. Encourage students to listen to each other and ask follow-up questions to find out more. For whole-class feedback, ask two or three students to share their opinions with the rest of the class.

WORKSHEETS

Lesson 11.1 Health tips

The body (W56)

should and *shouldn't* (W57)

Lesson 11.2 In it to win it

Present perfect (W58)

Irregular past participles (W59)

Lesson 11.3 Move it

Present perfect vs simple past (W60)

Sports (W61)

11.1 Health tips

Talk about the body and health

V the body **G** *should* and *shouldn't* **P** sentence stress

VOCABULARY
The body

A Label the picture with the words in the box.

arm ear eye foot head heart neck stomach

The Body

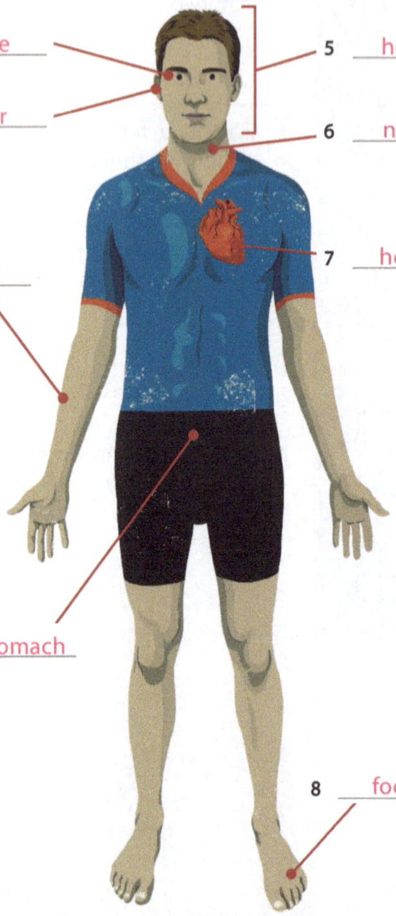

1 eye
2 ear
3 arm
4 stomach
5 head
6 neck
7 heart
8 foot

B Complete the sentences using the words for parts of the body in the box. There are two words you do not need.

blood brain hand legs nose skin

1 I run with my legs.
2 I think with my brain.
3 I smell with my nose.
4 I hold a pen with my hand.

Irregular plurals

We say *I have two feet* NOT *I have two foots*

C SPEAK Work in pairs. Take turns giving each other instructions.

A: Touch your neck.
B: OK … Point to your eyes.

LISTENING

A Work in pairs. Look at the items (1–7) from an article in a health magazine. Which parts of the body (a–g) do you think they match? Are these things good or bad for your body? Why?

1 a cell phone screen
2 sleep
3 a firm bed
4 classical music
5 a ball
6 yogurt
7 coffee

a eyes
b brain
c blood
d back
e stomach
f heart
g skin

11.1 **B LISTEN FOR KEY WORDS** Listen to Bianca and Ella talking about an article from a health magazine. Check your answers to Exercise A.

11.1 Health tips

LEAD-IN

Write *the doctor* on the board. Then ask students in groups to brainstorm other people or places we can get health tips and information from (e.g. *medical websites, apps, friends, family*). Build up the list on the board. Then have a whole-class discussion as to how useful each source of information is.

VOCABULARY

A Students label the picture with the words in the box. Check answers as a class. Check the pronunciation of *head* /hed/, *heart* /hɑːrt/ and *stomach* /ˈstʌmək/.

B Students complete the sentences. They then compare in pairs before checking as a class. Clarify the pronunciation of *blood* /blʌd/ and read through the *Irregular plurals* box to check the plural form of *foot* (*feet*). You could ask students if they can remember any other irregular plural nouns in English (e.g. *tooth – teeth; child – children; woman – women*).

C Students take turns giving each other instructions. Encourage them to use the vocabulary for body parts. Students should try to do as their partner instructs them. Use the **Vocabulary Worksheet** on W56 for extra practice.

LISTENING

A In pairs, students review the list of items. Ask them to match them to the parts of the body. Open up the discussion to the whole class. Do not confirm answers at this point.

11.1 **B** Play the recording. Students listen to the two people and check their answers to the previous exercise. Give feedback as a class.

TEACHING IDEA by David Seymour and Maria Popova

Vocabulary: Feet and feats

Use this activity to review the vocabulary section. Say this to your students:

Listen to these parts of the body and point to them on yourself.

feet, palm, nails, throat, ears, knuckles, eyes, knees, teeth, tongue, eyelids, lips, fingers, leg, shoulder, thumb

In pairs, suggest a verb for each part of the body and write a sentence, e.g. *feet – run. They ran onto the platform.*

Swap partners. Take turns reading your sentences and see if your partner can name the part of the body.

TEACHING IDEA by David Seymour and Maria Popova

Grammar: Annoying habits

Use this activity to prepare for the grammar section on *should* and *shouldn't*. Say this to your students:

In pairs, think of someone you know with annoying habits. Tell your partner about him/her. Don't choose someone in the class! Give each other some advice about how to deal with the person, e.g.

A: I hate him! He's always teasing me!

B: You should just ignore him.

I'm going to give you an adjective that describes a person. In pairs, write a sentence about this person's bad habits, e.g. *loud – He's always playing loud music until the early hours of the morning.* (Distribute the adjectives among the pairs. Allow the students to use dictionaries.)

boring, bossy, dirty, forgetful, greedy, grumpy, lazy, mean, messy

Read out your sentence and see if anyone can guess the adjective.

AUDIO SCRIPT

11.1

Listening, Exercise B
B = Bianca E = Ella

B: This article is called 'Look Good, Feel Good'. It has some nice clothes and some good health tips. You want a healthier lifestyle, don't you, Ella?

E: Mmm?

B: Actually, there are some really nice clothes in this article. What should I wear tonight? Those are nice pants. Should I wear pants tonight, Ella? Or a dress? I think I'll wear a dress. It's a party, after all.

E: Mmm.

B: Anyway, here's some good advice on how to take care of your body. Oh, you shouldn't spend too much
Ex A Q1; Ex C Q1 time on your phone – the screen is bad for your eyes.

E: Mmm?

Ex A Q2 **B:** I like this one. Sleep is good for your heart. I think your heart is very healthy, Ella. You're always asleep!
Ex A Q3; Ex C Q2 And sleeping on a firm bed helps with a bad back. Interesting.

E: Mmm?

B: And do you know how to improve your brain? You
Ex A Q4 should listen to classical music every day.

E: Oh?

B: Yes. It says it here. Ha! I didn't know Mozart could make you more intelligent!

E: Mmm.

B: Ooh! Rolling a small ball under your foot is good for
Ex A Q5; you. It helps the blood flow around your body.
Ex C Q3 **E:** Really?

Ex A Q6; **B:** You should eat yogurt to keep your stomach healthy.
Ex C Q5 Everyone knows that! Coffee is good for you. Is it?
Ex A Q7; Oh, I see. You should put it on your skin. It makes it soft.
Ex C Q5 **E:** Mmm.

B: But you shouldn't drink too much coffee – it keeps you awake. Ella. Coffee keeps you awake. Ella? Are you awake?

E: Mmm? Oh, yes, please.

B: What do you mean 'yes, please'? Are you listening to me?

E: Of course I am. You just offered me some cake.

B: I said 'awake'. You never listen to me. I'm giving you all of this great health advice for free and as usual, you're *not listening*!

E: Mmmmhmm. Sorry, what did you say?

11.1 **C** Students complete the sentences. Play the recording again. Students listen and check.

D In pairs, students discuss the questions. For whole-class feedback, ask each pair to share their ideas. Ask the rest of the class if they agree or not.

GRAMMAR

A Write the sentences on the board. Underline *should* in each and ask students the question from the task instructions. Elicit that we use *should* to give advice.

B Students work alone to complete the rule. Check answers as a class.

C Direct students to the **Grammar Hub** (see below). Read the examples and go through the rules with the class.

D Go through the task and example with students. Provide another example, e.g. *I have a headache*, and elicit advice. Encourage students to say what you should and shouldn't do (e.g. *listen to loud music*). Students then give advice in pairs. For whole-class feedback, ask pairs to share the best advice they discussed. Use the **Grammar Worksheet** on W57 for extra practice.

PRONUNCIATION

11.2 **A** Play the recording. Students listen and repeat the sentences. Ask which word is stressed: *should* or *shouldn't*. Play the recording again for students to check. Elicit that the answer is *shouldn't*.

You should go to the doctor.
You shouldn't watch so much TV.

11.3 **B** Allow time for students to read the sentences. They should predict where the stress will be in each one. Play the recording. Students repeat the sentences, focusing on correct sentence stress. Remind them that *should* is not usually stressed.

SPEAKING

A Read through the problems with students. Allow students time to brainstorm advice for each person. Monitor and assist with vocabulary as required.

B Students work alone to write two pieces of advice for each problem. Monitor and assist, focusing on the accuracy of the sentences produced.

C Put students into groups of four. Students take turns saying their problem and listening to advice from other group members. The student should then choose the best advice for the problem. For whole-class feedback, ask students to say what their problem was and the best advice they received.

GRAMMAR HUB

11.1 *should* and *shouldn't*

	Positive	Negative	
I/you/we/they	**You should drink** lots of water.	**You shouldn't smoke**.	
	Question	Short answers	
he/she/it	**Should I buy** a return ticket?	Yes, **you should**.	No, **you shouldn't**.

- We use *should* to give advice.
- We use *should/shouldn't* + base form.

Be careful!

You should rest. NOT ~~*You should to rest.*~~ NOT ~~*You should resting.*~~

11.1 *should* and *shouldn't*

A Complete the sentences with *should* or *shouldn't*.

1 That's a bad cough. You really ___should___ see a doctor.
2 You ___shouldn't___ smoke – it's really bad for your health.
3 If you want to lose weight, you ___should___ exercise more.
4 If you're sick, you ___shouldn't___ go to work today. You could make other people sick.
5 You look really tired. You ___should___ go to bed early.
6 A: ___Should I___ I take my medicine now?
B: Yes, you ___should___.

B Use the prompts to write sentences with *should* or *shouldn't*.

1 ___*You shouldn't eat*___ (you / not / eat) late at night.
2 ___We shouldn't listen___ (we / not / listen) to loud music.
3 ___Should I go___ (I / go) to the gym more often?
4 When ___should I take___ (I / take) my medicine?
5 ___She shouldn't have___ (she / not / have) four coffees every day.
6 ___They should drink___ (they / drink) lots of water.
7 ___He shouldn't watch___ (he / not / watch) so much TV.

➤ Go back to page 103.

11.1 **C LISTEN FOR DETAIL** Listen again. Complete the sentences with no more than three words from the conversation.

your foot healthy coffee bed on your phone

1 Spending a lot of time __on your phone__ is bad for your eyes.
2 Sleeping on a firm __bed__ can help with a bad back.
3 Rolling a ball under __your foot__ helps blood flow around the body.
4 Eating yogurt can help keep your stomach __healthy__.
5 Putting __coffee__ on your skin can help make it softer.

D SPEAK Work in pairs. What things are good for you? What things are bad for you?

A: Cold showers are good for your skin.
B: Yes, and for your heart, too.

GRAMMAR
should and *shouldn't*

A WORK IT OUT Look at the sentences from the conversation between Bianca and Ella. Do we use *should* to give orders or to give advice? To give advice

You should listen to classical music every day.
You shouldn't drink too much coffee.

B Choose the correct words to complete the rule.

should and *shouldn't*
Should / Shouldn't is followed by ***infinitive / base form.***

C Go to the **Grammar Hub** on **page 142**.

D SPEAK Work in pairs. Student A – ask for advice about your health. Student B – give your partner advice. Take turns.

A: I have breakout prone skin.
B: You should put coffee on it.

PRONUNCIATION
Sentence stress

11.2 **A** Listen and repeat the sentences. Is *should* or *shouldn't* stressed? *shouldn't* is stressed.

11.3 **B** Listen and repeat. Copy the sentence stress.

1 You should exercise every day.
2 You shouldn't eat much fat or sugar.
3 You should sleep eight hours every night.
4 You shouldn't use your phone at bedtime.
5 You should drink lots of water.

SPEAKING

A PREPARE Work in pairs. Look at the problems. What advice would you give each person?

1 My pants are too tight. *exercise more, eat less*
2 I can't see very well.
3 My head hurts.
4 I have a sore foot.

B PLAN Write two pieces of advice for each problem in Exercise A, one with *should* and one with *shouldn't*.

1 You should exercise more.
2 You shouldn't eat so much.

C DISCUSS Work in groups of four. Student A – read out a problem. Students B, C and D – give advice. Student A – choose the best advice for each problem.

Talk about the body and health

11.2 In it to win it

Talk about your experiences

G present perfect **V** irregular past participles **P** past participles

NoFear

Meet the players!

Every week on *No Fear*, 20 players climb, swim and jump as they race to the finish line. Only three people make it to the final each week. In the end, there can be only one winner! Let's meet the three fastest people from last week ... Ex B

Sam McGunn, 32

Sam is a firefighter. He works hard, but in his free time he's really active. He's jumped out of an airplane seven times, and he's run 23 marathons! Sam is very fit, but he's never won a competition. That's why he wants to win this. His wife, Tara, and son, Ben, are here to support him. What do you think? Is Sam the strongest player on the show?

Ex C Q1; Ex D Q2

Hana Hansen, 28

Hana hasn't played any sports in her life. But she owns a large farm and works on it seven days a week, 364 days a year. She often rides horses on the farm. Her husband, Raoul, spends a lot of time working in other countries, so she often has to take care of the animals, the house and their three young children on her own. Hana doesn't have any time for sports, but she's strong and she's a fighter. Can she beat Sam or Jude?

Ex D Q4; Ex D Q3

Jude Wexler, 31

Jude doesn't work, but he's traveled all over the world. He's climbed mountains in Africa and raced cars in the Middle East. Jude doesn't believe in hard work, he prefers to have fun. 'I travel all the time.' Have you ever flown an airplane? 'I have. I loved it.' Have you ever been to a gym? 'I haven't. I don't like exercising,' says Jude. 'To prepare for this type of challenge, you should do what you love. And I love having fun. I believe I can win.' Jude has won 14 competitions with this method. Can he make it 15?

Ex D Q5; Ex D Q6

Glossary

active (adj) someone who does a lot of different activities/sports and has a lot of energy and interests
challenge (n) something that needs a lot of skill and energy and determination to deal with or to achieve
firefighter (n) someone whose job is to put out fires and rescue people from dangerous situations

READING

A SPEAK Work in pairs. You're going to read an article about a TV show called *No Fear*. Look at the pictures. What do you think happens in the show?

B Read the article's introduction. Check your ideas from Exercise A. *No Fear is an extreme race which involves climbing, swimming and jumping. Only three out of twenty contestants progress to the final each week.*

C READ FOR GIST Read the text again. Complete the summaries with *Sam*, *Hana* or *Jude*.

1 __Jude__ doesn't have a job and thinks the best way to win is by having fun.

2 __Sam__ is fit, hardworking and has the support of his family.

3 __Hana__ isn't into sports, but is strong and works all year to manage a large farm.

D READ FOR DETAIL Read again. Are the sentences true (T) or false (F)? Correct the false sentences.

1 Sam won seven competitions. T / (F)
2 Sam is married with a child. (T) / F
3 Hana is often home alone. T / (F)
4 Hana likes to ride around on her motorcycle. T / (F)
5 Jude likes going to the gym. T / (F)
6 Jude came in first in 14 competitions. (T) / F

E SPEAK Work in pairs. Which player do you want to win the competition? Why?

I hope Jude wins because I hate going to the gym, too.

LEAD-IN

Show pictures of two adventurous activities (e.g. *hot-air ballooning* and *go-karting*) and two safer activities (e.g. *cooking* and *gardening*). Explain the word *adventurous* (new and exciting). In pairs students should talk about whether they like or would like to do each activity, and why.

READING

A Write *No Fear* on the board. Explain that this is the name of a TV show. Focus students on the article on page 104. Put students into pairs and ask them to quickly imagine what the show is about. Give them up to two minutes to make suggestions. Share answers as a class.

B Give students a minute to read the introduction to the article and check their ideas. Check answer as a class.

C Focus students on the fill in the blank sentences. Allow them up to three minutes to find the information in the article.

D Give students times to complete the exercise alone before checking their answers with a partner. Give feedback as a class.

1 F (He's never won a competition.); 2 T; 3 F (She often has to take care of the animals, house and her children.); 4 F (She likes to ride around her farm on her horses.); 5 F (He doesn't like exercising.); 6 T.

E Open up the discussion to the whole class and take a vote to find out who the favorite to win is.

GRAMMAR HUB

11.2 Present perfect

	Positive	Negative
I/you/we/they	**I've climbed** Mount Everest.	We **haven't visited** the Burj Khalifa.
he/she/it	**She's ridden** an elephant.	He **hasn't been** to Africa.

	Question	Short answers	
I/you/we/they	**Have you (ever) been** to New York?	Yes, **we have**.	No, **we haven't**.
he/she/it	**Has she (ever) eaten** sushi?	Yes, **she has**.	No, **she hasn't**.

- We use the present prefect to talk about past experiences.
- We use *have/has* + past participle.
- With the present perfect, we don't say when the action happened.

  I've ridden a motorcycle. NOT ~~*I've ridden a motorcycle yesterday.*~~
- We can use *ever* in questions to mean 'before now'.
- We can use *never* in negative statements.

  *I've **never** jumped out of an airplane.*

Be careful!

- We use *been* not *gone* to talk about places we have visited.

  *I have never **been** to China.* NOT ~~*I have never gone to China.*~~
- Be careful with the past participles of common irregular verbs.

  bring → brought *buy → bought* *do → done*
  go → gone/been *make → made* *think → thought*
  write → written

See **Irregular Verbs** on **page 121** for more information.

11.2 Present perfect

A Complete the sentences with the past participle form of the verbs in the box.

~~appear~~ climb do forget been visit

1 I've *appeared* on a TV show twice.
2 Have you ever climbed a mountain?
3 She's never forgotten her first airplane jump.
4 They haven't done any dangerous activities.
5 We have visited Korea three times.
6 Have you ever been to Greece?

B Complete the sentences with the present perfect form of the verb in parentheses. Use contractions where possible.

1 He hasn't played (not play) any sports in his life.
2 They 've never been (never go) to Iceland.
3 We 've swum (swim) in the Mediterranean Sea.
4 Have you ever driven (you ever drive) a sports car?
5 I 've met (meet) Taylor Swift.
6 She 's never played (never play) tennis on grass.

➤ Go back to page 105.

11.2 In it to win it

GRAMMAR

A If possible, display *No Fear* on the board. Focus students on the highlighted sentences. Then allow them time to complete the rule box on their own. Check answers as a class.

B Direct students to the **Grammar Hub** (see TB104). Read the examples and go through the rules with the class.

C Go through the example with students and elicit what has been added to or changed in the prompt. Students then work alone to write complete sentences from the other prompts. Monitor and assist, focusing on accuracy and the correct past participle forms. Students compare answers with a partner and then check with you if they do not agree on any answers.

D Go through the task. Allow students time to think about and write their sentences. Make sure they understand that one sentence needs to be false. Monitor and check for accuracy. Put students into small groups. They take turns reading aloud their sentences. Encourage students to ask each other questions to find out more information, before they decide if the sentence is true or not. Use the **Grammar Worksheet** on W58 for extra practice.

VOCABULARY

A Focus students on the table. Display it to the whole class, if possible. Students then work alone to complete the table. When they have done as much as they can, students compare answers in pairs. Encourage students to check their answers with the *Irregular Verbs* list on page 121. They can also use the list to make sure their spelling is accurate.

11.4 **B** Play the recording. Students listen and check the answers. Play the recording again for students to repeat the words.

C Direct students to the **Vocabulary Hub**. Give students time to complete the exercise alone before checking answers in pairs.

D Direct students to page 121. Students can work in pairs to test each other, with one student saying the verb and the other student saying the simple past form and then the past participle form. If you have time, you could put students into teams to do this and have a whole-class competition. Use the **Vocabulary Worksheet** on W59 for extra practice.

PRONUNCIATION

11.5 **A** Play the recording. Students listen to the past participles. Focus students on the table and the underlined syllables. Play the recording again for students to listen and repeat.

11.6 **B** Students add the words to the correct columns. Encourage students to work in pairs and say the words aloud in order to decide on the pronunciation. Play the recording for students to check their answers and repeat. If you have time, put students into pairs and ask them to practice using the past participles in sentences (e.g. *I've never ridden an elephant, My brother's been to New York five times*, etc). Monitor and practice correct pronunciation as necessary.

SPEAKING

A Write *Have you ever …?* on the board. Elicit ways to complete the question, using a past participle. For example, *Have you ever been skydiving? Have you ever ridden a motorcycle?* Ask students to write four questions of their own. Encourage students to write questions about exciting, dangerous or adventurous activities. Monitor, and assist with language as required.

B Read through the task instructions and example with students. Put students into groups, or ask them to mingle around the room. Tell them to ask and answer their questions with as many people as possible. They should ask follow-up questions in the simple past to find out more information.

C In pairs, students discuss their findings and decide who should take part in *No Fear*. For whole-class feedback, ask each pair to nominate two other students and give reasons.

TEACHING IDEA by David Seymour and Maria Popova

Vocabulary: Past participles

Use this activity to review the vocabulary section. Say this to your students:

In groups of four, make sentences using past participles in alphabetical order. If you can't think of one, you are out of the game, e.g.

A – *I've answered his letter.*

B – *He's blown the whistle.*

C – *I've cooked something special.*

D – *I've never driven a car.*

Work in two teams. I'm going to read a list of nouns. If you think you can use one in a present perfect sentence, put your hand up. If your sentence is correct, your team gets a point. If it's wrong, the other team gets a point and another attempt with the same word, e.g. *tea* – *I've made you some tea.*

cat, bags, dentist, hair, car, tree, shower, Roger, shirt, New York, love, house, road, Janet, café, person, phone, map, dinner, rain, factory, light bulb, egg, nose, computer, duck

In two teams, listen to these infinitives and yell out the past participle. If you're correct, your team gets a point. If you're wrong, the other team gets a point and another attempt at the same verb.

bite, leave, hide, steal, swim, win, put, see, wear, eat, think, know, show, buy, be, throw, drink, sit, ring, stand, let, grow, lose, give, do, shut, teach, speak, run, make, catch, go, bring, ride, rise, tell, shine, sell, fly, take, get, come, keep, break, fight

(Write some infinitives which have irregular past participles in a tic-tac-toe grid.)

Work in two teams to play tic-tac-toe. Take turns to choose a square. To win it you have to tell me the past participle of the verb in the square and use it in a sentence.

GRAMMAR

Present perfect

A WORK IT OUT Look at the highlighted sentences from *No Fear*. Then choose the correct words to complete the rules.

Present perfect

1. We use the present perfect to talk about ***present / past*** experiences.
2. We ***say / don't say*** when in the past the action happened.
3. We make the present perfect with subject + *have* + ***simple past / past participle***.
4. We use ***ever / never*** in questions.
5. We use ***ever / never*** in negative sentences.

B Go to the **Grammar Hub** on **page 142**.

C PRACTICE Use the prompts to write present perfect sentences. Use contractions.

1. I / not be / on a TV show
   I haven't been on a TV show.
2. I / never / jump / out of a plane
   I've never jumped out of a plane.
3. She / climb / a mountain / three times
   She's climbed a mountain three times.
4. He / not try / any dangerous activities
   He hasn't tried any dangerous activities.
5. They / visit / Africa / twice
   They've visited Africa twice.
6. I / never / watch / a game show
   I've never watched a game show.

D SPEAK Work in groups. Write three present perfect sentences about yourself. Two true, and one lie. Read the sentences to the group. See if they can guess the lie.

VOCABULARY

Irregular past participles

A Complete the table with the correct forms of the verbs.

Irregular verbs		
base form	**simple past**	**past participle**
be	*was/were*	been
break	broke	broken
do	1 did	done
eat	2 ate	eaten
3 forget	forgot	forgotten
go	4 went	gone/been
have	5 had	had
ride	6 rode	ridden
run	7 ran	run
8 see	saw	seen
9 take	took	taken
10 win	won	won

11.4 **B** Listen and check. Then listen and repeat.

C Go to the **Vocabulary Hub** on **page 153**.

D Go to **page 121** for a list of irregular verbs.

PRONUNCIATION

Past participles

11.5 **A** Listen and repeat the past participles. Notice how we say the underlined syllables.

/iːn/	/ən/	/ʌn/	/ɒn/
seen seen	broken eaten forgotten ridden taken	done run	gone

11.6 **B** Add the verbs in the box to the table in Exercise A. Then listen, check and repeat.

eaten forgotten ridden run won taken

SPEAKING

A PLAN Write four questions with *Have you ever …?*

B SPEAK Interview people in your class and write notes. Use simple past questions to get more information.

A: Have you ever ridden an elephant?
B: Yes I have.
A: Really? Where did you ride one?
B: In Laos! It was amazing!

C DISCUSS Choose two people in the class to take part in *No Fear*. Say why you chose them.

We chose Agata because she has done more dangerous things than anyone else.

Talk about your experiences

11.3 Move it

Talk about sports and hobbies

G present perfect vs simple past **P** contractions **V** sports **S** understanding the sequence of past events

READING

A SPEAK Work in pairs. What do you think 'ultra-running' is?

B READ FOR GIST Read *Spotlight*. Choose the correct words to complete the sentences.

1 Ultra-running *is* / *isn't* running farther than a marathon.
2 Ultra-running is *better* / *worse* for you than running marathons.
3 You *can* / *can't* walk when you do an ultra-run.
4 Karina *listens* / *doesn't listen* to music when she's running.
5 You *should* / *shouldn't* eat a lot during an ultra-run.
6 You *have to* / *don't have to* start training when you're young.

C Read again. Number the events (1–5) in the order Karina did them. Use the information in the box.

Understanding the sequence of past events

To understand the sequence of past events in a text, think about:
- the order the information is stated
- time references (e.g. *2016, ten years ago*)
- sequencing words (e.g. *then, after that*)

a She did her first ultra-run. 4
b Her children moved away. 1
c She ran a marathon. 3
d She ran in a competition in the desert. 5
e She started running. 2

D SPEAK Work in pairs. Would you try ultra-running? Why/Why not?

SPOTLIGHT

Karina Welch, ultra-runner

Are you bored of running marathons? Do you want to try something new? Ultra-running is becoming more and more popular. Ultra-runs are longer than marathons. They are usually in remote and beautiful places, like the Gobi Desert or the Rocky Mountains, so you can run and enjoy nature at the same time! Ex B Q1

This week, we're talking to Karina Welch, an ultra-runner, who is 66.

So, Karina, when did you start running?
Twenty-five years ago, when I was in my late 40s. My children left home and I needed a way to spend my time, so I decided to start running. I began in my local park, then I ran a few marathons and finally I started ultra-running.

How many ultra-runs have you done?
I've done around 20 races. My first run was in 2009 and it was really difficult. Ultra-runs are different from marathons, but they're better for your body. You normally run in the countryside and not on hard roads. Ex B Q2

Have you ever run a very difficult race? Where was it?
Yes, I have! Four years ago, I ran in the *Marathon des Sables* in the Sahara desert. I ran 250 km in six days, in very hot weather. I didn't actually run the whole time. I sometimes walked for a few kilometers, but that's normal in ultra-running. The important thing is to keep moving! Ex B Q3

Glossary

jogging (n) the activity or exercise of running at a slow steady speed
warm up (phr v) to prepare for a sport or activity by doing gentle exercises or practicing just before it starts

What do you do when you run for such a long time? Do you listen to music? Ex B Q4
No, I like the silence, especially when I'm running in a very quiet place. I like listening to the birds and the wind. I usually eat a lot when I run. You need food to keep your energy levels up. Ex B Q5

What are your tips for someone who is interested in ultra-running?
It's never too late to start! I didn't run when I was young and now I love it. Ex B Q6 Start with jogging, and slowly increase the number of kilometers. And always warm up before you run!

Finally, what do you like most about ultra-running?
I feel free. When I am running, I don't think about anything. It's just me, my legs and the sky.

11.3 Move it

LEAD-IN

Show images relating to your hobbies and the sports you play or enjoy watching. Elicit the names of each, adding any new vocabulary to the board and practicing the correct pronunciation. Tell students about why you like each hobby or sport and encourage them to ask you questions. Next, put students into pairs to discuss their own interests. Monitor, helping with any new or challenging vocabulary. Make a note of any useful emergent language, adding it to the board and using it to stimulate full class discussion wherever possible.

READING

A Write *ultra-running* on the board. Elicit students' ideas as to what this sport is. Encourage students to look at the picture on page 106 to help them develop their ideas. Point out that *ultra-* means 'extreme'.

B Give students time to read through Sentences 1–6 and understand what they need to read for. Then, give students up to three minutes to read the article and choose the correct words. Check answers as a class.

C Read through the *Understanding the sequence of past events* box with students. Point out that time expressions and sequencing words in a text help readers understand when things happened, so it is worth paying attention to them. Students then read through the events and the *Spotlight* article again, numbering the events in the order Karina did them.

D Put students into pairs to discuss the questions. Encourage students to ask follow-up questions to find out more. You can also ask students to list any other extreme sports they know and to say if they would like to try them. Open the discussion up to the whole class, and take a vote to find out how many people want to try ultra-running.

GRAMMAR HUB

11.3 Present perfect vs simple past

- We use the present perfect to talk about an action in the past, but we don't say when it happened.

  *Yes, I've **been** to Canada.* NOT ~~*Yes, I've been to Canada in 2015.*~~

- We use the simple past to talk about an action at a specific time in the past.

  *She went to Greece **in 2016**.* NOT ~~*She has been to Greece in 2016.*~~

- We use time expressions with the simple past, *not* the present perfect.

  *I went to Hawaii three years **ago**.* NOT ~~*I've been to Hawaii three years ago.*~~

  *We took the train to work **yesterday**.* NOT ~~*We've taken the train to work yesterday.*~~

Be careful!

- We often ask a general question about past experiences using the present perfect.
- Then we use the simple past to ask for or give more details.

A: Have you ever been to France?
B: Yes, I have.
A: When did you go?
B: Two years ago.

11.3 Present perfect vs simple past

A Choose the correct tense to complete the sentences.

1. She*'s been* / *went* to Denmark last year. (went)
2. They*'ve traveled* / *traveled* to Chile a long time ago. (traveled)
3. *Have you biked* / *Did you bike* to work yesterday? (Did you bike)
4. *Have you ever been* / *Did you ever go* to Vietnam? (Have you ever been)
5. We*'ve driven* / *drove* across Europe last summer. (drove)
6. *Have you tried* / *Did you try* snowboarding when you were in Switzerland? (Did you try)

B Complete the text messages with the present perfect or simple past form of the verb in parentheses.

Virginia: [1] Did you go (go) skiing last week?

Teresa: Yes, we [2] did. [3] Have you ever been (ever go) skiing?

Virginia: No, I [4] haven't. I [5] haven't done (do) any winter sports.

Teresa: Really? I [6] have tried (try) both skiing and snowboarding. They're really fun!

➤ Go back to page 107.

11.3 Move it

GRAMMAR

A Write the sentences on the board and ask students to identify the verbs. Underline them and elicit which ones are the present perfect (*'ve done, Have you ever run*). Ask students why the present perfect is used in some sentences and the simple past in others. Students then work through the rule box, choosing the correct words. Check answers as a class.

B Direct students to the **Grammar Hub** (see TB106). Read the examples and go through the rules with the class.

C Go through the example conversation with students. Show how there is a present perfect question and the follow-up questions are in the simple past. Students then ask and answer the questions in pairs. Make sure they ask follow-up questions to find out more information. Monitor and focus on the accuracy of the questions, both present perfect and simple past. Students can swap partners and ask the questions again. Use the **Grammar Worksheet** on W60 for extra practice.

PRONUNCIATION

11.7 **A** Point out that *I have* is contracted in normal spoken English to become *I've*. Explain that the apostrophe shows that letters are missing and that when we say these contractions, sounds are missing. Play the recording for students to listen and read the sentences.

11.8 **B** Allow students time to read through the pairs of sentences. Then play the recording. Students apply check marks to the sentences they hear. Check answers as a class.

Play the recording again. Students listen again and repeat. If you have time, you could ask students to underline the stressed words and syllables in the sentences. Then, students can repeat the sentences again, with stress on the correct words.

VOCABULARY

A Focus students on the photos and ask them to say what they can see. Ask students which verb goes with each sport. Check answers as a class. Before moving to the Vocabulary Hub, you could try to elicit more sports from students at this point. Add any new vocabulary to the board, showing images if possible to check that everyone understands each word.

B Direct students to the **Vocabulary Hub**. Give students time to complete the exercises alone before checking answers in pairs. If you have time, you could ask students to test themselves. One student says one of the sports from Exercise A. The other student points to the correct picture and says the correct verb (*go, do* or *play*) that goes with the sport.

C Model the answer for students, using target language from the lesson. Students then find out what sports their partner plays and how often. Use the **Vocabulary Worksheet** on W61 for extra practice.

SPEAKING HUB

A Go through the task with students. Focus on the example questions and ask students to identify the verbs' tenses and why they are used in each case. Students then work alone to write five questions. Monitor and assist, focusing on accuracy of grammar.

B Highlight that they will ask other students their questions and then ask follow-up questions to find out more. Demonstrate with one or two students as required. Put students into groups of four, or allow them to mingle around the room. Students interview three students, writing a note of the answers.

C For whole-class feedback, have a discussion on the information students found out. Ask follow-up questions to help students to extend their responses further.

TEACHING IDEA by David Seymour and Maria Popova

Vocabulary: Categories

Use this activity to review the vocabulary section. Say this to your students:

Choose one of these headings and write a list of different sports. Write a few notes describing any experience you have had of playing or watching them, e.g. *soccer – last Saturday in the park.*

winter sports, decathlon, water sports, animal sports, table sports, motor sports, ball sports, fighting sports, extreme sports

In pairs, compare your lists, and tell each other about your experiences.

TEACHING IDEA by David Seymour and Maria Popova

Guess the game

Use this activity to build on sports vocabulary and review question forms.

In pairs, take turns thinking of a sport for your partner to guess. You can ask 20 questions and your partner can only answer 'yes' or 'no'.

(With mixed nationality classes, find out how many of them know one of their national sports, e.g. sumo wrestling, boules, cricket, kabbadi, baseball, ice hockey. Put them into groups with students who do not know the sport so that they can explain it to them.)

TEACHING IDEA by David Seymour and Maria Popova

Grammar: Tell me more

Use this activity to review the grammar section. Say this to your students:

In pairs, ask and answer questions about whether you have ever done these things. If the answer is yes, find out some more information, e.g.

A: Have you ever broken a bone?
B: Yes, I have.
A: When was that?
B: When I was in school.
A: What happened?
B: I broke my arm playing rugby.

cut your finger, eat Indian food, get an injection, wear a fancy dress, live by the ocean, do anything brave, sleep in a tent, sail a boat, drive a tractor

Tell your partner something you've done which you don't think anyone else in class has done and something you've never done which you think another student in class has done, e.g. *I've been scuba diving. I've never played cricket, but I think Shaqil probably has.*

Tell us what your partner said and find out if his/her guesses are true.

GRAMMAR
Present perfect vs simple past

A WORK IT OUT Look at the sentences from *Spotlight*. Choose the correct words to complete the rules.

I've done around 20 races.

My first run was in 2009.

Have you ever run a very difficult race? Where was it?

Present perfect and simple past

1. We use the present perfect to talk about an action in the past. We *say / don't say* when it happened.
2. We use the simple past to talk about an action in the past. We *know / don't know* when it happened.
3. We use time expressions, like *ago, in 2010, last week* with the *present perfect / simple past*.
4. We often ask a general question about past experiences using the *simple past / present perfect*.
5. We then use the *simple past / present perfect* to ask for more details or to give more details (such as *where, when, how*).

B Go to the **Grammar Hub** on **page 142**.

C SPEAK Work in pairs. Take turns asking and answering questions. Discuss where and when you did them.

1. try / snowboarding?
2. run / in a race?
3. meet / a famous person?
4. win / a sports competition?

A: Have you ever tried snowboarding?
B: Yes, I have.
A: When did you go?
B: When I was in Andorra, last year.

PRONUNCIATION
Contractions

11.7 **A** Listen and read. Notice the pronunciation of the contractions.

1 a **I have** never been to Moscow.
  b **I've** never been to Moscow.

2 a **He has** never run a marathon.
  b **He's** never run a marathon.

3 a **We haven't won** the competition.
  b **We have not won** the competition.

11.8 **B** Listen and check (✓) the sentences you hear. Then listen again and repeat the sentences.

1 a ☑ I have been to New York five times.
  b ☐ I've been to New York five times.

2 a ☐ Elliott has never eaten sushi.
  b ☑ Elliott's never eaten sushi.

3 a ☐ She has not run a marathon.
  b ☑ She hasn't run a marathon.

VOCABULARY
Sports

A Complete the phrases with the verbs in the box.

do go play

1 __go__ running

2 __do__ karate

3 __play__ soccer

B Go to the **Vocabulary Hub** on **page 153**.

C SPEAK Work in pairs. Tell your partner what sports you play and how often you play them.

SPEAKING HUB

A PREPARE You are going to interview your classmates about sports and hobbies. Write five main questions.

Have you ever run a marathon?
When was the last time you went to the gym?

B DISCUSS Interview three students. Write notes about their answers. Try to ask follow-up questions to get more information.

A: What sports do you play?
B: I play soccer once a week and sometimes play basketball with my brother.
A: Do you play for a soccer team?
B: No, I just play with friends for fun.

C DISCUSS Have a class discussion. What is the most popular sport or hobby? Which is the most unusual? What is the most interesting thing that someone has done or made?

I think Pablo's hobby is the most unusual. He does Zumba ... underwater!

Talk about sports and hobbies

Café Hub

11.4 Get fit

F – ask for information P – stress and intonation

COMPREHENSION

A Watch the video. Correct the six mistakes in the poster.

B **SPEAK** Work in pairs. Are the sentences true (T) or false (F)? Correct the false sentences. Then watch the video again and check your answers.

1. Milly's sitting in the park with her back against a tree. (T) / F
2. Neena is sitting in ~~the kitchen~~. her bedroom T / (F)
3. Neena did yoga before and fell over. (T) / F
4. The Yoga Yoga Yoga receptionist has ~~short~~ long hair. T / (F)
5. At the beginning of the class, they put their hands on their chest. (T) / F

USEFUL PHRASES

A Change one word in each useful phrase. Use the words in the box.

calling coming eyes fired ~~last~~ legs

1. Oh, one final thing. *Oh, one last thing.*
2. Thanks for phoning Yoga Yoga Yoga. Thanks for calling Yoga Yoga Yoga.
3. What do you mean, you aren't working? What do you mean, you aren't coming?
4. You're sacked! You're fired!
5. Cross your arms. Cross your legs.
6. Close your mouth. Close your eyes.

B How do you say these useful phrases in your language?

FUNCTIONAL LANGUAGE

Asking for information

A 00.40–02:17 Complete Milly's questions. Then watch the video and check your answers.

1. What __time__ is the next slow yoga class?
2. How __much__ does it cost?
3. How __long__ is it?
4. Are __there__ any lockers for our bags?
5. How __many__ people are in the class?
6. Can __I__ book two places for Milly and Neena, please?

B Complete the questions. Use the questions in Exercise A to help you.

1. __What time__ do you open/close?
2. __Can I__ reserve a badminton court?
3. __How much__ is it for one lesson?
4. __What time__ does it start/finish?
5. __How many__ teams are in the league?

C **SPEAK** Work in pairs. Student A – ask a question from Exercise A or B. Student B – make up an answer. Swap.

A: What time do you open?
B: 9 am every morning.

MILLY

SAM

NEENA

ZAC

GABY

PRONUNCIATION

Stress and intonation

11.9 **A** Listen and complete the questions.

1 What time do you open?
2 How long does it last?
3 How much does it cost?
4 Who's the instructor?
5 How many people are in the class?
6 When does it start?

11.9 **B** Listen again and repeat. Copy the stress and intonation.

C **SPEAK** Work in pairs. Practice asking the questions in Exercise A. Remember to use the correct stress and intonation.

SPEAKING

DISCUSS Work in pairs. Take turns booking a lesson using the information below.

Student A – call to book a lesson. Say who the lesson is for and ask about:

- time
- cost
- length of lesson
- name of instructor

Student B – look at the information in the advertisements and answer Student A's questions.

Urban dance class

All ages!
Teacher: Nino
Every evening 7–8 pm
Adult: $7.50 Students: $4.00
Only 12 places per class

Boxing class

Beginners!
Small classes – five people.
Teacher: Max
3 pm to 4 pm every day
$12.50

Swimming lessons

City swimming pool
Teachers: Ahmed and Fraser
Every Saturday
10:30 am to 12:30 pm
Adult: $5 Child: $2

Tennis lessons

One-hour lessons with your coach, Andy
Maximum of two people per lesson
Every afternoon from 2 to 4 pm
Adult: $16 Child: $9

Ask for information

➤ Turn to page 170 to learn how to write a recommendation on a forum.

11.4 Get fit

LEAD-IN

Tell students about your weekly exercise routine. Do you go to classes? Do you play on any teams? Encourage students to ask you questions and write any new or useful emergent language on the board. Then, put students into pairs to discuss their own exercise routines. Monitor, writing a note of any interesting vocabulary that could stimulate a full class discussion.

COMPREHENSION

A ▶ Focus students on the poster, asking questions to check their understanding. Then go through the task and play the video. Students compare the list of mistakes they noticed with a partner. Check answers as a class.

B ▶ Allow students time to read through the sentences. They may be able to predict or recall which sentences are true or false at this point. They watch the video again to confirm the answers and correct the false sentences.

USEFUL PHRASES

A Read through the task and the completed example. Do the second one together as a class. Students then work alone to change the other phrases. Students compare answers with a partner before checking as a class.

B As far as possible, students work with other students with the same first language to discuss how to say the useful phrases.

FUNCTIONAL LANGUAGE

A ▶ 00:40-02:17 In pairs, students complete the questions Milly asks in the video. Then play the video again. Check answers as a class.

B Work through the first example together as a class, writing the answer on the board. Students then discuss and complete the questions in pairs, using Exercise A to help. Give feedback as a class. Take the time to practice more natural pronunciation at this point, focussing on the connected speech (e.g. saying *Can_I* as **/kənaɪ/** and … *do_you* as **/ʤʊ/**, etc).

C Students work in new pairs, asking questions from Exercise B and responding appropriately. Again, take the time to focus on natural pronunciation as well as accuracy of language here.

PRONUNCIATION

11.9 **A** Students read through the fill in the blank questions. Play the recording for students to listen and write the missing words.

11.9 **B** Play the recording again. Ask students to identify the word stress in the questions. Students underline the stressed syllables. Then play the recording again, pausing after each question. Students listen and repeat, focusing on producing the correct stress and intonation.

C Students practice the questions in pairs, helping to improve each other's use of stress and intonation. Encourage them to look at each other when speaking, instead of just reading from the page.

SPEAKING

Focus students on the information about different classes and lessons. Ask questions to check their understanding (e.g. *How much is a child's swimming lesson?*).

Explain that they are going to take turns role playing calling each other and booking a lesson. Focus on the information that students need to ask about. Remind students to use the useful phrases and *Functional Language* from earlier in the lesson.

Put students into pairs. As they perform the role plays, monitor and write notes on effective use of the target language and also of phrases which need reformulation. Use these as a basis for whole-class feedback at the end of the exercise.

Extra activity

Put students into pairs. Ask them to write new conversations using the *Functional Language* from this page in a different context (e.g. classes at a language school, going on a walking tour, etc). Monitor and assist with new vocabulary as necessary. Finally, ask students to perform their role plays for the class and vote on their favorite.

▶ VIDEO SCRIPT

D = DVD R = Receptionist M = Milly

D: … And lift your foot over your head …
R: Hello, yoga yoga yoga. How can I help?
M: Hi, there. I'd like to book a relaxing yoga class for two people.
R: OK. Have you done yoga before?
M: Yes, we have.
R: Great. You should try a slow yoga class! Good for the mind and good for the body!
M: OK cool. What time is the next slow yoga class?
R: 11 o'clock today.
M: OK great. And … how much does it cost?
R: £10 each.
M: And … how long is it?
R: One hour.
M: Are there any lockers for our bags?
R: Yes.
M: And … how many people are in the class?
R: Usually about six people but … it's nearly full so you should book now.
M: OK. Can I book two places for Milly and Neena, please?
R: Milly … and … Neena. Wonderful. See you later.
M: Oh, one last thing. Who's the instructor?
R: She's called Lucy. She's very good.
M: OK, thanks. See you at 11.
R: OK. Thanks for calling yoga yoga yoga. Bye bye bye. Lucy! Where are you? What do you mean, you're not coming? Again! This means I have to teach the class! Again! You're fired! Hello everyone. Let's get into a sitting position. Please sit down. Cross your legs, put your hands on your chest and slowly close your eyes.

11 Writing

write a recommendation on a forum

W adding information with *too*, *also* and *as well*

A SPEAK Work in pairs. Do you ever give or read advice on chat forums? Which ones? What do you write about? Tell your partner.

B Work in pairs. Read the post on a fitness website. What sports or activities do you think Martin should try?

Hi everyone. I'm 23 and I want to get fit. Can anyone recommend a sport or activity for me? I like doing things on my own and team sports, but I don't want to spend a lot of money. What should I try? Thanks!

Martin | June 15, 4:17

C Read the replies to Martin's question. Do they match any of the things you thought of in Exercise B?

Hi Martin! You should try yoga. It's really fun! You don't need any special equipment or clothes. One problem is that lessons are sometimes expensive. I found a yoga class in my town and I go twice a week. Now I can touch my toes!

Luis | June 15, 4:25

Hi there! I think you should try running. I've started a running club in my town. It's great! We go running together every week. Of course, you can also go running on your own. The best thing about running is that you can do it at any time you want! But be careful! Running is difficult, and it can hurt your knees as well. You should start slowly.

Caitlin | June 15, 4:27

What about soccer? I started five years ago and I love it. My friends and I play every week on a Saturday morning. Soccer is really good exercise, and it's fun, too! One problem is that you need to buy boots and sports clothes. You also need other people to play. You can't do it on your own. But I think it's more fun to exercise with friends!

Marta | June 15, 4:27

D Read again and answer the questions. Write notes.

1 What sports and activities do the writers think Martin should try?
2 What good things do the writers say about the sports or activities?
3 What bad things do the writers talk about?

E Work in pairs. Whose advice do you think is best? Why?

Adding information with *too*, *also* and *as well*

We can use *too*, *also* and *as well* to add information to an idea.
Too and *as well* come at the end of the sentence.
Also comes before the main verb, but after the verb *be*.

F Work in pairs. Read again. Find and underline sentences with *also*, *too* and *as well*.

G Rewrite the second sentence using the word in parentheses. Use the Language information box to help you.

1 Golf is expensive. You need a lot of time. (also)
You also need a lot of time.
2 Swimming is good for your heart. It's good for your arms and legs. (as well)
It's good for your arms and legs as well.
3 You can play basketball in the winter. You can play it in the summer. (too)
You can play it in the summer, too.
4 Rita is good at tennis. She's good at badminton. (too)
She's good at badminton, too.

WRITING

A PREPARE Read the post below. What sport or activity should Janice try? Write notes. Use the steps in Exercise D to help you.

I am a 53-year-old woman. I'd like to try a sport or activity. I don't like team sports and I have problems with my back. Does anyone have any advice for me? What should I try? Thanks!
Janice

B Write your recommendation. Use *also*, *too* and *as well* to add information.

170 WRITING

Answers

1 Yoga, running and soccer
2 Yoga is fun and you don't need special equipment; you can run on your own at any time; soccer is good exercise and fun.
3 Yoga can be expensive; running can be difficult and hurt your knees; you can't play soccer on your own and you need to buy boots and sports clothes.

Point out that although these words have a similar meaning, we put them in a different position in the sentence.

Refer students to these posts as models for the writing task.

Encourage students to read each other's recommendations.

WRITING

In this writing lesson, students will learn how to write a recommendation, paying attention to how they can use words like *too*, *also* and *as well* to add extra information.

A Students discuss the questions in pairs. Open up the discussion to the whole class and add your own experiences, too.

B Go through the task with students. Students then read the fitness website post and, in pairs, discuss which sports or activities they think Martin should try.

C Students read the three replies. Then, with the same partner from Exercise B, they identify any replies which match their own ideas. Share answers as a class.

D Students read the replies again and then answer the questions, writing notes as they do so.

E Put students into new pairs. They discuss the three replies and the advice given, trying to agree on which advice they think is the best. Open up the discussion to the whole class to find out how many students agree.

F Read through the box about adding information. In pairs, students find and underline sentences containing *also*, *too* and *as well* in the three replies from Exercise C. Check answers as a class.

G Go through the task and the completed example, highlighting how the second sentence has been rewritten to include the word in parentheses. Students work alone to rewrite the remaining sentences. Check answers as a class by writing the sentences on the board.

WRITING TASK

A Students read the post and write notes on the sport or activity they think Janice should try. Remind them to refer to Exercise D to organize their ideas.

B Students write their recommendations. Remind them to use *also*, *too* and *as well* to add information. If you have time, students could post their replies around the room and read each other's recommendations. They can 'like' (by adding a check mark) the ones they agree with. At the end, find out which replies are most popular.

Unit 11 Review

GRAMMAR

A Find and correct the mistake in each sentence.

1 You should to stop smoking.
You should stop smoking.

2 You don't should eat junk food every day.
You shouldn't eat junk food every day.

3 How often I should exercise?
How often should I exercise?

4 Do you think I should to join a gym?
Do you think I should join a gym?

5 She shouldn't drinks so much coffee.
She shouldn't drink so much coffee.

6 I shouldn't start going to bed earlier.
I should start going to bed earlier.

B Write the words in the correct order to make sentences.

1 jumped out of / three / He's / an airplane / times
He's jumped out of an airplane three times.

2 any / never / sports / He's / played
He's never played any sports.

3 She's / won / never / a competition
She's never won a competition.

4 you / been / Have / India / to / ?
Have you been to India?

5 you / Have / the new restaurant / to / been / in town / ?
Have you been to the new restaurant in town?

6 been / Japan / times / I've / to / five
I've been to Japan five times.

7 Have / an / you / elephant / ever / ridden ?
Have you ever ridden an elephant?

8 Mexican / never / eaten / food / She's
She's never eaten Mexican food.

C Use the prompts to complete the conversation. Use the present perfect and simple past where necessary.

Eloise: you / ever / try / yoga? [1] *Have you ever tried yoga?*
Michael: Yes,[2] I have.
Eloise: when / you / try / it? [3] When did you try it?
Michael: Three months ago. I / go / to a class near my house. [4] I went to a class near my house.
Eloise: you / enjoy / it? [5] Did you enjoy it?
Michael: Yes,[6] I did. I want to go again. You / ever / try / it? [7] Have you ever tried it?.
Eloise: No, [8] I haven't. Maybe we can go together.

D SPEAK **Work in pairs. Talk about sports and exercise and then give some advice.**

A: I want to exercise outside.
B: You should go running.

VOCABULARY

A Label the parts of the body (1–10) with words in the box.

arm brain eye foot hand
heart leg neck nose stomach

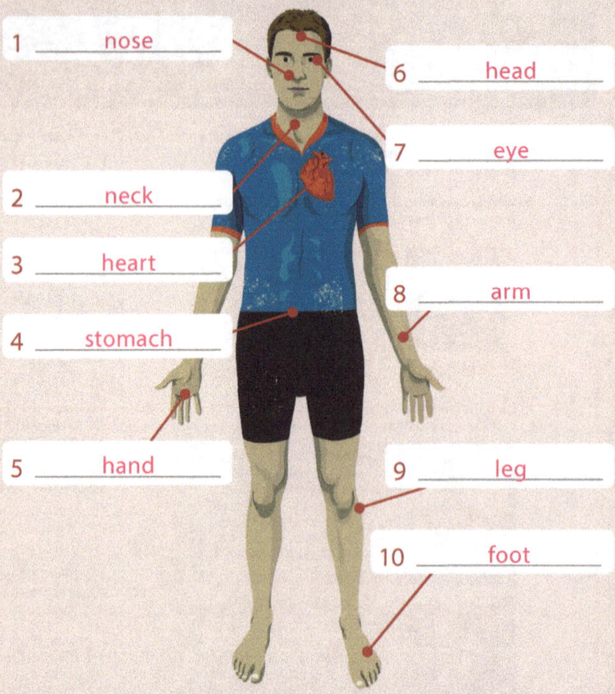

B Complete with the correct form of the verbs.

Ben is amazing. He's [1]*did* / *done* everything and he's [2]*been* / *went* everywhere. He's [3]*flew* / *flown* a plane and he's [4]*seen* / *saw* the Pyramids. I haven't ever [5]*win* / *won* a competition or even [6]*ridden* / *rode* a horse. But I have [7]*broken* / *broke* a bone, so I suppose that's something.

C Complete the table with the sports in the box.

bike riding ~~judo~~ badminton swimming ~~soccer~~
gymnastics basketball surfing tennis ~~running~~

play	go	do
soccer	*running*	*judo*
badminton	bike riding	gymnastics
basketball	swimming	
tennis	surfing	

FUNCTIONAL LANGUAGE

Complete the questions (1–6) with the words in the box.

any how cost time ~~when~~ who

1 *When* 's the next exercise class?
2 What time does the gym open?
3 How long is the class?
4 How much does it cost?
5 Do I need to bring any equipment?
6 Who 's the class instructor?

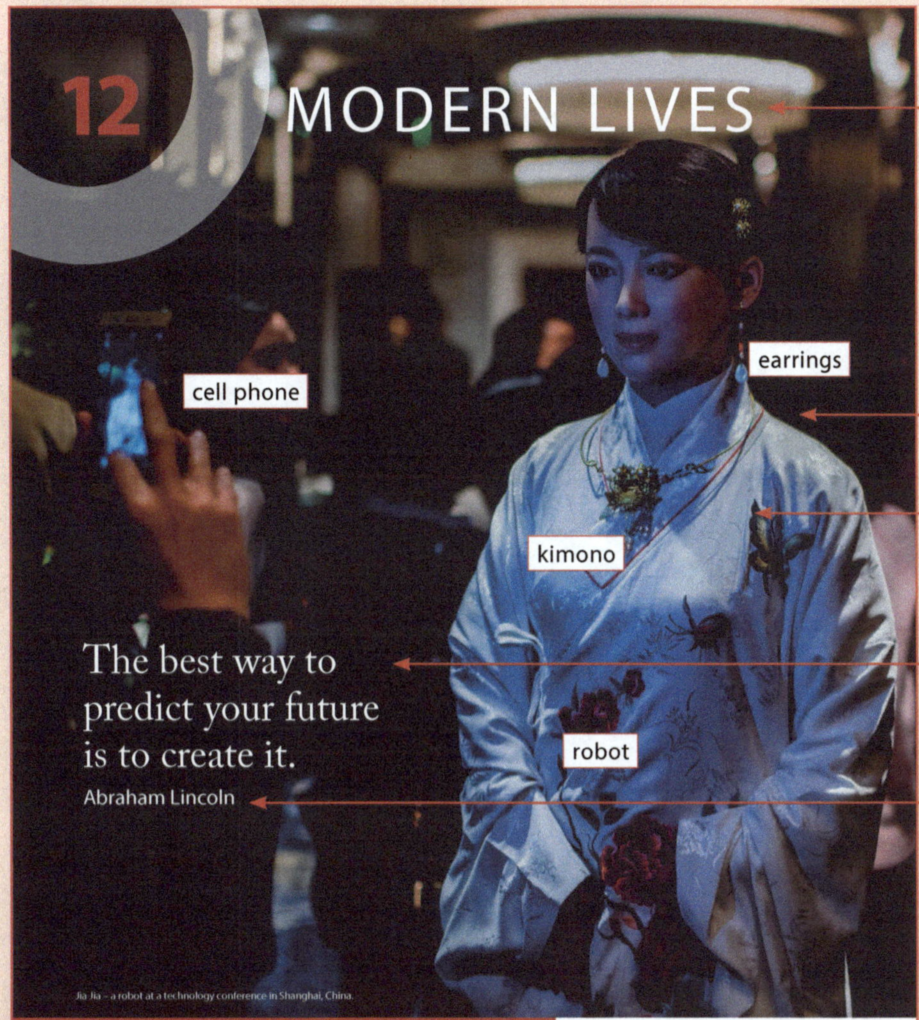

Jia Jia – a robot at a technology conference in Shanghai, China.

Modern (adj) using new styles that are different from the styles of the past
Synonyms: new (adj), up-to-date (adj)

Ask students to label the photo if you need time to set up the class.

Jia Jia – a robot at a technology conference in Shanghai, China.

The quote suggests that we have control over our future. We do not need to sit back and see what happens.

Abraham Lincoln (1809–1865) was the 16th President of the United States. He held office from 1861 until 1865 when he was assassinated. He has always been highly respected, particularly because he rose from an ordinary background to become president.

OBJECTIVES

- talk about future plans
- make predictions
- talk about social media habits
- show interest in something
- write a formal email

Work with a partner. Discuss the questions.

1. Where do you want to live in 10 years' time?
2. Look at the picture. Would you like a robot like this?
3. What do you want to do in the future?

MODERN LIVES 111

OBJECTIVES

Read the unit objectives to the class.

UNIT OPENER QUESTIONS

Ask students to look at the picture on the page and describe what they see. Write any new or useful emergent language on the board, including the phonemes, and practice good pronunciation. If possible, use the language as the basis for class-wide discussion.

Ask students to read the questions at the bottom of the page. Check that students understand the questions.

Put them into pairs to discuss the three questions. Monitor and help with grammar and vocabulary as required. Encourage students to listen to each other and ask follow-up questions to find out more. For whole-class feedback, ask two or three students to share their opinions with the rest of the class.

WORKSHEETS

Lesson 12.1 Life's too busy

going to (W62)

Future time expressions (W63)

Lesson 12.2 Everything will be shiny

will for predictions (W64)

Collocations with *get* (W65)

Lesson 12.3 Communication

Internet communication (W66)

might (W67)

12.1 Life's too busy

Talk about future plans

G *going to* P *going to*: weak and strong *to* V future time expressions

LISTENING

A Look at the picture. Work in groups and answer the questions.

- What problem does the person in the picture have?
- Are you a busy person? Why/Why not?
- How do you remember everything you have to do?

12.1 **B LISTEN FOR GIST** Listen to some friends talking. Who is the most organized person: Juliet, Mario or Kelly? Kelly

12.1 **C LISTEN FOR DETAIL** Listen again. Choose the correct answer to complete the sentences.

1 Juliet is working this weekend because

- a she always works on the weekend.
- b she was on vacation last week.
- c work is really busy at the moment.

2 Mario read an article about

- a how to work full time and study.
- b how to manage time.
- c how to get a better job.

3 According to the newspaper article, you should

- a make a short list of tasks.
- b make a long list of tasks.
- c never make a list of tasks.

4 Mario decides

- a to study this evening.
- b to learn to make lists.
- c to study in the mornings and work in the evenings.

D SPEAK Work in pairs. Do you agree with the advice? Why/Why not? What are some other ways to organize your time?

A: I agree with Kelly. You need to understand your body clock.

B: To organize my time, I use an app to make lists.

GRAMMAR

going to

A WORK IT OUT Read the sentences from the conversation. Underline the verbs. Does *going to* refer to the present or the future? future

1 I'm going to try that idea at work next week.

2 I'm definitely not going to finish it.

3 Are you going to finish your essay this weekend?

B Complete the rules with *be* or *base form*.

going to for future intentions and plans
We use [1] be + *going to* + [2] base form to talk about a future plan.

C Go to the **Grammar Hub** on **page 144**.

D Complete the sentences with the correct form of *going to*. Use the verbs in parentheses.

1 I'm going to go (go) to the movie theater on the weekend.

2 I'm going to meet (meet) friends after class.

3 I'm going to relax (relax) at home tonight.

4 I'm going to have (have) chicken for dinner.

5 I'm going to do (do) my homework this afternoon.

6 I'm going to buy (buy) a new car next year.

7 I'm going to travel (travel) around Europe this summer.

E SPEAK Work in pairs. Make the sentences in Exercise D true for you.

A: What are you going to do after class?

B: I'm going to meet my sister for lunch.

A: Oh, that sounds nice. I'm going to go to the gym.

12.1 Life's too busy

LEAD-IN

Write a 'To Do' list on the board, including things you have to do today, this week and this month. Ask if students have any similar things on their 'To Do' list. Students then write their own and share it in a group. For whole-class feedback, students decide who has the easiest and most difficult 'To Do' list.

LISTENING

A Focus students on the picture. Elicit how the person probably feels. In groups, students discuss the questions. Share ideas as a class. If you have time, find out if students use apps on their phones to help them remember everything they have to do.

12.1 **B** Go through the task and then play the recording. Check answers as a class. Elicit that it is Kelly who is most organized.

12.1 **C** Allow time to read through the questions and options. Students could discuss in pairs and predict the answers. Students then listen again. Check answers as a class.

D Students discuss the advice in pairs, explaining their views and giving suggestions for other ways to organize their time. For whole-class feedback, write student's suggestions on the board.

GRAMMAR

A Write the sentences on the board. Elicit the verbs and underline them. Encourage students to say what *going to* is used for in these sentences.

B Students work individually to complete the rules. Check answers as a class.

C Direct students to the **Grammar Hub** on page 144 (see TB113). Read the examples and go through the rules.

D Students work individually to complete the sentences. Allow time for students to compare answers with a partner before checking as a class.

E Put students into pairs. Students can either say the sentences as they are or change them to make them true. Encourage students to respond to each other's sentences in a natural way. Use the **Grammar Worksheet** on W62 for extra practice.

AUDIO SCRIPT

12.1

Listening, Exercise B
J = Juliet M = Mario K = Kelly

J: Guys! I'm so sorry I'm late. I needed to finish some things at work.

M: It's Saturday, Juliet. Why are you working on the weekend?

Ex C Q1 **J:** Oh, things are really busy at the moment. It's terrible. I'm at work all day, then I have to leave at five to pick up the children. Then in the evenings, I'm always busy with them. Well, actually, I'm usually in the car because I have to take them to their dance classes, or soccer, or swimming.

Ex C Q2 **M:** I read an article in the *Guardian* about time management. It had some useful tips.

K: Yeah, I saw that, too.

J: Well, I need some tips. Something has to change. Tomorrow, I'm going to make a long list of everything I need to do.

M: No, don't make long lists!

J: Why not?

M: Because you can't finish everything. The article said you have to make a list of five things.

Ex C Q3

J: Only five?

M: That's right. But I never make lists. What's the point?

K: I like making long lists because that way I remember everything. But maybe I should try the five-list idea.

J: I make lists, too, but I'm going to try that idea at work next week. My biggest problem is that I can't say no, so I have too much to do.

M: I'm like that, too. I agreed to work full time this week, but then I'm studying for my degree in the evening. I need to finish an essay. It's due in on Monday, but there just aren't enough hours in the day. I don't know what I'm going to do.

K: Are you going to finish your essay this weekend?

M: I think I can find time to plan it tonight, but I'm definitely not going to finish it. It's difficult to study when I'm tired.

K: You need to understand your body clock. When do you work best? I'm definitely a morning person.

M: Yes, I think I am, too.

J: Maybe you should ask your boss if you can work in the evenings, so you can study in the mornings?

Ex C Q4 **M:** That's a great idea! I'm going to see him tomorrow, so I can ask him then.

K: Or maybe you could take a day off? It's impossible to do everything, so don't worry about it!

Ex B **M:** But you're really organized, Kelly. I'm not! I find it hard to prioritize.

K: Just make a list, then decide which are the most important things.

M: Why make a list when everything is a priority. I can't decide what's most important, so I do nothing!

J: I know just what you mean!

12.1 Life's too busy

PRONUNCIATION

12.2 **A** Play the recording. Students listen and focus students on the word *to*. Play the recording again and ask them to listen and repeat.

12.3 **B** Students decide on the pronunciation of *to*. They should also identify any linking sounds. Students compare ideas with a partner. Then play the recording for students to check answers and repeat the sentences.

C In pairs, students take turns saying the sentences. Monitor and assist as required.

VOCABULARY

12.4 **A** Focus students on Andrew's list of things to do and read through the task. Play the conversation between Andrew and his manager. Students apply check marks to the things Andrew is going to do on the weekend.

B Read out the first line of the conversation, and ask students to identify the future time expression (*next month*). Students then work alone to complete the task.

C Read through the completed example with students. Elicit what has changed in the prompt and what has been added in order to make the question. Students work alone to complete the remaining questions. Monitor and assist as required.

D In pairs, students ask and answer the questions. Monitor and make a note of any errors. Use these as the basis for whole-class feedback at the end. Use the **Vocabulary Worksheet** on W63 for extra practice.

SPEAKING

A Put students into A/B pairs. Direct them to the **Communication Hub**. To see the exercises and answers go to pages TB157 and TB159. Explain that each student has some information missing and that they must ask their partner for the information. Encourage students to use *going to* in their questions and in their replies.

B Write a list of five things you want to do soon on the board. Invite students to ask you questions about each thing to find out more information. Ask students to write their own list and then share them with a partner and answer questions to give more information.

GRAMMAR HUB

12.1 *going to*

	Positive	Negative
I	**I'm going to travel** around Japan after college.	**I'm not going to work** in an office when I graduate.
he/she/it	**She's going to book** the tickets next week.	**She isn't going to visit** Kyoto during her trip.
you/we/they	**We're going to stay** in hostels.	**We aren't going to book** anything until we get there.

	Question	Short answers	
I	**Am I going to get** in trouble for this?	Yes, **you are**.	No, **you aren't**.
he/she/it	**Is he going to make** a reservation for both of us?	Yes, **he is**.	No, **he isn't**.
you/we/they	**Are you going to speak** to her next week?	Yes, **we are**.	No, **we aren't**.

- We use *going to* to talk about future plans and intentions.
- In the negative, with *you*, *he*, etc, we can also say: *You're not going to*, *He's not going to*, etc.

  *She **isn't** going to book anything until next month.* OR *She's **not** going to book anything until next month.*
- In negative short answers, with *you*, *he*, etc, we can also say: *No, you're not.*, *No, he's not.*, etc.

  *Are they going to visit the Guggenheim? No, **they aren't**.* OR *No, **they're not**.*

12.1 *going to*

A Reorder the words to make sentences.

1 go / going to / backpacking around Europe / she's
She's going to go backpacking around Europe.

2 study / at a university / going to / I'm / art history
I'm going to study art history at a university.

3 going to / the tickets / when / are you / book / ?
When are you going to book the tickets?

4 a new job / start / I'm / looking for / going to
I'm going to start looking for a new job.

5 build / they're / themselves / going to / it
They're going to build it themselves.

B Complete the sentences with the correct form of *be going to* and the verbs in parentheses. Use contractions where possible.

1 *Are you going to have* (you / have) a big birthday party?

2 She's going to finish (she / finish) her essay this weekend.

3 When are they going to travel (they / travel) to Bucharest?

4 What time are you going to get up (you / get up) tomorrow?

5 It isn't / It's not going to be (it / not / be) cold tonight.

6 We aren't / We're not going to arrive (we / not / arrive) until late.

➤ Go back to page 112.

PRONUNCIATION

going to: weak and strong *to*

12.2 **A** **Listen and repeat the sentences. Notice that *to* sounds different in each sentence.**

1 I'm going **to** finish my essay this weekend.

2 I'm not going **to** invite Paul and David to the barbecue.

12.3 **B** **Read the sentences and circle /tə/ or /tuː/. Draw a ‿ to show any sounds that link together. Then listen and repeat.**

1 I'm going to see the new Wes Anderson movie on the weekend. /tə/ /tuː/

2 Matt's going to study in Washington D.C. /tə/ /tuː/

3 I'm not going to eat anything until we get there. /tə/ /tuː/

4 He's going to open a restaurant in Cambridge. /tə/ /tuː/

5 I'm not going to stay long at the party. /tə/ /tuː/

C **SPEAK** **Work in pairs. Practice saying the sentences in Exercise B. Listen and check your partner's pronunciation. Be careful to say *to* correctly and to link sounds with /w/.**

VOCABULARY

Future time expressions

12.4 **A** **Listen to Andrew talking to his manager, Yasmin. Check (✓) the things Andrew is going to do this weekend.**

+ Add to list		
1	☐	Ask Jane about invitations
2	☐	Meet Chris
3	☑	Work at the conference

B **Read the conversation between Andrew and Yasmin. Underline seven future time expressions.**

Yasmin: So, Andrew. Are we all ready for the product launch next month?

Andrew: I think so. I still need to do a few things, like ask Jane about the invitations.

Yasmin: Are you going to speak to her soon?

Andrew: Yes. She's out at the moment, but I'm going to call her this afternoon.

Yasmin: Great. And what about Luis and Chris? Have you arranged a meeting with them?

Andrew: I'm going to meet Chris tomorrow, but I don't know about Luis. I think he's traveling at the moment. We've emailed each other a lot, but maybe I'll actually meet him one day!

Yasmin: OK. And what about the reception tonight? Are you going to be there?

Andrew: Yes, definitely. I'm looking forward to it.

Yasmin: I wanted to ask you … can you work this weekend? We need help with the conference.

Andrew: Uh, yes, that's fine.

C **Use the prompts to write questions with *going to* and future time expressions.**

1 What / do / tonight?
What are you going to do tonight?

2 How / travel / to class / next week?
How are you going to travel to class next week?

3 What time / get up / tomorrow?
What time are you going to get up tomorrow?

4 do / anything special / on the weekend?
Are you going to do anything special on the weekend?

5 go / on vacation / this year?
Are you going to go on vacation this year?

D **SPEAK** **Work in pairs. Ask and answer the questions in Exercise C.**

SPEAKING

A **SPEAK** **Work in pairs. Student A – go to the Communication Hub on page 157. Student B – go to the Communication Hub on page 159.**

B **DISCUSS** **Write a list of five things you want to do soon. Share them with a partner. Ask and answer questions to find out more.**

A: When are you going to start a photography course?
B: Next month. I love taking pictures!
A: Where are you going to do it?
B: At the art college.

Talk about future plans

12.2 Everything will be shiny

Make predictions

G *will* for predictions **V** collocations with *get* **P** contractions: *'ll*

1

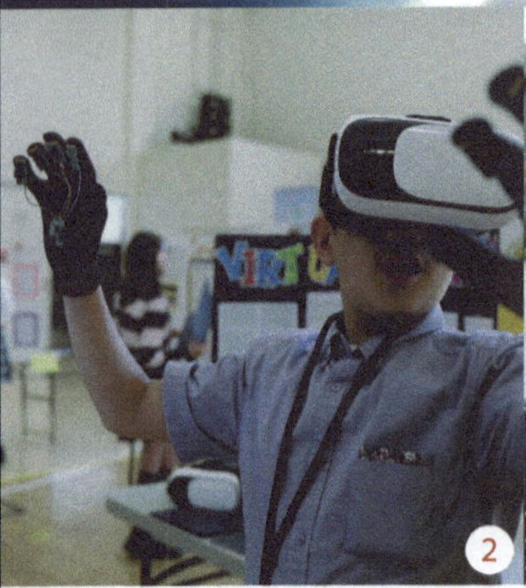

2

3

READING

A Work in pairs. Look at the pictures (1–3). Describe the technology in each and how it might improve the world.

B **READ FOR GIST** Read *Future life*. Check (✓) the topics that Michael made predictions about.

- [x] fashion
- [ ] virtual reality
- [x] houses
- [x] transportation
- [ ] video games
- [x] robotics
- [x] education
- [x] soccer

C **READ FOR DETAIL** Read again. Are the sentences true (T) or false (F)? Correct the false sentences.

1. Michael gave the essay to his mother on her birthday. T/(F)
2. Michael thought people would walk more in the future. T/(F)
3. Michael thought that people wouldn't need jobs in the future. (T)/F
4. Michael's prediction about machines in stores came true. (T)/F
5. Michael thought that there would be robot teachers in 2018. (T)/F

D **SPEAK** Work in pairs. Answer the questions.

1. Which of Michael's predictions came true and which didn't?
2. Do you think that making predictions is useful?

A: *Some of Michael's predictions came true. For example, every student here has a tablet.*

B: *Yes, but we don't all wear silver clothes!*

FUTURELIFE

About | Articles | Archives

What will the future be like?

No one knows, but we all like making predictions. In 1998, a young boy wrote an essay for a school competition with predictions about the year 2018. Michael Forster was ten years old when he wrote it. He didn't win the competition, Ex C Q1 but his mother saved the essay anyway and gave it to him on his 30th birthday. Some of Michael's predictions came true and others, well … read his essay below.

In 20 years' time, it will be 2018. I will be 30 years old. The world will be very different. Ex B *Everyone will wear silver clothes and will have silver hair. All houses will be metal and everything will be shiny.* Ex B *Cars won't drive on roads; they will fly in the air.* Ex C Q2 *People won't walk because they will fly around with jetpacks instead. People won't get sick, hungry or thirsty.* Ex C Q3 *And they won't need to get money or have a job.* Ex B *Robots will do everything. They will take care of the people and get them everything they need. In stores, there will be robot sales clerks. Children will get to school on their jetpacks. At school, there won't be desks. Every student will have a computer.* Ex C Q4 *The teachers will be robots. The teacher-robots won't get angry with the students.* Ex B *Tottenham will win the European Cup.*

Although Michael was wrong about a lot of his predictions – we don't all have silver hair, for example – some of his predictions were correct. Here at Futurelife, we love looking at past ideas about the future, so we asked Michael about his essay. 'I'm surprised that some of my Ex C Q5 ideas came true,' he said. 'We now pay machines for food at the grocery store. And many of us don't have desks; we work on computers all day.' What Michael's predictions show is that no one can predict the future, but a ten-year-old child's ideas aren't all crazy!

Glossary

essay (n) a piece of writing by a student about a subject
jetpack (n) a machine that someone wears on the back to make them fly
prediction (n) what you think will happen in the future

12.2 Everything will be shiny

LEAD-IN

Show students pictures of interesting modern technology (e.g. *smart watches*, *drones*, etc). Elicit the name of each and label the images. Next, put students into groups to discuss the following questions: *1 Do you own or use any of this technology? Why/Why not? 2 Is this technology popular in your country? Why/Why not? 3 Is this technology useful? Why/Why not?* Monitor, helping students with any challenging new vocabulary. Make a note of any useful emergent vocabulary and write it on the board. Give feedback as a class, encouraging class wide discussion wherever possible.

READING

A Focus students on the photos. In pairs, they describe what they can see and how the technology might improve the world. Share ideas as a class.

B Give students time to look through the list of topics. Then, allow students up to three minutes to skim *Future Life* and find out what topics are mentioned. Check answers as a class.

C Set a longer time limit of up to six minutes. Make sure students have seen the glossary at the end of the text, which helps them with some of the more difficult words in the article. Students read the text for detail and then decide if the sentences are true or false. They should identify the part of the text which gives the answer and also correct the false sentences. Allow time for students to compare answers in pairs. Check answers as a class.

1 F (Michael's mother gave him the essay on his birthday.); 2 F (He thought that people would fly around with jetpacks instead of walking.); 3 T; 4 T; 5 T.

D Students discuss the questions in pairs. Monitor and encourage students to extend their discussion with follow-up questions. Give feedback as a class, asking students to explain their answers. Encourage class wide discussion where appropriate.

TEACHING IDEA by David Seymour and Maria Popova

Grammar: Plans

Use these to review the grammar section on *going to*. Say this to your students:

Write a note of what you are going to do at these times.

after class, tonight, tomorrow, on Saturday, next week, next year

Mingle, and find someone who is going to do some of the same things as you, e.g. *Maria and I are both going ice skating on Saturday*.

On your own, think of an activity that people usually do on the weekend. Tell me what it is. (If someone repeats an activity that another student has already said, tell them they have to think of another one and come back to them when they've done so.) Mingle and find out how many students in the class are going to do the thing you thought of.

Do you make New Year's resolutions? Tell us a few typical resolutions people make.

In pairs, imagine it is New Year's Eve. Write down three resolutions for somebody famous, e.g. *I'm going to tell fewer lies to the newspapers. I'm going to get a better lawyer.*

Compare your resolutions with another pair. Can they guess the famous person?

METHODOLOGY HUB by Jim Scrivener

Studying your own teaching

Teaching English can be very exciting, but at 3:30 on a Monday afternoon, with a whole term ahead of you, it can seem a lot of other things too.

For the first two years or so in the profession, the demands of getting to grips with subject matter, technique, organization and school politics, not to mention students, can be very stressful and tiring. It may often feel as if you stand no chance as it becomes clear that you can't make every lesson perfect and that some students and some classes simply won't like what you do. And there are the days when you may have to struggle just to get through.

As time goes on, you will probably find that you have more experience to lean on, more tried-and-tested lessons in the bag to recycle endlessly. Then boredom and staleness are the dangers, once the challenge of becoming competent has faded. Twenty years of teaching experience can become no more than two years' experience repeated ten times over. Repeated venturing down well-traveled roads leads sooner or later to boredom, fossilization of routines, to increasing defensiveness and fear of change. The question becomes not 'How can I survive?' but 'How can I keep moving forward?' or 'How can I become the best teacher I can be?'. The most established and safer you are in your job, the harder it can become to take risks, to try something completely different.

The first important steps toward becoming a better teacher involved an increased awareness about what you do now and an openness to the possibility of change.

If you want to move forward, you have to be clear about what it is that you do now. Do you actually know what you are doing in class? Do you ever stop and examine your actions, your intentions, your motives, your attitudes? You keep planning for the next lesson, the next day, but to look back, to recall what happened, to reflect on it: this seems harder to do. What did happen in that class? What were you like as a teacher? Did you enable learning or prevent it? Why did you do the things you did? What were the other options, the ones that you didn't take?

12.2 Everything will be shiny

GRAMMAR

A Read through the first prediction with students. Point out that it was made in 1943. Elicit opinions on whether it came true. Encourage further discussion through the use of follow-up questions. Students then discuss the other predictions in pairs. Open the discussion up to the whole class to see if everyone agrees.

B Work as a class to complete the rules.

C Direct students to the **Grammar Hub** (see below). Read the examples and go through the rules with the class.

D Students work alone to complete the sentences. Allow students time to compare in pairs before checking answers as a class.

E Students discuss the predictions. Then put pairs into groups to share and discuss their ideas further. For whole-class feedback, find out which predictions are most and least likely. Use the **Grammar Worksheet** on W64 for extra practice.

VOCABULARY

A Display or write the sentences on the board and underline *get* in each one. Read through the *get* box with students. Students then review *Future Life* and find two more examples of *get*.

B Direct students to the **Vocabulary Hub**. Give them time to complete the exercise alone before checking answers in pairs.

C Invite a student to ask you the three questions. Provide model answers, adding extra information as appropriate using target language from the unit. Students then ask and answer the questions in pairs. Use the **Vocabulary Worksheet** on W65 for extra practice.

PRONUNCIATION

12.5 **A** Play the recording for students to listen and repeat.

12.6 **B** Play the recording for students to apply check marks to the sentences they hear.

SPEAKING

A Write *2050* on the board. Ask students what they think the world will be like in this year. In groups, students discuss the topics in the box.

B Students write predictions using *will* and *won't*. Monitor and assist as required.

C Put students into new groups. Students share their predictions and discuss which ones they agree with and why.

D The group selects three of the most likely predictions. They present these to the class, explaining why they think these predictions will come true.

GRAMMAR HUB

12.2 *will* for predictions

	Positive	Negative
I/you/he/she/it/we/they	Rock music **will be** popular forever.	Students **won't go** to school in the future.

	Question	Short answers	
I/you/he/she/it/we/they	**Will they visit** Mars in our lifetime?	Yes, **they will**.	No, **they won't**.

- We use *will* + base form to make predictions.
  Germany will win the next World Cup.
  In 10 years' time, most people will drive electric cars.
- In the positive, we often contract *will* to *'ll* in informal writing and speech.
- In the negative, we can also say *will not*. This is more formal.
  Schools ***will not*** *teach the same subjects in the future.*

Be careful!

- We often use *will* after *Do you think …* .
  Do you think the party will be fun?

12.2 *will* for predictions

A Reorder the words to make sentences.

In the year 2025 …

1 there / flying / cars / be / will
There will be flying cars.

2 won't / be / school / there / books / any
There won't be any school books.

3 cities / other / have / planets / on / we'll
We'll have cities on other planets.

4 robots / do / work / all / the / will / us / for
Robots will do all the work for us.

5 come / true / will / our / predictions / all
Our predictions will all come true.

6 with / people / will / around / jetpacks / fly
People will fly around with jetpacks.

B Use the prompts to write questions and short answers with *will*.

1 we / finish / on time?
Will we finish on time? (?) *Yes, we will.* (+)

2 she / read / your diary
Will she read your diary? (?) Yes, she will. (+)

3 you / work and study / at the same time
Will you work and study at the same time? (?) No, I won't. (-)

4 his predictions / come true
Will his predictions come true? (?) No, they won't. (-)

5 he / get / a better job
Will he get a better job? (?) Yes, he will. (+)

6 Chris / be / at the party
Will Chris be at the party? (?) No, he won't. (-)

➤ Go back to page 115.

GRAMMAR
will for predictions

A Read these predictions about the future. Which ones came true? What has happened?

Computers are tools for scientists. Nobody will want to buy one for their home.
– **Henrik Andersson,** head of the American Telegraph Association (1943)

Lots of people have computers at home now.

People want to go out to dinner, see their friends … maybe go to the movie theater. They won't stay at home watching TV.
– **Guy Chandler,** movie producer (1946)

People often stay at home to watch on-demand TV.

Bitcoin is the future. In five years' time, Bitcoin will be the only way to buy things online.
– **Yoichi Katayama,** author of *The Eco Futurist* (2009)

People buy things online with bank cards or other services.

Will we ever put a man on the moon? Maybe, but not for another 100 years.
– **Elliott Shaw,** writer for *The Boston Times* (1965)

The US put a man on the moon in 1969.

Sadly, we won't have flying cars any time soon. They're just too expensive.
– **Sarah Kalensky,** writer for *The Forecaster* (2017)

This is true so far.

B **WORK IT OUT** Choose the correct words to complete the rules.

***will* for predictions**

1 For positive sentences, we use subject + *will* + ***infinitive*** / ***base form***.

2 For negative sentences, we use subject + ***won't not*** / ***won't*** + base form.

3 For questions, we use ***will*** / ***do*** + subject + base form.

C Go to the **Grammar Hub** on **page 144**.

D **PRACTICE** Complete the sentences with *will* or *won't*.

In the future, …

1 there ___won't___ be cars. Everyone will have jetpacks.

2 students won't go to school. They ___will___ study at home.

3 human teachers ___won't___ exist. All teachers will be robots.

4 other languages won't exist. Everyone ___will___ speak English.

5 there ___won't___ be any books in schools. Every student will have a tablet.

E **SPEAK** Work in pairs. Do you agree or disagree with the predictions in Exercise D?

VOCABULARY
Collocations with *get*

A These sentences use phrases with *get*. Find two other sentences in *Future Life* that use phrases with *get*.

People won't ***get sick, hungry*** *or* ***thirsty****.*

And they won't need to ***get money*** *or have a job.*

They will take care of the people and get them everything they need.

Children will ***get to school*** *on their jetpacks.*

The teacher-robots won't get angry with the students.

get

The verb *get* has three different meanings: **become** (*get sick*), **buy or obtain** (*get money*) or **arrive** (*get to school*).

B Go to the **Vocabulary Hub** on **page 153**.

C **SPEAK** Work in pairs. Ask and answer the questions.

- What time you will get home today?
- What time do you usually get tired in the evening?
- What do you want to get the next time you go shopping?

I'll get home at 8 pm today. What about you?

PRONUNCIATION
Contractions: *'ll*

12.5 **A** Listen and repeat. Notice the difference between simple present and simple future with a contraction.

They like the movie. They'll like the movie.

12.6 **B** Listen and check (✓) the sentence you hear.

1 a ☑ We work together.
  b ☐ We'll work together.

2 a ☐ We leave early on the weekend.
  b ☑ We'll leave early on the weekend.

3 a ☐ We live in a big house.
  b ☑ We'll live in a big house.

4 a ☑ I travel a lot.
  b ☐ I'll travel a lot.

SPEAKING

A Work in groups. Think about the world in 2050. Make predictions about the things in the box.

houses technology the weather transportation

B **PLAN** In your groups, write predictions about what *will* and *won't* happen in 2050.

C **DISCUSS** Work with students from other groups. Discuss their predictions. Do you agree with them? Why/Why not?

D **PRESENT** In your new group, choose three predictions you think will come true. Present your ideas to the class and explain why you think they will happen.

Make predictions

12.3 Communication

Talk about social media habits

V internet communication P diphthongs G *might* S predicting

VOCABULARY

Internet communication

A SPEAK Work in pairs. Look at the infographic. How many of the social networks do you use? Do you use any others?

B DISCUSS Work in pairs and discuss the questions. Write notes.

Which network …

1 has the largest number of users? Facebook
2 is most popular with younger people? Snapchat
3 is useful for professional people? LinkedIn
4 is useful to read the news? Twitter
5 is most popular in Asia? WeChat

C Quickly read the infographic and check your answers.

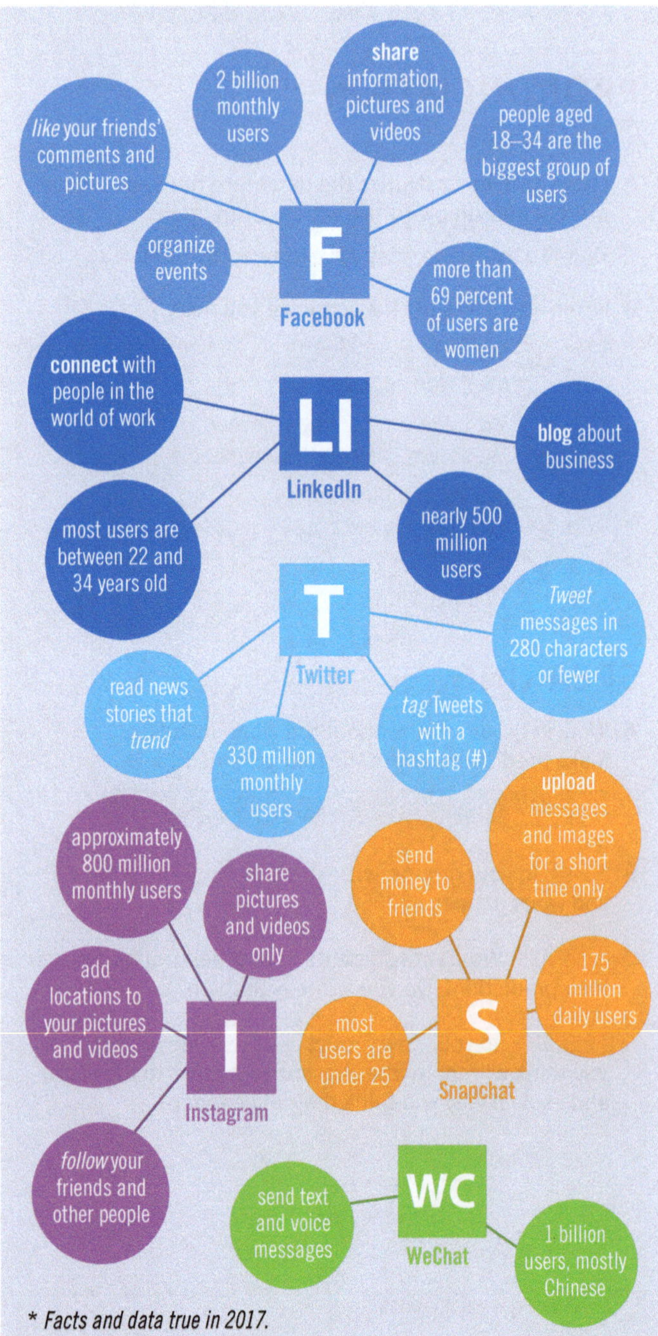

D Match the words in the box to the icons (1–10).

blog chat connect follow like share tag trend tweet upload

1 share
2 follow
3 tag
4 trend
5 like
6 tweet
7 upload
8 blog
9 chat
10 connect

E Complete the sentences with words from Exercise D.

1 When I upload a picture, I only share it with my friends.
2 I follow comedians on *Twitter*. They tweet really funny comments and videos.
3 I blog about music once a week.
4 On *Facebook*, I usually just 'like' a few posts from family and friends.
5 I chat with my friends on the phone not on social media.
6 I hate it when my friends tag me in pictures.

F SPEAK Work in pairs. Which sentences in Exercise E are true for you?

PRONUNCIATION

Diphthongs

12.7 **A Listen and repeat the words in the table. Notice how we say the underlined letters.**

/uw/	/eɪ/	/ɔɪ/	/oʊ/
new true	place Facebook	boy point	nose follow
/ju/	**/aɪ/**	**/aʊ/**	
cute users	my like	mouth mouse	

Diphthongs are two vowel sounds that are said together. There are seven diphthongs in American English – **eɪ / aɪ / oʊ / ɔɪ / aʊ / ju** / and **/ uw /**. Practicing these sounds will improve your pronunciation.

12.8 **B Work in pairs. Add the words and phrases in the box to the table in Exercise A. Then listen and repeat.**

true Facebook follow like mouse point users

12.3 Communication

LEAD-IN

Tell the class about your own social media habits. Explain which apps you use, what you use them for, etc. Write any new or useful language on the board. Encourage students to ask you questions. Next, put students into groups to discuss their own social media habits. Monitor, helping them with any challenging or new vocabulary. Make a note of any useful emergent language and use it as the basis for class-wide discussion when all groups have finished talking.

VOCABULARY

A In pairs, students discuss the types of social media on the infographic, saying which they use. Open up the discussion to the whole class and find out the most popular. Give your own opinions, too.

B Students discuss the questions in pairs. As they do so, ask them to write notes on what they think the answers might be. Don't confirm any answers at this point.

C Students read the infographic and check their ideas. Ask the class if they found any of the information surprising.

D Draw one of the icons on the board and write the word *icon*. Elicit a definition of *icon* (a small picture on a computer screen which opens a particular program). Students label each of the icons. Check answers as a class.

E Students complete the sentences. Check answers as a class.

F Allow students time to look through the sentences again, ticking those which are true for them. Students then discuss the sentences in pairs or small groups, explaining why they are or aren't true. Use the **Vocabulary Worksheet** on W66 for extra practice.

PRONUNCIATION

12.7 **A** Play the recording. Students listen and repeat the words. Read through the information about diphthongs and how two vowel sounds are brought together to make one new sound. Say the diphthongs individually and practice with students, asking them to look at how your mouth moves to produce the different sounds. Then play the recording again for students to listen and repeat the diphthongs within words.

12.8 **B** In pairs, students add the words from the box to the table. Encourage students to say the words aloud, focusing on the vowel sound. Point out that students can also sometimes use the spelling as a clue to the vowel sound. Play the recording for students to check and repeat.

TEACHING IDEA by David Seymour and Maria Popova

Vocabulary: The internet

Use this activity to review the vocabulary section. Say this to your students:

In small groups, imagine you are going to give a course on how to use the internet to a class of complete beginners. Before you start, you want to explain the following vocabulary. Prepare your notes.

ISP (Internet Service Provider), password, to log on, virus, hacker, links, spam, to browse, to download, online, website, surf, bandwidth, worldwide web, home page, HTTP (Hypertext Transfer Protocol)

Compare your notes with another group. Who has the clearest explanations? In small groups, write a list of the top ten uses of the internet. Compare your lists.

TEACHING IDEA by David Seymour and Maria Popova

Grammar: Our future

Use this activity to review the grammar section. Say this to your students:

Create a list of ten major changes that you think will take place during the next hundred years. Include these things.

- *technology, war and peace, culture, economics, the United States, the environment*

In pairs, tell each other about your hopes and plans for the future, including marriage, ambitions, home, travel and work. Use these expressions. (Write them on the board.)

I think I'll … Maybe I'll … I hope I'll … … I'll never … I expect I'll … I might …

In small groups, write five questions with *Do you think … + will that you might ask a friend*, e.g. *Do you think you'll ever settle down somewhere?* Here are some possible topics to ask about.

- job, housing, children, money, English, fame

METHODOLOGY HUB by Jim Scrivener

Working with phonemes

Here are some general ideas for working with phonemes:

- Integrate phonemic work into all your teaching of grammar and lexis. Always work on helping the students to achieve good pronunciation, and encourage them to make a record of the phonemic transcription as well as the spelling of new items.
- Observation of mechanics: let students watch how you and they make particular sounds.
- Ear-training: get students to listen to and distinguish words which have sounds that seem to them very similar (e.g. *hat* vs. *hut; thin* vs. *tin*; examples of this kind are known as **minimal pairs**).
- Tongue twisters, to work on particular sounds or to contrast sounds (e.g. *Three thin trees and three tall trees*).
- Transliteration: get students to write out a word or sentence in phonemic script. Jokes seem to work well.
- Train learners in using a dictionary to find pronunciation as well as spelling.
- Keep a phonemic chart on the wall of your classroom. Focus briefly on one phoneme each lesson.
- Tap out words on the chart and ask students to say the words.
- Use the chart for pointing out correct sounds when students pronounce something wrong.

12.3 Communication

LISTENING

A Focus students on the photos. In pairs, they discuss what might be each person's favorite social media network. Share ideas as a class. Then read through the *Predicting* box with students, highlighting that this is what the students have just done.

12.9 **B** Play the recording. Students listen and check their predictions.

12.9 **C** Before listening again, allow students time to read through the questions and predict the answers.

D Students discuss the questions in pairs. Encourage students to ask follow-up questions to find out more. For whole-class feedback, ask groups to summarize the main points of their discussion and see if there is cross-class consensus.

GRAMMAR

A Give students time to complete the rules before checking as a class.

B Direct students to the **Grammar Hub** (see below). Read the examples and go through the rules with the class.

C In pairs, students discuss their own social media habits. Monitor and assist as necessary. Use the **Grammar Worksheet** on W67 for extra practice.

SPEAKING HUB

A Direct students to the **Communication Hub** (TB158) for further practice.

B In groups, students summarize their research. Ask each group to report back to the whole class.

AUDIO SCRIPT

12.9

Listening, Exercise B

S = Shani L = Luke W = Wai J = Jean M = Maria

S: I use Facebook for news about friends and family and sometimes Twitter, to see what's trending, but I don't post much. I studied business at a university (Ex B Q1) and now I work for a large bank so my number one social network is LinkedIn. (Ex B) I like to see what's happening in the business world. I blog about business and one day I'd love to teach it.

L: I connect with friends on Instagram – or face to face at our local café. I follow loads of people on Twitter. I love it. A friend of mine is an actor and he tweets about the acting world and the theater He's so funny! And I follow the latest news stories. I teach eight-year-old children (Ex C Q2) and they know all the news. I might sign up to Snapchat so I can keep up-to-date!

W: I don't mind Facebook, but I much prefer Instagram. (Ex B) I like taking pictures and Instagram is a great place to share them. (Ex C Q3) I also use WeChat a lot. It's really popular back home in China, so I use it to keep in touch with my friends and family. A lot of the people at work also use LinkedIn, so I might set up an account too. I don't want to miss out!

J: I only use Facebook. (Ex B) Sometimes I use it to catch up with my five friends, but usually it's to see my family. I have four children and six grandchildren. (Ex C Q4) They put photos on Facebook and I get to see what they're doing. Sometimes I 'like' a photo, but I can't do much more than that, I'm afraid. I might try some other social media networks, but at the moment I don't really know how to use them.

M: I check Facebook every two hours! It's a great way to keep in touch with old school friends you haven't seen for ten years. However, for photos, I like Snapchat best (Ex B) because pictures only stay online for ten seconds (Ex C Q5) after I send them.

GRAMMAR HUB

12.3 *might*

	Positive	Negative
I/you/he/she/it/we/they	**I might stop** using Facebook.	**She might not read** my tweets.

- We use *might* to talk about something that is not definite but possible.
- We use *might* + base form.

12.3 *might*

A Complete the sentences with *might* or *might not*.

1 I might not be able to come on Saturday, because I have to help my friend move.

2 Do you want me to give Tom a message? I might see him at the conference.

3 I'll try, but I might not be able to get everything finished in time.

4 I might be home late tonight because I have lots of work to finish.

5 You should call Sarah. She might think you've forgotten her!

B Complete the sentences with the correct form of *might* and a verb in the box.

go take have ~~see~~ send wait

1 OK, great. I *might see* you later then.

2 You're right. I might send her an email to check the flight time.

3 It's hot in here. I might wait outside.

4 I might take the bus, because it's cheaper than a taxi.

5 She might not have time to finish everything.

6 I might not go tonight. I'm not feeling very well.

➤ Go back to page 117.

LISTENING

A PREPARE You are going to listen to five people talking about social media. Look at the pictures and guess what their favorite social media network is.

Predicting

Before you listen, use information such as pictures, questions, what you already know to help you predict the topic or guess information.

B LISTEN FOR GIST Listen to the people. How many predictions in Exercise A did you get right?
12.9

C LISTEN FOR DETAIL Listen again. Choose a, b or c to complete the sentences.
12.9

1 Shani …
- a studied business.
- b runs a business.
- c teaches business.

2 Luke works in a …
- a café.
- b theater.
- c school.

3 Wai likes sharing his pictures on …
- a Facebook.
- b Instagram.
- c LinkedIn.

4 Jean has … grandchildren.
- a four
- b five
- c six

5 Maria likes that pictures only stay on Snapchat for …
- a ten years.
- b two hours.
- c ten seconds.

D SPEAK Work in pairs and discuss the questions.

1 Which age group do you think spends the most time on social media? Why?

2 How long do you think they spend on social media each week?

GRAMMAR

might

A WORK IT OUT Look at these sentences about social media. Then choose the correct words to complete the rules.

A: I might sign up to Snapchat so I can keep up to date!
B: A lot of the people at work also use LinkedIn, so I might set up an account, too.
A: I might try some other social media networks, but at the moment, I don't really know how to use them.

might

1 We use *might* for ***definite plans / possible plans*** or wishes.
2 We use *might* ***before / after*** the base form.

B Go to the **Grammar Hub** on **page 144**.

C SPEAK Work in pairs. Think about your own use of social media. Tell your partner what you *are going to / might* use more (or less) in the future.

A: I'm so busy. I spend a lot of time on Facebook. I might try to use it less.
B: I'm going to start using Twitter.

SPEAKING HUB

A Go to the **Communication Hub** on **page 158**.

B Work in groups. Compare the results of your survey to the information in the infographic.

Like the infographic, we found that the most popular social network was Facebook. Some people in the class use Facebook and Twitter for their work, not LinkedIn.

Talk about social media habits

12.4 Party time

F– show interest in something   P– stress and intonation

COMPREHENSION

A ▶ **SPEAK** Work in pairs. What is happening in each picture? Put the pictures in the order (1–6) you think they happen. Then watch the video and check your answers.

a 4

b 5

c 3

d 2

e 6

f 1

B **SPEAK** Work in pairs. Retell the story from the pictures.

FUNCTIONAL LANGUAGE

Showing interest in something

▶ Complete the conversations with the words in the box. Then watch the video again and check.

did great love matter poor problem shame terrible thanks worry

Replying to bad news

Zac: Did you get tickets to the festival?

Sam: No, I didn't. All the tickets were sold out.

Zac: That's a 1 ___shame___. Sorry about that.

Sam: Ah, it doesn't 2 ___matter___.

Milly: I fell off my bike.

Gaby: Oh no! 3 ___Poor___ you. Are you OK?

Milly: I'm fine. I fall off my bike all the time.

Gaby: Really? That's 4 ___terrible___!

Replying to good news

Dad: Yeah, we're here for the weekend.

Sam: That's 5 ___great___!

Apologizing

Milly: Hey! I'm really sorry I'm late.

Neena: No 6 ___problem___. You missed Sam's face. He was so surprised!

Milly: I'm so sorry I'm late.

Gaby: It's all right. Don't 7 ___worry___.

Giving compliments

Milly: That's a cool dress.

Gaby: Thanks, I 8 ___love___ it.

Milly: Mmmm … and this cake is so good!

Gaby: 9 ___Thanks___. I made it!

Milly: 10 ___Did___ you? That's awesome!

MILLY

SAM

NEENA

ZAC

GABY

PRONUNCIATION

Stress and intonation

12.10 **A** **Listen and repeat the replies. Copy the stress and intonation.**

1 That's amazing!
2 I love it!
3 That's terrible.
4 Poor you.
5 That's a shame.
6 It doesn't matter.
7 No problem.
8 Don't worry.

B **SPEAK** **Work in pairs. Student A – tell your partner some good or bad news. Student B – reply to your partner with one of the phrases in Exercise A. Remember to use the correct stress and intonation. Swap.**

A: I got a new job.
B: That's amazing!

SPEAKING

A **PREPARE** **Work in pairs. Write two conversations. Use the ideas below or your own ideas. Use the Functional language to help you.**

Conversation 1

- You arrive late at the party because you got lost.
- You get lost all the time.
- You like your partner's jacket.
- You think the food is great.

Conversation 2

- You arrive late at the party because you left your bag on the bus.
- You lose things all the time.
- You like your partner's shoes.
- You think the music is great.

B **PRESENT** **Practice your conversations. Then choose one and perform it for the rest of the class.**

A: I'm really sorry I'm late.
B: It's all right – don't worry.
A: I got lost.
B: Oh no, poor you! Are you OK?

Show interest in something

➤ Turn to page 171 to learn how to write a formal email.

12.4 Party time

LEAD-IN

Tell students about a surprise party you have been to or organized. Explain who it was for, whether you managed to keep it a surprise, how the person reacted to the surprise, etc. Next, put students into groups to share their own experiences. Monitor and help students with any new language.

COMPREHENSION

A Students work in pairs to discuss the pictures. They should describe what is happening in each picture and decide on the order they go in. Give feedback as a class, nominating different pairs to give their ideas about each picture. Don't confirm anything at this stage. Play the video for students to check.

B In pairs, students retell the story using the pictures. For whole-class feedback, nominate pairs at random to tell the story of each picture. Try to elicit as much detail as students can remember about each scene.

FUNCTIONAL LANGUAGE

Highlight the four different sections of the conversation, and check understanding of *compliments* (something nice that you say to praise someone). Students then complete the conversation. Allow students time to compare answers in pairs before watching the video again to check.

PRONUNCIATION

12.10 **A** Play the recording. Students listen and repeat the replies. After doing this once, focus on each reply and elicit where the stress is. Play the recording again. Students listen and copy the stress and intonation. Encourage students to be as expressive as possible with their pronunciation.

B Students tell their partner some good or bad news. Their partner responds with one of the phrases from Exercise A, focusing on correct stress and intonation. They then swap roles and do the task again. Monitor, assist and praise as appropriate.

SPEAKING

A In pairs, students write two conversations. Point out that they don't have to use the ideas given, if they have better ones. Remind students to use the phrases from the *Functional Language* section. Monitor and assist as required.

B Students practice their conversations. They could record themselves on their phones, in order to play the conversations back and notice things to improve. Remind them to focus on using correct stress and intonation. Pairs then choose one of the conversations to perform for the whole class.

VIDEO SCRIPT

N = Neena Z = Zac S = Sam D = Sam's Dad
Mi = Milly G = Gaby Mu = Sam's Mum

N: Quickly! They're coming soon!
Z: Did you get tickets to the festival?
S: No, I didn't. All the tickets were sold out.
Z: Ahhh … That's a shame. Sorry about that.
S: Ah, it doesn't matter.
Z: Oh … no! I left my bag at the café. Sorry, I need to go back.
S: Yeah. It's OK. WOW! How did you …?
All: Surprise!
Z: The key.
S: Wow. I don't know what to say … Mum? Dad!
D: Hi Sam.
S: Are you staying in London?
D: Yeah, we're here for the weekend.
S: That's great!
Z: She won't come.
N: Milly? I'm sure she'll be here soon. Don't worry.
Mi: Hey. I'm really sorry I'm late!
N: No problem. You missed Sam's face. He was so surprised.
Mi: Hey, Zac. Are you OK?
Z: OK. Yeah. I'm OK.
Mi: OK!
G: Oh hi, you must be Milly? I'm Gaby, would you like some cake?
Mi: Yeah, I'd love some. I'm so sorry I'm late.
G: It's alright. Don't worry.
Mi: I fell off my bike.
G: Oh no! Poor you. Are you OK?
Mi: I'm fine. I fall off my bike all the time.
G: Really? That's terrible!
Mi: I know! Hey! That's a cool dress.
G: Thanks, I love it.
Mi: Mmm … and this cake is so good!
G: Thanks. I made it.
Mi: Did you? That's awesome!
Mu: We're going. Are you free tomorrow afternoon?
S: Yes. Text me?
Mi: Hey. I'm leaving now. I'm going to France tomorrow. Really nice to meet you, Gaby.
G: Lovely to meet you.
Mi: Bye Zac …
Z: Oh … Bye, Milly … Hey, Milly?
Mi: … Yeah?
Z: Ask her out. Ask her out. Ask her out. NOW ZAC! NOW! Thanks … Thanks for coming.
Mi: No problem. It was really cool. See you again … Sometime … Bye …
Z: Yeah … Bye …
S: That was awful.
N: There'll be another time.
Z: I am going to marry her.
S: Cheesecake?

12 Writing

Write a formal email

structuring emails

A Read the invitation. What is it for?

1 an anniversary 2 a birthday 3 a wedding

hosted by Ray and Marcia
May 15, 12:00 pm–6:00 pm
Old Creek Golf Club
20 Ocean Drive, Tampa, Florida, US

The ceremony will take place at 12 noon. After the ceremony, there will be a lunch at the Clubhouse, followed by a reception. Formal dress.
For more details, please contact our wedding planner, Kelly Olson: kelly@floridaweddings.nett

B Work in pairs. Read again and answer the questions.

1 Whose wedding is it?
2 When is the wedding?
3 Where is the wedding?
4 Who do you contact for more details?

C Read Justin's email to the wedding planner. Number the steps 1–6.

Dear Ms. Olson,
I am writing to ask you for some information.
My wife and I are going to attend Ray and Marcia's wedding in Tampa on May 15. We would like to book a double room in a hotel nearby. Could you please recommend somewhere?
Also, we are going to arrive at Tampa airport late at night. Is there public transportation at that time? Or should I take a taxi?
I look forward to hearing from you.
Kind regards,
Justin Blake

3 Ask for a recommendation
1 Start a formal email with the title and the last name of the person you're writing to
5 Friendly phrase before the end of the email
2 Reason for writing
4 Ask about transportatioin
6 End a formal email with the full name of the writer

D Complete the email with the words in the box.

cost could dear information look regards writing

[1] Dear Mr. Young,
I am [2] writing to ask for some [3] information about a reception room in your hotel.
I am going to be 30 years old this year, and I want to have a big party to celebrate. I am going to invite around 150 people.
[4] Could you please tell me how much the room costs?
Also, could you tell me how much food would [5] cost for the guests?
I [6] look forward to hearing from you.
Kind [7] regards,
Gemma Lai

Structuring emails

We usually write formal emails to people we don't know, often to ask for information.
We start formal emails with *Dear* + *Mr./Mrs./Ms.* + last name.
We often give a reason for writing and then ask some questions.
Before the end of the email, we use a friendly phrase (*I look forward to seeing / hearing from you.*)
You can end formal emails with any of these phrases: *Sincerely yours, Regards, Kind regards.* Then your full name.
We don't usually use contractions in formal emails.
I am writing to ask for information **NOT** *I'm writing to ask for information.*

WRITING

A PREPARE Read the invitation. What is it for? A ten-year anniversary.

Hosted by Sophie and Nadim August 6, 6:00 pm–10:00 pm
10 Jack McClure Place, Northbridge, New South Wales, Australia

Come and celebrate ten wonderful years together!
We hope you can all come!
P.S. The Tired Traveler is a great small hotel nearby. Write to Mr. and Mrs. Foster for reservations.

B Write an email to *The Tired Traveler* hotel to make a reservation. Write about the following:

- What kind of room would you like?
- How long do you want the room for?
- When and how are you going to arrive?
- What else do you want to know?

C Work in pairs. Read each other's emails. Did your partner use formal language?

WRITING 171

Answers
1 Ray and Marci's; 2 May 15, 12:00 –6:00; 3 Old Creek Golf Club, 20 Ocean Drive, Tampa, Florida, US; 4 kelly@floridaweddings.nett

Refer students to this email as a model for the writing task.

Remind students that it is always important to decide who you are writing to, because this changes the style you use.

Allow students to read each other's work and comment on the effect it has on them.

WRITING

In this writing lesson, students will learn how to write a formal email, paying attention to how to write in a formal style.

A Students read the invitation and decide what it is for. Check answer as a class.

B Students read the invitation again in more detail and answer the questions. Allow students time to discuss answers in pairs before checking as a class.

C Go through the task and check understanding of a *wedding planner* (a person whose job it is to organize other people's weddings). Students then read Justin's email and put the steps in order. Check answers as a class.

D Read through the *Structuring emails* box with students. Point out that it can be rude to write in an informal style to someone you don't know. At the same time, it can seem rude to write in a formal style to someone you know very well. Ask students to review Justin's email and identify examples of formal language. Students then complete the email.

WRITING TASK

A Students read the invitation and think about its purpose. Check answer as a class.

B Go through the task with students. First, they write notes to answer the questions. Then, using these notes and the example emails in the lesson, along with the information about structuring emails, students write an email to *The Tired Traveler* hotel. Monitor and assist as required.

C In pairs, students read each other's emails. Ask them to say if they think the email feels polite and formal, or too friendly. If you have time, students could swap emails with a new partner and write the reply from *The Tired Traveler*, in a formal style.

Unit 12 Review

GRAMMAR

A Complete the conversation with the correct form of *going to* and the verbs in parentheses.

Erin: What [1] *are you going to do* (*you/do*) when you graduate?

Niall: I [2] 'm going to work (*work*) for my uncle's company in Australia for the summer, then in September I [3] 'm going to start (*start*) a course at the university there.

Erin: Wow! What [4] are you going to study (*you/study*)?

Niall: Medicine. I [5] 'm going to be (*be*) a doctor one day! How about you? [6] Are you going to look (*you/look*) for a job?

Erin: No, I [7] 'm going to travel (*travel*) around Asia with some friends for a few months.

Niall: Wow! That sounds amazing. You [8] 're going to have (*have*) an amazing time.

Erin: Yes, and maybe I can visit you in Australia!

B Use the prompts to write predictions about the world in ten years' time. Then compare your ideas with a partner. Do you agree?

1 The weather / hotter
The weather will be hotter.

2 Food / more expensive

3 Clothes / cheaper

4 Robots / do a lot of jobs that humans do now

5 Children / use pens and pencils at school

6 People / drive electric cars

C SPEAK Work in pairs. Ask and answer questions about the future. Think about:

- your plans for the summer
- predictions for your life ten years from now

D Complete the sentences with *going to*, *might* or *will*.

1 I met Gianni on *Facebook*. We aren't sure yet, but we *might* meet face-to-face soon.

2 I start as my own boss next week, so *LinkedIn* will certainly be the social media network that I use the most.

3 I 'm going to send her a message now.

4 There's a new social media network. It might be popular in the future, but it will be difficult to catch up with *Facebook* and *Twitter*.

5 I think people will probably use social media more and more in the future.

VOCABULARY

A Complete the future time expressions with *a*, *e*, *i*, *o* or *u*.

1 I rarely exercise o n th e w e e k e nd.

2 I'm planning to buy a house n e xt y e a r.

3 I'd like to climb Mount Everest o n e d a y.

4 I have to go home s o o n.

5 I'm going on vacation th i s s u mm e r.

B SPEAK Check (✓) the sentences in Exercise A that are true for you. Discuss your answers with a partner.

C Use the words in the box to complete the phrases with *get*.

home	hungry	lost	money
organized	sick	~~to college~~	wet

1 I usually get *to college* at nine in the morning.

2 It's raining. Let's go inside – I don't want to get wet.

3 I'm not very busy today. I think I'll get home early tonight.

4 Let's take a map so we don't get lost.

5 The five-list plan really helps me to get organized

6 I always get hungry at about 3 pm.

7 Don't give her too many – she'll get sick.

8 I have to work. I don't get any money from my parents.

D Choose the correct words to complete the text.

I'm a designer and I have my own website. I [1]***connect / blog*** about art and design.

I sometimes use *Facebook* when I want to [2]***upload / chat*** pictures and [3]***follow / share*** them with my friends and family. It makes me happy when my friends [4]***blog / like*** my pictures. I have a *Twitter* account. I [5]***follow / upload*** my friends. They [6]***twitter / tweet*** a lot!

E Work in groups. Discuss the questions.

1 Who do you follow on social media? Why?

2 Do you think social media is the best way to connect with friends and family? Why/Why not?

3 What kind of things do you upload to social media?

4 Do you ever get angry when friends tag you in photos online?

5 What topic could you blog about?

FUNCTIONAL LANGUAGE

Match sentences (1–5) with replies (a–e).

1 I'm sorry I'm late.
2 I lost my phone yesterday.
3 I'm sorry, but I don't have any money.
4 My brother's going to be on TV tonight.
5 I passed all my exams.

a Don't worry. I can pay for this.
b Wow! That's great.
c That's OK.
d Really? That's interesting. Is he an actor?
e Oh, no. That's awful.

Vocabulary and Communication Hub

Contents

Vocabulary Hub

1.1 Countries and nationalities

A Match countries (1–12) with the words in the box.

Brazil Chile China Egypt France India Italy Japan Portugal Spain Thailand Turkey

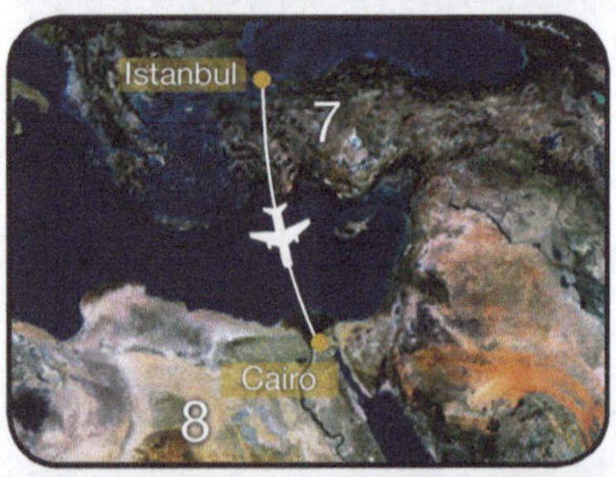

1 Portugal
2 Spain
3 France
4 Italy
5 China
6 Japan
7 Turkey
8 Egypt
9 India
10 Thailand
11 Brazil
12 Chile

B Complete the table with the words in the box.

British Greek Russia Poland ~~South Korean~~ Swedish Switzerland Vietnamese

Country	Nationality
	-ian/-an
Colombia	Colombian
South Korea	1 South Korean
2 Russia	Russian
	-ish
Finland	Finnish
3 Poland	Polish
Sweden	4 Swedish
	-ese
Sudan	Sudanese
Vietnam	5 Vietnamese
	Other
The Netherlands	Dutch
Greece	6 Greek
7 Switzerland	Swiss
the UK	8 British

➤ Go back to page 2

2.2 Describing appearance

A Complete the table with the words in the box.

bald a beard glasses large a mustache short slim tall

Face / head:	bald; a beard; glasses; a mustache
Height:	short; tall
Build:	large; slim

B Match the descriptions (1–5) with the pictures (a–e).

1 She's tall and has curly hair. c
2 She has long, straight hair and glasses. d
3 He has red hair and a mustache. e
4 He has light hair and blue eyes. a
5 He's short and bald. b

➤ Go back to page 14

3.1 Everyday activities

Match photos (1–9) with the activities.

5 listen to music 1 watch TV 9 take a shower 8 go to the movie theater 4 go for a run 6 have coffee with friends 7 go to bed 2 read a book 3 have lunch

➤ Go back to page 22

4.1 Work and jobs

Match the photos (1–8) with the words in the box.

3 dentist 8 designer 1 hairdresser 6 journalist 7 mechanic 2 nurse 4 police officer 5 sales clerk

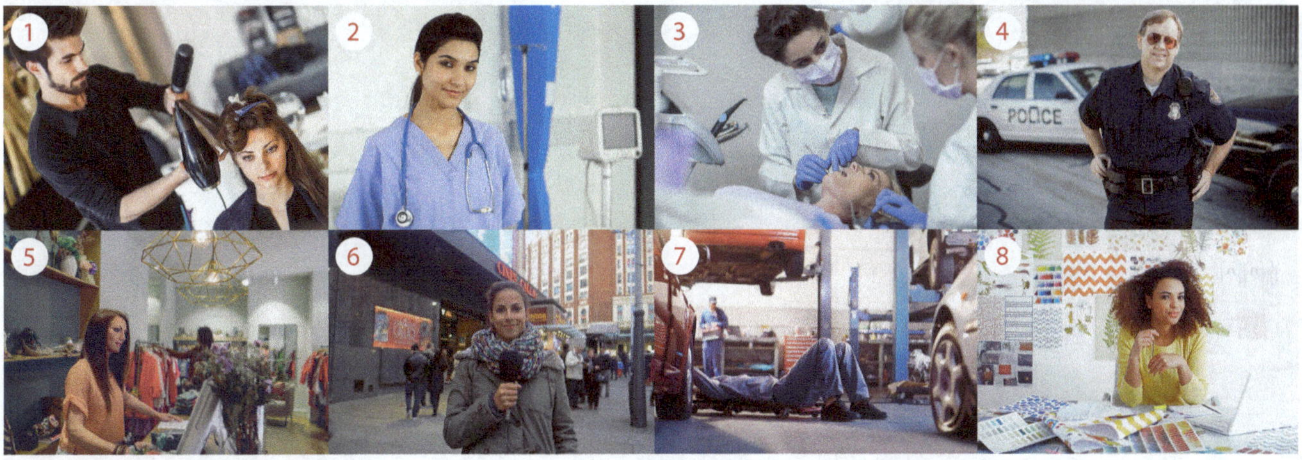

➤ Go back to page 32

Vocabulary Hub

5.1 Rooms and furniture; prepositions of place

A Label the rooms (a–e) with the words in the box.

bathroom bedroom dining room kitchen living room

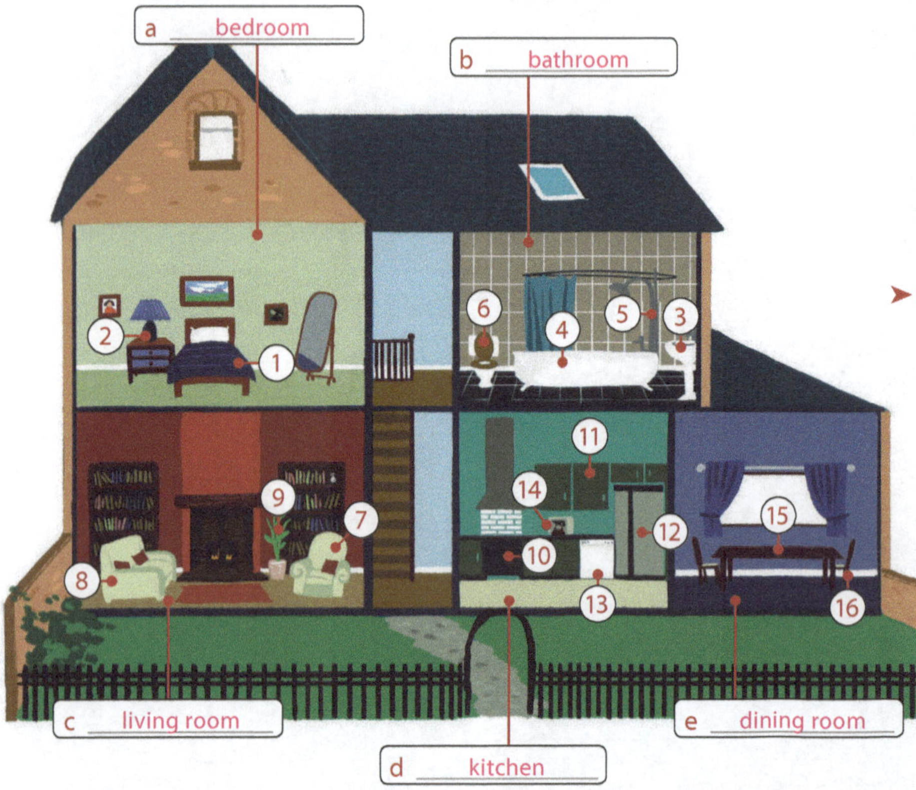

B Look at the picture again. Number the words 1–16.

7 armchair	2 lamp
4 bathtub	9 plant
1 bed	5 shower
16 chair	3 sink
14 coffee machine	8 couch
10 oven	15 table
11 cupboard	6 toilet
12 fridge	13 dishwasher

➤ Go back to page 42.

5.2 Places in a town or city

Match photos (1–12) with the places.

1 café 3 movie theater 11 gym 4 hospital 5 library 10 market 6 museum 7 park 9 restaurant 2 grocery store 12 theater 8 subway station

➤ Go back to page 44.

7.1 Transportation

Match pictures (1–12) with the words in the box.

2 bicycle   6 boat   11 bus   1 car   9 ferry   10 motorcycle
3 plane   12 cruise ship   5 taxi   8 train   7 trolley   4 subway

1

2

3

4

5

6

7

8

9

10

11

12

➤ Go back to page 62.

7.2 Travel phrases

Complete the email using the past tense of the verbs in the box.

arrive   leave   miss   return   take

To: Samantha

Dear Samantha,

We're back! We visited my parents last week. Our journey home was terrible. It took a long time. We [1] left my parents' house on Saturday evening. We [2] took a bus and then a train to Caracas. We [3] arrived in the city at lunchtime on Sunday. Unfortunately, the traffic on the way to the airport was really bad, and we [4] missed our flight! So we [5] returned to the city and stayed in a hotel. In the end, we got home on Wednesday, four days after leaving my parents' house!

Talk to you later.

Rose

➤ Go back to page 65.

Vocabulary Hub

8.1 Food and drink

A Label the images (1–15) with the words in the box.

an apple butter cake cheese chicken chips eggs lettuce mushrooms pasta potatoes shrimp rice tea tomatoes

1 
butter

2 
lettuce

3 
tea

4 
potatoes

5 
mushrooms

6 
shrimp

7 
chips

8 
eggs

9 
chicken

10 
an apple

11 
rice

12 
cheese

13 
tomatoes

14 
pasta

15 
cake

B Complete the table with words from Exercise A.

Dairy	butter
	cheese
	eggs
Meat and fish	shrimp
	chicken
Fruits and vegetables	lettuce
	potatoes
	mushrooms
	an apple
	tomatoes
Drinks	tea
Other	chips
	rice
	pasta
	cake

➤ Go back to page 72.

8.2 Containers

Complete the labels (1–8) with words from the box.

a bag a bottle a box a carton a jar a package a container a can

1 a bottle of water

5 a container of yogurt

2 a box of cereal

6 a bag of rice

3 a carton of milk

7 a can of beans

4 a package of cookies

8 a jar of jam

➤ Go back to page 75.

9.1 Clothes

A Match pictures (1–18) with the words in the box.

9 boots 4 coat 3 dress 12 gloves 18 hat
16 headscarf 10 sweater 5 scarf 11 shirt
8 shoes 17 shorts 7 skirt 14 socks 15 sunglasses
6 T-shirt 2 tie 13 sneakers 1 pants

B Complete the descriptions with words from Exercise A.

I like Nobel Peace Prize winner Malala Yousafzai's style. It's traditional and beautiful. She usually wears a 1 headscarf, a long 2 dress, a pair of 3 pants and some simple shoes.

I prefer simple styles, like Mark Zuckerberg's. He usually wears a 4 T-shirt, a pair of blue jeans and a pair of sporty 5 sneakers.

Emma Watson is so stylish. She looks great when she wears a black 6 dress and a pair of black 7 shoes.

➤ Go back to page 82.

9.3 Stores and services

Match the words in the box with pictures (1–12).

2 bakery 3 bank 4 bookstore 5 butcher's 7 department store 12 dentist's
8 hairdresser's 9 library 1 market 10 newsstand 6 pharmacy 11 grocery store

➤ Go back to page 87.

10.2 Seasons and weather

A Label the images with the words in the box.

fall spring summer winter

B Match phrases (1–8) with pictures (a–h). Some phrases can go with more than one picture.

1 It's cloudy. h
2 It's cold. b, f
3 It's foggy. e
4 It's hot. a
5 It's raining. d
6 It's snowing. b
7 It's sunny. a, g
8 It's windy. c

➤ Go back to page 95.

10.3 Phrasal verbs

Choose the correct phrasal verbs to complete the text.

Around two years ago, my husband and I went hiking in Austria. When we [1]*set off* / *gave up*, it was fairly cold, but then it got hotter and I [2]*put on* / *took off* my jacket. The mountain air felt so nice! We walked for a really long time. In fact, we got lost! We [3]*found out* / *looked for* our car, but we couldn't find it. We met a man and we tried to talk to him. We wanted to [4]*find out* / *look for* where the nearest village was, but he didn't understand us. In the evening, it got really cold. I [5]*put on* / *took off* my jacket, but it wasn't enough. We were frightened and we were ready to [6]*set off* / *give up*, but then we found a village! The police officer told us that our car was only a three minute walk from the police station!

➤ Go back to page 97.

11.2 Irregular past participles

Complete the sentences with the past participle form of the verbs in the box. There are two verbs you do not need.

be do go have ride see take win

1 I've never ___ridden___ a horse and I don't want to.
2 She's ___won___ three running races.
3 I've ___been___ to more than ten countries.
4 They've ___seen___ the sun rise in Africa.
5 I've never ___had___ a meal that cost more than $100.
6 He's ___taken___ a picture of a famous person.

➤ Go back to page 105.

11.3 Sports

A Label the pictures with the words in the box.

badminton basketball bike riding golf gymnastics judo ice skating skiing surfing ~~swimming~~ tennis yoga

1 ___*swimming*___

2 ___judo___

3 ___basketball___

4 ___golf___

5 ___skiing___

6 ___tennis___

7 ___surfing___

8 ___ice skating___

9 ___gymnastics___

10 ___badminton___

11 ___yoga___

12 ___bike riding___

B Match the sports in Exercise A with the correct verb – *do*, *go* or *play*.

Play	badminton basketball golf tennis
Do	gymnastics judo yoga
Go	bike riding skiing surfing swimming ice skating

➤ Go back to page 107.

12.2 Collocations with *get*

A Write the phrases with *get* in the correct place.

get home get hot get lunch get some coffee get there get tired

Become	Buy or obtain	Arrive
get hot get tired	get lunch get some coffee	get home get there

B Think of two more phrases for each meaning of *get*. Add them to Exercise A. **Suggested answers:**

become: get wet, get lost; **buy or obtain:** get a haircut, get a job; **arrive:** get to the station, get to the end

➤ Go back to page 115.

Communication Hub

2.2 Student A and B

Student A – look at the photos. Choose one person and describe them to your partner.
Student B – listen and guess who your partner is describing.
Then switch roles.

➤ Go back to page 15.

5.3 Student A and B

DISCUSS Work in pairs. Answer the questions about buildings (1–6). Use the adjectives in the box to help you.

1 Describe the buildings.
2 What happens inside?
3 Which building is your favorite? Why?
4 Which building don't you like? Why?

amazing   beautiful   big   boring   cool   interesting   funny   modern   old   small   strange   tall   terrible   ugly

➤ Go back to page 47.

6.1 Student A and B

A SPEAK Work in pairs. Read the *City Guide* and choose one thing to do together on the weekend. Explain what you like and don't like to help you decide.

A: Let's go out this weekend!
B: Good idea. What's going on?
A: There's a rock concert in the park on Saturday.
B: Oh, I don't like rock music. Let's go to a nightclub. I love dancing.
A: Sorry, I'm a terrible dancer!

B SPEAK Take a class vote. Which events are popular?

➤ Go back to page 53.

City Guide

Movies
French Film Festival ★★★
A festival of French movies, with famous movies like *Amélie*, *That Man from Rio* and *Two Days in Paris*.

Art
Van Gogh – the last years ★★★★★
An exhibit of Van Gogh's paintings from 1888 to 1890.

Clubs
70s disco ★★★★
The 70s disco craze continues. Dance all night to your favorite tunes!

7.2 Student A and B

Work in pairs. Follow these instructions to play the game:

- Use a dice and counters to play the board game.
- Complete the sentences with the simple past form of the verbs in parentheses.
- Every time you get the answer right, roll again!

25 SPIN AGAIN!	**26** didn't take They (not take) the train to Spain; they (go) by bus. went	**27** You missed the train. Go back to **6**.	**28** didn't see I (not see) the Colosseum when I (be) in Rome. was	**FINISH**
24 There's a storm. Go back to **8**.	**23** I (go) to Thailand last year. went	**22** didn't fly We (not fly) to Mexico; we sailed.	**21** You're in a traffic jam. Go back to **12**.	**20** SPIN AGAIN!
15 didn't book We (not book) a hotel; we (stay) with friends. stayed	**16** You forgot your passport. Go to **3**.	**17** SPIN AGAIN!	**18** didn't go We (not go) to Malaysia by train; we (go) by car. went	**19** They (take) the ferry. took
14 He (not go) to Rome. didn't go	**13** He (miss) the train. missed	**12** You only have a carry-on bag. Go to **18**.	**11** SPIN AGAIN!	**10** didn't arrive They (not arrive) in Bogotá until 5 am.
5 SPIN AGAIN!	**6** didn't take They (not take) much luggage.	**7** missed They (miss) their flight to France.	**8** She (leave) at 8 am. left	**9** Your flight arrived 30 minutes early. Go to **18**.
4 SPIN AGAIN!	**3** I (travel) to Dubai by plane. traveled	**2** You have a first-class ticket. Go to **8**.	**1** She (take) a train to London. took	**START**

➤ Go back to page 65.

7.3 Student A and B

SPEAK Work in pairs. Use the pictures to tell the story of Max and Sarah's vacation.

➤ Go back to page 67.

Communication Hub

2.1 Student A

A Read about another famous family. Answer Student B's questions about the family.

Bebel Gilberto is a famous Brazilian singer. She was born on May 12, 1966. Her father is the singer, songwriter and guitarist, João Gilberto and her mother is the singer Miúcha Buarque. Her uncle is the singer, writer and poet, Chico Buarque.

B Ask Student B questions about a famous family. Write the answers.

1 What's his name? Matthew Centrowitz Jr.
2 What is his dad's name? Matt Centrowitz Sr.
3 What is his sister's name? Lauren
4 Why are they famous? They are athletes.

➤ Go back to page 13.

8.1 Student A

Look at the picture. Ask Student B what's in their fridge. Answer Student B's questions. What is the same? What is different?

➤ Go back to page 73.

In Student B's fridge: two apples, cheese, fish, butter, four tomatoes, three oranges, two cartons of apple juice, one carton of milk, eggs

They both have cheese, apples, tomatoes and milk.

The differences are that Student B has one carton of milk, whereas Student A has two, and Student B has four tomatoes, whereas Student A has two.

10.2 Student A

A Use the prompts to make superlative questions.

1 small / city / in the world? What's the smallest city in the world?
2 hot / city / in Europe? What's the hottest city in Europe?
3 wet / place / on Earth? What's the wettest place on Earth?
4 high / city / in South America? What's the highest city in South America?
5 old / city / in Africa? What's the oldest city in Africa?
6 remote / city / in the world? What's the most remote city in the world?
7 big / jungle / in the world? What's the biggest jungle in the world?

B SPEAK Ask Student B your questions and write down the answers. Answer Student B's questions using the information box below.

Tokyo, Japan – 37 million people
Argos, Greece – 6th century BC
Winnipeg, Canada – minus 45°C (1966)
El Azizia, Libya – 58°C
Lhasa, Tibet – 3,600 m
Singapore
The Sahara Desert – 9 million km²

A: What's the biggest city in the world?
B: The biggest city in the world is Tokyo, Japan. Thirty-seven million people live there.

➤ Go back to page 95.

12.1 Student A

Look at Andrew's list of five things he has to do. Ask and answer questions to find the missing information.

A: What's Andrew going to do on Friday?
B: He's going to …

1 *This afternoon – call James Smith.*
2 Email the design company *on Friday.*
3 *Send out the conference invitations next week.*
4 *Tomorrow morning –* arrange a meeting with Max
5 *Today –* write the PRS report *!*

➤ Go back to page 113.

9.2 Student A and B

A You are going to interview your partner about their job/studies. Write questions using the prompts (1–7).

1 What / do? What do you do?
2 Where / (work/study)? Where do you work/study?
3 What / do / every day? What do you do every day?
4 What / enjoy / about / (job/course)? What / not enjoy? What do you enjoy about your job/course? What do you not enjoy?
5 Where / live / at the moment? Where do you live at the moment?
6 What / interest / in? What are you interested in?
7 What / do / today? What are you doing today?

B SPEAK Interview your partner using the questions from Exercise A. Write notes.

C SPEAK Work in small groups. Imagine two students in the class are going to swap jobs for a day. Use your notes from Exercise B to help you choose which students should swap jobs. Explain why.

Fumi is interested in art and Alex works in a museum. Maybe they should swap jobs.

Good idea!

➤ Go back to page 85.

10.3 Student A and B

A Work in pairs. Which of the following places do you think is the most difficult to survive in? Why?

a forest | an island | a jungle | a mountain

B PLAN Work in pairs. Imagine you are lost in one of the places in Exercise A. What are the dangers? What can help you? Choose three items to take with you.

Location	
Dangers	
Things to take	

C ORGANIZE Write a survival plan.

SURVIVAL PLAN
We can use the pocketknife to cut up fruit.
We can use the matches to light a fire – wild animals won't like the fire!

D PRESENT Tell the class your ideas.

➤ Go back to page 97.

12.3 Student A and B

A SPEAK Interview your classmates about how they use social media. Write notes. Ask for more information.

SOCIAL MEDIA HABITS

1 Which social network do you use the most?
a Facebook
b Twitter
c LinkedIn
d other

2 How often do you 'like' things?
a fewer than 5 times a day
b 5–10 times a day
c 11–20 times a day
d more than 20 times a day

3 What do you share the most?
a pictures
b videos
c news stories
d funny stories

4 How many people do you follow?
a fewer than 50
b 50–100
c 101–300
d more than 300

5 How often do you chat?
a fewer than 5 times a day
b 5–10 times a day
c 11–20 times a day
d more than 20 times a day

6 In the future, how much do you think you'll use social media?
a more
b less
c the same amount
d not at all

B ORGANIZE Work in groups. Compare your answers. Organize them into statistics.

Most people share news stories.

Nobody tweets every day.

➤ Go back to page 117.

2.1 Student B

A Ask Student A questions about a famous family. Write the answers.

1 What's her first name? Bebel
2 Where is she from? Brazil
3 What are her parents' names? Joao Gilberto and Miúcha Buarque
4 Why is she famous? She is a singer.

B Read about another famous family. Answer Student A's questions about the family.

Matthew Centrowitz Jr.

Matthew Centrowitz Jr. is an Olympic athlete from the US. In 2016, he won a gold medal for the 1,500 meters. His father, Matt Centrowitz Sr., is also an Olympic athlete who won a gold medal in the 1979 Pan-American games. Matthew Centrowitz Jr.'s sister Lauren Centrowitz, is also an athlete.

➤ Go back to page 13.

8.1 Student B

Look at the picture. Ask Student A what's in their fridge. Answer Student A's questions. What is the same? What is different?

➤ Go back to page 73.

In Student A's fridge: a container of yogurt, a pitcher of juice, cheese, two apples, chicken, bowl of rice, two tomatoes, lettuce, two cartons of milk

They both have cheese, apples, tomatoes and milk.

The differences are that Student B has one carton of milk, whereas Student A has two, and Student B has four tomatoes, whereas Student A has two.

10.2 Student B

A Use the prompts to make superlative questions.

1 big / city / in the world? What's the biggest city in the world?
2 old / city / in Europe? What's the oldest city in Europe?
3 cold / city / in North America? What's the coldest city in North America?
4 hot / place / in the world? What's the hottest place in the world?
5 high / city / in Asia? What's the highest city in Asia?
6 expensive / city / in the world? What's the most expensive city in the world?
7 big / desert / in the world? What's the biggest desert in the world?

B SPEAK Ask Student A your questions and write down the answers. Answer Student A's questions using the information box below.

Vatican City, Rome – 800 people
Athens – 22°C average temperature in summer
Mawsynram, India – 11,871 mm of rain every year
La Rinconada, Peru – 5,101 m
Luxor, Egypt – 3200 BC
Auckland, New Zealand – 2,153 km from Sydney
The Amazon rainforest – 5.5 million km²

A: *What's the smallest city in the world?*
B: *The smallest city in the world is the Vatican City in Rome. Eight hundred people live there.*

➤ Go back to page 95.

12.1 Student B

Look at Andrew's list of five things he has to do. Ask and answer questions to find the missing information.

A: *What's Andrew going to do this afternoon?*
B: *He's going to …*

1 *This afternoon –* call James Smith.
2 *Email the design company on Friday.*
3 Send out the conference invitations *next week.*
4 *Tomorrow morning – arrange a meeting with Max.*
5 *Today – write the PRS report!*

➤ Go back to page 113.

1.1 Vocabulary

Countries and nationalities

A Match the countries (1–8) with the nationalities (a–h).

1 Australia	**a** Greek
2 Chile	**b** Filipino
3 Greece	**c** Moroccan
4 Denmark	**d** Australian
5 Germany	**e** Chilean
6 Morocco	**f** South Korean
7 South Korea	**g** German
8 Philippines	**h** Danish

B Write the nationality. Then label the flags (1–8) to match the sentences.

1 I'm from Australia. I'm … ______________________.

2 I'm from Chile. I'm … ______________________.

3 I'm from Greece. I'm … ______________________.

4 I'm from Denmark. I'm … ______________________.

5 I'm from Germany. I'm … ______________________.

6 I'm from Morocco. I'm … ______________________.

7 I'm from South Korea. I'm … ______________________.

8 I'm from the Philippines. I'm … ______________________.

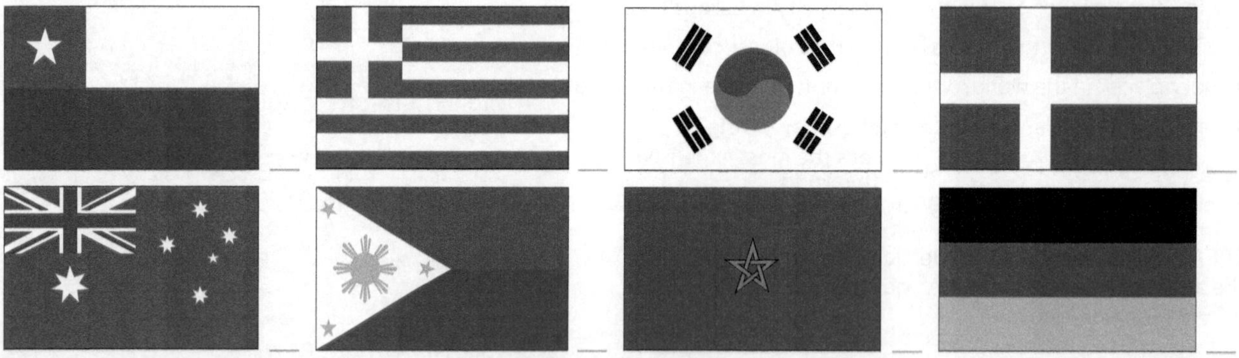

C Work in pairs. Practice saying the sentences in Exercise B.

1.1 Grammar

Simple present *be*: positive and negative

A Work in pairs. What are the pictures of? Complete the words with *a, e, i, o* or *u*.

1

2

3

4

5

1 *M__pl__ syr__p*

2 *P__zz__*

3 *Sp__ __n*

4 *__ __str__l__ __n fl__g*

5 *Pyr__m__ds __f G__z__a*

B Complete the sentences with *is, isn't, are* or *aren't*.

1 Pizza ____________ Italian.

2 The Pyramids of Giza ____________ in Mexico. They ____________ in Egypt.

3 Maple syrup ____________ British. It's Canadian.

4 We ____________ from Spain.

5 This ____________ the Australian flag.

C Work with a partner. Cover the sentences. Look at the pictures and say the sentences. Then make new sentences.

Pizza is Italian.

Correct! Can you think of a new sentence?

Uh, pasta is Italian!

Big numbers

A Write the numbers in words.

1 9,000 *nine thousand*

2 300 *three hundred*

3 5,000 ______________

4 128 ______________

5 70,000 ______________

6 68,000 ______________

7 125,000 ______________

8 2,000,000 ______________

B Write five numbers that are important to you in the circles below. Use the prompts to help you or your own ideas.

- your house number
- your grandmother's age
- your favorite number
- the number of friends you have on Facebook
- the number of brothers you have

C Work in pairs. Student A: Say a number from Exercise A. Student B: Try to guess why that number is important. Swap and repeat.

76

Is it your house number?

Haha! No. Try again …

1.2 Grammar

Simple present *be*: questions

A Complete the conversation with *am*, *is* or *are*.

Vijay:	Hi. How [1]________ you?
Andy:	I [2]________ fine, thanks. And you?
Vijay:	Good. What's your name?
Andy:	My name [3]________ Andy.
Vijay:	Andy? My name [4]________ Vijay.
Andy:	Hi Vijay. Where [5]________ you from?
Vijay:	I [6]________ from India. [7]________ you from Germany, Andy?
Andy:	No, I [8]________ from the US.

B Work in pairs. Practice the conversation in Exercise A.

C Work in pairs. Write a new conversation using your own names and nationalities.

D Practice your conversation from Exercise C.

Everyday items

A Work with a partner. You are going to a museum. Choose five items to take. Number the items in order of importance, from 1 (most important) to 5 (least).

a bottle of water

a watch

keys

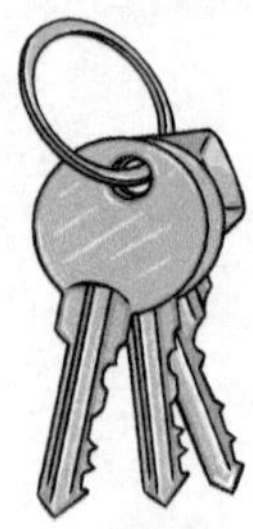

money

an umbrella

a laptop

tissues

headphones

a magazine

a credit card

a cell phone

a bag

B Work with a partner. Choose a new place to visit. Decide on the five most important things to take with you.

Let's go to the movie theater.

Good idea! OK, so we need money …

Definitely … and some tissues in case the movie is sad

a/an and plural nouns

A Complete the sentences with *a*, *an* or –.

What's in your BAG?

This week, we speak to **Mark Pinder** – a 28-year-old businessman from New York, US.

I have a lot of things here. I have [1]______ bottle of water, [2]______ money, [3]______ tissues, [4]______ wallet, [5]______ umbrella, [6]______ headphones, [7]______ credit card, [8]______ keys, [9]______ laptop, [10]______ cell phone and [11]______ watch.

B Work in pairs. Tell your partner what's in your bag using *a* or *an*.

C Work in groups. Take three things from your bag and put them on the table. Then ask questions with *this/that* and *these/those*.

Is this your laptop?

No, that's my laptop!

Family

A Complete the table with the words in the box.

aunt brother child children cousin daughter father grandchildren granddaughter grandfather grandparents grandson mother nephew niece parents sister son uncle

female	male	male or female

B Work in pairs. One person chooses a word from the box, and the other makes a true sentence about it.

Uh … uncle!

My uncle's name is Tom.

Possessive adjectives and apostrophes

A Complete the sentences with a possessive apostrophe and a word from the box.

Brian Ellen father grandmother grandson husband mother Richard sister son

Richard is married to Ellen. They have a daughter, Faye, and a son, Brian. Brian has a cat named Mia. Richard has a mother, Emma, and a father, Derek.

1 Richard is ______________________ husband.
2 Ellen is Faye ______________________.
3 Derek is Richard ______________________.
4 Emma is Faye ______________________.
5 Mia is ______________________ pet.
6 Derek is Emma ______________________.
7 Faye is Brian ______________________.
8 Brian is Emma ______________________.
9 Richard is Derek ______________________.
10 Ellen is ______________________ wife.

B Work in pairs. Use some of the words from the box and a possessive apostrophe to tell your partner about your family, friends and pets.

best friend brother cat daughter dog father grandfather grandmother husband mother sister son wife

Describing appearance

A Work in pairs. Complete the diagram with the words in the box. Sometimes words can be used in more than one category. Then add your own ideas.

bald beard ~~blond~~ blue brown curly fat green
gray mustache short slim straight tall

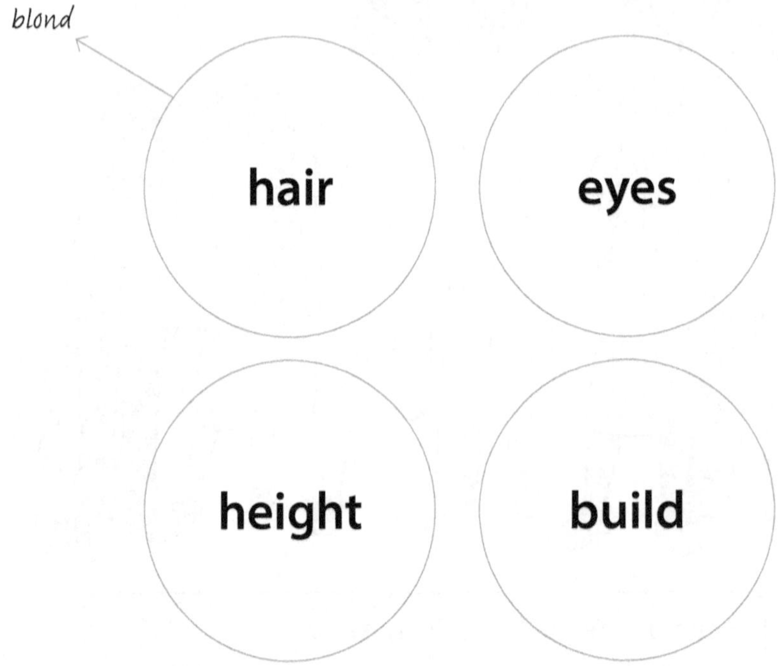

B Choose a person from the class. Write a short description of the person. Use phrases from Exercise A and any other words you know.

C Work in pairs. Take turns describing the person. Don't say their name. Guess the person your partner is talking about.

2.2 Grammar

have/has

A Complete as many sentences as possible about people in your family.

1 My ______________ has ______________ hair.
2 My ______________ is tall.
3 My brother has ______________.
4 My sister has ______________ and ______________.
5 My ______________ has glasses.
6 Nobody in my family is ______________.
7 My uncle has ______________.
8 ______________ is tall.
9 ______________ has long hair and glasses.
10 My grandfather has ______________ hair.
11 My grandmother is ______________.
12 I have ______________ and I am ______________.

B Walk around the class and find someone who has the things in the table. Write the student's name.

Find someone who has…

	Student's name
a grandfather with gray hair	
two brothers with short hair	
a father with a beard	
a mother with long hair	
an aunt with blond hair	
an uncle with a mustache	
parents with glasses	
a friend with blue eyes	
grandparents with brown eyes	
a father who is bald	
a sister with red hair	
a mother who is tall	
a brother who is short	

2.3 Vocabulary

Personality adjectives

A Complete the table with the adjectives in the box.

friendly funny happy messy neat noisy quiet sad serious unfriendly unhappy

Positive	Negative	Both

B Work in pairs. Ask and answer questions about people in your family and your friends.

Is your father funny?

Yes, he's very funny.

Why?

C Tell the class about the person you would most like to meet.

I would like to meet Anna's brother.
He's friendly and happy, but he's very noisy.

2.3 Grammar

Using adjectives

A Put the words in the correct order to write captions for pictures (1–6).

1 a / dress / expensive / It's / very

____

2 boyfriend / really / My / tall / is

____

3 movie / It's / very / a / sad

____

4 fairly / sister's / bedroom / My / is / messy

____

5 grandmother's / really / My / neighbors / noisy / are

____

6 think / tired / I / he's / fairly

____

B Work in pairs. Describe someone in the class using *fairly, very* and *really* with adjectives. Try to guess who the other person is describing.

3.1 Vocabulary

Everyday activities

A Check (✓) the activities you do every day.

- ☐ get up
- ☐ go to work
- ☐ leave home
- ☐ have breakfast
- ☐ take a shower
- ☐ watch TV
- ☐ have lunch
- ☐ go to bed
- ☐ have dinner

B Complete the table with activities from Exercise A and your own ideas. Put the activities in the order you do them and write a time next to each activity.

Activity	Time

C Work in pairs. Ask when you do the activities.

3.1 Grammar

Simple present positive

A Find and correct the mistakes. You will not need to change two of the sentences.

1 My friend listen to the radio every morning.

2 My English class starting at 5:30 pm every day.

3 I do drive to work in the morning.

4 My parents are live in an apartment in the city center.

5 My sister likes playing video games.

6 My brother does cooks dinner every night.

7 I have breakfast before I goes to work.

8 My best friend is listens to classical music.

9 I work at a desk all the day.

10 I to watch TV with my roommates every night.

11 My teacher talks about soccer every day.

B Rewrite the sentences in Exercise A so they are true for you. You can change the verbs, nouns or adverbs.

C Work in pairs. Discuss your sentences from Exercise B. Ask questions for more information.

My English class starts at 9:00 am every morning.

Oh, really? I start at 10:00 am.

Adverbs of frequency

A Complete the sentences so they are true for you, using the adverbs in the box.

always never often rarely sometimes usually

I ____________ listen to music.

I ____________ use the internet.

I ____________ drive to work.

I ____________ do homework.

I ____________ go out with my friends.

I ____________ exercise.

I ____________ get up before 7:00 am.

I ____________ start my day with yoga.

I ____________ drink strong coffee.

I ____________ eat out.

I ____________ use my cell phone in class.

I ____________ eat a big breakfast.

I ____________ use Facebook or Instagram in cafés.

B Walk around the class and find someone who:

	name
1 never uses a cell phone in class	
2 sometimes eats out	
3 rarely gets up before 7:00 am	
4 never listens to music	
5 always exercises	
6 rarely drinks strong coffee	
7 often eats out	
8 always does homework	
9 sometimes starts the day with yoga	

Prepositions of time

A Add the prepositions *in*, *at* or *on* to the questions in the questionnaire.

1. Do you work ______ Mondays?
2. Do you go out ______ weekdays?
3. What do you do ______ eight o'clock in the evening?
4. Where are you usually ______ Sunday morning?
5. What do you always do ______ the weekend?
6. Where do you go ______ the weekend?
7. Do you listen to music ______ the evening?
8. Do you watch television ______ the morning?
9. Do you use your cell phone ______ night?
10. Do you play games ______ Saturdays?

B Work in pairs. Ask and answer the questions in Exercise A.

C Work in new pairs. Ask questions to find five things you both usually do at the same time or day.

Simple present negative

A Check (✓) the things you do. Put an (✗) on the things you <u>do not</u> do.

watch television every night ☐	enjoy playing video games ☐
cook for my family on Sundays ☐	speak Spanish ☐
eat meat ☐	play the guitar ☐
live in an apartment ☐	live with my parents ☐

B Work in pairs. Make five negative sentences about people in your class, using the prompts in Exercise A.

1 *Juan doesn't live with his parents.*

2 *Haruka doesn't enjoy playing video games.*

C Are your guesses in Exercise B correct? Ask people in the class questions to find out.

Juan, do you live with your parents?

No, I don't. I live with friends from work.

3.3 Vocabulary

Big celebrations

A Complete collocations (1–7) with the verbs in the box.

eat give have put up watch (x2) wear

1 ____________ decorations

2 ____________ fireworks

3 ____________ a party

4 ____________ special food

5 ____________ presents

6 ____________ traditional clothes

7 ____________ a parade

B Write five sentences which are true for you or your country.

We never have a party on a birthday in my country.

C Work in pairs. Compare your sentences. Are they the same or different?

4.1 Vocabulary

Work and jobs

A Complete jobs (1–6) with *a, e, i, o* and *u*.

1 p__l__t
2 t____ch__r
3 d__s__gn__r
4 d__ct__r
5 b__s__n__ssw__m__n
6 __ct__r

B Match sentences (a–f) with the jobs in Exercise A.

a I work in a hospital.
b I sometimes work in an office, but I go out and meet a lot of people.
c I travel to many different countries.
d I work in an office, and I love art.
e I work in movies and television.
f I work with children.

C Work in pairs. Student A: mime a job from Exercise A. Student B: guess the job. Swap.

4.1 Grammar

Simple present *yes/no* questions; short answers

A Complete the questions and answers with the correct form of *do*.

1 __________ you work from home? ✓
2 __________ she wear a uniform? ✗
3 __________ he travel a lot? ✓
4 __________ you like your job? ✗
5 __________ he go out and meet people? ✗
6 __________ she work in a hospital? ✓

B Match questions (1–6) with answers (a–f).

a No, he __________.
b Yes, she __________.
c Yes, he __________.
d No, I __________.
e Yes, I __________.
f No, she __________.

C Work in pairs. Ask and answer questions about each other's jobs using the prompts in the box.

go out and meet people | like your job | travel a lot | wear a uniform | work at a computer | work from home | work in an office | work with children

Do you work from home?

No, I don't.

4.2 Grammar

have to/don't have to

A Complete conversations (1–4) with the correct form of *have to*.

1
A: ________________ (you / wear) a uniform at work?
B: No, ________________

2
A: ________________ (you / work) on the weekend?
B: Yes, ________________

3
A: ________________ (your husband / travel) a lot for work?
B: Yes, ________________

4
A: ________________ (your sister / work) nine to five?
B: No, ________________

B Write sentences that are true for you using *have to* and the ideas below:

- meet new people every day
- wear a uniform
- get up early on the weekend
- work in the evenings
- pay for lunch at work

C Walk around the class. Ask and answer questions using the prompts in Exercise B. Ask follow-up questions for more information.

Do you have to wear a uniform at work?

Yes, I do.

Oh, really? What do you do?

I'm a firefighter.

D Work in pairs. Tell each other five interesting things you found out in Exercise C.

Juan has to wear a uniform at work because he's a firefighter.

Time expressions

A Match the time expressions (1–5) to the times (a–e).

1 nine to five	**a** 12:00 am
2 early in the morning	**b** 12:00 pm
3 late in the afternoon	**c** 5:00 am – 7:00 am
4 midnight	**d** 4:00 pm – 6:00 pm
5 noon	**e** 9:00 am – 5:00 pm

B Complete the sentences with time expressions from Exercise A.

1 Most people in offices have to work from ________________.

2 I start work at 6 am, so I have to get up ________________.

3 Morning finishes at ________________.

4 Most people go to bed before ________________.

5 A lot of people come home from work ________________.

C Walk around the class. Ask and answer questions to find someone who sometimes does these things and someone who never does.

	name
works until midnight	
sleeps until noon	
gets up early in the morning	
works from nine to five	

Question words

A Write questions using *How, What, When, Where, Who* or *Why* and the prompts in the box.

1 favorite kind of music? ______	
2 languages you speak? ______	
3 English course finish? ______	
4 you want to learn English? ______	
5 favorite writer? ______	
6 get to work every day? ______	
7 parents live? ______	
8 exercise you do every week? ______	
9 father do? ______	
10 favorite movie? ______	

B Work in pairs. Ask and answer the questions in Exercise A. Write notes.

Education collocations

A Complete the sentences with the verbs in the box.

get (x2) go study take (x2) train

1 I don't want to ______________ business.

2 I want to ______________ a degree.

3 I don't want to ______________ to college.

4 I want to ______________ to be a teacher.

5 I don't want to ______________ a certification.

6 I want to ______________ a course in my free time.

7 I don't want to ______________ a lot of exams.

B Rewrite the sentences in Exercise A so they're true for you.

C Work in pairs. Ask and answer questions using the collocations in Exercise A. Ask follow-up questions to find out more.

Do you want to train to be a teacher?

Yes, I do.

Why?

5.1 Vocabulary

Rooms and furniture: prepositions of place

A Complete the table with the words in the box.

apartment bathroom bed bedroom caravan chair couch dining room
house lamp living room swimming pool table TV yard

places to stay in	rooms and outdoor things	furniture

B Work with a partner. Ask questions about the things from the table.

Do you have a house or an apartment?

I have an apartment. It's nice, with three bedrooms and large windows.

How many chairs do you have in your house?

Ten, I think. We have six in the dining room and four in the living room.

there is/are

A Write sentences about your home using the words and *there is/there are/there isn't a/ there aren't any.*

1 bathroom *There is a bathroom in my home.*

2 swimming pool ____________________

3 dining room ____________________

4 living room ____________________

5 yard ____________________

6 chair ____________________

7 TV ____________________

8 bedroom ____________________

9 dishwasher ____________________

10 armchair ____________________

11 lamp ____________________

12 bed ____________________

B Work in pairs. Say which objects you think the other person has in their home. Correct your partner.

I think there are two bedrooms in your home.

Yes, that's right. There are two bedrooms.

There are five lamps in your living room.

No, there aren't, there are only two.

5.2 Vocabulary

Places in a town or city

A Match the places in the box with the pictures (1–15).

airport café grocery store gym hospital library market movie theater museum park restaurant school store subway station theater

B Work in pairs and tell them about your places. Use prepositions of place from the box.

across from behind between near next to

In my town, we have a grocery store across from the bus station, but we don't have a museum.

We have a small museum next to the park. We have a lot of grocery stores.

can

A Complete the sentences with a verb from the box and *can* or *can't*.

make	play	ride	speak	swim	work

1 Can you __________ the piano? Yes, I __________ but I'm not very good.

2 Can you __________ at home? No, I __________. I'm a teacher.

3 Can you __________ a cake? Yes, I think I __________.

4 Can you __________ a bicycle? No, I __________. I never learned.

5 Can you __________ another language? Yes, I __________ speak English!

B Change the answers in Exercise A so they are true for you. Then ask and answer the questions in pairs.

C Complete the sentences with *can* or *can't* for your hometown or city.

You __________ go to a park.

You __________ take a train.

You __________ go to a good museum.

You __________ eat in a Japanese restaurant.

You __________ study at a university.

You __________ shop in a market.

You __________ catch a plane.

D Work with a partner. Ask and answer questions to find out what you can and can't do in each other's hometowns or cities.

American Language Hub Level 1 Teacher's Book.

5.3 Vocabulary

Adjectives to describe the appearance of things

A Write an example of each thing below.

1 a big animal ________ *Elephant* ________

2 a boring sport ____________________

3 a beautiful city ____________________

4 an amazing vacation ____________________

5 a modern painting ____________________

6 a small car ____________________

7 a terrible idea ____________________

8 an old person ____________________

9 an interesting website ____________________

10 an ugly building ____________________

B Work with a partner and exchange ideas. Do you have the same examples?

C Think of the opposite of each example in Exercise A.

An elephant is a *big* animal.

And a mouse is *small* animal!

Imperatives

A Match the imperative sentences (1–7) with the responses (a–g).

1 Don't watch the TV.
2 Read your book.
3 Please sit down.
4 Give that to me.
5 Please tell me your name.
6 Please spell your name for me.
7 Stand up when he comes in.

a Thank you. Is there a chair?
b No, I don't want to read.
c A – L – I – C – E.
d No, I need it.
e Okay!
f It's Jason.
g Why not? There's a good show on.

B Work in pairs and follow the instructions below:

1 In the left-hand side of the box below, draw the furniture to make a picture of a bedroom, dining room, bathroom or living room. Do not show your picture to anyone!

2 Work in pairs. Describe your pictures to each other and draw your partner's room in the right-hand side of the box. Remember not to show them your picture!

'Draw a TV between the bed and the armchair'.

across from armchair bed behind between chair coffee draw
lamp machine near next put to TV washing machine write

Your room	Your partner's room

3 Compare your pictures. Are they the same?

6.1 Vocabulary

Entertainment

A Complete descriptions (1–7) with the words in the box.

comedy concert exhibit festival
internet magazine movie theater theater

1 ________________ You watch one of these when you want to see something funny.

2 ________________ You go to one of these to listen to music.

3 ________________ You read this in a café or at home.

4 ________________ You go to this to have fun for a day.

5 ________________ You look at this to get information.

6 ________________ You go here to watch movies.

7 ________________ You go to one to see paintings and art.

B Work in pairs. Say how often you do each activity and why.

I never go to exhibits.
They're boring.

6.1 Grammar

Likes and dislikes

A Write sentences with *like, love* or *hate* for these. Use … *ing* where necessary.

comedy   go to a park   go to festivals   jazz music   read magazines
rock music   Shakespeare   watch fireworks   watch movies

B Work in pairs. Read your sentences to each other. Do you like/dislike the same things?

6.2 Grammar

was/were

A Complete conversations (1–4) with the correct from of *was/were*.

1

A: Where ____________ you last night?

B: I ____________ at the gym until 9 pm.

2

A: Hey! How ____________ your weekend?

B: It ____________ really boring!

3

A: ____________ Tom at the party on Saturday?

B: No, he ____________.

4

A: Wow! That ____________ a terrible game.

B: I know. It ____________ so boring!

B Work in pairs. Ask and answer your own questions using *was/were*.

6.2 Vocabulary

Past time expressions

A Complete the brainstorm with the words in the box.

~~10 minutes~~	2006	four months	July of last year
month	Saturday	six years	the summer	year

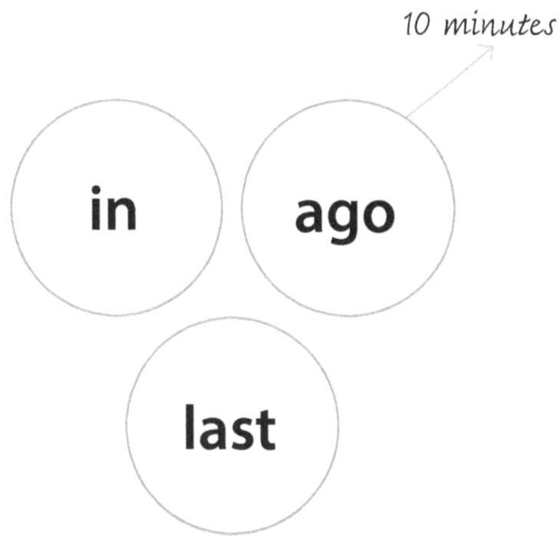

B Work in pairs. Ask and answer questions with *Where were you…* and time expressions in Exercise A.

6.3 Grammar

Simple past regular and irregular verbs

A Complete the table with the simple past form of the verbs in the box.

ask be become buy decide get give go have join
live meet move play practice send start study work

irregular	regular with *-ed*	regular with *-d*	regular with *-ied*

B Work in pairs. Say a verb, and your partner makes a sentence using the simple past, without looking at the table. If your partner gets it right, they continue. Count the number of correct answers.

Go.

I went to school ten years ago.

Correct! That's one point. OK, next … become.

Life events

A Complete the sentences with the simple past form of the verbs in parentheses.

1 Tom (be) __________ born in New York in 1983.

2 He (go) __________ to school in Queens, New York.

3 He (learn) __________ French in high school.

4 He (study) __________ French in college.

5 He (become) __________ a French teacher.

6 He (start) __________ working at his old school.

7 He (buy) __________ an apartment in Brooklyn, New York.

8 He (get) __________ married to Emily in 2005.

9 They (have) __________ a baby girl named Sarah.

10 They (move) __________ to a big house in the country.

11 The child (go) __________ to school nearby.

12 She (finish) __________ school and (go) __________ to college.

B Write sentences about the key events in your life in order.

C Tell your story to a partner. Compare your stories.

7.1 Vocabulary

Transportation

A Label the images with the words in the box.

bicycle   boat   bus (x2)   motorcycle   plane   scooter   ship   train

1 ______________

2 ______________

3 ______________

4 ______________

5 ______________

6 ______________

7 ______________

8 ______________

9 ______________

B Work in pairs. Tell the story of a trip from your school to another country. Take turns saying one sentence in the past using a different transportation method each time.

7.1 Grammar

could

A Which of these could you do 70 years ago? Which of these couldn't you do? Write sentences.

buy things online drive a car eat fast food eat traditional food
fly to another country learn a language study at a university use the internet at home
watch a movie at a movie theater watch TV on a computer

1 *You couldn't use the internet at home.*

B Work in pairs. When was the first time people could do the things in Exercise A? Discuss your ideas.

I think you could use the internet at home in the 1990s.

No, I think it was the 1980s.

7.2 Grammar

Simple past negative

A Rewrite the sentences in the simple past negative.

1 I liked rock music when I was younger. ____________________

2 He went to work last week. ____________________

3 They studied French at school. ____________________

4 I lived with my parents when I was a teenager. ____________________

5 I went on vacation last summer. ____________________

6 She studied at Harvard University. ____________________

7 They came here by boat. ____________________

8 She became a professional dancer. ____________________

9 We took a lot of luggage. ____________________

10 We arrived on time. ____________________

B Write five sentences about things you did and didn't do yesterday. Two sentences should be true and three should be false.

C Work in pairs. Read your sentences from Exercise B. Try to guess which are true and which are false.

I went on a plane.

Haha! You didn't go on a plane!

Travel phrases

A Complete the story with the simple past form of the verbs in the box.

arrive	leave	miss	return	take

Hello. I'm in Milan again after my trip to London, England. I [1]_____________ there two weeks ago at Heathrow Airport. It was very, very big and cold! I [2]_____________ my flight, but I almost did, because the taxi I [3]_____________ to Milan airport was late, and I [4]_____________ my house until eight o'clock. In London, I went shopping, saw some famous landmarks and visited my friends – it was fun. I [5]_____________ to Milan yesterday, and now I miss London a lot.

B Write a story about a trip you took last year. Use the story in Exercise A to help you.

C Work in pairs. Read your story to your partner, but don't say the five simple past verbs. Your partner guesses the words you left out.

Simple past questions

A Correct the simple past questions.

1 *Did you went to Canada on your last vacation?*

2 *You meet many people last year?*

3 *Did fly you anywhere last year?*

4 *You arrived late at the airport last time you went?*

5 *Did you be happy yesterday?*

6 *Did you went swimming last week?*

7 *What time you got up this morning?*

8 *You visited a museum last month?*

9 *Did you had a good time on vacation last year?*

10 *When you arrive here today?*

B Work in pairs. Ask and answer the questions from Exercise A. Ask follow-up questions to find out more.

Did you go to Canada on your last vacation?

No, I didn't. I went to Japan.

Oh, wow! How long did you go for?

Two weeks – it was amazing!

Verb phrases

A Choose the correct verbs to complete the sentences.

1 I like to ***swim / have*** in the ocean when I'm on vacation.

2 Most people ***meet / visit*** museums when they go to a big city.

3 We didn't ***take / read*** any pictures on our last trip.

4 Did you ***eat / read*** a good book on your last vacation?

5 They didn't ***get / meet*** lost in Rome because they had a good map.

6 How many people did you ***lose / meet*** at the hostel?

7 We ***had / got*** a really good time in Tokyo last summer.

8 They ***went / took*** shopping before they went to dinner.

B Think about your last vacation. Write a postcard to your partner using the verb phrases from Exercise A.

8.1 Vocabulary

Food and drink

A Complete the table with the words in the box.

apple banana beans bread broccoli butter cake carrot chicken chips coffee egg mushroom onion orange pasta pizza sandwich shrimp tea tomato water

fruits	vegetables	meat and fish	drinks	other

B Check (✓) the items in Exercise A that you have at home now.

C Work in pairs. Write three foods you think your partner loves, three they like and three they hate.

Your partner loves …	
Your partner likes …	
Your partner hates …	

D Swap your answers with your partner's. How many were correct?

8.1 Grammar

Countable and uncountable nouns; *some* and *any*

A Complete the table with the words in the box.

banana bean bread broccoli cake carrot chicken
chocolate pasta sandwich shrimp tea water

Countable	Uncountable	Both

B Decide on a meal to make. Make a shopping list.

Shopping list

- (x5) eggs
- some flour

C Show another student your list. Can they guess what you want to make?

8.2 Vocabulary

Containers

A Complete the table with the words in the box. Some may be in more than one container.

beans cake carrots chips coffee cola eggs mushrooms
onions orange juice pasta shrimp tea tomatoes water

a bag of	a bottle of	a can of	a can of	a carton, package or box of

B Write a list of the items in Exercise A that you have in your kitchen at home.

C Work in pairs. Ask each other questions to find out what is on your partner's list.

Do you have a can of tomatoes?

8.2 Grammar

much, many, a lot of

A Complete the questions in the diet questionnaire with *How much* and *How many*. Then write three more questions with *How much* or *How many*.

Diet questionnaire

1 ______________ liters of water do you drink every day?

2 ______________ fruit do you eat every week?

3 ______________ pasta do you eat every month?

4 ______________ cups of coffee do you usually drink every day?

5 ______________ bags of chips do you eat every month?

6 ______________ cans of cola do you drink every week?

7 ______________ meat do you eat every month?

____

____

____

B Work in pairs. Ask and answer the questions in Exercise A. Who has the healthiest diet?

8.3 Grammar

a/an, the, no article

A Complete the recipe with *a, an, the* or – (no article).

METHOD

To make [1] ______________ tomato sauce for [2] ______________ pasta, open [3] ______________ can of tomatoes and put them in [4] ______________ small bowl. Chop [5] ______________ onion and some [6] ______________ garlic and fry in [7] ______________ pan with some [8] ______________ olive oil. Add [9] ______________ tomatoes from [10] ______________ bowl, stir and cook for [11] ______________ fifteen minutes. Add [12] ______________ salt and [13] ______________ pepper and stir again. Cook some [14] ______________ pasta, and put it in [15] ______________ big serving bowl. Add [16] ______________ tomato sauce, stir, and serve with cheese.

B Complete the questions with *a/an, the* or –. Then work in pairs to ask and answer the questions.

1 What kind of ______________ pasta do you like?

2 How often do you eat ______________ chicken?

3 Do you ever eat ______________ eggs for breakfast? How do you like to cook ______________ eggs?

4 Do you ever have ______________ pizza for dinner? What kind of ______________ pizza do you like?

5 Do you ever have ______________ cup of tea or coffee after dinner? Do you put sugar in ______________ it?

Food preparation

A Choose the correct options to complete the recipe.

SPANISH OMELETTE

INGREDIENTS

- Three eggs.
- Two potatoes.
- Some olive oil, salt and black pepper.

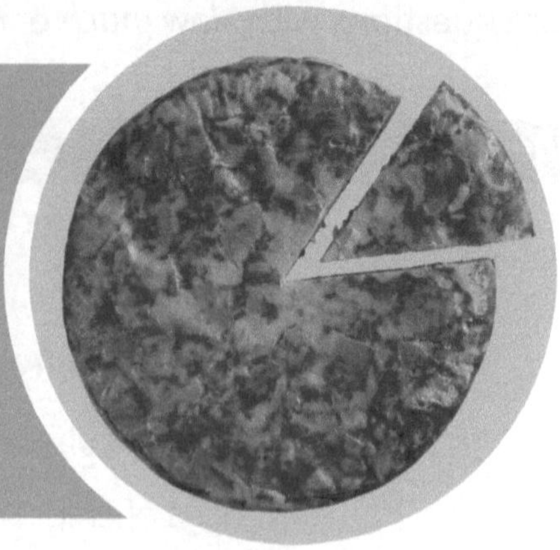

METHOD

1 ***Crack / Fry*** three eggs into a bowl and beat them, along with some salt.

2 ***Peel / Put*** two potatoes and cut into slices.

3 ***Fry / Put*** the potato slices into the eggs and mix.

4 ***Put / Crack*** some olive oil into a pan and ***add / chop*** the eggs and potatoes.

5 Slowly ***fry / serve*** the eggs and potatoes. Turn them over in the pan.

6 ***Add / Peel*** salt and black pepper and ***serve / chop***. Enjoy!

B Think of a recipe you know well. Write the name, ingredients and how to make it.

____

INGREDIENTS

- _______________
- _______________
- _______________
- _______________
- _______________

METHOD

1 _______________

2 _______________

3 _______________

4 _______________

5 _______________

C Work in pairs. Explain your recipes from Exercise B.

9.1 Vocabulary

Clothes

A Label pictures (1–12) with the words in the box.

cap coat dress gloves hat pants scarf
shorts skirt sneakers socks sunglasses

1 ____________

2 ____________

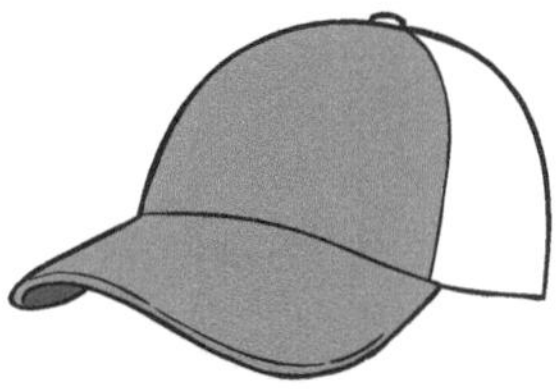

3 ____________

4 ____________

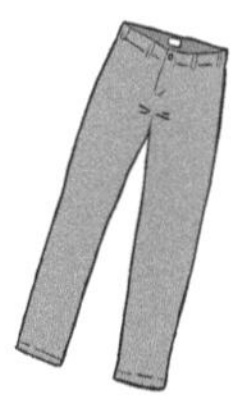

5 ____________

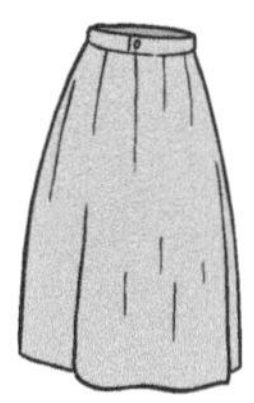

6 ____________

7 ____________

8 ____________

9 ____________

10 ____________

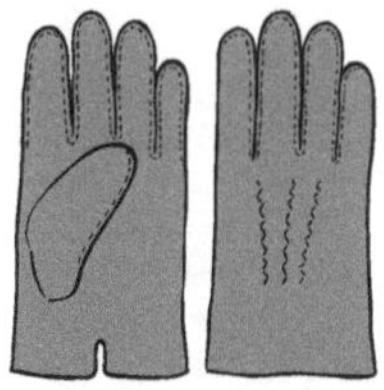

11 ____________

12 ____________

B Work in pairs. Ask and answer the questions. Use words from Exercise A to help you.

- What do you wear on a cold day?
- What do you wear on a hot day?
- What do you wear to work?
- What do you wear at home?
- What do you wear when you play sports?
- What do you wear when you go to a restaurant?
- What do you wear at the movie theater?
- What do you wear when you are happy?

Present progressive

A Use the prompts to write present progressive sentences and questions.

1 She / play / video games in her bedroom. ____________________

2 I / not go / to the party on Saturday. ____________________

3 You / watch / the news? ____________________

4 They / play / soccer in the yard. ____________________

5 He / listen / to music on his phone. ____________________

6 What / you / do now? ____________________

7 He / wait / at the bus stop. ____________________

8 She / wear / a Prada jacket. ____________________

9 He / not work / today. ____________________

10 What / you / make / for dinner? ____________________

B Write five present progressive sentences.

1 ____________________

2 ____________________

3 ____________________

4 ____________________

5 ____________________

C Work in pairs. Student A: mime a sentence from Exercise B. Student B: try to guess what your partner is doing. Swap.

9.2 Vocabulary

Present time expressions

A Choose the correct time expressions to complete the blog post.

What's Going On This Month?

EMILY STEVENS – November 10

Last year was hard, but my life is great [1]***today / at the moment***. I'm [2]***currently / at the moment*** spending a lot of time studying, and my friend is visiting for a few days [3]***today / right now***. [4]***At the moment / these days*** she's out shopping – she loves staying here near the mall. It is raining [5]***today / these days***, so it's a good day for shopping. My father is away [6]***these days / at the moment*** on a business trip, and [7]***right now / these days*** my mother is sleeping, so the house is quiet – it's easy to study. I'm really enjoying my college course [8]***at the moment / today***, because this semester we are learning about Japan, which I love.

B Complete the questions with the words in the box.

days moment now right these today

1 What are you reading at the ______________?

2 Where do you have lunch these ______________?

3 What is your family doing ______________ now?

4 What are you studying ______________?

5 What is your teacher doing right ______________?

6 What are you doing in your free time ______________ days?

C Work in pairs. Ask and answer the questions in Exercise B. Try to ask follow-up questions for more information.

What are you reading right now?

I'm reading *The Secret History* by Donna Tartt. It's amazing!

Oh, really? What's it about?

Simple present vs present progressive

A Complete the sentences with the simple present or present progressive form of the verbs in parentheses.

1 I ____________ (read) a magazine at the moment.
2 My friend ____________ (go) to the movie theater every Saturday.
3 Why ____________ you ____________ (drive) so fast – we have a lot of time.
4 My sister always ____________ (tell) me what to eat.
5 We ____________ (work) in a different office these days.
6 I ____________ (watch) TV right now – can you call back later?
7 I think my father ____________ (talk) to someone downstairs.
8 My brother ____________ (love) soccer and tennis.
9 She ____________ (work) as a doctor in the city hospital.
10 What time ____________ you ____________ (get up) every day?

B Write six questions in the simple present or present progressive, using a verb from box A and a time expression from box B.

A	B
eat	after work
do	right now
read	every day
wear	today
work	tonight

1 ____
2 ____
3 ____
4 ____
5 ____
6 ____

C Work in pairs. Ask and answer your questions from Exercise B.

What are you reading right now?

I'm reading an amazing book by Haruki Murakami called, *Norwegian Wood*.

Object pronouns

A Complete the table with the words below.

he her it me them we you

subject	I		she		it		they
object		you		him		us	

B Choose the correct pronouns to complete the sentences.

1. ***I / Me*** like Jimmy because ***he / him*** is funny, but I don't think ***he / him*** likes ***me / I***.
2. My father is working right now, so ***I / me*** can't speak to ***he / him*** until 6:00 pm.
3. Where is your friend – is ***she / her*** at home?
4. ***We / Us*** don't talk to ***he / him*** or ***she / her***, because ***they / them*** are not friendly.
5. The cat is great – I love ***him / he*** but the dog isn't so nice – ***she / her*** always bites ***me / I***!
6. What time can ***we / us*** come over?
7. Do ***they / them*** live in a big house?
8. I don't like vegetables, but I have to eat ***they / them***.

C Complete the questions with appropriate pronouns.

1. What is your best friend's name? Why do you like ____________?
2. What is your favorite place? Why do ____________ like ____________?
3. What is your favorite food? Can ____________ cook ____________?
4. Which friends do you like to go out with? When do ____________ see ____________?
5. What clothes do you usually wear? Where did ____________ buy ____________?
6. Do you have a hat? When do you wear ____________?

D Work in pairs. Ask and answer the questions in Exercise C. Try to ask follow-up questions to get more information.

What is your best friend's name?

Uh, his name's Laurence.

Why do you like him?

He's pretty quiet sometimes, but he's also really funny!

Stores and services

A Match stores and services (1–6) with the things you can buy or do there (a–f).

1 bakery	**a** buy meat
2 pharmacy	**b** buy bread and cakes
3 market	**c** buy magazines and newspapers
4 butcher's	**d** borrow books
5 library	**e** buy medicine
6 newsstand	**f** buy cheap clothes and food

B Work in pairs. Imagine you're having a surprise party for someone in the class. Make a list of food, drinks and other things you need to buy.

Shopping list

Food

-
-
-
-

Drinks

-
-
-
-

Other things

-
-
-
-
-

C Think of five more things you need to buy for the party (e.g. decorations, clothes). Include a present for the person you want to surprise. Add your items to the list.

D Using the words in the box, decide where you can buy the things on your list.

bakery butcher's department store grocery store market online store

E Present your shopping list to the rest of the class. Explain how many stores you need to go to.

Landscape features

A Label pictures (1–9) with the words in the box.

beach desert forest hill island jungle lake mountain ocean

1 ______________

2 ______________

3 ______________

4 ______________

5 ______________

6 ______________

7 ______________

8 ______________

9 ______________

B Work in pairs. Think of a place you went to, with some of the landscape features from Exercise A. Say where you went, when and why. Try to ask follow-up questions to get more information.

I went to a mountain in Kenya, in 2015, for a vacation.

Oh, wow! Who did you go with?

10.1 Grammar

Comparatives

A Complete the sentences with the comparative form of the adjectives in the boxes.

big cheap close

1 My new office ____________ to the station ____________ my last one.

2 Canada ____________ Spain.

3 Taking the ferry to France ____________ flying.

big expensive traditional

4 A Ferrari ____________ most other cars.

5 Print newspapers ____________ online articles.

6 Mount Everest ____________ K2.

crowded hot wet

7 The Amazon Jungle ____________ the Arctic.

8 The city center ____________ my town.

9 Rainforests ____________ normal forests.

B Work in pairs. Student A: name two things for your partner to compare. Student B: make a comparative sentence about the things your partner says. Swap.

Paris and Dubai.

Paris is older than Dubai.

Japanese food and French food.

Japanese food is better than French food.

10.2 Vocabulary

Seasons and weather

A Complete captions (1–8) with *a, e, i, o* or *u*.

1 It's r____n____g.

2 It's s__nny.

3 It's sn__w__ng.

4 It's cl____dy.

5 It's h__t.

6 It's f__ggy.

7 It's w__ndy.

8 It's c__ld.

B What's the weather like in your country? Complete the table below with words from Exercise A and your own ideas.

winter	spring	summer	fall
		It's hot	

C Work in pairs. Talk about weather in your country using the notes in Exercise B.

What's the weather like in the summer?

It's really hot. Sometimes it reaches 42 degrees Celsius.

10.2 Grammar

Superlatives

A Complete the table with the superlative form of the adjectives in the box.

amazing bad ~~beautiful~~ boring cold ~~dry~~ expensive
~~good~~ high hot remote small traditional wet

short adjectives	long adjectives	irregular
the driest	*the most beautiful*	*the best*

B Can you add any more adjectives and superlatives to the table in Exercise A?

C Work in pairs. Take turns making superlative sentences with the words in Exercise A. Try to find three things you agree about.

Stephen Curry is the best basketball player in the world!

I agree!

10.3 Vocabulary

Phrasal verbs

A Complete the definitions with the phrasal verbs in the box.

give up look for put on set off take off

1 ______________ to start wearing clothes or shoes

2 ______________ to remove clothes or shoes

3 ______________ to stop trying to do something

4 ______________ to start a journey

5 ______________ to try to find someone or something

B Complete the questions with phrasal verbs from Exercise A.

1 When you go on a trip, do you ______________ early or late?

2 When you try to do something difficult, do you sometimes ______________?

3 When you lose something, do you usually ______________ it or buy a new one?

4 What clothes do you ______________ when the weather is cold?

5 Do you ______________ your sunglasses when you go inside?

C Work in pairs. Ask and answer the questions in Exercise B.

Verb + infinitive

A Correct the sentences.

1 *I plan go to Italy on vacation next year.*

2 *You don't need to leaving home before six o'clock.*

3 *Please remember bringing warm clothes – it's cold here.*

4 *I decided not cook meat, because she doesn't like it.*

5 *If you want watch TV, you can.*

6 *What time do you plan to arriving at the concert?*

7 *I don't think my mother remembered add sugar!*

8 *Do you think we need buy some cake for the children?*

9 *I really want for go to Paris one day, to see the Eiffel Tower!*

10 *Did you decide wear a tie for your interview?*

B Work in pairs. Talk together and think of one example of the things below.

- Something you plan to do next week.
- Something you need to remember to do next week.
- Something you need to do before tomorrow.
- Something you want to do this year.

11.1 Vocabulary

The body

A Label the body parts (1–8).

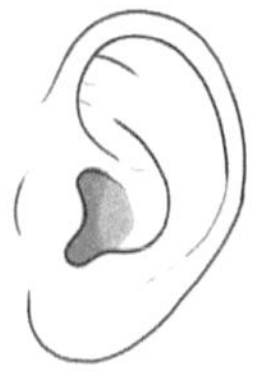

1 ______________

2 ______________

3 ______________

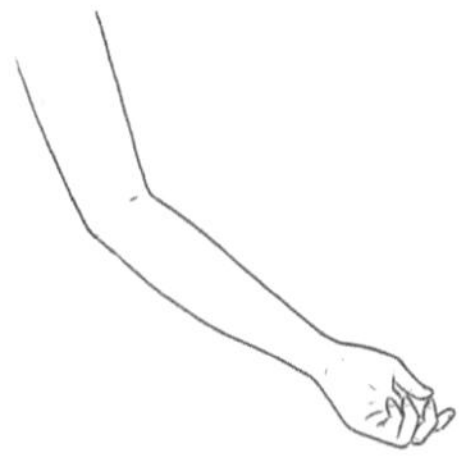

4 ______________

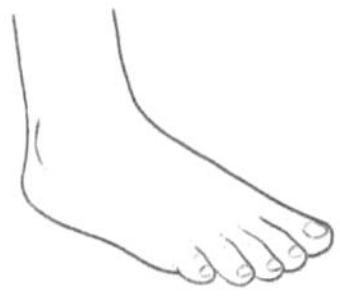

5 ______________

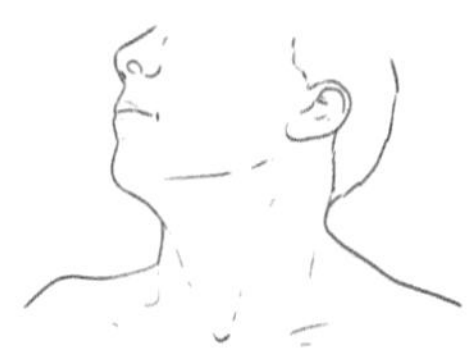

6 ______________

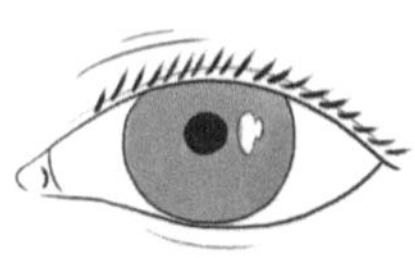

7 ______________

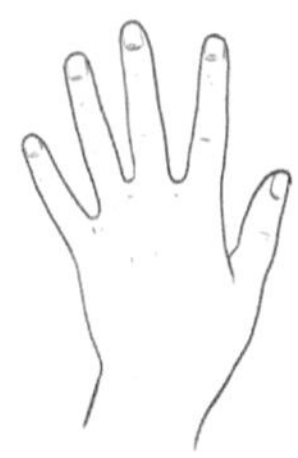

8 ______________

B Work in groups. Take turns miming the words below. Score one point for every word your group guesses correctly.

head

heart

neck

stomach

blood

back

brain

skin

finger

toe

should and *shouldn't*

A Complete the sentences with *should* or *shouldn't*.

Top Ten Tips
for a Better Life

1 You ________________ sleep for eight hours every night.
2 You ________________ use your phone before going to bed.
3 You ________________ drink a lot of coffee.
4 You ________________ do exercise like yoga every day.
5 You ________________ smoke.
6 You ________________ drink 10 glasses of water a day.
7 You ________________ smile and be nice to other people.
8 You ________________ take a break when you get tired at work.
9 You ________________ go on vacation more often.
10 You ________________ eat a lot of junk food like pizza and chips.

B Choose one of the topics from the box. Write six sentences giving advice about it, three negative and three positive.

feel good   get a job   get in shape   have a good vacation   help other people   help the world
learn a language   learn to cook   open a restaurant   pass an exam   start a business

1 ________________
2 ________________
3 ________________
4 ________________
5 ________________
6 ________________

C Work in pairs. Read out your sentences one by one. Guess which topic your partner is giving advice about.

Present perfect

A Use the prompts to write present perfect questions.

	notes
1 you / see / the sunrise?	
2 you / live / in another country?	
3 you / make / a meal for more than five people?	
4 you / try / to give something up?	
5 you / ride / a motorcycle?	
6 you / eat / a terrible meal?	
7 you / met / a famous person?	
8 you / win / a competition?	
9 you / spend / a lot of money on one thing?	
10 you / see / a movie more than five times?	
11 you / break / a bone in your body?	
12 you / cry / during a movie?	

B Work in pairs. Ask and answer the questions from Exercise A. Give details if possible, using the simple past. Write notes about your partner's answers.

Have you ever ridden a motorcycle?

Yes, I have. I rode one every day when I lived in Vietnam.

C Work in a new pair. Explain to your partner what you found out in Exercise B.

11.2 Vocabulary

Irregular past participles

A Match bases (1–12) to their past participles (a–l).

1 be	**a** won
2 break	**b** ridden
3 do	**c** taken
4 go	**d** had
5 take	**e** forgotten
6 win	**f** seen
7 have	**g** done
8 eat	**h** been
9 forget	**i** broken
10 ride	**j** gone
11 see	**k** run
12 run	**l** eaten

B Work in pairs. Student A: say a base form of a verb. Student B: ask your partner a present perfect question using the verb they say. Use simple past to give or get more information. Swap.

Eat!

Have you ever eaten anything strange?

Yes, I have. I ate crickets in Vietnam.

Yuck! What did they taste like?

Uh … a little like onions.

11.3 Grammar

Present perfect vs simple past

A Complete conversations (1–5) with the correct form of the verbs in parentheses.

1

A: ________________ (you / win) a competition?

B: Yes, I have. My team ________________ (win) the league last year.

2

A: ________________ (you / go) to the gym last night?

B: No, I didn't. I ________________ (go) to dinner with some friends.

3

A: ________________ (you / go) on vacation last year?

B: Japan. We ________________ (stay) in an amazing hostel in Tokyo.

4

A: ________________ (you / live) in another country?

B: No, but my brother has. He ________________ (work) in China for a year.

5

A: ________________ (be / your) first trip to Sweden?

B: No, it wasn't. I ________________ (be) to Stockholm for work three times now.

B Write five present perfect questions to ask your partner.

1 ________________

2 ________________

3 ________________

4 ________________

5 ________________

C Work in pairs. Ask and answer your questions from Exercise B. Ask follow-up questions and use the simple past to give more information.

Sports

A Complete the table with the sports and activities in the box.

badminton basketball bike riding boxing dancing horseback riding judo karate running soccer swimming tennis yoga

do	play	go

B Add any other sports you know to the table in Exercise A.

C Work in pairs. Ask about each sport in turns, using *Have you ever … ?* Ask follow-up questions, to find out more.

Have you ever done karate?

Yes, I have. I'm very good at it.

Have you ever won any competitions?

12.1 Grammar

going to

A Correct the mistake in each sentence.

1 *Where you going to have dinner tonight?*

2 *I is going to play basketball with my friends this afternoon.*

3 *What time you are going to arrive?*

4 *Your friend are going to be very happy when he sees you!*

5 *Why are you going watch that boring movie?*

6 *When you going to do your homework?*

7 *I'm not going swim a kilometer this evening.*

8 *That man going to fall off his chair!*

9 *We aren't go to eat chicken tomorrow, we are go to eat fish.*

10 *Why isn't your brother going study at a university?*

B Walk around the class. Ask and answer questions using *going to* to complete the table. Write notes.

Find someone who's going to …

	name	notes
travel to another country next year.		
watch a movie tonight.		
go to bed late.		
learn a new skill this year.		
call their parents on the weekend.		
cook dinner for someone this week.		
take an exam soon.		
look for a new job this year.		
go to a concert this month.		
do some exercise this evening.		
stop doing something unhealthy this year.		
listen to music on the way home.		
spend a lot of money soon.		

Future time expressions

A Put the time expressions in order of time, starting with the earliest. Which one is different?

_____ next month _____ next week _____ next year _____ on the weekend
_____ one day _____ this afternoon _____ this evening _____ tomorrow _____ tonight

B Write five questions with *going to* using a verb from box A and a time expression from box B.

A

do
eat
go
live
watch

B

after your course finishes
in five years' time
next year
this summer
tonight

1 ______________________________

2 ______________________________

3 ______________________________

4 ______________________________

5 ______________________________

C Work in pairs. Ask and answer your questions from Exercise B.

Where are you going to go on vacation next year?

I'm not sure. I think we're going to go to Iceland.

12.2 Grammar

will for predictions

A Match predictions (1–7) to reasons (a–e).

Predictions

1 One day, I will be rich.

2 People will never stop reading books and newspapers.

3 I think Jamie will become a doctor.

4 Sorry, I think I'll be late home tonight.

5 I think Italy will win the soccer game tomorrow.

6 He won't finish college and he won't get a degree.

7 I won't finish all this chicken.

Reasons

a I just have so much work to do.

b He doesn't like studying and he wants to get a job.

c They are better than the internet.

d They have a great team.

e I had a really big lunch.

f He always helps me when I'm sick.

g I have a great idea for a business!

B Work in pairs. Make two predictions about three of the topics in the box using two different times for each one. Does your partner agree?

Times

this evening

tomorrow

next week

next month

next year

one day

Topics

the weather

your town or city

your job

sports

your country

clothes and fashion

Collocations with *get*

A Complete the sentences with *get* and the words in the box.

cold home hungry lost money
organized sick thirsty to school wet

1 Have fun on your trip, but take a map so you don't ______________.
2 It's raining – we are going to ______________.
3 If you ______________, drink some water.
4 I have to ______________ before classes start at 9:00!
5 What time do you ______________ after work?
6 When my children ______________, I make them a sandwich.
7 You need to wear warm clothes and eat healthy food – I don't want you to ______________.
8 I need a job to ______________ to pay for my new car.
9 I'm going to the store to buy books and things I need to ______________ before I start college.
10 In the winter, when I ______________, I put on a scarf, a hat and gloves.

B Match questions (1–6) to answers (a–f).

Questions

1 What do you do when you get cold?
2 What do you do when you get sick?
3 How did you get here today?
4 What do you eat when you get hungry in the afternoon?
5 Have you ever gotten lost?
6 What time do you get home in the evening?

Answers

a I came by bus.
b Yes, in New York – I didn't have my GPS.
c At five or six o'clock, usually.
d I stay in bed and drink a lot of hot tea.
e Chocolate!
f I don't get cold – it's never cold here.

C Work in pairs. Ask and answer the questions, and give your own answers.

12.3 Vocabulary

Internet communication

A Label pictures (1–8) with the words in the box.

chat connect like share tag trend tweet upload

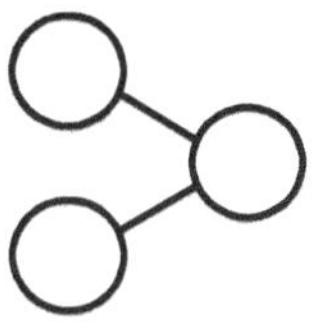

1 ____________

2 ____________

3 ____________

4 ____________

5 ____________

6 ____________

7 ____________

8 ____________

B Complete the questions with words from Exercise A.

1 What apps do you use to ____________ with friends?

2 Do you always ____________ your friends in pictures? Why/Why not?

3 What's the funniest ____________ you've ever read?

4 Do you always ____________ with people who ask you to be friends on Facebook? Why/Why not?

5 What kind of things don't you ____________ on social media? Why?

C Work in pairs. Ask and answer the questions in Exercise B.

What kind of things don't you share on social media? Why?

I don't upload pictures of my family, because I think they should be private.

might

A Complete conversations (1–5) with the correct form of *might* and a verb from the box.

get go have make see

1

A: Are you going to the party on Saturday?

B: Yes, definitely.

A: OK, great. I ______________________ you there.

2

A: What are you going to have for lunch?

B: Hmm … I don't know. I ______________________ some sushi from that store by the bus station.

3

A: Do you have any vacation plans?

B: Yes, I think we ______________________ to Italy to see Macro's parents.

4

A: Hey! How's the report going?

B: Not well. I ______________________ time to finish it all today.

5

A: I ______________________ some coffee. Do you want some?

B: No, thanks. I just had a cup.

B Work in pairs. Take turns making sentences with *might* using the time expressions in the box.

next year this afternoon this summer tomorrow tonight

Answer key

1.1 Vocabulary

A

1 d 2 e 3 a 4 h
5 g 6 c 7 f 8 b

B

1 Australian 5 German
2 Chilean 6 Moroccan
3 Greek 7 South Korean
4 Danish 8 Filipino

From left to right: Chilean flag **2**, Greek flag **3**, South Korean flag **7**, Danish flag **4**, From left to right: Australian flag **1**, Filipino flag **8**, Moroccan flag **6**, German flag **5**

1.1 Grammar

A

1 Maple syrup 2 Pizza 3 Spain
4 Australian flag 5 Pyramids of Giza

B

1 is 2 aren't / are 3 isn't 4 are 5 is

1.2 Vocabulary

A

3 five thousand
4 one hundred and twenty-eight
5 seventy thousand
6 sixty-eight thousand
7 one hundred and twenty-five thousand
8 two million

1.2 Grammar

A

1 are 2 'm / am 3 is / 's 4 is / 's
5 are 6 'm / am 7 Are 8 'm / am

1.3 Grammar

A

1 a 2 – 3 – 4 a 5 an 6 – 7 a
8 – 9 a 10 a 11 a

2.1 Vocabulary

A

female: aunt, daughter, granddaughter, niece, mother, sister
male: father, son, uncle, grandson, grandfather, nephew, brother
male or female: children, parents, child, grandchildren, grandparents, cousin

2.1 Grammar

A

1 Ellen's 2 's mother 3 's father
4 's grandmother 5 Brian's
6 's husband 7 's sister 8 's grandson 9 's son 10 Richard's

2.2 Vocabulary

A

hair: bald, curly, brown, gray, mustache, short, straight, (green), (blue)
eyes: blue, green, brown, gray
height: short, tall **build:** fat, slim

2.3 Vocabulary

A

positive: happy, friendly, funny, neat
negative: messy, sad, noisy, unhappy, unfriendly **both:** quiet, serious

2.3 Grammar

A

1 It's a very expensive dress.
2 My boyfriend is really tall.
3 It's a very sad movie.
4 My sister's bedroom is fairly messy.
5 My grandmother's neighbors are really noisy.
6 I think he's fairly tired.

3.1 Grammar

A

1 My friend listens to the radio every morning.
2 My English class starts at 5:30 pm every day.
3 I drive to work in the morning.
4 My parents live in an apartment in the city center.
5 ✓
6 My brother cooks dinner every night.
7 I have breakfast before I go to work.
8 My best friend listens to classical music.
9 I work at a desk all day.
10 I like to watch TV with my roommates every night.
11 ✓

3.2 Vocabulary

A

1 on 2 on 3 at 4 on 5 on
6 on 7 in 8 in 9 at 10 on

3.3 Vocabualry

A

1 put up 2 watch 3 have 4 eat
5 give 6 wear 7 watch

4.1 Vocabulary

A

1 pilot 2 teacher 3 designer
4 doctor 5 businesswoman 6 actor

B

a 4 b 5 c 1 d 3 e 6 f 2

4.1 Grammar

A

1 Do 2 Does 3 Does 4 Do
5 Does 6 Does
a doesn't b does c does d don't
e do f doesn't

B

1 e 2 f 3 c 4 d 5 a 6 b

4.2 Grammar

A

1 Do you have to wear / I don't
2 Do you have to work / I do
3 Does your husband have to travel / he does
4 Does you sister have to work / she doesn't

4.2 Vocabulary

A

1 e 2 c 3 d 4 a 5 b

B

1 nine to five 2 early in the morning
3 noon 4 midnight 5 late in the afternoon

4.3 Grammar

A

1 What's your favorite kind of music?
2 How many languages do you speak?
3 When does your English course finish?
4 Why do you want to learn English?
5 Who's your favorite writer?
6 What time / When / How do you get to work every day?
7 Where do your parents live?
8 How much exercise do you do every week?
9 What does your father do?
10 What's your favorite movie?

4.3 Vocabulary

A

1 study 2 get 3 go 4 train
5 get 6 take 7 take

5.1 Vocabulary

A

places to stay in: house, caravan, apartment
rooms and outdoor things: swimming pool, living room, bathroom, yard, bedroom, dining room
furniture: chair, bed, lamp, TV, couch, table

5.2 Vocabulary

A

1 airport 2 theater 3 library 4 park 5 museum 6 restaurant 7 café 8 subway station 9 market 10 grocery store 11 school 12 store 13 gym 14 hospital 15 movie theater

5.2 Grammar

A

1 play / can 2 work / can't 3 make / can 4 ride / can't 5 speak / can

5.3 Grammar

A

1 g 2 b 3 a 4 d 5 f 6 c 7 e

6.1 Vocabulary

A

1 comedy 2 concert 3 magazine 4 festival 5 internet 6 movie theater 7 exhibit

6.2 Grammar

A

1 were / was
2 was / was
3 Was / wasn't
4 was / was

6.2 Vocabulary

A

in: 2006, July of last year, the summer
ago: four months, six years
last: month, Saturday, year

6.3 Grammar

A

irregular: became, got, met, went, gave, sent, had, was/were, bought
regular with *-ed*: joined, played, started, asked, worked
regular with *-d*: moved, practiced, decided, lived
regular with *-ied*: studied

6.3 Vocabulary

A

1 was 2 went 3 learned 4 studied 5 became 6 started 7 bought 8 got 9 had 10 moved 11 went 12 finished / went

7.1 Vocabulary

A

1 bus 2 train 3 boat 4 ship 5 bus 6 scooter 7 bicycle 8 plane 9 motorcycle

7.1 Grammar

A

You could drive a car.
You could watch a movie at a movie theater.
You couldn't use the internet at home.
You could fly to another country.
You could study at a university.
You could eat traditional food.
You couldn't eat fast food.
You couldn't watch TV on a computer.
You couldn't buy things online.
You could learn a language.

7.2 Grammar

A

1 I didn't like rock music when I was younger.
2 He didn't go to work last week.
3 They didn't study French at school.
4 I didn't live with my parents when I was a teenager.
5 I didn't go on vacation last summer.
6 She didn't study at Harvard University.
7 They didn't come here by boat.
8 She didn't become a professional dancer.
9 We didn't take a lot of luggage.
10 We didn't arrive on time.

7.2 Vocabulary

A

1 arrived 2 didn't miss 3 took 4 didn't leave 5 returned

7.3 Grammar

A

1 Did you go to Canada on your last vacation?
2 Did you meet many people last year?
3 Did you fly anywhere last year?
4 Did you arrive late at the airport last time you went?
5 Were you happy yesterday?
6 Did you go swimming last week?
7 What time did you get up this morning?
8 Did you visit a museum last month?
9 Did you have a good time on vacation last year?
10 When did you arrive here today?

7.3 Vocabulary

A

1 swim 2 visit 3 take 4 read 5 get 6 meet 7 had 8 went

8.1 Vocabulary

A

fruits: banana, orange, apple, **vegetables:** broccoli, beans, carrot, mushroom, onion **meat and fish:** chicken, shrimp **drinks:** water, coffee, tea **others:** sandwich, bread, pizza, cake, chips, egg, butter, pasta

8.1 Grammar

A

Countable: banana, shrimp, bean, carrot, sandwich; **Uncountable:** water, tea, broccoli, bread, pasta; **Both:** chicken, cake, chocolate

8.2 Vocabulary

A

a bag of	a bottle of
chips	orange juice
pasta	water
carrots	cola
shrimp	
onions	
beans	

a can of	a carton, package or box of
tomatoes	mushrooms
beans	tea
cola	pasta
	cake
	eggs
	coffee

8.2 Grammar

A

1 How many 2 How much 3 How much 4 How many 5 How many 6 How many 7 How much

8.3 Grammar

A

1 – 2 – 3 a 4 a 5 an 6 – 7 a 8 – 9 the 10 the 11 – 12 – 13 – 14 – 15 a 16 the

B

1 – 2 – 3 – / the 4 – / – 5 a / –

8.3 Vocabulary

A

1 Crack 2 Peel 3 Put 4 Put / add 5 fry 6 Add, serve

9.1 Vocabulary

A

1 hat 2 sunglasses 3 cap 4 sneakers 5 pants 6 skirt 7 scarf 8 coat 9 dress 10 socks 11 gloves 12 shorts

9.1 Grammar

A

1 She's playing video games in her bedroom.
2 I'm not going to the party on Saturday.
3 Are you watching the news?
4 They're playing soccer in the yard.
5 He's listening to music on his phone.
6 What are you doing now?
7 He's waiting at the bus stop.
8 She's wearing a Prada jacket.
9 He's not working today.
10 What are you making for dinner?

9.2 Vocabulary

A

1 at the moment
2 currently
3 right now
4 At the moment
5 today
6 at the moment
7 right now
8 at the moment

B

1 moment **2** days **3** right **4** today **5** now **6** these

9.2 Grammar

A

1 'm reading **2** goes **3** are / driving **4** tells **5** work **6** 'm watching **7** is talking **8** loves **9** works / 's working **10** do / get up

9.3 Grammar

A

subject	**object**
I, you, she, he, it, we, they	me, you, her, him, it, us, them

B

1 I, he, he, me **2** I, him **3** she **4** We, him, her, they **5** him, she / me **6** we **7** they **8** them

C

1 him/her **2** you/it **3** you/it **4** you/them **5** you/them **6** it

9.3 Vocabulary

A

1 b **2** e **3** f **4** a **5** d **6** c

10.1 Vocabulary

A

1 beach **2** desert **3** jungle **4** ocean **5** hill **6** mountain **7** lake **8** forest **9** island

10.1 Grammar

A

1 is closer, than **2** is bigger than **3** is cheaper than **4** is more expensive than **5** are more traditional than **6** is bigger than **7** is hotter than **8** is more crowded than **9** are wetter than

10.2 Vocabulary

A

1 raining
2 sunny
3 snowing
4 cloudy
5 hot
6 foggy
7 windy
8 cold

10.2 Grammar

A

short adjectives
the coldest
the hottest
the smallest
the highest
the wettest

long adjectives
the most amazing
the most boring
the most remote
the most expensive
the most traditional

irregular
the worst

10.3 Vocabulary

A

1 put on **2** take off **3** give up **4** set off **5** look for

B

1 set off **2** give up **3** look for **4** put on **5** take off

10.3 Grammar

A

1 I plan to go to Italy on vacation next year.
2 You don't need to leave home before six o'clock.
3 Please remember to bring warm clothes – it's cold here.
4 I decided not to cook meat, because she doesn't like it.
5 If you want to watch TV, you can.
6 What time do you plan to arrive at the concert?
7 I don't think my mother remembered to add sugar!
8 Do you think we need to buy some cake for the children?
9 I really want to go to Paris one day, to see the Eiffel Tower!
10 Did you decide to wear a tie for the interview?

11.1 Vocabulary

A

1 ear **2** nose **3** leg **4** arm **5** foot **6** neck **7** eye **8** hand

11.1 Grammar

A

1 should **2** shouldn't **3** shouldn't **4** should **5** shouldn't **6** should **7** should **8** should **9** should **10** shouldn't

11.2 Grammar

A

1 Have you ever seen the sunrise?
2 Have you ever lived in another country?
3 Have you ever made a meal for more than five people?
4 Have you ever tried to give something up?
5 Have you ever ridden a motorcycle?
6 Have you ever eaten a terrible meal?
7 Have you ever met a famous person?
8 Have ever won a competition?
9 Have you ever spent a lot of money on one thing?
10 Have you ever seen a movie more than five times?
11 Have you ever broken a bone in your body?
12 Have you ever cried during a movie?

11.2 Vocabulary

A

1 h **2** i **3** g **4** j **5** c **6** a **7** d **8** l **9** e **10** b **11** f **12** k

11.3 Grammar

A

1 Have you ever won / won
2 Did you go / went
3 Did you go / stayed
4 Have you ever lived / worked
5 Was that / 've been

11.3 Vocabulary

A

do	**play**
yoga	soccer
judo	badminton
boxing	basketball
karate	tennis

go
swimming
bike riding
horseback riding
running
dancing

12.1 Grammar

A

1. Where are you going to have dinner tonight?
2. I'm going to play basketball with my friends this afternoon.
3. What time are you going to arrive?
4. Your friend is going to be very happy when he sees you!
5. Why are you going to watch that boring movie?
6. When are you going to do your homework?
7. I'm not going to swim a kilometer this evening.
8. That man is going to fall off his chair!
9. We aren't going to eat chicken tomorrow, we are going to eat fish.
10. Why isn't your brother going to study at a university?

12.1 Vocabulary

A

1. this afternoon
2. this evening
3. tonight
4. tomorrow
5. on the weekend
6. next week
7. next month
8. next year
9. one day

one day is different because it is not a fixed point in the future

12.2 Grammar

A

1 g **2** c **3** f **4** a **5** d **6** b **7** e

12.2 Vocabulary

A

1 get lost **6** get hungry
2 get wet **7** get sick
3 get thirsty **8** get money
4 get to school **9** get organized
5 get home **10** get cold

B

1 f **2** d **3** a **4** e **5** b **6** c

12.3 Vocabulary

A

1 share **2** tag **3** trend **4** like
5 tweet **6** upload **7** chat
8 connect

B

1 chat **2** tag **3** tweet **4** connect
5 share

12.3 Grammar

A

1 might see **2** might get **3** might go
4 might not have **5** might make